The Chambered
CAIRNS
of the
CENTRAL
HIGHLANDS

FRONTISPIECE. Balnuaran of Clava North-east (INV 9), view from the west.

The Chambered
CAIRNS
of the
CENTRAL
HIGHLANDS

An Inventory of the Structures and their Contents

A. S. Henshall
and
J. N. G. Ritchie

EDINBURGH UNIVERSITY PRESS

© A. S. Henshall and J. N. G. Ritchie, 2001

Edinburgh University Press Ltd
22 George Square, Edinburgh

Typeset in Plantin
by Pioneer Associates, Perthshire, and
printed and bound in Great Britain by
The Bath Press, Bath

A CIP Record for this book is available from
the British Library

ISBN 0 7486 0643 2 (paperback)

Contents

Part Two

The Inventory of the chambered cairns
in Ross and Cromarty and
Inverness-shire

Acknowledgements

Many institutions and friends have helped in the preparation of this volume. Several funding bodies have made grants available that have made the survey possible: the Binks Trust, Historic Scotland, the Russell Trust, the Society of Antiquaries of London, and the Society of Antiquaries of Scotland.

Land-owners and tenants have, as ever, been helpful in allowing access to monuments. The Forestry Commission allowed access to the cairns on their land. Dr D. Alston drew our attention to Brown's Survey of 1816, and to his discovery of Cairnside (ROS 60). Dr A. Robb contacted us on identifying the remains of Taradin (ROS 61), and we are grateful to Lord Burton for allowing us to visit and plan this site. Mr J. Jack readily gave permission for the re-excavation of Kilcoy South (ROS 24). This was undertaken by GUARD, The Department of Archaeology, The University of Glasgow, and we are grateful to the directors, Dr H. Loney and Mr G. MacGregor, and their team of volunteers. Historic Scotland gave Scheduled Ancient Monuments Consent for the work on condition that the drystone wall that formerly crossed the site be reinstated, and this was done splendidly by Mr B. Wilson, Wildland. Dr A. A. Woodham kindly gave the records of the earlier excavation to the National Monuments Record of Scotland, and discussed his findings on site in 1997.

We are particularly grateful to Professor Richard Bradley, and other members of his team, for showing us the monuments at Balnuaran of Clava under excavation on several occasions. Professor Bradley generously allowed us access to his excavation report at pre-publication stage and our discussion has greatly benefited from this. We have tried not to duplicate information and hope that the two accounts will complement one another, though our interpretations are perhaps less optimistic. In the course of other work it proved possible for colleagues in the Royal Commission on the Ancient and Historical Monuments of Scotland to assist in the recording of the Balnuaran of Clava monuments both photographically (including the use of the Commission's Hi-Spy camera) and with ground survey (figure 45). Colleagues within the Royal Commission have provided information and illustrations from the National Monuments Record of Scotland, notably Dr. I. Fraser, Mr K. McLaren, Mr R. Mowat, and members of the Photographic Department; Mr J. B. Stevenson gave permission to reproduce his unpublished plan of the prehistoric landscape at Kinrive (figure 12). The staff of the Map Library of the National Library of Scotland responded with their unfailing courtesy to many requests.

Examination of the finds in the former National Museum of Antiquities of Scotland (now part of the Museum of Scotland in the Royal Museum of Scotland) was facilitated, at a time of considerable inconvenience because of the imminent move to the new building, by Dr A. Sheridan and Mr T. G. Cowie. Mr I. A. G. Shepherd kindly advised on beaker pottery and on long cairns in Aberdeenshire.

Other friends have helped our project: Mr I. Fraser advised on Gaelic place names, and Dr J. and Mr R. W. Munro provided historical detail for Appendix 4.

We are very grateful for the skill and patience of Mr K. H. J. Macleod in preparing the line illustrations for digital publication, which has enabled consistent presentation, particularly of the plans in Part 2, and he has also undertaken the preparation of the maps. Miss M. O'Neill has allowed us to reproduce her drawings of the querns from Kilcoy South first published in Close-Brooks 1983.

Figures 2–3, 5–7, 12 are from the collections of the National Monuments Record of Scotland and are Crown Copyright, Royal Commission on the Ancient and Historical Monuments of

Scotland. The watercolours reproduced in Figure 4 are in the collections of the Royal Museum of Scotland and are reproduced by permission of the Trustees of the National Museums of Scotland. Figures 8–9 were provided by the Public Record Office, London.

The Frontispiece is the work of Mick Sharp.

Plate 1 was provided by the Society of Antiquaries of London. Plate 16 is reproduced with the permission of Dr J. Close-Brooks. Plate 19 is from the collections of Historic Scotland. The other plates are from the National Monuments Record of Scotland.

PART ONE

1. Introduction

1.1) The oldest visible structures in the Scottish landscape, as indeed in many parts of western Europe, are the remains of the immensely ancient burial places built by the earliest farming communities in our land. These structures were built of stone and covered by a cairn. For some five or six millennia they have been conspicuous features in the landscape, either as unnatural-looking mounds or (when ruined) groups of large stones. After knowledge of their original purpose had been lost, they were still perceived as mysterious and awesome, and might be explained as the work of supernatural beings, or later as temples erected by the druids. In Scotland serious investigation of chambered cairns only began, spasmodically, a hundred and fifty years ago. Since then understanding of the cairns, and more importantly of the people who built them, has increased at an ever quickening pace, and is now aided by skills from a range of disciplines outside archaeology.

1.2) In the north mainland of Scotland, the Outer Hebrides, Skye, and the Northern Isles, there are the remains of about four hundred and fifty chambered cairns, more are known to have existed, and an unknown number (perhaps as many again or even more) have been destroyed without trace. All the authenticated chambered cairns have been plotted on the distribution map (figure 1), and, apart from a very few around the western seaboard with which we are not concerned (the Clyde cairns), they all belong to the widespread international family of passage-graves (so-called because the chambers are approached down a passage rather than directly from outside). Another contemporary type of funerary monument, long mounds that may or may not contain a stone-built chamber, are also plotted on the map.

1.3) The great importance of all these cairns to the peoples who built them is indicated by their numbers, by their size and elaborate design, and by the long periods during which we know that they were in use. This was the time that husbandry began, and was to become increasingly the economic basis of society. The cairn-builders had neither metal tools nor wheeled transport, and the construction of the cairns represents a very considerable investment by these small communities in terms of the man-hours and organisation needed, and the consequent loss of work-time and effort from tasks that were essential for their physical welfare. Even now the cairns remain mysterious, and their purposes are only partially understood. There are uncertainties about the burial customs, about the reasons for the disturbance of the deposits in the chambers, about the deliberate sealing of the chambers, and most elusive of all, the significance of the entombed ancestors and their perceived influence on the welfare of the community. Some scholars are seeking much more wide-ranging interpretations from the cairns.

1.4). In the near absence of evidence from settlement sites in the north mainland, chambered cairns are potentially one of the prime archaeological sources for an understanding of the people of the neolithic period. Besides the architectural sophistication of the cairns, they may preserve the physical remains of the cairn-users and some of their artefacts, material for radiocarbon dating, and perhaps more importantly they are likely to preserve valuable environmental evidence. In the Northern and Western Isles, where settlement sites have been excavated, the integration of domestic and spiritual life begins to be revealed.

1.5) The theoretical basis for much archaeological writing and teaching has been expanded and enhanced in recent years. In particular megalithic burial monuments of all categories, as well as the deposits found in them, are being examined from many different points of view,

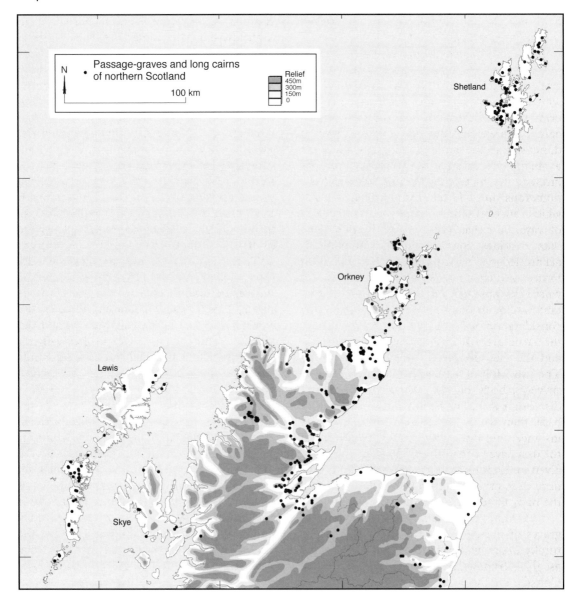

FIGURE I. The distribution of northern Scottish passage-graves and long cairns.

and there is discussion of a much wider range of possible interpretations than formerly, sometimes probing the unknowable. One of the stances most critical of detailed field recording, which is the objective of our work, is taken by Parker Pearson and Richards: 'despite the obsessive practice of recording architecture and physical features in the greatest detail imagin-

able, archaeologists were somehow missing the point in their substitution of description for understanding' (1994, xi). Much current archaeological writing involves generalisations in order to explore the relationships between the artefacts of the past (be they monuments or small finds) and the people who created or used them (Hodder 1992, 15). Justification for field-survey of the sort that we have undertaken is clearly necessary.

1.6) A study such as ours attempts to make available a body of data, firmly grounded in archaeological observation in the field, from which generalisations may be made and theories tested. Consistency of survey across a compact area provides an unusual sense of dimension to the study. The information from a single unexcavated site may in itself be limited, yet incrementally information from numerous sites will build into a body of data, which can, of course, be interpreted in a variety of ways, ways that satisfy today's fashions. The data provides consistent descriptions (with acknowledged inadequacies), that will allow future workers to make some assessment of what is, or was, actually present. This is important in questions of monumentality, the consideration of the impact and significance of the structures themselves, their distribution, and the intended use of space within them. The provision of a consistently described and surveyed body of material allows theoretical discussion to be continued on a more reliable basis than would otherwise be the case. For instance, sites that have been misinterpreted in the past have been identified by us and reasons given for their rejection; newly discovered sites have been critically examined and included in the body of accepted evidence.

1.7) The great majority of the passage-graves of northern Scotland belong architecturally to one group, for half a century known as the Orkney-Cromarty group of cairns. Considering the large area over which they are spread and the length of time over which they were built, it is hardly surprising that they vary widely in size and design. In the later part of the neolithic period there seems to have been a shift in social structure, at least in some areas, from an egalitarian society of small and relatively isolated communities to one where some centralising of power can be detected. This shift was expressed by an interest in circular ritual sites or temples, astronomy, and in Orkney by developing some uniquely impressive chambered cairns, of which Maes

Howe is the supreme example. Later still in Inverness-shire, the concepts that gave rise to the building of temples and chambered cairns coalesced, and another unique form of monument was produced, the cairns of Clava type.

1.8) If the Scottish chambered cairns are so important in heritage terms and for future research it is highly desirable to record the surviving remains individually and in detail. Erosion is an ongoing process, even for the relatively few that are in state care: weathering, invasion by shrubs and trees, damage by sheep and cattle, and human interference all take their toll. Quite minor damage, such as the destruction of a short length of original walling, may be a significant loss. In the Central Highlands the difficulties presented by the ruined state of the vast majority of the cairns, those of Orkney-Cromarty type, are particularly acute. These cairns are vulnerable, and individually the remains are often difficult to interpret: there is no well-preserved example to be seen in this region. Comparison of data from both within and outside the region enables the true potential of many monuments to be appreciated, and it is possible to rediscover the three-dimensional design and original appearance of most of the ruined tombs, and thus to begin to perceive the scale and skill, and the accumulated experience, of the builders. These monuments were not crude or haphazard structures, but were the first carefully planned and ambitious architecture in the land. Our publications are offered to all those who are concerned with understanding, respecting, and preserving a unique range of field monuments which have survived from the remotest past.

1.9) An overall view of the Scottish chambered cairns, with a brief description of each monument, was prepared between 1951 and 1968 (Henshall 1963, 1972), and since then many scholars have worked on the subject. In 1981 Davidson and Henshall started a revision of Henshall's first volume, county by county, with fuller accounts of the monuments: Orkney was published in 1989 and Caithness in 1991. The campaign was continued by Henshall and Ritchie, and Sutherland was published in 1995. The present volume, covering the Central Highlands (the mainland part of the former counties of Ross and Cromarty and Inverness-shire) is the fourth and last in the series. In all these volumes the cairns are identified by a 'county' code and number: ORK Orkney, CAT Caithness, SUT Sutherland, ROS Ross and Cromarty, INV Inverness-shire, etc., and this code is quoted throughout the present volume. The writers regret that it is not possible for them to treat the rest of the Scottish chambered cairns and long cairns (over three hundred if the many Shetland cairns are included) in the same way.

1.10) Several administrative changes in local government have, over the years, caused confusion in the cairn records. Currently the area that we have called the Central Highlands forms part of Highland Council. In 1975 the former county of Ross and Cromarty became the District of Ross and Cromarty as a constituent part of Highland Region: the parish of Kincardine was transferred to Sutherland District. At this time too the Western Isles, formerly divided between the counties of Ross and Cromarty and Inverness-shire, was created as an independent administrative unit. Also in 1975 the county of Inverness-shire was divided into to a number of Districts within Highland Region. Since the creation of Highland Council in 1996 the whole of the mainland part of the former county is within that Council's administration. In this volume the monuments are listed in two groups, those in Ross and Cromarty (usually abbreviated to Ross-shire), and those in Inverness-shire. One monument in the former county of Banffshire and now in Moray Council has also been included for the sake of completeness.

1.11) Our prime purpose is the presentation of a record of each cairn as it was at the time of our visit, and this forms an Inventory in Part 2 of the volume. As mentioned above, the great majority of the cairns covered by the present work belong to the Orkney-Cromarty group, but in the southern part of the region

there are cairns of the Clava group. Only some of the latter contain chambers, while others do not, but are ring-cairns. Yet these contrasting forms of cairn clearly belong to one distinct tradition, and this tradition also embraces other cognate monuments widespread to the south and east. The Clava-type monuments thus presented us with a difficult decision, whether to include them, exclude them, or to include only the chambered cairns. All of the options were unsatisfactory, but inclusion of all the Clava-type cairns would have enlarged the undertaking beyond our resources, and in any case they were the subject of a wide-ranging study undertaken simultaneously by Professor Richard Bradley and his team. To have excluded examination of the group would have deprived us of considering them in relation to the Orkney-Cromarty cairns; thus it was decided to include only the passage-graves of Clava type (though in the upshot, for exceptional reasons, two ring-cairns were also included in the Inventory). It so happens that in the Central Highlands there are only three chambered cairns in the care of Historic Scotland, carefully presented for public inspection after excavation, and all three are impressive monuments of Clava type.

1.12) The satisfactory examination of upstanding monuments such as ruined chambered cairns, without any disturbance of the surface, depends on a number of skills as well as an open mind. Undoubtedly the most important asset for the fieldworker is experience, gained during visits to many examples over many years, by which significant features are recognised and sifted and the irrelevant are discarded. The confidence of experience has to be tempered by an awareness that it may engender an expectation that certain features will be present, and that hitherto unknown features will tend to be overlooked. Experience of the landscape, too, is required, and of the variety of structures likely to be found in it. This enables judgement of what is likely to be natural (particularly relevant in determining which features may or may not be cairns, and in tracing the shape and size of cairns), and identification of superimposed or contrived structures at ruined cairns (such as round houses or lambing pens) which can be misleading. It is also desirable to balance awareness of the less common plans and features that may be present against an inclination to perceive more interesting features than is justified (for instance concave forecourts are particularly difficult to identify). Nor is it helpful to disguise the difficulties in interpretation, to present as certain what may only be probable or possible, or to present in vague terms what is clear. One of the most difficult tasks is to determine, at greatly ruined sites or at those that are virtually complete, which of them may or may not be chambered cairns or long cairns. Over-zealous recording, either in the identification of very dubious chambered cairns or in planning irrelevant detail, only serves to muddy the waters.

1.13) Our fieldwork presented as an Inventory in Part 2 has three components, the plan, photographs, and verbal description of each cairn. Our visits were made in spring or in autumn, when the vegetation that may obscure features, or indeed may entirely overwhelm some cairns, was at its lowest, but daylight was not at its shortest. The plans (with three exceptions) have been drawn from specially prepared plane table surveys by Graham Ritchie and Audrey Henshall. They are published with the cairn material shown stippled, and unless the edge is vague or is obviously distorted, it is edged by dashes. The chambers are shown without stipple even when they are filled with displaced cairn material. Details that are no longer visible are shown by lines of dots. It should be noted that the size and shape of chambers where the walls cannot be seen are indicated very approximately. True north is shown on the plans. All the finished drawings are by Audrey Henshall. The original plans, at a larger scale (10 feet to 1 inch, or about 3 m to 25 mm), and the photographic negatives and slides have been deposited in the National Monuments Record of Scotland.

1.14) The verbal descriptions, after discussion on site, were the responsibility of Audrey Henshall. The text aims to be concise and clear, with interpretations mainly reserved for Part 1. Many measurements have been given, because it was felt that they may help those unfamiliar with north Scottish chambered cairns to recognise, or interpret otherwise, newly discovered sites. All upright structural stones (orthostats) are recorded with the major horizontal measurement as 'length' and the transverse measurement as 'thickness'. With paired orthostats the left one is described before the right one, as seen looking into the chamber from the entrance. When it is reasonably certain that the tops of orthostats are intact, this has been stated; a broken upper edge, unless obviously shattered, is not significant as it may have been so originally.

1.15) The bald descriptions of cairns can sometimes be expanded by meagre additional information, either published or in manuscript. The 1st edition OS 6-inch maps and the ONB are sometimes more informative on little-known monuments than might be expected. For a few cairns fuller additional information is available, in the cases of ROS 12, INV 8–10, 17, 52 drawn from excavation reports, or, in the case of INV 51, from plans preserved in the National Monuments Record of Scotland. We were fortunate to be able to visit the important excavations at Balnuaran of Clava (INV 8–10) at the invitation of the excavator. Exceptional circumstances occurred that enabled us to commission the re-opening of the chamber and forecourt area of Kilcoy South (ROS 24), to obtain a detailed plan and elevation of an unusual structure and to test the hypothesis that it was built in two phases. In the upshot the results of this small investigation were surprising. The few finds that have come from the excavated sites are listed with the museum registration number given in brackets, and our list number is quoted in italics in our text. Photographs and illustrations of monuments, and drawings of artefacts, are in Part 1 of the volume which offers a synthesis of the material in the Inventory. The heading of each entry in Part 2 includes the site number in the National Monuments Record of Scotland (NMRS) to aid identification of the cairn. There are also short references to publications, with minimal references in the following text to allow identification of the source or a page within a source, and the full references are listed at the end of the volume.

2. Development of the study of the cairns

2.1) The two groups of cairns with which this book is concerned received very different levels of interest during the eighteenth and nineteenth centuries. Many of the Clava-group cairns with their spectacular rings of standing stones (and in this Section both passage-graves and ring-cairns are included) were easily accessible from Inverness, and were the subject of much discussion. The cairns of the Orkney-Cromarty group, on the other hand, were mostly to be found further north, and whether intact or in ruin, they must have seemed largely featureless, and they were paid little attention.

Early notices of cairns of Clava type

2.2) During the eighteenth century the Highlands were being opened up, as far north as the Great Glen, as a matter of government policy, primarily by means of a massive road-building programme connecting a series of strategically-placed forts and garrisons. Inverness, as one of the pivots of this strategy, emerged from relative isolation, with increasing commercial and industrial prosperity, and with a stratum of well-educated citizens. One consequence of the improving conditions was the adventurous Highland Tours made by gentlemen from the south. Because several of the monuments were beside the 'government roads' along which they were travelling, the first passing references to cairns of Clava type occur in their accounts, as 'Druidical Circles' or 'Druids' Temples'. In 1760 Bishop Richard Pococke briefly described Kinchyle of Dores, and he also saw Culloden, Cullearnie and Stoneyfield (INV 37, 25, 23, 47) (p. 104), and nine years later Thomas Pennant mentioned Kinchyle of

Dores (named Durris) and Stoneyfield (p. 275). The best known of these tours was made by Boswell and Johnson in 1773. On 30 August they stopped at Kinchyle of Dores, and Boswell's oft-quoted record of this visit cannot be resisted: 'Dr Johnson justly observed that, "to go and see one druidical temple is only to see that it is nothing, for there is neither art nor power in it; and seeing one is quite enough" ' (Boswell 1785, 143).

2.3) Before the mid-nineteenth century there was little information in print. It is evident that to the south and east of Inverness many of the monuments were well known, and further afield a few more were known in the valleys of the River Beauly and the River Spey. Because most of the monuments had been robbed of their cairn material, the obvious features were the circular settings of large stones, and the insignificant remains of the internal structures were generally ignored. Thus the monuments were regarded as either single or double stone circles (the inner circles being the cairn kerbs). The earliest extant plan, of Newton of Petty (INV 45), was made in 1750 by Paul Sandby, the landscape surveyor, but has only been published in a redrawn version (Bradley 2000, 131, illustration 114; the original water colour is in the National Library of Ireland). Numerous 'circles' were noted in vague terms in the descriptions of parishes in the *Statistical Accounts* published respectively in the 1790s and in 1845, and an unusually helpful description of Delfour (INV 29) was given in the latter. Cairns were regarded as a different category of monument. The well-preserved cairns at Balnuaran of Clava, each surrounded by standing stones (INV 8–10), were considered to be exceptional and puzzling, one explanation being that the burial cairns had been inserted into much earlier circles/temples after their primary function had ended (NSA 14, 1845, 450). Within the framework of contemporary thinking, at a time when there was little perception of the chronological depth of pre-Roman antiquity, but when there was great interest in circles in other parts of Britain, the 'circles' were subjects of endless

speculation. The concept of temples for druidical worship lingered on in the popular mind
throughout the nineteenth century.

2.4) In January 1824 George Anderson,
later Rector of Inverness Academy, read a pioneering but modest paper to the Society of
Antiquaries of Scotland on some of the stone
circles in the neighbourhood of Inverness
(Anderson 1831). His aim was to give 'a correct
account of some of the structures', and it is
only to be regretted that his initiative was
not continued to give 'correct accounts' of
more monuments before the interference or
complete destruction that they were soon to
suffer. Most of the monuments he described
were denuded cairns of Clava type, some
cannot now be classified, and a few are now
known to be monuments of other types;
indeed he included the Orkney-Cromarty-type
cairn at Leachkin (un-named, INV 38) which
he mistook for a stone circle.

2.5) Anderson was an alert observer, he
provided plans, and his measurements are reasonably accurate (figure 2). For its date
Anderson's approach was notably sensible and
concise. He recorded in some detail Kinchyle
of Dores (INV 37), Druidtemple (Leys,
INV 30), Cullearnie (un-named, INV 23), and
Newton of Petty (un-named, INV 45) and he
mentioned, without comment, other 'circles'
including INV 2 and 47. He drew attention to
the wealth of remains on the Clava estate, only
8 km east of Inverness, but without providing
details.

> The most imposing and complete associa-
> tion of circles and cairns [is] to be met
> with ... The whole of this plain, for
> upwards of a mile in extent, is covered over
> with large cairns, encircled by rows of
> immense slabs of sand-stone. Among these,
> numerous temples are seen; and small
> detached circles, half covered by grass and
> heath, occur between them. Stones of
> memorial, or single columns, are perceived
> stretching along the field. . . . (ibid., 219)

In conclusion, Anderson noted that at all the

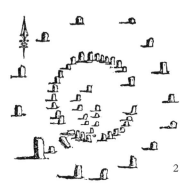

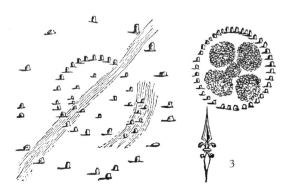

FIGURE 2. Plans of Clava-type cairns drawn
before 1824. 1, Kinchyle of Dores, INV 37; 2,
Druidtemple, INV 30; 3, Cullearnie, INV 23.
From G. Anderson, 1824.

'circles' he had visited the size of the stones
decreased from west to east, and that in general
the stones of the outer ring were taller than
those of the inner ring (i.e. that the circle of

FIGURE 3. The passage and chamber at Balnuaran of Clava South-west, INV 10. From T. D. Lauder, 1830.

standing stones was taller than the kerb of the overlooked cairn). Except for Balnuaran (INV 9, 10), where cairns of considerable size remained within the circles, Anderson did not doubt that the monuments were temples, though 'there seems reason to suspect that the structures . . . are not, as is generally believed, entirely Druidical or Celtic', but 'the works of Scandinavian settlers or pirates'.

2.6) In the late 1820s the south-west cairn at Balnuaran (INV 10) was investigated for the landowner, Mrs Campbell. The passage and chamber were revealed (figure 3), and pieces of two pots and cremated bone were found. A description of the circular chamber, with 'the wall converging to the centre in a rude dome about 12 feet (3.6 m) high', was published rather obscurely by T. D. Lauder, accompanied by engravings of the chamber and the pots (1830, 15, 418). In 1834 Anderson supplemented his earlier account of the Clava monuments in an appendix to a substantial *Guide to the Highlands* (p. 446–51). He noted that in the other two cairns at Balnuaran (INV 8, 9) an inner circular setting of stones

could be seen defining the central structures. Anderson made a forward step in suggesting that, if the loose cairn material were removed from these three cairns they would appear as three concentric stone circles, and consequently that several of the Druidical temples 'may be *emptied* cairns' (p. 450–1). This view was re-stated emphatically by William Jolly over forty years later: 'so-called Druidical circles are simply dismantled cairns. They may be seen in all stages – some of them perfect cairns, others partially dismantled, and others totally dismantled' (ISSFC 1880a, 32). Even then his colleagues were not really convinced.

2.7) It was not until 1858 that a description of the cairns at Clava, all too slight and largely repeating Anderson, was brought before a learned society by Innes (1860, 47–50). He noted Culdoich (INV 21), the westernmost of the monuments, for the first time, with the cairn 'as yet undisturbed' and a single huge monolith standing beside it. He saw the enigmatic sites at Miltown of Clava (INV 43, 44), and (he thought) eight more cairns each with a circle of standing stones (but his observations were limited and some-what misleading). The passage and chamber of the north-east cairn at Balnuaran (INV 9) had been exposed by this time, and Innes illustrated the two cairns (INV 9, 10), still in a heathery landscape free of trees, by two prints made from the charming water-colours painted for him by the Rev. Burnett Stewart (figure 4). Innes compared 'these chamber-cairns' to Newgrange in Ireland where the huge chambered cairn is surrounded by a free-standing circle of stones. By this time, with the introduction of the three-age chronology and especially after the publication in 1851 of Daniel Wilson's *Archaeology and Prehistoric Annals of Scotland* in

which the remains of Scotland's remote past were first presented systematically, it was now possible for the well-informed to begin to perceive the great antiquity of some monuments. Although he was able to quote relatively few examples, Wilson placed both stone circles and chambered cairns in the Age of Stone.

Clava-type cairns in the later nineteenth century

2.8) Progress in recording the monuments was gradual, and their interpretation continued to be debated. Both matters were largely in the hands of the professional gentlemen based in

FIGURE 4. Balnuaran of Clava. Above, the cairn and circle of the South-west cairn, INV 10; below, the passage and chamber of the North-east cairn, INV 9. By the Rev. Burnett Stewart, 1857.

and around Inverness. Whilst on holiday in Strathspey in 1866, Dr Arthur Mitchell (a distinguished antiquary and Inspector of Lunatic Asylums, who had family connections with the area) had visited a 'curious' and 'unique' structure at Grenish (INV 34) which he recorded with a sketch plan and section (1874, 685–7). It was a well-preserved cairn with a hollow centre defined by a circular setting of stones, and he introduced the term 'ring cairn' to describe it. There were two prostrate stones outside the cairn, and if more of the circle of standing stones had survived, the connection with the 'stone circles' in the Inverness area would have been clear. Delfour (INV 29), also in the Spey valley, presented the same problem with a fairly well-preserved ring-cairn and a single standing stone outside it (NSA 14, 1845, 87). About the same time Mitchell visited Corrimony (INV 17) in Glen Urquhart, and recorded, with a sketch plan, a substantial cairn surrounded by a circle of standing stones. However, his main interest in the monument was the cupmarked stones, and thus he drew attention to another distinctive feature of the cairns of Clava type (1874, 643–4). Professor J. Y. Simpson (of the University of Edinburgh, the pioneer of anaesthesia) had been taking a vigorous interest in cupmarked stones throughout Britain, and in a long essay presented in 1864 he included one cupmarked stone in each of the chambered cairns at Balnuaran (INV 9, 10), and more cupmarked stones at Bruiach and Culburnie (INV 14, 19, later recognised as ring-cairns), though he had not seen them himself (1866, 26–7, pl. x).

2.9) The 1870s and 1880s were stimulating decades. The Inverness Scientific Society and Field Club was founded in 1875, 'generally to promote scientific study and investigation, and specially to explore the district for the purpose of inquiring into its Geology, Botany, Natural History, Archaeology etc'. Field excursions were an important part of the programmes for many years, and were fully reported in the Transactions. These reports give glimpses of the monuments as they were when visited, and the lively discussions which arose. The first

FIGURE 5. Sketch of Druidtemple, INV 30, about 1870. From the Object Name Book.

edition of the Ordnance Survey maps were appearing in the later 1870s, giving greater topographical detail as well as recording many antiquities. Without exception the Clava-type cairns were titled 'Stone Circle', though at Balnuaran 'and cairns' was added. Useful additional information (including rare illustrations, figure 5) is sometimes to be found in the Object Name Books, which were the authority for the details shown on the maps. No less than thirty monuments certainly or possibly of Clava type were shown, and only one cairn certainly of this type has been identified since. All this activity provided the stimulus for important publications by Jolly and Fraser.

2.10) Progress and regress may come simultaneously. 1875 saw the publication of a sumptuous volume on hill forts and stone circles by Miss C. Maclagan. This energetic, eccentric and unreliable lady from Stirling made a contribution to the data on Inverness-shire 'circles' by publishing plans of Gask and the centre cairn at Balnuaran (INV 32, 8), and also the first plan to show the relationship of the three Balnuaran cairns (p. 74–7, pls. xxv, xxvi, xxx). She provided brief descriptions of these and four other monuments (INV 18, 28, 30, 48) though fuller accounts of them were soon to follow. Less helpful was her bizarre proposition, supported by drawn reconstructions, that the circles and cairns were the bases of denuded broch-like dwellings. As late as 1878 a minor rearguard action was fought in Inverness by James Ross (1880) on behalf of the 'druidical temples' interpretation of the 'circles'.

2.11) By 1877 Angus Grant, schoolmaster at Aviemore and subsequently at Drumnadrochit, had recognised the relationship, and also the differences, between the 'circles' at Grenish, Aviemore and Tullochgorm (INV 34, 6, 49) in the Spey valley and those 'circles' to the north which were known to surround chambered cairns, i.e. the Balnuaran cairns and Druid-temple (INV 9, 10, 30), and also Corrimony (INV 17) where the existence of a chamber was anticipated (Grant 1880); unknown to him the Corrimony chamber had been opened and filled in probably at the beginning of the century. Grant rightly pointed out that the diameters of the central areas of the three Spey valley monuments were too great for them to have been roofed over. He had identified one of the persistent problems in understanding the Clava-type cairns, that the central structure may be either a chambered cairn or a ring-cairn. However, Grant drew the wrong conclusion, that the roofed chambers had been constructed within pre-existing cairns, a variant of the explanation offered in 1845 (and Grant's interpretation was repeated in a major publication as late as 1951 by W. L. Scott, p. 44 fn.). The distribution of Clava-type cairns was now apparent, with Corrimony and a second 'circle', Carn Daley (Gartalie, INV 16, mentioned casually by Grant in 1881, published in 1883), at the western limit in Glen Urquhart, and with Carn Urnan (Carn Inenan, ROS 13) on the Black Isle to the north, recorded with plans and sections by Beaton in 1882.

2.12) William Jolly, Inspector of Schools and first president of the Inverness Scientific Society and Field Club, published in the same year, 1882, a comprehensive fully illustrated inventory of over eighty cupmarked stones in the Inverness neighbourhood, an impressive

achievement. In the first and second sections of his paper he dealt with the many cupmarked stones which he had found incorporated into the structure at nine Clava-type monuments. Additionally, Jolly described the three cairns at Balnuaran, and (following Maclagan) he provided a plan of the centre cairn (INV 8) with the strange radial 'causeways' which had recently been exposed in clearing the site. As well as a plan of Corrimony (INV 17), he provided the first plans of Bruiach and Culburnie (INV 14, 19). Jolly drew attention to the number of cupmarked stones found in other contexts or isolated, and also to a number of Clava-type cairns at which there were no cupmarked stones, and finally he summarised his observations.

2.13) In May 1884, exactly two years after Jolly had read his paper to the Society of Antiquaries of Scotland, James Fraser, a civil engineer living in Inverness, read an invaluable paper to the same Society. He provided the first detailed overall view of Clava-type cairns, which he still referred to as 'circles', in their core area. Eleven monuments (INV 48, 18, 32, 42, 28, 21, 8–10, 15, 30) were covered by descriptions, plans and sections or elevations, and he added plans of three more (INV 37, 47, 45), all drawn to a professional standard and published to a uniform scale (figure 6). Four of these sites, Croftcroy, Midlairgs, Daviot, and Cantraybruich (INV 18, 42, 28, 15) were described for the first time. In all, Fraser listed and tabulated thirty-eight monuments within the drainage area of the River Nairn and westwards to the River Ness, though for various reasons not all of them are included in our lists. A number of the structures included by Fraser had been very badly damaged or totally removed, and it seems that too much reliance was placed on the confident titling of them as 'Stone Circles (Remains of)' on the OS maps. Except for Midlairgs and Stoneyfield (INV 47), subsequent damage has been slight, which must in part be due to Fraser's industry and presentation.

2.14) Fraser had shown the variation in both the size of the monuments, and the numbers of

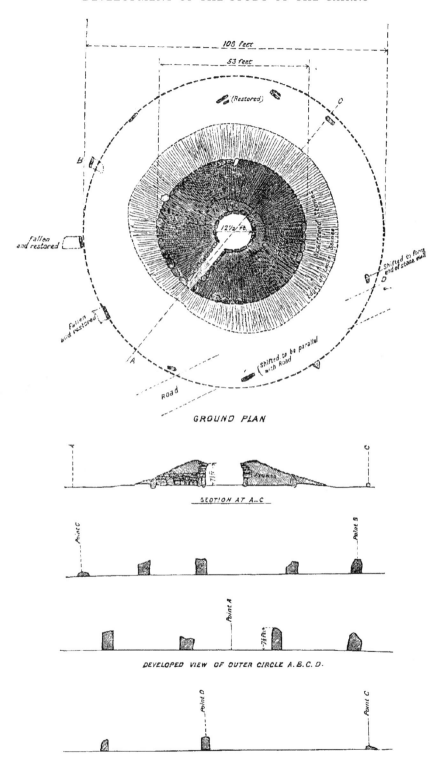

FIGURE 6. Balnuaran of Clava South-west, INV 10. Surveyed by Fraser in 1883 and published in 1884.

stones in the circles. He was satisfied that the 'intermediate rings' of close-set stones had been the kerbs of cairns, and thus that the circles of standing stones had surrounded substantial cairns (though cairn material was observed at only four monuments besides those at Balnuaran). He had seen remains of passages leading into the interiors at four or five cairns, with some variation in the direction of the entrances. Yet he listed only the two Balnuaran cairns (INV 9, 10) as chambered cairns, and cautiously did not commit himself as to the form of the central constructions at other cairns (or more likely his comments were edited out, see his discussion in Fraser 1883). He had found that at a few monuments the stone settings were not strictly concentric. His final comments are surprising in view of the intense mathematical and cosmological studies which were to follow.

One thing is certain, from the various irregularities of construction which have just been referred to, and that is, that there was no mathematical correctness or precision applied in the laying out or building of these singular structures. From the occasional excentricity of the different rings it might be further inferred, with some probability, that the outer rings were first set up and afterwards the interior rings. This seems to be as much as can be fairly inferred from mere measurements, so far as the group of circles in this district is concerned.

2.15) Fraser's publication was followed by two backward-looking papers given to the Gaelic Society of Inverness, which nonetheless have points of interest. At last Grenish, Culdoich, Gask, Delfour and the centre cairn at Balnuaran (INV 34, 21, 32, 29, 8) were all recognised as ring-cairns, and Grenish was described fairly fully with an improved plan by Alexander Macbain, the distinguished Gaelic scholar (1885). A variant and unlikely chronological scheme was put forward: chambered cairns surrounded by stone circles were succeeded by ring-cairns and then by triple-circle structures without cairns, quoting Druidtemple (INV 30) as an example of the last. Drawings of Balnuaran, Grenish, and especially that of Druidtemple, by Mr Smart, enhanced the publication (figure 7). G. Bain, having studied the layout of the Balnuaran cairns, proposed that the 'rays' and the stone circle at the centre cairn (INV 8) together formed a 'sun calendar' (1887).

2.16) When John Stuart, the Secretary of the Society of Antiquaries of Scotland, was ending his fact-finding tour of northern Scotland in the autumn of 1866 (see ¶ 2.32), he visited only four Clava-type cairns (Carn Urnan, Druidtemple and probably Bruiach and Culburnie, ROS 13, INV 30, 14, 19) (1868, 301–3). The first Inspector of Ancient Monuments, General A. H. Pitt Rivers, with his assistant W. S. Tomkin, made northern tours in 1884 and 1885 in order to inspect and record the monuments proposed for protection by scheduling under

FIGURE 7. View of Druidtemple, INV 30, from the NNE. Drawn by Mr Smart in or before 1884. From Macbain 1885.

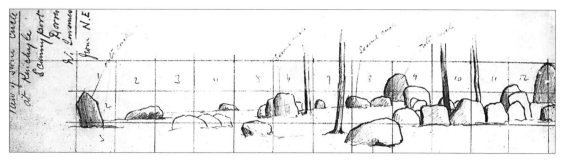

FIGURE 8. Kinchyle of Dores, INV 37. Part of the illustration by Tomkin in 1885 during Pitt Rivers' official tour.

the new Ancient Monuments Act. They visited five of the best known and most accessible cairns, Druidtemple, Kinchyle of Dores (figure 8) and Balnuaran of Clava (INV 30, 37, 8–10) (Thompson 1960, 106–7).

2.17) Joseph Anderson, the greatly respected Keeper of the National Museum of Antiquities of Scotland, used the Rhind Lectures of 1881 and 1882 to present a coherent up-to-date outline of Scottish prehistory. When considering the Clava-type cairns he saw that the passage-graves, represented by the Balnuaran cairns (INV 9, 10), were of a form distinct from the several other types of chambered cairn that he was able to define in Scotland. He reversed the emphasis when considering the Clava monuments, because he thought of the stone circles as adjuncts to the cairns, and 'it is the chamber which is the central idea and the essential object of the composite construction'. From this it followed that chronologically they lay between neolithic 'unencircled' cairns and bronze age 'uncairned circles', that is, between the late neolithic and the beginning of the bronze age (1886, 300–3). However, he implied that all of the Clava-type cairns were chambered and he ignored the ring-cairn element in the Clava group.

2.18) After a gap of over twenty years, three ring-cairns in the Spey valley, Grenish, Aviemore and Delfour (INV 34, 6, 29), received further attention in the same dilettante spirit as previous field investigations. C. G. Cash, an Edinburgh schoolmaster holidaying in the area in 1905, prepared fuller descriptions and detailed plans, though unfortunately Delfour had been partly covered with field-gathered stones since it was first described in 1845 (1906). The following year Cash found and excavated a Clava-type chambered cairn at Avielochan (INV 5). It had been greatly reduced and nothing was found in the primary levels in the chamber. The cairn lacked a circle of standing stones, but it is unknown whether or not this was originally the case (1910).

2.19) By this time the distribution and the numbers of cairns of Clava type in Inverness-shire and Ross-shire were nearly entirely known, and the structures were (for the period) well recorded, in contrast to the other groups of chambered cairns in Scotland. Only Dalcross Mains (INV 26) in the Nairn valley, Carn Daley (INV 16) in Glen Urquhart, and Belladrum North (INV 11), which was not an obvious member of the group in the Beauly valley, had been largely overlooked, and a few cairns to the east in the former counties of Nairn and Banff awaited recognition as outlying members of the group. It was generally accepted that all the monuments had consisted of a burial cairn surrounded by a circle of standing stones. Some of the cairns were chambered, and some of the cairns were ring-cairns; the latter was a class of monument without, as yet, parallels elsewhere. Unlike other groups of chambered cairns amongst which the excavated chambers had produced burials and artefacts, nothing was known of the builders of Clava-type cairns; the two recorded excavations had produced only some cremated bone and two uninformative pots now known only from an engraving.

Progress on Clava-type cairns in the twentieth century

2.20) A new phase in the study of Scottish chambered cairns began with the appointment in 1927 of V. Gordon Childe to the newly established Chair of Prehistoric Archaeology in the University of Edinburgh. He brought an international perspective to his consideration of Scottish monuments, and as far as chambered cairns were concerned he sought to integrate them and their builders with the European scene. A number of scholars wrestled over several decades with the problem of the origins and development of chambered cairns in Europe, and widely differing conclusions were offered as the data expanded and perceptions changed (helpfully summarised in Piggott 1954, 124–7). The arguments, persuasive in their day, now seem hardly more relevant than the nineteenth-century speculations. Until the mid 1970s, when the revolutionary implications of radiocarbon dating were imposing a radical re-interpretation of the neolithic period, the Mediterranean area was generally perceived as the source of movements of peoples westwards and northwards along the Atlantic seaboard, and as these movements could be dated only by insecure links with those distant lands, this had resulted in an extremely compressed time-scale.

2.21) In *The Prehistory of Scotland*, published in 1935, Childe defined four groups of passage-graves on a geographical basis. Those in Caithness together with some in Sutherland were deemed 'classical' because they were thought to be architecturally close to tombs in southern Spain, Portugal and western France, and he interpreted the Clava passage-graves as a specialised derivative form (p. 24), but he was uncertain of their immediate origin. The ring-cairns, lacking an entrance passage and roofing, he interpreted as degenerate versions of the passage-graves (p. 51–3). The cairns of both forms were now named after the Clava

estate on which the best known examples are situated. Childe introduced a new problem when he rightly recognised that there must be a link between the Clava-type cairns and the recumbent-stone-circles of Aberdeenshire and adjacent counties (ibid., 174–5). Detailed information on these monuments had become available through surveys by F. R. Coles, published between 1900 and 1907. Recumbent-stone-circles consist of a stone circle (which includes a huge prone block between a pair of tall 'flankers' on the south-west quadrant), within which is a low cairn with a hollow centre, and they often include cupmarked stones. The recumbent-stone-circles thus echo the four distinctive features of the Clava-type cairns: the circle of standing stones, the grading of stones to emphasise the south-west side, the ring-cairn and cupmarkings. Childe proposed that the recumbent-stone-circles derived from Clava-type cairns, and from this it followed that, because recumbent-stone-circles were thought to be late bronze age in date, Clava-type passage-graves must be late within the chambered cairn tradition. Childe subsequently suggested that Clava passage-graves were built by colonists from the Boyne region of Ireland, who were probably engaged in early metalwork trade (1940, 75).

2.22) A few years later it was convincingly argued that simple corbelled passage-graves, known to be wide-spread in western Europe, derived from similar tombs in Almeria, and that they held a primary position amongst the chambered cairns in whatever region they were found (Daniel and Powell, 1949). The Clava passage-graves were seen as classic examples of primary passage-graves. Stuart Piggott, who succeeded Childe in Edinburgh, when discussing the Clava cairns in his *Neolithic Cultures of the British Isles* (1954, 257–62, but the text completed in 1951), suggested that the supposed link with Spanish monuments was supported by the occurrence in the same part of Spain of circular graves which might be comparable to the ring-cairns. Childe's fieldwork in 1943 in eastern Ross-shire (¶ 2.38) had emphasised the individuality of the Clava type of passage-graves. Instead of being late among Scottish passage-graves, the Clava cairns were now thought to be early. With hindsight, it seems astonishing that, due to the chronological framework then in use, Piggott should have placed them about 1750 BC, and it is ironic that, for the wrong reasons, both Childe and Piggott were indeed not far off the mark in their dating.

2.23) Because there was no internal evidence to support any of the hypotheses, a campaign of excavation was clearly the only way to advance understanding of the Clava cairns, and this was initiated by Piggott under the auspices of the Society of Antiquaries of Scotland. The three cairns at Balnuaran (INV 8–10) had passed into State care in 1925, by which time they were in a neglected condition, and some conservation work and limited excavation in the two chambers had followed under the supervision of Kathleen Kennedy (only published in 1990, by Barclay). Attention was therefore concentrated on Corrimony (INV 17), the Clava-type cairn that appeared to have suffered least interference, and Piggott excavated there in 1952. He was disappointed to find that the chamber had been previously opened, though the sandy floor was undisturbed and, for the first time in Britain, the stain of a totally decayed skeleton was recorded. It seemed that a crouched inhumation had been the sole burial. Piggott also investigated the chambers of two greatly ruined passage-graves, Druidtemple and Kinchyle of Dores (INV 30, 37), but the floors had been dug over, and only scraps of cremated human bone were found. The following year Piggott examined the central areas of the ring-cairns at Balnuaran and Culdoich (INV 8, 21) with equally uninformative results; only cremated bone was found, even though the deliberate infilling above the floor remained at Culdoich. In his report (1956) Piggott included new plans of the Balnuaran passage-graves and the first plan of the passage-grave at Dalcross Mains (INV 9, 10, 26).

2.24) During his campaign Piggott inspected most of the monuments listed by Fraser, and

concluded that ten were passage-graves and nine were ring-cairns, while twelve were unclassifiable. The rough equality in numbers and their propinquity led him to the conclusion that the ring-cairns were not degenerate passage-graves but 'that we are dealing with two tomb-types which were current at the same time' (1956, 196). If so, the ring-cairns did not represent an intermediate stage between the passage-graves and the recumbent-stone-circles, though he acknowledged that there was some connection between them. The then current view of Clava-type cairns was concisely presented by Daniel (Piggott ed. 1962, 59–60, 62–3).

2.25) The cairns of the Clava group were visited again in the late 1950s as part of Henshall's survey of the chambered cairns of the north of Scotland (1963), but she did little more than provide somewhat fuller descriptions and plans to a uniform scale. The distribution of Clava-type cairns was extended eastwards into the former counties of Nairn and Banff, particularly by the identification of an outlying passage-grave at Lagmore (BAN 1). The cairns of the Clava tradition and the cairns and circles of other traditions in eastern Scotland were no longer physically separate. In the same year (1963) a paper by Walker sought to place the cairns in a wider archaeological perspective. In the second volume of Henshall's survey the cairns were considered in relation to other groups of chambered cairns and a range of other monuments, and this introduced a change of perspective (1972, 270–6, 283–4), already hinted at in 1963. In the highland zone of Britain, as more information was emerging on ring-cairns, enclosed cremation cemeteries, and kerb-cairns (Ritchie and MacLaren 1972; Kenworthy 1972), it seemed to her that the dominant element in the design of the Clava cairns came from this tradition rather than from the passage-grave tradition. The concept of roofed central areas, and the skills to build stone vaults, were assumed to have come to the builders of the Clava-type ring-cairns from the builders of Orkney-Cromarty cairns. From this standpoint it followed that the Clava passage-graves had evolved locally, and were among the latest chambered cairns to be built in Scotland; a tentative date in the late third or early second millennium was suggested.

2.26) The opposite view was taken by Aubrey Burl after studying the ring-cairns and recumbent-stone-circles in north-east Scotland. Provided with much more information, he came to the same conclusions as Childe, that the Clava passage-graves were the progenitors of both the Clava-type ring-cairns and the recumbent-stone-circles, and that the builders of Clava-type passage-graves were pioneer settlers who had come from the west up the Great Glen (1970, 56, 59, 65; detailed in 1972; 1976, 160–1). Henshall's view was extended by Barclay, as a consequence of his increasing appreciation of the ring-cairn element in a variety of burial mounds to the south and east of the area under consideration (1990, 30–1; 1992); he even expressed a doubt that the passage-graves had been roofed.

2.27) From the time that the circles around the Clava cairns, and for that matter all stone circles in Britain, were thought of as pagan temples, it was accepted that their design was likely to be related to solar or lunar events. The cairns at Balnuaran (INV 8–10) were among the monuments studied by Rear-Admiral H. B. Somerville in 1910 (published in 1923). By superimposing the plans he demonstrated the remarkable similarity of the three cairns, including the orientation of the two passage-graves, which he was satisfied aligned on sunset at the winter solstice. From the mid-twentieth century there was intense study of the design and implied astronomical purposes of stone circles by a number of highly respected academics, and (to their prehistoric colleagues) their publications are overwhelming in quantity and erudition. Alexander Thom, Professor of Engineering Science at the University of Oxford, was one of the most influential, through a series of publications between 1954 and 1980 (conveniently listed in Thom, Thom and Burl 1980, 11–12). His claims that many monuments were designed in complex geo-metrical layouts rather than as true circles, and

that these designs indicate a highly sophisticated understanding of astronomy, are felt by many to have been extravagant. Among over two hundred meticulous surveys made by Thom fifteen were of Clava-type cairns. Druidtemple (INV 30) provides an example of his analysis of a non-circular setting (Thom 1967, 68–9), and the designs of the settings at other cairns were tabulated (ibid., 137). Burl, in his comprehensive study, *The Stone Circles of the British Isles* (1976), drew on Thom's work, and showed that the Clava circles together with those at recumbent-stone-circles are of an architectural tradition which is distinct and geographically restricted within the stone circle phenomenon (p. 162–3). He examined the orientations of the monuments in relation to both solar and lunar events.

2.28) Since Piggott's excavations in the early 1950s there have been excavations at three more cairns, and also further work at Culdoich (INV 21), and most importantly at Balnuaran (INV 8–10). The cairn at Stoneyfield (Raigmore, INV 47) was totally excavated by D. D. A. Simpson in 1972 and 1973 (1996), and most of the remains of Miltown of Clava North (INV 43) were excavated by N. M. Sharples in 1990 (1993); it was shown that neither monument was a Clava-type cairn in the strict sense. At Culdoich work by J. Barber in 1982 was restricted to the investigation of the one standing stone, and the possible existence of a stone circle, but no evidence for this was found. The ring-cairn at Newton of Petty (INV 45) was excavated by J. E. Thawley in 1975–7, and the delay in publication turned out to be an advantage when it was integrated into Bradley's massive study of Clava-type cairns (2000, 131–59).

2.29) In 1994–6 Richard Bradley and a team from the University of Reading undertook three seasons of excavation and fieldwork with two main objectives. Firstly, he sought greater insight from an intensive study of the cairns themselves, concentrating on the three at Balnuaran (INV 8–10). He wished to prove that they were of unitary construction, and most importantly, the excavation produced material for radiocarbon dating with a totally unexpected result: the cairns had been built about 2000 BC in the early bronze age and long after the last Orkney-Cromarty cairns, and they had been reused in the late bronze age. In attempting to penetrate the underlying intentions behind the design of the cairns, attention was given to the significance of the colours of the stones used, the placement of cupmarked stones, the orientation, and the layout of the monuments clustered at Clava. It was during this campaign that Culdoich South (INV 55), a cairn which is probably a Clava-type passage-grave, was discovered only 1.5 km south of the Balnuaran cairns. Secondly, the study was widened to place the cairns in their settlement environment, and this involved the analysis of field-work over a large area extending to the coast. Bradley's project was thus infinitely more extensive than ours, and his approach was very different; our work, undertaken at the same time, is complementary, concentrating on the planning and detailed description of the surviving structure of all the passage-graves. Whilst working at the Balnuaran cairns MacCarthy saw the evidence for their unitary construction and he investigated the possibility that this was not so at all Clava-type cairns. His conclusion that a good case could be made for the circle of standing stones sometimes being an addition, and the possible implications, were published in 1996 before Bradley's work had been completed.

Early notices of cairns of
Orkney-Cromarty type

2.30) Before the mid nineteenth century few cairns or denuded chambers had been noted, far less described, to the north of Inverness, though many of them must have been well known locally. Many of the cairns were still virtually intact and appeared featureless, and appreciation of more complex antiquities was difficult without any framework for classification. Even so, information from the eastern part of Ross-shire is surprisingly scant. Chambered cairns are numerous on the Black

Isle and on the north side of the Cromarty Firth, and this area is prosperous and relatively accessible, though before the railways and motorised transport the Beauly Firth may have been more of a barrier than is appreciated now. There are a few Orkney-Cromarty-type cairns to the south of the Beauly Firth in Inverness-shire, but except for the sheer size of one long cairn they are unspectacular compared with the Clava-type cairns, and so tended to be ignored. Long cairns without visible chambers have been included in the following paragraphs.

2.31) A cairn near Evanton, probably chambered and probably that later known fancifully as The Priest's Sepulchre (ROS 35), was visited by Pococke on his Scottish tour of 1760. The only plan of an exposed chamber to be published before 1882 was that of Tarradale (ROS 61) (plate 1). It was accurately recorded in 1831 by James Logan, a native of Aberdeen, who later moved permanently to London. He was a gifted, unstable, and exasperating man with influential friends and patrons, who became a respected authority on Scottish gael-dom, and made his livlihood by journalism. As a young man he had a lively interest in antiquarian matters, including Pictish stones, and wandered widely in the Scottish Highlands collecting material (DNB 12, 1967–8, 83; Cruickshank ed. 1941, xiii–xliii). The ruined chamber at Leachkin (INV 38), just outside Inverness, was noted before 1824, but was not illustrated. Inevitably, the nature of the remains at Tarradale and Leachkin was not understood. Five chambered cairns (ROS 6, 7, 12, 24, 60) are recorded on Brown's Survey of part of the Black Isle in 1816 as 'Cairns', and may be assumed to have been little robbed at that time. Although some chambers must have been explored, generally in the course of destruction, only two are known to have been investigated at the behest of the landowner (ROS 42 and probably 7). In the Statistical Account and New Statistical Account, published in the 1791 and in 1845, the meagre notes on antiquities include the only descriptions of two destroyed monuments, the denuded chamber of Clachan Biorach (ROS 14) and the

PLATE I. Tarradale (ROS 61). Watercolour by James Logan (1831) of 'Clachan more na Taradin, a singular collection of stones on a small and rather steep conical hill at Taradin, parish of Kilearnan, Ross-shire'. Folio 117 of the portfolio *Primeval Antiquities* in the Library of the Society of Antiquaries of London. (Printed inverted for comparison with the plan in Part 2.)

long cairn at Heights of Dochcarty (ROS 58). Other chambered cairns were merely noted as 'cairn', 'stone circle', 'stone coffins', or 'enclosure'.

2.32) By the mid nineteenth century chambered cairns were recognised as a distinct and widespread class of monument in western Europe, though even in 1851 Wilson knew of few examples in Scotland. This was soon to change; in the north the two Clava-type passage-graves at Balnuaran (INV 9, 10) were known by 1858, and in the 1850s and 1860s pioneering investigations were producing fine examples in Orkney and Caithness. A bequest by A. H. Rhind to the Society of Antiquaries of Scotland was intended to fund excavations in the three counties of the northern mainland 'where the remains are mostly unknown to the general student, [and] are often in good preservation' (Stuart 1868, 289). This led to the Secretary of the Society making a tour in 1866, to assess the variety and quality of monuments in this huge and difficult region. He was shown much of interest in Caithness and Sutherland, but he visited relatively few monuments in Ross-shire, probably because there was no antiquary there of the calibre of those active further north. He did see the long cairn in Morangie Forest (ROS 45), probably Carn Glas (ROS 12), and probably the two cairns at Boath (ROS 10, 11), though no chambers were visible. At Ballachnecore (ROS 3) 'there was a cairn, of which the two ruined chambers remain'. He drew attention to the earlier descriptions of other monuments in the area (ROS 14, a 'remarkable structure'; ROS 58, a long cairn; ROS 22 and 52, both without comment), but did not visit them. Evidently he heard of Upper Park (ROS 51) but the description did not indicate the nature of the remains. He then continued his journey into Inverness-shire (¶ 2.16). The upshot was that the cairns of Ross-shire continued in obscurity.

2.33) The survey work for the first edition of the 6-inch Ordnance Survey maps covering north-east Inverness-shire and east Ross-shire was undertaken between 1868 and 1875. Although thirty-seven chambered cairns or long cairns, now classified as belonging to the Orkney-Cromarty group, were shown as antiquities on the maps, none was titled as 'Chambered Cairn'. Some were titled 'Cairn' and may have been too intact for further classification, but others were misleadingly titled 'Stone Circle, Remains of', and yet others were given their specific name in gothic lettering, thus avoiding the need to classify them. The surveyors took an unusual interest in the antiquities they were mapping, and entries in the Object Name Books sometimes give useful details about the monuments. Indeed, one

puzzling structure was dug out at the behest of an officer, and was shown to be a burial monument, though it was not recognised as a denuded chamber (ROS 52).

2.34) It might have been expected that the founding of two learned societies in Inverness in the 1870s would have advanced the study of these cairns, but there was little interest in them, and even when seen, there was a surprising failure to recognise their character. From 1876 members of the Inverness Scientific Society and Field Club visited several during their excursions, but always incidentally to their main objectives. They went several times to Essich Moor (INV 31), and did recognise that it was a long cairn containing chambers and that it could be compared to the long cairns in Caithness. On a rare excursion farther afield in 1899, visits were made to Scotsburn House and Kinrive West long cairn (ROS 46, 27), but the nearby impressive chamber in the King's Head Cairn (ROS 25) was only mentioned, not visited.

2.35) Angus Beaton, a civil engineer living in Munlochy in the Black Isle, took members of the Society to see some of the antiquities in his locality. He prepared descriptions of a range of monuments, accompanied by careful plans and sections, which were published by the Society of Antiquaries of Scotland in 1882. Four chambered cairns were published for the first time: Carn Glas (ROS 12) was still intact; at Balnaguie and Belmaduthy (ROS 6, 8) greatly reduced cairns contained settings of large orthostats (referred to as 'enclosures'), and it seems strange that they were not recognised as denuded chambers, perhaps because their plans were rectangular rather than round; The Temple at Tore (ROS 37) was understandably baffling due to its very reduced condition. In 1886 Roderick Maclean, factor at Ardross, gave a paper to the Gaelic Society of Inverness on the parish of Rosskeen, and though he was mainly concerned with other matters, he mentioned nine chambered cairns, several of which were on the Ardross estate (ROS 18, 25, 27, 32, 44, 49, 52, 54, 55). He gave minimal descriptions, and referred to most of them only

FIGURE 9. The denuded chamber at Ballachnecore, ROS 3, from the south-east. Drawn by Tomkin in 1885, with Pitt Rivers himself to give scale, during Pitt Rivers' official tour.

as 'cairns', although he realised that one had contained 'a vault', but several he did not recognise as remains of cairns at all. Nonetheless, his paper is useful for the only record of two destroyed cairns, and in giving slight information on other cairns which were not to be examined for another fifty or even eighty years.

2.36) On his northern tour of 1885 Pitt Rivers visited Ballachnecore (where Tomkin made two delightful drawings, figure 9), Heights of Brae, and Contin Mains (ROS 3, 22, 19), all of which he identified as burial chambers, though he considered that ROS 3 and 19 had never been covered by a cairn.

2.37) By the end of the nineteenth century it was possible to infer, by reading carefully many snippets of information which were mainly obscurely published, that there were a few chambered cairns and two long cairns north of the Beauly Firth in eastern Ross-shire. South of the Beauly Firth, in Inverness-shire, there was certainly one long cairn, but three monuments recorded as antiquities had not yet been identified as chambered cairns of Orkney-Cromarty type. The records made by

the officers of the Ordnance Survey and by Pitt Rivers were, of course, unpublished. The situation in Sutherland, where a number of chambered cairns had been identified and several had been investigated, was to be transformed in 1911 by the publication of an inventory of monuments by the recently established Royal Commission on the Ancient and Historical Monuments and Constructions of Scotland. Ross-shire and Inverness-shire were not to receive this comprehensive treatment, so that the imbalance of archaeological information continued.

Progress on Orkney-Cromarty-type cairns in the twentieth century

2.38) There matters rested until, at the height of the second world war, it was realised that antiquities in military training areas were under threat. So, in 1943, an emergency survey concentrating on the monuments recorded on the OS 6-inch maps was undertaken for the Royal Commission by V. G. Childe, a Commissioner, and Angus Graham, Secretary of the Commission, in selected areas between the Dornoch Firth and the Beauly Firth. The result, to professional surprise, was that the apparent gap between the well known Orkney-Cromarty-type cairns to the north of the Dornoch Firth and the Clava-type cairns south of the Beauly Firth was found to contain many chambered cairns. Almost all were of Orkney-Cromarty type, though several long cairns had no chamber visible. To show clearly the significance of these discoveries, i.e. the contrasting chamber design in Orkney-Cromarty-type and Clava-type cairns, and the almost mutually exclusive distribution of the two groups, Childe published brief descriptions of thirty cairns (counting INV 31 as one monument) and six plans (1944). These included eight chambered cairns and three long cairns without visible chambers, all recognised for the first time (ROS 2, 4, 29–32, 36, 38–42), ten cairns of which there was slight and unreliable information (ROS 3, 6, 8, 19, 22, 25, 27, 37, INV 31, 38), and one site which has been dropped from our list (ROS 26), and also six or seven Clava-type cairns to the north and west of Inverness. It had become clear that the one group of cairns did not derive from the other, as had seemed possible until now (Childe 1935, 53).

2.39) In the early 1950s A. A. Woodham undertook a survey of the prehistoric monuments of the Black Isle (1956a). He was able to add six cairns to Childe's list (ROS 7, 12, 23, 24, 33, 34), and supplied nine chamber plans and one complete plan. Woodham followed up by excavating the disturbed chamber at Carn Glas (ROS 12) in 1955 and 1956. Besides revealing the bipartite plan, he recovered some beaker sherds and flints. In 1956–8 Woodham excavated a more rewarding cairn, the nearby Kilcoy South (ROS 24). The chamber had an unusual three-part plan, and retained its filling associated with sherds of a number of beakers. The cairn appeared to have a horned forecourt, but further work in 1997 (reported in ¶ 5.23 and in the Inventory) showed that this was a misconception caused by curious sequences of robbing and dumping field-gathered stones. In 1963 Woodham excavated an almost totally

ruined chamber, Tomfat Plantation (INV 52), which he had found south of Inverness; it produced a few beaker sherds. The last cairn to be excavated, in 1965, was the newly discovered Balvraid (INV 51), seemingly isolated in west Inverness-shire but really an outlier of the Hebridean passage-graves. The excavator, J. X. W. P. Corcoran, died before a report was written.

2.40) During Henshall's fieldwork in the later 1950s seven more scattered chambered cairns (ROS 5, 9–11, 18, INV 12, 46) were added to the known list, three of them as a result of a visit to Boath by Woodham, and in the following years officers of the Ordnance Survey identified another nine (ROS 44, 46–49, 51–3, 55). As part of Henshall's country-wide survey, all the known chambered cairns in Ross-shire and Inverness-shire were described, and most of them were illustrated by a plan which in many cases had been specially prepared (published in 1963 with additional material in 1972). Three more cairns (ROS 57, 59, INV 53) were recorded by the Royal Commission in the late 1970s, another was found by D. Coghill in 1993 (INV 54), and as late as 1997 the long cairn at Cairnside (ROS 60) was found by D. Alston using Brown's map of 1816, and lastly in 1999 the lost cairn recorded by Logan in 1831 (ROS 61) (¶ 2.31) was rediscovered by A. Robb. Three destroyed cairns (ROS 54, 56, 58) have been tentatively identified as chambered from inadequate sources, and are noted in the present volume. This brings to fifty-nine the number of cairns of Orkney-Cromarty type (including long cairns without chambers) recorded in our Inventory.

*Synthesis and assessment of the
Orkney-Cromarty cairns*

2.41) The background to Childe's and Piggott's approach to the Scottish passage-graves has been summarised in ¶ 2.20–3. Piggott recognised that the northern chambered cairns were passage-graves belonging to one architectural family distributed through eastern Ross-shire, Sutherland, Caithness, to

Orkney, and he introduced the term 'Orkney-Cromarty group' to emphasise their geographical spread (Piggott 1954, 232–52; but he also included the small number of cairns of Maes Howe type, confined to Orkney, which are generally regarded as a distinct group). The chambers of the Orkney-Cromarty group were normally divided by pairs of transversely-set orthostats into two or three compartments, and in most cases parts of the chambers were vaulted (apart from the extreme developments of this plan on Orkney). Because vaulted chambers under round cairns were thought to be an early form of passage-grave, they were interpreted as the burial places of peoples settling along the western seaboard of mainland Europe and around the Irish Sea area, ultimately colonising the north of Scotland by way of the Great Glen. However, a puzzling feature of the northern passage-graves was the form of some of the cairns. Besides those with normal round cairns, some chambers were covered by long cairns, huge structures greatly in excess of the size needed to enclose the chamber. It seemed probable, as suggested by previous writers, that this cairn form, inappropriate to passage-graves, derived from the 'gallery graves' in south-west Scotland or north-east Ireland. Consequently Piggott regarded the chambered cairns with long cairns as hybrid monuments, which suggested that they were later in date than the passage-graves with round cairns. There was a further complication in that long cairns generally, and round cairns occasionally, had forecourts to the front and rear, the so-called horned long cairns and short horned cairns. The confusing variety of cairn plans and chamber plans was in fact even less amenable to typological arrangement than was suggested in Piggott's diagram (1954, figure 37).

2.42) By the time that his *Neolithic Cultures of the British Isles* was published in 1954, a century of investigations had shown that the burial rites were by either inhumation or cremation, and that the chambers might contain quantities of pottery, or very little, occasionally stone artefacts, or nothing at all. Some of the gravegoods indicated a late date for the use of the tombs, and on the chronological table at the back of his book Piggott placed them, in the framework then current, in the middle or late neolithic, between about 1700 and 1450 BC. He felt that the Orkney-Cromarty and the Clava cairn-builders could not have arrived in the Beauly Firth area at the same time, but which was the earlier he left an open question.

2.43) In 1963 a synthesis of the more detailed information which had accumulated since 1954 was offered, but the interpretaion of the cairns was little changed (Henshall 1963, 61–76, 113–7). In 1972 Henshall reviewed the whole chambered cairn phenomenon in Scotland. The Orkney-Cromarty group of cairns was now seen to include the passage-graves of the Hebrides and the west coast of the mainland, hitherto considered as a separate group. By this time radiocarbon dating was an established tool, and the understanding of European prehistory was being transformed. Although the internal chronology of the Orkney-Cromarty-type cairns was far from clear, it was accepted that the earliest Scottish passage-graves belonged in the early neolithic and must have been built not later than 3000 BC (at that time a rather daring proposition, but the dating of the cairns continues to be pushed ever earlier), and it seemed likely that they continued to be built to the end of the third millennium or even later (Henshall 1972, 280–3). Finds from chambers were seen to be unhelpful for dating the constructional phases, as mostly they had been introduced long after the first burials.

2.44) The recognition that cairn-building had extended over a long period made it easier to accept the evidence, which had been accumulating in Scotland and elsewhere, that chambered cairns were sometimes multiperiod structures. Notably for the Orkney-Cromarty-group cairns, Corcoran's excavation of Tulach an t-Sionnaich in Caithness (CAT 58) had demonstrated that a long cairn had been added to, and had sealed, an earlier small passage-grave (Corcoran 1966, 5–22). This new approach offered escape from the typological dead-end, because it allowed the chambers and the long cairns (which belonged to a mortuary tradition unconnected with passage-graves and not directly derived from the chambered cairns of south-west Scotland) to be considered separately (Henshall 1972, 201–4, 286). The designs of the Orkney-Cromarty-type chambered cairns now seemed to be the result of local isolated developments of two basic traditions, and the search for prototypes abroad was an obsolete exercise; the remote impulse which gave rise to the building of chambered cairns lay outside the scope of these studies. The structural relationship of long cairns and passage-graves was clearer, but the relationship of their builders remained obscure.

2.45) As far as the cairns in Ross-shire and Inverness-shire were concerned, in 1963 it could be seen that in general terms they were in accord with those in the rest of the Orkney-Cromarty province, though they were known almost entirely from surface examination. There were a few long cairns and one or two short horned cairns; the chambers were normally bipartite, and were built with orthostats linked by panels of walling. Misguidedly, in 1972 an external origin was sought to explain the presence of rectangular chambers, which are hardly known further north, and it was suggested that they were likely to be early in any sequence (Henshall 1972, 260–1, 277). It was suggested with more probability that small single-compartment chambers were also likely to be early, both in this region and elsewhere, and the possibly two-period chamber at Kilcoy South (ROS 24) was quoted in support of this hypothesis (ibid., 257–9). A typological sequence was put forward in general terms, in which the design of chambers developed from south to north, including Orkney and ultimately Shetland (ibid., 263–4, 279–83), with a tentative chronology spanning the third millennium and continuing into the early second millennium. There now seemed to be little doubt that the passage-graves of Clava type were contemporary with the latest of the

Orkney-Cromarty-type cairns in the south of the province.

2.46) The chambered cairns of Caithness and Sutherland (the latter more closely related to those of Ross-shire) were investigated in greater detail in the 1980s and 1990s (Davidson and Henshall 1991, Henshall and Ritchie 1995). The designs of these chambers were now more thoroughly understood, but no major changes in their interpretation emerged. However, detailed consideration of multi-period cairns in both regions increased awareness of their monumental quality and of their structural complexity, especially of the long cairns covering chambers, and also of the extent of our ignorance (Davidson and Henshall 1991, 55–9; Henshall and Ritchie 1995, 41–9). A number of radiocarbon dates from Sutherland, Caithness and Orkney showed that tombs which are certainly not among the earliest were in use during the mid fourth millennium BC; the building of the first passage-graves must therefore lie considerably earlier (Henshall and Ritchie 1995, 74–6).

2.47) Whilst we were working on our surveys during the last two decades, the theoretical basis of British neolithic studies has radically altered. Stuart Piggott's *The Neolithic Cultures of the British Isles* published in 1954 had set a framework that was to remain the foundation for study for many years. The neolithic was thought of as intrusive and firmly linked to agricultural practices. Piggott's pessimistic assessment of the limited inferences possible from the observed data in chambered cairns may not be appreciated today, but it is still very relevant (1973, 9–15). The recent changes in perspective with a shift to a more theoretical approach, now concerned with processes of cultural change rather than with the description and classification of artefacts or monuments, has been concisely outlined by Whittle (1999, 61–2). Another approach which attempts to understand in philosophical as well as environmental terms the responses of ancient societies to the landscapes around them probes the many possible relationships between people and monuments over the centuries (discussed for example by Tilley 1994). An engaging new study by Edmonds (1999, although choosing southern English examples) has taken this approach, with neolithic monuments, landscapes, and the notions of the collective memories of the people around them interwoven in several layers of interpretation.

Similarly, the sorts of statements that may lie behind the creation of a monument, such as a chambered cairn or stone circle, in relation to its surrounding landscape have been explored by Bradley using Scottish examples as well as those from a much wider canvas (1993).

3. The land, the environment and the locations

The character of the Central Highlands

3.1) The area covered by this volume stretches from coast to coast across Scotland from the Moray Firth in the east to the shores of the Minch in the west and from the Dornoch Firth in the north to the southern end of the Great Glen. The environment ranges from the fertile coastlands of the Moray Firth to the inhospitable Monadhliath Mountains to the south and the mountains of Wester Ross and Lochaber to the west. In effect, however, the monuments under discussion are with few exceptions found only in the Firthlands of the east (figures 10, 11), and there is no need to attempt to characterise the geology and soil cover for the whole of Ross-shire and Inverness-shire. The area termed the Firthlands includes the firths and the lower valleys of the rivers that flow into them; the firths in question are the Dornoch Firth that forms the boundary between Sutherland to the north and Ross-shire to the south, the Cromarty Firth that separates Easter Ross from the Black Isle (not in fact an island but a large peninsula) with Cromarty at its north-east tip, and the Moray Firth with its inner arm, the Beauly Firth, with Inverness-shire to the south. Until recent times with the building of impressive bridges, road travel involved long loops round the heads of the firths, but in prehistoric times, when seaborne travel was probably the norm, cross-firth communication would have been relatively easy.

3.2) The solid geology of the lower part of the Dornoch Firth, the Cromarty Firth and the Moray Firth is of Old Red Sandstone. There is older rock to the east, the Moine

schists, and Ben Wyvis, an important landmark to the north-west of the Cromarty Firth, is of this hard rock. The headlands of the North and South Sutors that flank the entrance to the Cromarty Firth are also formed of Moine schist. The Old Red Sandstones are part of a fold running north-east to south west and described as the Black Isle Syncline. The fossil fish that occur in nodules within the Middle Old Red Sandstone beds were discussed by Hugh Miller of Cromarty in his volume *The Old Red Sandstone* published in 1841, which first put on record the geology of the region. The complex Great Glen Fault and the associated Strath Glass parallel fault shaped the generally north-east to south-west dominant formations that are such features of the area. Glaciations played a further major part in shaping the landscape as we know it today, forming the broad U-shaped valleys of the Central Highlands. The firths themselves are described as glacially over-deepened and drowned ancient river valleys. The glaciers were also responsible for the deposition of boulder clay.

3.3) In the east the subsequent adjustments in land levels relative to the sea allowed raised beaches to be formed, now often the basis of good quality well-drained soils. The west coasts and central massifs have contrasting geology which has offered less favourable soil formation, the contrast between the peaty podsols and associated soils of Wester Ross and the Firthlands of Easter Ross being particularly marked (Gillen 1984, 40, fig 5); poor drainage and higher rainfall have also had a detrimental effect on soil formation in the western part of the area. Only around Kishorn and in a few other pockets have there formed lime-rich soils comparable to those of the Knockan-Inchnadamph area of western Sutherland; there is a concentration of cairns in the latter, but none have yet been found in Wester Ross. A comparison of Gillen's map of soil types (1984, 40, fig. 5) with the map of cairns in Ross-shire (figure 11) tellingly makes the point that the distribution of monuments relates to humus-iron podsols and brown forest soils formed above the Old Red Sandstone. The

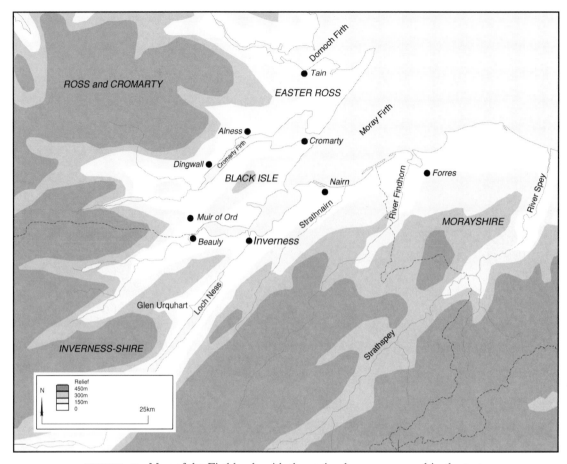

FIGURE 10. Map of the Firthlands with the main place-names used in the text.

coasts of the inner Moray Firth are drier and warmer than the western areas, and there is every reason to believe that this would also have been so in the neolithic period. (¶ 2 and 3 are based on information in Gill 1975; Gillen, 1984; 1986; Price 1976; Sissons 1967; Smith 1975.)

The evidence for pre-neolithic peoples

3.4) The final retreat of glacial conditions about 10,000 years ago allowed mosses and small shrubs to become established. Little by little tree cover increased, first birch and pine, later oak, hazel, ash and alder. Mammals too, including deer, wolves and bears, colonised the new lands long before man began to explore

the northern parts of Scotland to harvest the natural resources of the forests and firths and rivers about 8000 BC. Evidence of mesolithic hunting and fishing activity is slight in the Central Highlands (Gourlay 1984, 100–2). Excavations in Inverness revealed two occupation horizons as well as a microlithic assemblage (Wordsworth 1985). Otherwise the only evidence of these people around the Firthlands comes from field walking, with scatters of lithics found at Balnaglack and Allanfearn on the south side of the Moray Firth, and sparser scatters from a number of coastal locations in the same area and around the Black Isle, and also inland in Strathnairn; shell middens (though of unconfirmed date) are known on the coast of Easter Ross, the Black Isle, and

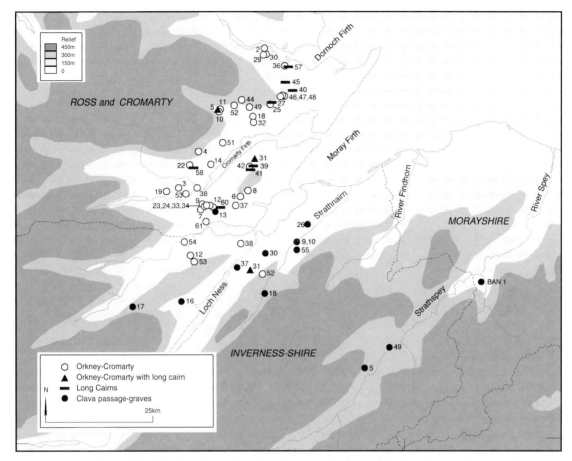

FIGURE 11. Map of the Firthlands showing the chambered cairns with the code numbers used in the text.

near Inverness (Bradley 2000, 200–4, with references, illustration 168, for Inverness-shire; Gourlay 1984, 102, for Ross-shire). In the west an extensive settlement has been excavated on the Isle of Rhum (Wickham-Jones 1990). Scatters of mesolithic flint tools have been found at Redpoint and Shieldaig in Wester Ross (Wickham-Jones 1994, 62–3, 73–4), and in 1999 many sites in the Applecross peninsula and on the Crowlin Islands were identified by Scotland's First Settlers Project during field walking and by test excavations. The success of the Project suggests that the apparent absence of evidence in other coastal areas may be explained by the lack of field work (Finlayson et al. 1999). Traces of mesolithic occupation

are insubstantial in the northern counties, there are a few mesolithic sites in Orkney (Saville 1996), and none as yet in Shetland. In both the Northern Isles and the Western Isles the locations of possible sites may have been lost to the sea.

Neolithic settlement and the distribution of cairns

3.5) Previous assumptions about the transition from mesolithic ways to neolithic farming have been questioned recently, and from a specifically Scottish viewpoint by Armit and Finlayson (1996). Although the traces of a mesolithic presence in northern Scotland may be sparse, the indications are that a long established mobile mesolithic population was present when farming practices, and presumably a more permanent settlement pattern, was being established about 4000 BC. Farming was not introduced into an empty landscape, and the patterns of interaction between the different ways of life were likely to have varied. There is little doubt that in some areas of the north the assumed benefits of a sedentary agricultural life would have been weighed against the millennia of successful exploitation of what the land and sea had to offer, and the skills of hunting and fishing would have been carefully maintained. With the near absence of neolithic settlement sites in the north, apart from Orkney, the sedentary nature or otherwise of the neolithic inhabitants is difficult to gauge. The neolithic period is characterised by the cairns, and the cairns are by nature permanent features. Any interpretation is thus very impressionistic. A cairn that may seem a marked feature in today's landscape in a valley with a couple of farms may seem confirmation of a sedentary population. But it may equally be the spot where widely-ranging population groups made irregular stops for a number of reasons, not all of which may have been related to burial at all. To take the matter further in an area where settlement of either period is exiguous would be unwise.

3.6) The distribution of cairns around the Firthlands indicates the main areas of settlement in neolithic times, and several of the more inland cairns are located in valleys with good agricultural potential. But there is no doubt that originally there were a great many more cairns, and that their loss has been proportionately greater from the land that has been intensively farmed in modern times (see ¶ 6.10, 9.3). The distribution of cairns is therefore distorted, and though the extent is unquantifiable, this has to be borne in mind. The absence of cairns in the harsher environments of the west is no surprise, and the single cairn in the far west of our area (INV 51, included in this volume for administrative completeness) is linked to the monuments in

the Hebrides. Woodland cover of the Firthlands around 3000 BC was of birch, hazel and oak (Tipping 1994, 12, illustration 3), but very few pollen studies have been carried out in the area. Work at Lairg in Sutherland has shown that a farming economy was certainly underway early in the fourth millennium BC (McCullagh 1992, 6). Little by little a pattern of neolithic settlement will undoubtedly emerge, but at present the evidence is very slight. At Kinbeachie, near the Woodhead cairns (ROS 41–2) in the Black Isle, a rectangular structure defined by posts was excavated in 1998, along with pits, neolithic pottery and a miniature polished stone axe, and a radiocarbon date within the neolithic period (Dalland 1998a, 1998b). At Stoneyfield, near Inverness, excavation of a cairn with a massive kerb (INV 47) revealed a setting of some fifty-two posts as well as occupation debris including grooved ware pottery. The excavator stressed, however, that the interpretation of the function of this setting as either domestic or funerary is problematic (Simpson 1996, 63). Bradley has also considered that some of the material found around the cairns at Balnuaran indicates settlement in the immediate vicinity at some time before they were built (2000, 120–1). Although evidence of settlement, or at least of timber structures, is increasing, the cairns still remain the primary source of information for the neolithic period in the northern mainland.

The siting of cairns

3.7) The siting of cairns is an important aspect of any evaluation of their relationships within the landscape, however subjective any assessment may be, and it is particularly difficult at the many Orkney-Cromarty-type cairns which are now within dense forestry plantations. Most of the cairns are on hillsides at moderate elevations, generally on a level site or on a small knoll. Given the geography of the Firthlands with high hills rising close to the shores, many cairns almost inevitably have an extensive outlook over low-lying land and the firths, with high mountains in the background.

PLATE 2. Heights of Brae (ROS 22), the orthostats of the inner compartment from the north-east.

This is generally true also of the cairns on lower flat ground, for instance in the open landscapes at the west end of the Black Isle. The views from cairns are very beautiful and tend to beguile the modern visitor. Yet the impression grows that neither the outlook, nor their visibility when seen from afar, were prime considerations, and the landscape would have retained much open woodland which would obstruct distant viewing. Proximity to a settlement is likely to have been the main siting determinant. There are a few exceptions where a prominent site seems to have been chosen, for instance Heights of Brae (plate 2), Upper Park or Leachkin (ROS 22, 51, INV 38) set on the top of ridges dividing valleys, or Essich Moor (INV 31) spectacularly fitted along a rocky ridge, or Cnoc Navie (ROS 18) on the brow of a dominant hill. There are several close clusters of cairns, notably at Boath, where three cairns (ROS 5, 10 and 11) are situated on a terrace above the Alness River, and at Scotsburn (ROS 46–8). The group of cairns at Kilcoy (ROS 12, 23–4) is part of a concentration of cairns (including one of Clava-type, ROS 13) in the gently undulating farmland at the west end of the Black Isle.

3.8) There are seven apparently unchambered long cairns in Easter Ross and the Black Isle. They have a similar range of location and siting as the cairns already discussed. At several (and the three long cairns known to contain chambers can be included) the builders seem to have taken advantage of a break in slope to emphasize the form of the cairn, as at Kinrive West (ROS 27) for example. Edderton Hill (ROS 57) is set along the contour of a steep hill, and even in its much damaged state it is possible to appreciate its commanding position. One of the oddest situations is that of Morangie Forest (ROS 45) which is set slightly skew across the grain of the slope of the hillside. Cairnside (ROS 60) is in flat agricultural land. Topography played a vital part in the creation of the chambered long cairn on Essich Moor (INV 31), for two of the elements of the cairn were placed on independent knolls at either end of a ridge with linking linear cairn material built along the crest of the ridge.

3.9) In the past the siting of Clava-type cairns has tended to be contrasted with that of the Orkney-Cromarty-type cairns, but as far as the Clava-type passage-graves are concerned this is only partly true. Certainly the Balnuaran

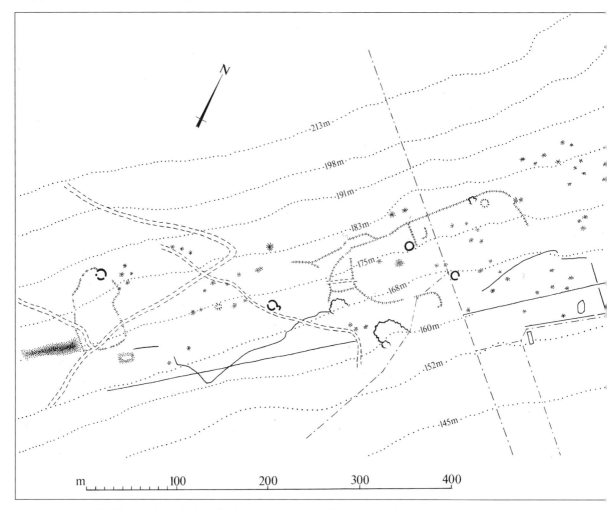

FIGURE 12. Prehistoric hut-circles, field-systems and small cairns to the east-north-east of Kinrive West, ROS 27, as surveyed by the Royal Commission on the Ancient and Historical Monuments of Scotland in 1979.

cairns, Corrimony and Croftcroy (INV 9, 10, 17, 18) are on valley floors, but Carn Urnan, Dalcross Mains, Druidtemple and Lagmore (ROS 13, INV 26, INV 30, BAN 1) are in open upland situations, and Culdoich South (INV 55) is high on a hillside above the River Nairn. This is not to imply that choice of location or site was not important to the builders, but that the intricacies of choice cannot be explained. This takes us well beyond the results of field evidence alone, but even the

old-fashioned surveyor standing all day at a plane-table allows the surrounding landscape of a chambered cairn to make a deep impression while the measurements are taken and the description is prepared; the landscape allows consideration of many changing possibilities in the interplay between settlement and ritual practice. Phillip's study of all the Clava-type cairns (in Bradley 2000, 171–84), which included monuments of doubtful or mistaken identity to enlarge the data-base, takes us little further.

·137m·

Cairns and ancient landscapes

3.10) The ancient landscapes around many of the cairns have been destroyed long ago by agricultural improvements and by forestry. The cairns, and in some cases only the chambers, have survived because of their size, and also perhaps because of superstitions about their origin. Only between Clava and the coast has field walking taken place to try to identify possible settlement areas (Bradley 2000, 185–210). The Royal Commission on the Ancient and Historical Monuments of Scotland has undertaken one detailed survey, which indicates what might be expected in areas of marginal ground that have escaped the improvers and the foresters. On the terrace that runs NE from Kinrive West (ROS 27) a series of small cairns, plot boundaries and hut-circles gives an impression of the density of settlement in rather later periods of antiquity than the long cairn itself (which is to the left side of the plan figure 12) (RCAHMS 1979a, no. 158, 20). There are few surviving ancient landscapes in the Firthlands, but detailed archaeological field survey in what are now marginal areas may lead to the discovery of further examples, and indeed further chambered cairns. Only in the eastern part of Ross-shire and Inverness-shire, and only in recent years, has archaeological survey been undertaken with the same intensity as in Sutherland and Caithness.

4. The passages and chambers of the Orkney-Cromarty group

Introduction and terminology

4.1) In this section the passages and chambers of cairns which are not of Clava type are considered. The majority undoubtedly belong to the Orkney-Cromarty group, and probably all of them do, though at first glance some of those with simple plans might suggest otherwise. Out of fifty cairns, four or five cairns contain two chambers, and one cairn contains three chambers; in addition there are also two or three chambers which are now considered to be of two periods, and thus each of these offer (when dissected) two structures for consideration. Against this total, five cairns that have been destroyed, or nearly so, provide no information (ROS 33, 54–6, 59), and indeed their classification as chambered cairns is not beyond doubt. This Section is thus based on data from at least fifty-three chambers.

4.2) Despite the large number of chambered cairns in eastern Ross-shire and north-east Inverness-shire, their generally poor condition and the paucity of information from excavation means that at first sight structural information seems to be limited. Only four passages and chambers have been excavated, and the results from three have been disappointing. Two are small chambers and there had been severe interference before excavation (ROS 12, INV 52), and the third (INV 51), for which there is no excavation report, is a simple structure near the west coast which relates to the cairns of the Isle of Skye and the Hebrides rather than to those in the east. The chamber at Kilcoy South (ROS 24), though roofless, is a more impressive structure which was re-opened in 1997, forty years after the excavation, to obtain a detailed description. All in all it has to be admitted that

the circumstances of the chambered cairns in the Central Highlands are discouraging. Nonetheless, by collation of piecemeal information, and by drawing on data from well-preserved monuments in other parts of the Orkney-Cromarty province, it is possible to present a more comprehensive view of the chambers than might be expected, and also to begin an appreciation of what has been lost.

4.3) The following terminology is used to describe the passages and the chambers to which they led. *Chamber*: the entire structure beyond the passage, consisting of one, or two, or rarely three, compartments. *Compartment*: the separately roofed part of a chamber entered between portal stones. *Ante-chamber*: the outer compartment of a bipartite chamber when it is markedly smaller than the inner compartment. *Main chamber*: the inner compartment of a bipartite chamber when it is markedly larger than the outer compartment. *Cell*: an adjunct to the main chamber in the form of a small single-compartment chamber. *Portal stones*: a pair of upright stones generally set with their longer axes more or less at right angles to the axis of the passage or chamber, and designed to carry a lintel. Portal stones may be at the passage entrance (*entrance portal stones*), between the passage and the chamber (*outer portal stones*), or between the compartments of a bipartite chamber (*inner portal stones*). *Orthostat*: an upright stone which forms part of the wall of a passage or chamber (or the edging of a cairn). *Eke-stone*: a small slab inserted to level up a major structural stone.

4.4) The majority of the chambers are bipartite in plan, with the passage leading to two compartments, all on the same axis. These chambers are described first (¶ 4.17) followed by chambers that may have been built in two periods (¶ 4.37), single-compartment chambers (¶ 4.40), and finally those which at present cannot be precisely classified (¶ 4.44).

Construction methods

4.5) Most of the chambers have been reduced to a basic skeleton of orthostats. The orthostats had formed the major parts of the walls, but the arrangement of them, as now visible, is generally incomplete. When a considerable depth of cairn material remains some of the structure may be hidden, or only the tips of much larger stones may be exposed. When the cairn is greatly denuded some of the orthostats are likely to have been removed, or to have been reduced to stumps. These various uncertainties inevitably present a challenge to understanding the observable remains. Many of the orthostats are large, and their true size is often concealed by the remains of the cairn; they may be over 2 m high, and sometimes as much as 2 m long. Depending on the available stone, and thus on the local geology, the orthostats are boulders, occasionally split boulders, or heavy rectangular blocks, or relatively thin slabs, and there may be a mixture in one chamber, or occasionally even in paired portal stones. It is noticeable that the flattest surfaces of orthostats were carefully set to face into the chambers. Excavation has revealed at Carn Glas and Kilcoy South (ROS 12, 24) that one or more of the orthostats, which at first sight are among the most regular and largest, are set on narrow rounded bases and are dependant on substantial chock-stones and walling to maintain their position (figures 16, 18). This is all the more surprising at Kilcoy South where one of the orthostats is an unsually large block, another is the back-slab, and two are portal stones which were required to support lintels; clearly the purpose in most cases was to provide horizontal upper edges. It is not known, of course, whether this treatment of orthostats may be rare or more widespread.

4.6) The chamber walls were completed by walling, usually neatly built of relatively small slabs, laid horizontally. Sometimes very little walling was needed, just to fill gaps caused by irregularities in the shape of the orthostats, and sometimes considerable panels were built to link widely spaced orthostats. Some walling remains at a number of chambers (e.g. ROS 11, 24, 47), though once it has been exposed it generally disintegrates fairly rapidly.

4.7) Above the orthostats and walling, from a height of a metre or so, there were layers of corbel stones. These large flat slabs were generally laid with their longer axes radially to the wall-face, their inner ends slightly overhanging, and their outer ends projecting into the cairn core which secured them by acting as a counterweight. They are often 0.2 m or more thick, and 1 m or much more long. Their purpose was to gradually reduce the span of the roof. Except at the unusually well preserved chamber at Boath Short (ROS 11), only a few of the lowest corbel stones may remain in place (as at ROS 24, 47, 51), and more often the corbel stones are to be seen lying displaced either outside or inside the chamber. The core of the cairn, immediately surrounding the chamber, was built of densely-packed slabs and was an integral part of the chamber structure (see ¶ 10.6–8); the core can be glimpsed at the back of recently fallen orthostats at ROS 24 and 48.

4.8) Pairs of portal stones are a characteristic and easily recognised feature of the passages and chambers. Typical portal stones are quite substantial but relatively low boulders; the orthostats in the chamber walls are almost always taller, and sometimes are very much taller. If they survive, the portal stones are generally intact, and frequently they have flat or slightly rounded upper surfaces that are either horizontal or slope gently down away from the entry. The portal stones bore lintels (some of which remain in place), and together they formed low narrow entries to the several parts of each structure. The lintels were placed directly on the portal stones, or were raised on one or two eke-stones (a necessary arrangement when the paired stones differed slightly in height).

4.9) The roofing of the chambers was the most challenging part of the building operation. With the exception of Boath Short (ROS 11), to be described later, nothing remains of the roofing at the chambers in the Central Highlands, and therefore it is necessary to turn for information to several closely similar but more complete chambers in Sutherland, and at a further remove, to some chambers in Caithness (discussed and illustrated in

Henshall and Ritchie 1995, 22–5; Davidson and Henshall 1991, 22–30). Each compartment of the chamber was roofed separately. In a few of the small compartments the roof would have been quite low (judging by examples in the north mainland), and only a layer or two of corbel stones would have been required to support the lintels or capstone, or indeed sometimes no corbel stones may have been used. Most of the compartments were roofed by a vault constructed with oversailing layers of corbel stones, and the precise technique varied somewhat according to the size and shape of the space to be spanned.

4.10) Many of the vaults in the north mainland, including the Central Highlands, were built over compartments that were roughly round or square in plan. The roofs of compartments of moderate size were more than 2 m high, and the largest compartments are estimated to have been roofed at heights of between 3 to 4 m. At Achaidh (SUT 2) the roof was found intact at a height of about 2.2 m, and at The Ord North (SUT 48) the chamber walls still stood to a height of 3 m. At both, above the orthostats in the walls, layers of corbel stones had been laid in rings with the corbel stones tilted slightly downwards into the cairn. Each layer oversailed that below to reduce the span, until the roof could be closed by a capstone. Besides the counterweight of the cairn material on their outer ends, any inward shift of the corbel stones was checked by pressure against their neighbours, and the construction was theoretically very stable. In several cases the lintel over the entry is known to have been placed on its narrow side, so that the tall vertical face formed part of the vault with oversailing corbel stones butted up against it. This was also done in the Central Highlands. However, nowhere is it clear how the roofing problem posed at large bipartite chambers, where the vaults over two compartments are juxtaposed, was managed. In Sutherland there are some large compartments with an elongated plan, but there is little evidence of precisely how they were roofed. It so happens that the only compartment in the

Central Highlands to retain its roof almost complete (Boath Short, ROS 11) has a long oval plan, and it is possible to see how the circular vault was adapted to cover longer spaces (¶ 4.21).

The passages

4.11) Because they are near the edge of the cairns, passages are especially vulnerable, either to accidental destruction from encroaching cultivation, or to deliberate destruction as an easy source of building stone. Only two passages, though lacking their roofs, have been completely exposed (ROS 24, INV 51).

4.12) The passage entrances are generally 3 to 5 m, and exceptionally 7.5 m, within the present edge of the cairns. This may be due to the spread of the cairn beyond its original limits, and in many cases to blocking material placed deliberately outside the entrance, and sometimes also to the enlargement of the cairn in prehistoric times. The entrance was between a pair of portal stones, which bore the first lintel of the passage roofing. Seen from outside, the portal stones and lintel together defined the entrance, and were designed to be flush with a wall-face edging the cairn. The passage entrance at Kilcoy South (ROS 24) is 0.55 m wide between a fine pair of portal stones, square in plan and 1 m high, with horizontal upper surfaces (figure 18, plate 5). It is more usual for the portal stones to be rectangular in plan, and to be set transversely to the passage to offer a stable seating for the lintel. Occasionally, as at Kilcoy South or Scotsburn Wood West (ROS 48), the paired stones are set slightly splayed, producing a somewhat funnel-shaped entrance. The widths of the entrances range between 0.53 and 0.9 m (at ROS 29 and 49); the heights, where they can be observed or calculated (at ROS 9, 24, 29, 44, 48), indicate that the normal range was 0.8 to 1.2 m.

4.13) At Balvaird (ROS 7) there is a stone parallel to, and in front of, one of the portal stones. This additional stone has the appearance of being one of a second pair of portal stones, implying that the passage may have been lengthened by a metre or so to bring the entrance to the edge of an enlargement of the cairn. The alternative, that the chamber was tripartite and entered through a very short passage, seems unlikely.

4.14) At the inner end of the passages, forming the entry into the chambers, there was a second pair of portal stones. The shortness of many passages is surprising, and it may be noted, too, that some of the shortest passages lead to some of the largest chambers (e.g. ROS 18, 29, 31). The approximate lengths of sixteen passages are known, and they vary between about 1.5 and nearly 3 m including the portal stones at either end (at ROS 29 and 25), and the length of the passage walls between the portal stones may be as little as 0.9 m. The passage at Kilcoy South (ROS 24), revealed by excavation, was built of walling, rather unusually with the lower part on each side consisting of a larger stone stretching the whole length with smaller stones carefully laid above and filling the irregular gaps, a method that was also used elsewhere in the chamber. At most of the cairns nothing can be seen of the passage walls, which may suggest that walling of horizontal slabs was usual, and at Baldoon (ROS 44) a fragment of such walling is just visible. An alternative, seen at four passages (ROS 7, 48, INV 38, 51), was for an orthostat to form most of each wall, once supplemented by a small amount of walling. In other passages there might be two orthostats in a wall (ROS 34), or a mixture of orthostats and walling (ROS 12, ?8). The width of the passages was often generous and considerably greater than the width of the entries at either end; at ROS 7, 24 and INV 38 the passages were between 1.5 and 1.2 m wide, contrasting with the passages at ROS 12 and 34 which were at most only about 0.7 m wide, but roughly in scale with the small size of the chambers.

4.15) The passages at three long cairns require particular comment, because their interpretation, if correct, also affects the interpretation of the chambers. The passage at Boath Long (ROS 10), as presently exposed, has an unusual appearance, with a large regular slab forming the whole of each wall with no portal stones visible at either end. There is no reason to think the passage was ever appreciably longer than the slabs, and its dimensions are not exceptional. The passage at the north end of the Essich Moor cairn (INV 31) is also built of large rectangular slabs, and is unusually long, and certainly is without portal stones at the inner end (figure 20). At the east end of Mid Brae (ROS 31) there are three orthostats which appear to belong to one side of a passage, which presumably led to a chamber now completely destroyed. They were probably an entrance portal stone, an unusually large side slab (which can be almost matched for size at ROS 8 and 10), and a prone slab which may have been a portal stone at the inner end.

4.16) Some well preserved passages in Sutherland and Caithness retain their roof lintels, and these are generally set progressively slightly higher from the outer to the inner end. It may be assumed that the passages in the Central Highlands had similar roofs. Short passages, such as that at Lower Lechanich North (ROS 29), would require only three or four lintels, and here (as at one or two other chambers) the innermost lintel remains in place over the entrance to the chamber. No lintels remain over passage entrances, though a displaced lintel can be seen at Baldoon (ROS 44). The heights of the passage roofs, indicated by the heights of the portal stones at each end, were between at least 0.8 and 1.3 m.

Bipartite chambers

4.17) In the Central Highlands there are at least seventeen bipartite chambers (ROS 3, 6, 7, 9, 12, 18, 19, 22, 29, 34, 38, 44, 48, 49, 61, INV 38, 54), and thirteen more chambers (ROS 2, 4, 5, 10, 11, 14, 23, 42, 51, 53, INV 12, 52, 53) are probably or possibly of this plan. Each chamber consisted of two compartments on the same axis as the passage, roofed separately, and linked through a narrow low entry. The destroyed monument, Clachan Biorach (ROS 14), has been included on the basis of a convincing late eighteenth century description, but it is not mentioned again. Three more chambers (ROS 24, 25, 47) which have unusual three-compartment plans are also included in the following descriptions, because in each of them the two outer compartments replicate bipartite chambers. Their entire plans, and the probability that the third innermost compartment is of earlier date, are considered in ¶ 4.37–9.

4.18) As mentioned already, the entries from the passages into the chambers were between the pair of outer portal stones, and an inner pair of portal stones formed the entries from the first to the second compartments. Thus at each cairn there were three pairs of portal stones (including the entrance portal stones at the outer end of the passage), and there is a tendency for them to increase slightly in height from front to rear. The heights of the few outer portal stones that can be measured or estimated range between somewhat over 1.2 m at ROS 25 and 0.53 m at ROS 12, which are themselves unusually large and small chambers. The widths of the entries into the chambers are mostly about 0.7 m, with extremes of 1.3 and 0.45 m at the same two chambers. It is unlikely that any of the inner portal stones was over 1.5 m high, and the entries between them vary from 1.35 to 0.6 m wide (at ROS 25 and 47), and exceptionally they are only 0.46 m wide at ROS 12 and INV 53. At chambers where some entries seem impracticably narrow this is due to slight displacement of the stones (at ROS 22, 38), but there is no obvious explanation for the gap of only 0.23 m at Boath Long and Tarradale (ROS 10, 61). On the whole the portal stones are well-matched pairs and symmetrically placed, but sometimes there are irregularities in the planning, which is particularly noticeable at King's Head Cairn (ROS 25).

4.19) The lintel still in place over the outer portal stones at Lower Lechanich North (ROS 29) is small and rather irregular in shape, 1.35 m long. At the inner end of the passage at Balvaird (ROS 7) a lintel nearly 2 m long is probably *in situ* resting on hidden outer portal stones. At Ardvanie (ROS 2) there is a fallen

lintel which does not appear to have been subsequently disturbed; as neither the portal stones which supported it nor the passage can be seen it is uncertain whether it was at the inner end of the passage, or (less likely) at the outer end (in which case the chamber had only one compartment). The first two of these lintels, and possibly also the third, were set on their narrow sides to provide vertical faces 0.8 to 1 m high. The enormous lintel at Boath Short (ROS 11) is about 3 m long, and is no less than 1.63 m high in the centre. Although it is *in situ*, there is uncertainty whether it is over inner or outer portal stones. Other notably large lintels, at ROS 24, 25, and 53, certainly are displaced from over inner portal stones; the last two also appear to have been set on their narrow sides, and their vertical faces would have been 1.2 and 0.94 m high. One lintel at least (at ROS 7) seems to have been placed flat, and yet others are irregular in shape or damaged, or are nearer square in cross-section. The lintels over the inner portal stones were of particular structural importance because they were at the junction of the two compartments and at most chambers they were required to carry part of both vaults. It may seem surprising that lintels were set on their narrow sides, but this gave them greater strength, and also reduced the amount of roof corbelling needed in this difficult area of the structure.

4.20) The vault at Boath Short (ROS 11) survives almost complete, and it must have been among the largest. The chamber is enclosed within a cairn which is still 3.3 m high, and the internal structure was evidently discovered from above by removing the top of the roof. It is possible to stand on the top of the cairn and look down into what is still an impressive building, even though the floor is choked with loose stone, and one wall is in a perilous state of collapse. The entry below the lintel is blocked by stones, and nothing can be seen of the passage, nor of an outer compartment. It is assumed here that the visible compartment is the inner part of a bipartite chamber, which its size suggests, and that the outer part has been greatly damaged and is

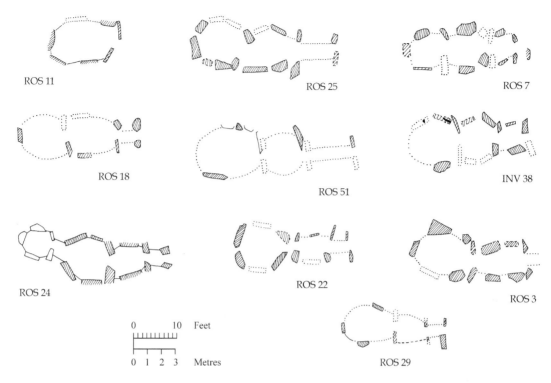

FIGURE 13. Bipartite chambers with polygonal compartments.
Key: extant orthostats, hatched with solid outline; orthostats not *in situ* (either fallen or previously recorded), hatched with dashed outline; hypothetical missing orthostats or walling, dotted.

completely hidden in disturbed cairn material. There is at least one parallel for a chamber of this form and size in the Central Highlands (ROS 51). Single-compartment chambers may be expected to be smaller, but analysis of the exceptional chamber at Brahan Wood (ROS 53) (¶ 4.41), if correct, indicates that very large single-compartment chambers were not unknown.

4.21) Whatever the status of the visible structure in Boath Short (ROS 11), it provides a rare opportunity to appreciate the appearance and impact of the large chambers in the Central Highlands. The compartment at Boath Short is 4.2 m long by at least 2.5 m wide (figure 13). The entrance is at least 1.2 m high between well-matched portal stones. They bear the massive lintel already mentioned, which, with the portal stones, reaches to almost 3 m

above the floor. The walls of the compartment are built of spaced boulders, the tallest at the rear about 2.2 m high. Up to the level of their shoulders the orthostats are linked by stretches of neat walling. Above this, the character of the walls changes and looks cruder as larger and thicker corbel stones are used. These are either flat boulders or split slabs laid end-on to the line of the wall-face. The compartment is a long oval in ground plan, but above the orthostats the vault becomes more rectangular in plan. At the east end the lintel provides a straight vertical wall; along the south side the corbel stones form an almost straight line with an overhang of 0.75 m; the west wall is straight with the two uppermost corbel stones overhanging so much that some displacement is probable; the north wall was presumably parallel to the south wall, but it has moved inwards *en masse* and is distorted (plate 3). This structural failure is partly due to the absence of the stabilising influence of corbel stones set on a horizontal curve, and partly to the lack of bonding between the walls at the corners of the vault. The side-walls butt against the face of the lintel at one end, and at the other end they are inadequately bonded with the straight wall-face rising above the rear orthostat. The walls retain what was almost certainly their original height of 3.3 m, and it can be estimated that the gap to be roofed was about 1.6 m wide by about 3 m long, and it would have needed a row of three or four lintels to cover it. In effect this was a barrel vault.

4.22) There are a number of variants of the bipartite design, none of which can be neatly isolated. Probably the commonest is that with two polygonal compartments (figure 13). In each chamber the compartments are of much the same size, with either the outer or the inner slightly the larger, and a few of them are as large as that at Boath Short (ROS 11). Chambers of this type are well known in Sutherland and have been named after a well preserved chamber at Skelpick (SUT 53) (Henshall and Ritchie 1995, 29–30). The entry into the chamber through a narrow portal led to the first vaulted compartment, at the back of which was another low entry leading to the second vaulted compartment. In these chambers the orthostats in the walls are mostly spaced out rather than contiguous, and thus linking walling was required. One of the most impressive chambers, for its large scale and the massive size of the sandstone blocks and boulders of which it is built, is at King's Head Cairn (ROS 25) (plate 4). It stands romantically in a birch wood, free of its cairn, but encumbered with huge corbel stones which have been displaced to lie at all angles inside and outside the chamber. In its present state of chaotic ruin it is difficult to appreciate the grandeur of its design. The relatively long passage led to a chamber 6.7 m long. As at Boath Short, there is a large lintel between the compartments which, before it tilted, would have presented

PLATE 3. Boath Short (ROS 11), the inner end of the chamber showing two orthostats and corbelling, photographed in 1957.

vertical faces reaching to at least 2 m above the floor. The vaults were intact when the chamber was first investigated in the mid nineteenth century, and the larger covered an area of roughly 3.65 by 2.56 m. Orthostats of a chamber of the same plan are exposed at Balvaird (ROS 7), where lintels are probably *in situ* over both the outer and the inner portal stones. The chamber is on a smaller scale than King's Head Cairn, but it is still quite large at 5.6 m long. The chamber at Scotsburn Wood East (ROS 47) (figure 17) is smaller, 4.5 m long. The walls are probably complete, but it is surrounded by deep cairn material and partly filled with large stones, and only parts of the structure are visible. These three chambers show the size range of chambers of Skelpick type.

PLATE 4. King's Head Cairn (ROS 25), view from north.

4.23) Sufficient remains of two very ruined chambers, Ussie and Leachkin (ROS 38, INV 38), to indicate that they were also of the Skelpick design, and were of much the same size as Balvaird (ROS 7). The large cairn at Upper Park (ROS 51) almost conceals a huge chamber, probably slightly bigger than that at King's Head Cairn (ROS 25). All that can be seen of the inner compartment is part of a very large orthostat on one side, the tip of another orthostat, and some corbel stones defining a stretch of the wall at a height of 1.6 m or so. The outer compartment is represented by one large tall orthostat set at a slight angle to the axis. It is assumed that both the outer and inner portal stones are hidden beneath the deep cairn material. The few orthostats that remain at the almost demolished Cnoc Navie chamber (ROS 18) suggest that the chamber was of similar size and design.

4.24) Some orthostats belonging to a chamber which may be the largest in the Central Highlands can be seen at Brahan Wood

(ROS 53) (figure 19). It certainly consisted of two polygonal compartments, and it was probably somewhat longer than the existing 7.85 m. It is unique in having two pairs of portal stones between the compartments, if the damaged central part of the structure has been correctly understood. Presumably they carried two parallel lintels, one of which survives displaced. This arrangement may have been a solution to the structural problem posed by adjoining vaults, but it is perhaps more likely that the chamber is a two-period construction (discussed in ¶ 4.41), in which case it is not directly comparable with the chambers mentioned above.

4.25) Some bipartite chambers with polygonal inner compartments have outer compartments which are rectangular rather than polygonal (figure 13). The chamber at Kilcoy South (ROS 24) is of this plan. The outer compartment is almost square, and the larger inner compartment measures 3 by 2.4 m; it is unusual in having a gap at the back which leads to the

PLATE 5. Kilcoy South (ROS 24) from east-south-east (the farthest ranging pole rests on the displaced lintel).

innermost part of the structure (discussed in ¶ 4.38). This handsome excavated chamber of medium size (now filled in) gives an impression of spaciousness and confidence (figure 18, plates 5, 6). It is built with closely-set large blocks, rectangular in plan and varying from rectangular to nearly diamond-shaped in elevation. The flat-topped portal stones are about 1 m high, and the wall orthostats are up to 1.4 m high. A few corbel stones survive in both compartments, and until quite recently the lintel between the compartments was in place. The walling which fills the small gaps between the orthostats is of fine quality, and the awkwardness of placing several of the orthostats on narrow bases, which required the support of substantial chock-stones, is hardly noticeable (plate 7).

4.26) One of the two chambers at both Heights of Brae and Tarradale (ROS 22, 61) seem to have been similar to Kilcoy South (ROS 24). The chamber at Ballachnecore (ROS 3) is the longest of all the bipartite chambers. The large spaced boulders, most of them intact, project from the remains of the cairn. When the leaning orthostats of the outer compartment

are restored in the mind's eye to approximately their original positions, it can be seen that the compartment was almost rectangular, long and relatively narrow, 3.5 m by 1.8 m. The Ballachnecore chamber may be rivalled for size by Upper Park (ROS 51), where most of the chamber is hidden, and at Woodhead Round (ROS 42), where there is probably a ruined inner compartment. The chamber at Lower Lechanich North (ROS 29) is mainly concealed, but both compartments evidently had elongated plans, and stretches of walling and corbelling were once visible.

4.27) Amongst all the chambers that have been described so far, a back-slab set across the axis of the chamber does not seem to have been of particular significance; they occur in only about half the chambers. In two cases where there is no back-slab (ROS 24, 47) this may have been to allow access to an inner structure, though if a back-slab had been considered desirable it could have been contrived. At ROS 22 the arrangement of the innermost orthostats on each side of the axis seems to have been by choice, and at ROS 3 and 61 an orthostat is a little to the side of the axis. Nor are the back-slabs necessarily the tallest orthostats in the chamber, though damage allows only a few firm statements. The tallest orthostats seem to be placed in the inner compartments, and at least six of them, including one at Boath Short (ROS 11), are 2 m or even more in height. Of these six, five were not on the axis (notable examples are at INV 38 and ROS 51), and though in three cases the

PLATE 7. Kilcoy South (ROS 24). Detail of the south-west wall of the main chamber and the entry to the inner compartment on the right.

back-slab may formerly have been taller, the bulk of the tallest extant stone suggests that it was the most impressive. The number of orthostats in the walls of inner compartments varies between three and six.

4.28) There need be no hesitation in assuming that the polygonal compartments with roughly circular plans were roofed by vaults of the type which have been described on the evidence from Sutherland. Over the larger spans the capstones would have been at heights of between 3 and 4 m. Even the relatively small and angular outer compartment at Kilcoy South (ROS 24) had some oversailing corbel stones, though the roof height here, as at other smaller compartments, is likely to have been nearer 2 than 3 m. Other compartments were longer in proportion to their width, and it may be assumed that some of these, such as the outer compartment at ROS 3, and the inner compartment at ROS 29, would have had elongated vaults, similar to that observed at Boath Short (ROS 11). A number of compartments are intermediate in their proportions, and for them the roof was presumably oval in form and closed by one or two capstones.

4.29) Two chambers, Bishop Kinkell and Stittenham (ROS 9, 49), appear to differ somewhat in concept from those that have been described. Unfortunately observations are restricted to a few orthostats projecting

PLATE 6. Kilcoy South (ROS 24) from west-north-west. The inner compartment is in the foreground (the east orthostat lying on the floor) with the main chamber behind and the displaced lintel filling the ante-chamber. The portal stones are just visible at the top of the photograph.

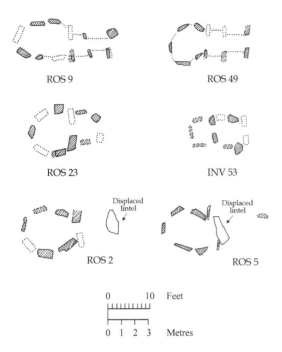

ROS 9   ROS 49

ROS 23   INV 53

Displaced lintel   Displaced lintel

ROS 2   ROS 5

0   10   Feet

0 1 2 3   Metres

FIGURE 14. Miscellaneous bipartite, or possible bipartite, chambers.

from the amorphous remains of the cairns, but it is clear that the outer compartments, or ante-chambers, are very small (figure 14). The plans of these chambers can be compared to a few in Sutherland and Caithness, and indeed these have been referred to as Caithness-type bipartite chambers (described in Henshall and Ritchie 1995, 25, 28–9). The ante-chambers are 1 m or a little more long, hardly wider than the passages, and are more or less square in plan. They must have been roofed at a low level by a single lintel between those resting on the outer and inner portal stones, and in effect the roof was a continuation of the passage roof. The ante-chambers gave access to polygonal main chambers of medium size. While the design of these chambers clearly differs from that of such chambers as Balvaird and King's Head Cairn (ROS 7, 25), it is not intended to imply that the designs are totally distinct. The outer compartments or ante-chambers at Kilcoy South and Heights of Brae (ROS 24, 22) can be seen as intermediate in size and form.

4.30) Insufficient is visible of the chamber at Kilcoy North (ROS 23) to do more than note the bipartite somewhat asymmetrical plan, and an ante-chamber that seems to have been short but wide (figure 14). The remains at Allt Eoghainn (INV 53), in an idyllic woodland setting, are virtually devoid of cairn material, and four of the chamber orthostats have simply fallen outwards, house-of-cards fashion, and have been left undisturbed. The plan can be partly reconstructed, and it is evident that the chamber was small and irregular in plan, and was probably unusual in having an inner compartment markedly smaller than the outer compartment (figure 14, plate 8).

4.31) Three greatly ruined chambers present the same difficulty as Boath Short (ROS 11): at each a polygonal setting of spaced orthostats may belong to the inner compartment of a normal bipartite chamber, the outer part of which is either hidden or destroyed (figure 14), or they may belong to a single-compartment chamber of which only the passage is missing. The former interpretation seems the more likely at Balnagrotchen (ROS 5) where at one time a quite large compartment, a pair of portal stones, and a displaced lintel could be seen. An orthostat that was visible 3.3 m in front of the portal stones may have belonged to the passage wall, and its position would support the suggestion that there was once an outer compartment. At Ardvanie (ROS 2) one portal stone is visible at the entrance to a compartment, and a tipped-over lintel 1.8 m in front of this stone may have been displaced from either outer portal stones or entrance portal stones. The Belladrum chamber (INV 12) has been reduced to only five orthostats, one of which is known to have been re-erected; no useful comment can be made.

4.32) A small group of bipartite chambers differs in some respects from those that have been described. In these both the outer and inner compartments are rectangular or square in plan, they are symmetrical on an axis which is emphasized by a transverse and often notably tall back-slab, and the orthostats are generally shapely rectangular blocks which are

PLATE 8. Allt Eoghainn (INV 53), view from east.

(ROS 6) had two blocks on each side of the inner compartment, and the very large back-slab, when upright, was 2.1 m high (just taller than the next highest orthostat). It is unfortunate that the outer portal stones and the passage are missing because a very short passage is implied by the presence of two stones that may be part of a façade outside the entrance (discussed in ¶ 5.25): a passage as short as that at Scotsburn Wood West could just be accommodated. The fourth chamber, Baldoon (ROS 44), is the most damaged. It was built of smaller but still quite substantial boulder orthostats, with two in each side of each compartment, and the prone back-slab would have been 1.75 m high, a little higher than the adjacent orthostats.

4.34) The excavated chamber at Carn Glas (ROS 12) is a small version of this type of chamber, only 2.6 m in total length and half the size of Balnaguie (ROS 6). The sandstone slab orthostats fit so closely that only tiny gaps

generally set close together so that a minimum of walling was required (figure 15). Four of these chambers are impressive for their overall size and for the precise setting of the massive stones of which they were built; fortunately the orthostats are fully exposed and almost all are intact.

4.33) Scotsburn Wood West (ROS 48), which retains its short passage and only lacks one chamber orthostat, is the most complete example. The back-slab, before it fell, was 2 m high, the tallest stone in the chamber by 0.5 m or more. Although it is a substantial block, it is rather unusual in this group of chambers because it did not stretch the whole width of the compartment. Contin Mains (ROS 19), bizarrely secure within the high walls and locked gate of a private burial ground, has, like ROS 48, one orthostat on each side of each compartment, and these are exceptionally large. The back of the chamber is missing, but the proportions of the chamber do not suggest that it was ever longer. The Balnaguie chamber

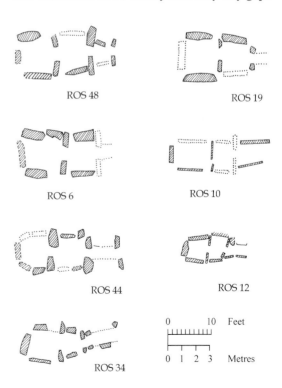

ROS 48

ROS 19

ROS 6

ROS 10

ROS 44

ROS 12

ROS 34

0   10 Feet

0 1 2 3 Metres

FIGURE 15. Bipartite chambers with rectangular compartments.

had to be filled with walling. The orthostats in the walls are relatively low, so the chamber is unusual in that the portal stones are roughly the same height. The wallhead along each side is noticeably level, achieved in two cases by setting the more rounded edge of an orthostat as the base. The most striking feature, however, is the large sharply-pointed back-slab which rises 0.75 m above the side-slabs (figure 16). The chamber in Tomfat Plantation (INV 52) had been disastrously damaged before it was excavated, and it has also suffered from the slab orthostats flaking, which has reduced their size to an unknown extent. The plan was not recovered, and there is no certainty that it was bipartite. If it were not for the impressive pointed back-slab, just over 2 m high and towering 1.5 m above the pitifully inadequate side-slabs, the remains would hardly be seriously considered. Here, too, orthostats have been set with a rounded edge as the base. The breadth of the chamber has probably been reduced by the slight displacement of a side slab, and the chamber may have been much the same size as Carn Glas, though it evidently differed in the greater use of walling.

4.35) The Balblair Wood and Muir of Conan chambers (INV 54, ROS 34) are midway in size between the extremes of these rectangular bipartite chambers. There is little of the former to be seen apart from the tall back-slab and a low side-slab butting against it, and the latter, because the chamber orthostats are damaged, provides no additional information. At Boath Long (ROS 10), where the spacious slab-built passage has been mentioned already, the chamber is almost hidden in cairn material. Two inner portal stones are only 0.23 m apart, so one of them is presumably displaced. Beyond them is a slab forming one side of the inner compartment, and the back-slab which is 0.4 m taller. Several more chambers may belong to this group, but, lacking any definitive features, comment is postponed to ¶ 4.44–5.

4.36) The only evidence that these rectangular chambers were roofed in much the same way as other bipartite chambers is provided by Scotsburn Wood West (ROS 48). A lintel,

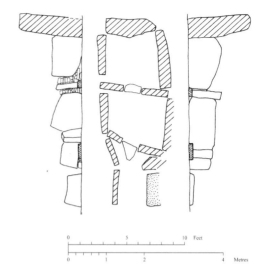

FIGURE 16. Carn Glas, ROS 12. Plan and elevations of the chamber, redrawn from Woodham and Woodham 1957a.

roughly square in cross-section, lies displaced from the inner portal stones, indicating that the two compartments were roofed separately. The great difference in the heights of the back-slab and the side-slabs at some chambers means that, at least in the inner compartments, there must have been a considerable amount of walling and corbelling to bring the sides level with the top of the back-slab, if not higher still. On the other hand, whatever the type of chamber, the presence of a very short passage implies that in these cases the outer compartments were roofed at a lower level.

Chambers with cells at the rear

4.37) Three chambers that have been included with the bipartite chambers have been found to possess a further element at the rear, a small compartment or cell entered through a short passage. These puzzling features raise the possibility that in each case the chamber was built in two phases, with a bipartite chamber placed immediately in front of an earlier structure. The bipartite chamber at King's Head Cairn (ROS 25) is one of the largest (figure 17). Behind it is a polygonal cist-like cell built with four small slab orthostats linked by walling, and which measures only about 1.4 by 0.95 m. The former existence of a short passage is indicated by a pair of slabs which can be interpreted as portal stones at its outer end. It is very unlikely that the passage was accessible from the back of the chamber; this would have involved squeezing through a gap of only 0.35 m between orthostats in the main chamber, and into an extension of the passage which would have had a total length of 2 m. This difficulty, together with the contrasting scale and building materials of the cell and the chamber, and the difference of about 30° in their axes, strongly suggests that the cell was an earlier independent structure. It may also be noted that it is only due to unusual circumstances, the removal of the cairn material and subsequent lack of disturbance, that the cell can be recognised.

4.38) Kilcoy South (ROS 24) appeared to be a normal bipartite chamber until an inner third compartment was revealed during excavation (figure 18, plate 6). The inner compartment, or cell, is smaller than the main chamber, and is approached from it by a short passage. The cell is about 1.7 m in diameter, built with three quite substantial orthostats linked by walling, and is entered between a pair of portal stones. The entry to the passage is between two large orthostats that form part of the wall of the main chamber. These orthostats have horizontal upper surfaces suitable for bearing a lintel, and indeed the horizontal surfaces were achieved very deliberately by setting the orthostats on slanting bases. The cell and the chamber proper are in the same relationship as at Kings's Head Cairn (ROS 25). The non-alignment of the two parts at Kilcoy South, together with the approach by a passage, suggested to Henshall in 1972 (p. 257, 259, before the cell at ROS 25 had been recognised) that the cell had been an earlier independent structure, and that the chamber built immediately in front of it had been designed to allow access to it. Examination of the chamber in 1997 raised doubts about this interpretation because the two parts of the

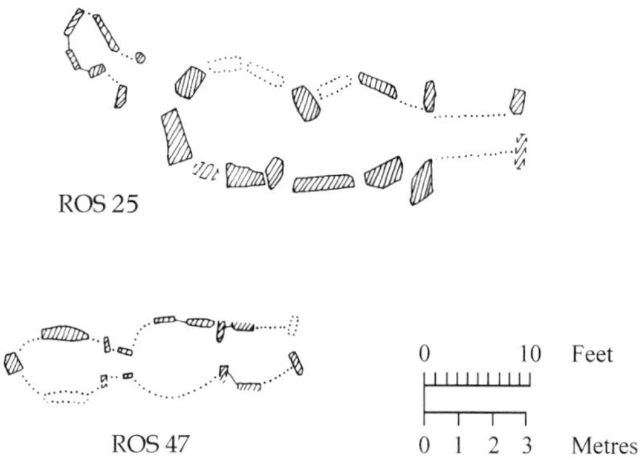

ROS 25

ROS 47

| 0 | | 10 | Feet |
| 0 | 1 2 3 | | Metres |

FIGURE 17. Chambers with cells at the rear: above, King's Head Cairn, ROS 25; below, Scotsburn Wood East, ROS 47.

structure appear to be closely integrated, and the building techniques are the same throughout. Apart from the general impression, two structural details may be noted: in both parts of the chamber portal stones were set with a horizontal upper surface by chocking a slanting base, and in the panels of fine walling a thin upright stone is generally used as the basal course. Curiously, the back-slab of the cell was raised on chock-stones to a little above ground level.

4.39) The arrangement of the chamber and cell differs at the relatively small chamber at Scotsburn Wood East (ROS 47) in that they are on the same axis, and the entry to the passage leading to the cell is in the centre of the rear wall of the main chamber (figure 17). The cell, which is only partly visible, is about 2.6 m long, and was probably oval with a substantial orthostat on each side and a slightly taller back-slab. The access passage is the same size as those at the other two chambers, about 0.9 m long by 0.6 m wide, and there is a pair of portal stones bearing a lintel at the inner end. However, the rather make-shift appearance of the passage does suggest that it was a contrived link with the chamber, and that two phases of building were involved. At all three cairns extensive excavation of the cairn material around the chambers is necessary before any firm conclusions can be voiced. Even if they

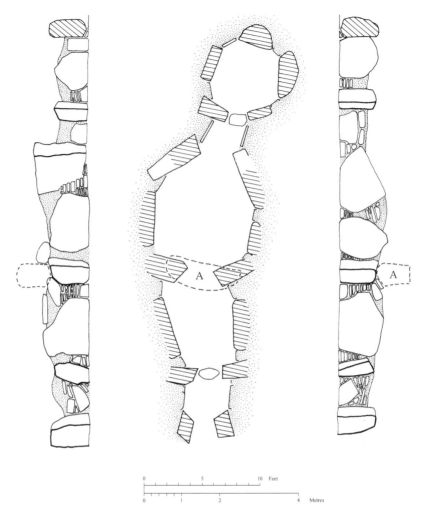

0   5   10 Feet

0   1   2   4   Metres

FIGURE 18. Kilcoy South, ROS 24. Plan of the chamber after Woodham 1958, and ASH and JNGR 1995. Elevations after MacGregor and Loney 1997. 'A' indicates the approximate position of the lintel, now displaced.

are contemporary with the main chambers, the inner structures approached down awkward small passages are distinguished from the other compartments of the chambers, and a difference in function is to be expected. It is possible that the S chamber at Tarradale (ROS 61) is yet another version of the bipartite chamber with a cell at the rear. If so, the cell is aligned on the axis but is not approached by a passage, and the whole structure (as far as it can be seen) has a unitary appearance (see ¶ 4.45).

Single-compartment polygonal chambers (figure 19)

4.40) It is perhaps surprising that only one certain example of a polygonal single-compartment chamber occurs in the Central Highlands, and that example is in an isolated chambered cairn near the west coast, Balvraid (INV 51) (figures 19, 30). This excavated chamber is about 2 m in diameter, built with five closely-set orthostats, and is entered between splayed portal stones. The capstone has fallen

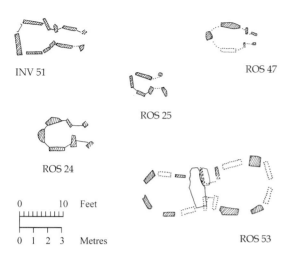

INV 51

ROS 47

ROS 25

ROS 24

0   10   Feet

0   1   2   3   Metres

ROS 53

FIGURE 19. Single-compartment, and possible single-compartment, polygonal chambers.

inside the chamber after the partial collapse of some of the orthostats, and it is unlikely that the roof height was much over 2 m. Three greatly ruined chambers of moderate size (ROS 2, 5, INV 12) may be of either the single-compartment plan, or bipartite and lacking their outer compartments; they, together with the large chamber at Boath Short (ROS 11), have been noted already in ¶ 4.31. When considering the three bipartite chambers with cells (¶ 4.37–9) it was suggested that in one or more cases the cells may originally have been free-standing units, in effect single-compartment chambers, which were later incorporated into cairns with larger chambers. The cells, if regarded as chambers, are very small, and in one case there are no transverse portal stones at the entrance. No chambers of this size are known as independent monuments in the Central Highlands, though two chambers of similar size are known in Sutherland (SUT 63, 74). It has to be recognised, too, that their size militates against their survival, or their recognition if surviving.

4.41) The existence of much larger single-compartment chambers is implied by the suggestion that Brahan Wood (ROS 53) is a two-period structure (¶ 4.24). This suggestion rests on the interpretation of the remains

between the two polygonal compartments of the very ruined monument (figure 19). The chamber axis runs roughly north to south, and it is not even certain that the entrance was from the south. If this were the case, the inner compartment would have been oblong, and designed without a back-slab, in which it would be similar to the inner compartment at Heights of Brae (ROS 22). A fallen lintel lies across the outer end of the compartment. In front of it is a leaning slab that has every appearance of being one of the portal stones on which the lintel, set on its narrow side, once rested. The outer compartment was nearly round, and one portal stone remains at the inner end, about 1 m from the base of the leaning portal stone. Thus it appears that there were two pairs of portal stones between the compartments, presumably each bearing a lintel, and presumably linked by walling, to make a passage about 1 m long. This arrangement is unique as far as is known, and the most likely explanation is that the outer compartment was an addition built in front of an existing chamber. Even if the chamber were entered from the north, the two-period interpretation is not affected.

Single-compartment rectangular chambers (figure 20)

4.42) There are three chambers resembling rectangular bipartite chambers, in that they are rectangular in plan, the building material is large rectangular blocks that are closely set, and the back-slabs are markedly taller than the side-slabs. The chambers in this group differ, however, in being undivided; it is not the case that the portal stones are missing because there are no gaps in the side walls to accommodate them. It follows that barrel vaults up to 6 m long were constructed over these chambers. Some corbel stones remain at ROS 31.

4.43) The ruins of the Mains of Ardross and Belmaduthy chambers (ROS 52, 8) each stand starkly in a field. They are large and simple structures, and each has been reduced to five orthostats. The chambers are similar in size, 5

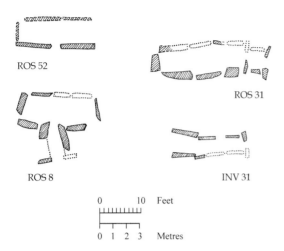

ROS 52

ROS 31

ROS 8

INV 31

0   10   Feet

0   1   2   3   Metres

FIGURE 20. Plans of three single-compartment rectangular chambers, and a chamber of uncertain plan.

and 5.6 m long, and virtually the same size as Balnaguie (ROS 6), the largest of the bipartite rectangular chambers. The Mains of Ardross chamber was built with two orthostats on each side, the tallest 1.6 m high, and a back-slab which, before it fell, fitted the end of the chamber exactly and stood 2.15 m high. It is assumed that the entrance was at the opposite end, but nothing more remains. Belmaduthy is exceptional in that the passage approaches at right angles to the axis of the chamber, and enters it through the centre of one side. (At Mains of Ardross a gap of 0.55 m between the orthostats on one side would theoretically allow a side entrance, though not with precisely the same arrangement of the ends of the passage orthostats protruding into the chamber.) At Belmaduthy one side wall consists of an orthostat on either side of the entrance, and the opposite wall presumably consisted of three orthostats, of which only one remains. The side-slabs are up to 1.27 m high, and the orthostat across one end is over 2 m high; because of damage the height of the orthostat at the opposite end is unknown. The chamber at Mid Brae (ROS 31) is larger, 6 m by about 1.8 m. One wall consists of three large blocks of stone, the other wall is largely obscured, and

the back-slab rises 0.4 m above the tallest side-slab. The chamber is entered between portal stones, from a very short passage aligned on the axis.

Unclassified chambers

4.44) There are three chambers in the long cairn at Essich Moor (INV 31), all rectangular rather than polygonal in plan, but only partly exposed. At the north end, in a considerable depth of cairn material, there are two almost parallel lines of large slabs, which can be interpreted tentatively as the walls of a particularly spacious passage and a chamber (or part of a chamber) (figure 20). There are no portal stones separating the passage and chamber, and at the junction, most unusually, a passage orthostat overlaps an adjacent chamber orthostat. The chamber, as visible, is 1.8 m long by 1.3 m wide, but, although there are no signs that it was ever longer, this must remain a distinct possibility. At the opposite end of the cairn the deep cairn material conceals all but the inner end of a chamber which may be quite large. A massive back-slab is well over 2 m high, and two much shorter slabs along one side have almost certainly been displaced inwards, making the chamber appear misleadingly narrow; its length is unknown. The third chamber, in the centre of the long cairn, consists of a long back-slab, its height uncertain but 0.4 m higher than the adjacent side-slab. On the edge of the cairn, and 3.3 m from the back-slab, is a pair of small portal stones; there may, then, have been a short passage leading to a small chamber, perhaps a little over 2 m long. A second chamber in the cairn at Heights of Brae (ROS 22) is similarly represented by a back-slab, adjacent side-slab, and a pair of small portal stones. The back-slab is over 0.5 m higher than the side-slab. There is no indication whether the portal stones were at the entrance to the chamber or to a passage, so the length of the chamber is uncertain.

4.45) The S chamber at Tarradale (ROS 61) is impressive for its overall size and for the massive nature of some of its orthostats, but

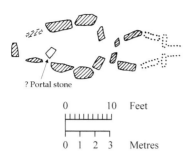

? Portal stone

0   10   Feet

0   1   2   3   Metres

FIGURE 21. Tarradale, ROS 61. The south chamber.

the plan is unusual and its interpretation is uncertain (figure 21). There was an outer compartment, probably somewhat polygonal in plan, but the outer part and the entrance are missing. At its inner end there is a gap between the inner portal stones and the inner compartment, a feature also seen at Heights of Brae (ROS 22). It is the large inner compartment which is exceptional. Its plan is almost wedge-shaped, and no less than 5.45 m long. The question arises whether the rear part was divided off to form a small compartment or cell. The sides of the part that in this view would be the centre compartment are built of particularly massive blocks, contrasting with the two relatively small surviving orthostats of the putative inner compartment. At the junction of the two parts there is an upright stone, partly exposed and slightly displaced, which may be the S member of a pair of portal stones. The length of the whole chamber cannot have been less than 9 m.

4.46) A number of chambers are so much obscured or so incomplete that they permit little useful comment. The large cairn at Lower Lechanich South (ROS 30) is curiously sited on a steep slope. Four orthostats at the lower side are all that can be seen of the internal structure aligned along the contour. There is a pair of portal stones, and behind one of them are two orthostats not quite in line, the inner taller. They may have formed the walls of the outer and the inner compartments of a rectangular bipartite chamber (with a portal slab missing from the gap between them), or they may

represent the wall of a rectangular single-compartment chamber. It is perhaps less likely that the outer orthostat was part of a passage because its relationship to the adjacent portal stone suggests that the structure would have been too wide at about 1.6 m.

4.47) The cairn at Red Burn (ROS 36) is largely intact, and only part of the outer compartment of a chamber can be seen in an excavated hollow. There is an orthostat on each side and a lintel that has fallen forwards from hidden inner portal stones. In the grounds of Reelig House, where there are good reasons to believe there was once a chambered cairn (INV 46), there is a fanciful wedge-shaped setting of slabs known as The Giant's Grave. The three slabs at the wider end may be *in situ*, and may have formed the inner end of a rectangular chamber. At Millcraig (ROS 32) the relationship of the two remaining orthostats of a demolished chamber suggest that it was rectangular in plan, but it is mainly notable for the size of the larger orthostat, nearly 3 m long by over 2 m high when it was vertical, and of unknown thickness since one face has been deliberately split away. At The Temple (ROS 37) three large blocks, one about 2 m high, are visible within a very disturbed cairn, and it can hardly be doubted that they are part of a chamber, but its plan is unclear. The remains at Muir of Allangrange and Scotsburn House (ROS 33, 46) are too slight for helpful comment.

4.48) The last monument, Balnacrae (ROS 4), seen in a ruined and denuded state, is one of the most impressive for the scale of the structure, and is also one of the most enigmatic (figure 22, plate 9). It is in rough pasture, not far from a deserted croft, and after the cairn material had been removed its site was cultivated. Consequently considerable damage is to be expected, but the sheer size of the largest of the remaining orthostats, both upright and prone, makes it unlikely that these have been moved. The orthostats extend for over 15 m from north-east to south-west.

4.49) The first impression is that the orthostats belong to a passage and chamber (A and B on the plan, figure 22) separated by

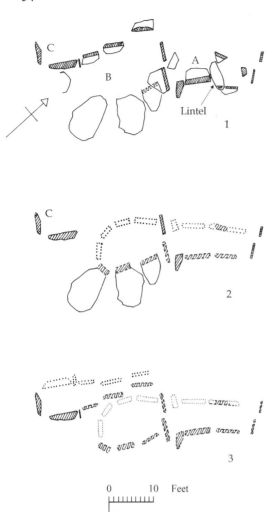

0   10   Feet

0   1   2   3   Metres

FIGURE 22. Balnacrae, ROS 4. 1, the chamber and passage as planned. 2, a tentative reconstruction with a passage leading to an oval chamber (the leaning and prone slabs restored, 'missing' stones dotted). 3, a tentative reconstruction with the stones on the northwest side of the monument forming part of a rectangular chamber approached by a passage.

portal stones, and this was the interpretation that accompanied the first published plan in 1943. The chamber would have been almost rectangular, 7.6 m long by about 3 m wide, with four orthostats on one side, and three

(now prone) on the other. Doubts about this interpretation arise from the unprecedented size of the area to be roofed, and the positioning of the orthostats and their relationship to the portal stones. There is no indication that the chamber was subdivided and roofed as two compartments, and the height of the orthostats (when upright) means that oversailing to reduce the span could not have started at less than 2.7 m above the floor. The nearest chambers that had roofs approaching the implied length at Balnacrae are the few stalled chambers in Caithness (Davidson and Henshall 1991, 33) which benefit from an ideal building stone, and there are several very large oval chambers in the Hebrides that come near to it in size (SKY 10, UST 23). Another difficulty with this interpretation is the failure to account for the largest of the upright stones (C on the plan).

4.50) Stone C is an imposing regular intact slab, over 2 m high, and has the appearance of the back-slab of a chamber. Beside it is a substantial slab which is 1 m lower. These two orthostats strongly suggest the inner end of a rectangular chamber. If so, the surviving orthostats represent two chambers, and the monument must be regarded as multi-period, but a satisfactory interpretation of the remains is elusive. It might be suggested that area A is the passage (or possibly the passage and ante-chamber) of an oval chamber of a size similar to that at Boath (ROS 11). The three leaning and prone slabs on the south side of the monument could be seen as part of the wall of this chamber, which would have been of exceptional height. In this interpretation it has to be assumed that the other side of the chamber is missing, because none of the smaller orthostats in the row opposite the prone orthostats could belong to a chamber of this plan. The row of four orthostats, which runs eastwards from stone C, might be seen as forming one side of the putative rectangular chamber and its passage, the other wall of which has been removed.

4.51). The relationship of these two hypothetical chambers, almost parallel and virtually

PLATE 9. Balnacrae (ROS 4), view from south.

contiguous, poses a critical problem. On structural grounds, the oval chamber must have been incomplete, either unfinished or partly destroyed, when the rectangular chamber was built. Conversely, the positions of the chambers within the cairn imply that the rectangular chamber was the earlier. These unresolved difficulties may indicate that a totally different explanation of the remains should be sought. Nontheless, there is a similar but less acute problem at the neighbouring cairn, Heights of Brae (ROS 22), where a rectangular and a polygonal chamber are side by side, and again at Tarradale (ROS 61) in the Black Isle where the cairn encloses both a polygonal chamber and a large chamber of unusual design. In each cairn the two chambers are only 2 m apart, and it is very doubtful whether both could have stood entire at the same time.

5. The cairns covering chambers of the Orkney-Cromarty group

5.1) The cairns in the Central Highlands have, in general, suffered interference and robbing to a greater extent than in other parts of northern Scotland. Gradual destruction was accelerated by the agricultural improvements in the nineteenth century, when cairns provided handy material for both the substantial stone walls that enclosed the new fields and for the new buildings. Sometimes the bare stones of the cairn interior were removed, leaving a matted rim of cairn material undisturbed except for a gap to allow access for carts; in these circumstances the former plan of the cairn may be preserved, as at ROS 6 and 32. More often the edge may be indefinable, or obviously curtailed by ploughing or other activity, as for instance at ROS 3 and 8. In other cases, after partial demolition, there followed a desire to clear the ground for cultivation. The remains of a few chambers, such as ROS 19, 52, and INV 12, survive without any sign of the cairns which once covered them. A different recording problem is posed by the universal use of ruined cairns as convenient dumps for field-gathered stones, and these may mask the original edges, and may even create an entirely misleading appearance, as happened at ROS 24. There can be little doubt that the majority of cairns were round in plan, one cairn is nearly square with short projecting horns, another is certainly square, and a number are long.

Round and heel-shaped cairns

5.2) Eleven cairns, the edges of which can be traced with confidence for the whole circuit, or for sufficient of it to record the shape, are certainly round (ROS 6, 12, 18, 29, 30, 32, 34,

36, 48, 49, 51), and fifteen more cairns can probably be included (ROS 2, 4, 5, 22, 24, 25, 37, 42, 44, 47, 53, 61, INV 38, 52, 54). They vary in diameter from about 16 m (ROS 44, 49) to about 30 m (ROS 4, 6), with an even progression from one extreme to the other, and two cairns are larger still (ROS 12, 32). Only eight cairns survive much over 1 m high. Red Burn and Upper Park (ROS 36, 51) are the most complete, and though their summits have been reduced, they are still quite impressive at 3 m or so high. Their sides, where undisturbed, rise in an even steep slope. Carn Glas (ROS 12) was an immense cairn, reliably recorded by a civil engineer as about 36 m in diameter and 6.4 m high; Cnoc Navie (ROS 18) is 23 m in diameter, and was once about 6 m high. The observed heights of cairns will generally be slightly less than the real heights because of the difference between the present land surface and the old land surface: this is well demonstrated at ROS 48 where a hole has been dug down to the old ground surface inside the chamber. In order to cover the chamber vaults the cairns must originally have been at very least 3 m high, and it may be assumed that they were normally considerably more. (The height of cairn material has normally been recorded by us from in front of the entrance because this position may be expected to give a fair average around the chambers where these are aligned along the contour on sloping sites.)

5.3) Judging by what is known of chambered cairns in the north of Scotland, and particularly in Sutherland where the building material is similar (see Henshall and Ritchie 1995, 37–9), the cairns in the Central Highlands, if excavated, would be revealed as carefully designed structures. The outer part of the cairn was a casing, built of loose stone, usually cobbles and boulders, contained by an outer wall-face, at least 1 m high. The observed diameters of cairns are likely to be greater than their original diameters by 3 m or more, due to the outward spill of loose stones following the collapse of the outer wall-faces; indeed the full spread of displaced stones will have been greater still, but the outermost part is likely to

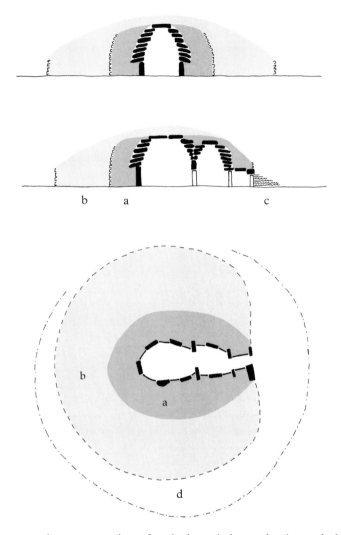

FIGURE 23. Diagrammatic reconstruction of a single-period round cairn and chamber (based on Lower Lechanich North, ROS 29); a, cairn core; b, cairn casing; c, blocking; d, visible extent of collapsed cairn material.

be hidden. On sloping sites there may also be some distortion of the plan where there is greater slippage downhill.

5.4) Structural considerations, confirmed by information from the northern cairns, indicate that the core of each cairn, immediately around the chamber, was an integral part of the chamber itself (see ¶ 10.6–8). The core was necessary to support the chamber walls, and was essential to provide a base for the lowest corbel stones, and at a higher level, to provide

the weight to counterbalance the overhang of corbel stones forming the chamber roof (figure 23). The cairn cores were about 2 to 3 m thick, and were carefully built for maximum stability with outer wall-faces that were not intended to be seen when the cairns were completed. The cores would normally be oval in plan, reflecting the line of the chamber walls. In the Central Highlands the inner core of carefully packed cobbles or slabs has only been glimpsed twice, behind fallen orthostats at Kilcoy South and Scotsburn Wood West (ROS 24, 48). Some of the completed cairns were surprisingly small, considering the size of the chambers within them, and the sides of the cairns must have risen steeply above the outer wall-faces. Some cairns, then, were no larger than was required to encase and protect the core and the chamber, and possibly to bring the roofing slabs into position.

5.5) Three of the smaller cairns in the Central Highlands, in which the relationship of the chamber to the cairn edge is clear (Stittenham, Scotsburn Wood West and Lower Lechanich North, ROS 49, 48, 29), appear to be uncomplicated single-period constructions contemporary with the chambers exposed within them (figure 24, 1). Allowing for minor distortion (in one case an old drain clipping the edge), their original diameters may be estimated as about 15, 16 and 14 m; their observed diameters are about 18, 19 and 16 m. In each case the centre point is in the middle of the inner compartment, which was presumably the highest part of the internal structure. At all three cairns the entrance to the passage is well inside the margin of a truly circular cairn, and the explanation may be that the cairns were flattened or even slightly concave across the front. Such a plan has been shown to exist at Kilcoy South (ROS 24) where the concave frontage has produced a modest heel-shaped plan (discussed later, ¶ 5.23) (figure 29). The completion of the round plan is likely to be due to deliberate blocking outside the entrance, as was revealed by excavation at Camster Round (CAT 13) in Caithness and The Ord North (SUT 48) in Sutherland, supplemented by stone fallen from over the entrance.

5.6) It is likely that several cairns with less clearly defined edges than the three described are of the same minimal type (ROS 5, 34, INV 52, 54). Cnoc Navie and Upper Park (ROS 18, 51) have larger cairns, probably about 19 or 20 m in diameter before spreading, and they cover unusually large chambers. The cairn at Cnoc Navie and probably that at Upper Park are also centered on the inner compartments. There is no reason to suspect

that these cairns have been enlarged after they were first built. The short passages that are characteristic of all the chambers of Orkney-Cromarty type, as noted in ¶ 4.14, and the consequent position of the entrance portal stones unexpectedly far within the outer edges of round cairns, indicate that all these round cairns were designed to be flattened or concave across the entrance.

5.7) On the other hand there can be little doubt that a number of cairns were built in more than one phase. The cairns at Heights of Brae and Tarradale (ROS 22, 61) each cover two chambers with differing plans. Though it is unfortunate that the limits of the cairns are vague, in both cases the centre appears to lie between the chambers. At Heights of Brae the earlier chamber is probably the smaller more damaged one, which, together with its cairn, was presumably partly demolished to build the larger chamber. There is no indication of the sequence at Tarradale, but it can be guessed that the larger atypical chamber is the later. The quite large final cairns were over 26 m and about 25 m in diameter. In whatever way the remains at Balnacrae (ROS 4) are interpreted, the structure must be of more than one period, and possibly there was a sequence of chambers similar to that at Heights of Brae and Tarradale (see ¶ 4.48–51). The cairn, almost totally removed, seems to have been round with a diameter of about 30 m.

5.8) At other cairns the off-centre position of a chamber is probably an indicator that the cairn was a multi-period construction. This anomaly is particularly noticeable at Red Burn (ROS 36) (figure 24, 2). The hidden inner compartment of the chamber cannot be central within the relatively well preserved cairn. This strongly suggests that the cairn has been enlarged, and that other structures, whether primary or secondary, are hidden within it. Stones belonging to the basal course of a wall-face can be seen round part of the perimeter of the cairn, and 2 m within it a very short length of a concentric wall-face is visible; both are features of the last building phase. The cairn at Lower Lechanich South (ROS 30) is

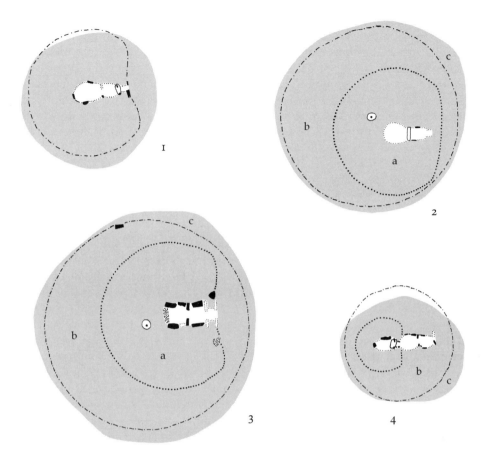

FIGURE 24. Round cairns. 1, a small single-period cairn (Lower Lechanich North, ROS 29). 2–4, cairns probably of multi-period construction (Red Burn, Balnaguie, Scotsburn Wood East, ROS 36, 6, 47). a, the hypothetical extent of the cairn assuming that the chamber is primary; b, the approximate extent of the cairn in its final form; c, the visible extent of cairn material. The centre points of cairns 2 and 3 are shown as large dots.

most unusually sited on a steep slope. Again, the chamber is only partly exposed, but on any reconstruction the centre of the cairn must lie outside it. The chambers in two particularly large cairns, Balnaguie and Millcraig (ROS 6, 32), are off-centre (a safe observation even at Millcraig where the chamber is too ruined to interpret the plan); once more there is the implication that the cairns have been enlarged (figure 24, 3). The badly ruined cairn at Woodhead Round (ROS 42) is puzzling at first sight, but it appears to have been round and to have covered a bipartite chamber. If the chamber orthostats have been correctly interpreted, the

centre of the cairn is over 3 m from the centre of the inner compartment. It is tempting to assume that in all these cairns the chambers, together with cairns of appropriate size, are the primary structures, but there is no clear evidence that this is so. Indeed, two cairns (ROS 25, 47) alert us to other possibilities.

5.9) When describing the large chamber at King's Head Cairn (ROS 25) in ¶ 4.37, it was pointed out that the tiny structure behind the chamber had almost certainly been an earlier independent chamber or cell, presumably under a very small cairn (figure 25, 1). At Scotsburn Wood East (ROS 47), too, the innermost compartment of the chamber is likely to have had an earlier existence. At the former cairn the inner compartment of the bipartite chamber seems to be more or less central, and the cairn was so large that it was considerably bigger than was necessary to include the structures of both phases. In contrast, the cairn at Scotsburn Wood East (figure 24, 4) is no larger than the smallest single-period cairns. It appears to be oval, though the shape may have been distorted by the slope of the ground. These two cairns, and possibly also Kilcoy South (ROS 24), may offer a clue as to the nature of earlier unidentified phases in other cairns suspected of being of more than one period.

5.10) The largest cairn of all, Carn Glas (ROS 12), was remarkable for its size, and remarkable also for the very small chamber exposed centrally within it. Even though no great depth of cairn material remains, there are no signs of another chamber; yet it is inconceivable that the final size of the cairn, 36 m in diameter, was not the result of extensive and repeated enlargements. Perhaps the most likely explanation is that it was increased in size for the addition of single-grave and cremated burials, possibly over many centuries.

5.11) It follows that enlargement of cairns may not be unusual, and cairns with diameters over 23 m or so may be suspected of being of more than one period. There are nine cairns of this relatively large size, eight of which have been mentioned above as giving hints of multiperiod construction. Mostly they are round, but King's Head Cairn (ROS 25) (figure 25, 1) appears to be heel-shaped, though its edges are now rather vague. This tentative interpretation of the plan of King's Head Cairn finds some support in the recognition that two possibly heel-shaped cairns of similar size, and one certainly heel-shaped larger cairn, exist as components of cairns of other shapes (ROS 11, 31, INV 31), and are mentioned later (¶ 5.12, 18, 20). On the other hand, Scotsburn Wood East (ROS 47) indicates that a multiperiod history does not necessarily involve a large cairn. Although not visible, the cairns

enclosing tiny chambers, such as those at this cairn and King's Head Cairn, would have been very much smaller than the smallest recognisable round cairn. The visible cairn at Balvraid (INV 51) offers a somewhat similar situation; excavation revealed that it was an addition to a small round chambered cairn, only 8 to 9 m in diameter, but in this case the outer cairn was square in plan (figure 25, 2). Again, the Essich Moor long cairn (INV 31) appears to incorporate a round cairn, about 12 m in diameter (figure 28).

Short horned and square enlargements of cairns

5.12) The Boath Short cairn (ROS 11) is a most remarkable structure, both for its size and its plan (figure 25, 3). The inner compartment of a very large bipartite chamber, or maybe a large single-compartment chamber, is roughly central to the monument. The cairn enclosing it is impressive, 3.3 m high, but its edges merge indefinably into the surrounding platform and there has been considerable disturbance (plate 10). The shape and size of the cairn are thus uncertain, but it gives the impression of being heel-shaped because of the apparent flattening on the side where the passage entrance is to be expected; the diameter may be roughly estimated as at least 28 m. The platform is about 1 m high, formerly with clear edges all round. It is trapezoidal in plan with wide short horns projecting from each corner. It was designed on the same axis as the chamber, with a wide straight face across the front, gently narrowing sides, and a straight rear edge. In effect, the horns form a very wide shallow forecourt at the front, and, though not now so obvious, a similar but smaller forecourt at the rear. The plan is a version of the short horned cairn plan known in Sutherland and Caithness (Henshall and Ritchie 1995, 41; Davidson and Henshall 1991, 42–3), but on an immense scale. Overall, the platform is 50 m wide at the front and 35 m from front to back, double the size of the next largest short horned cairn. The northern cairns of this plan have

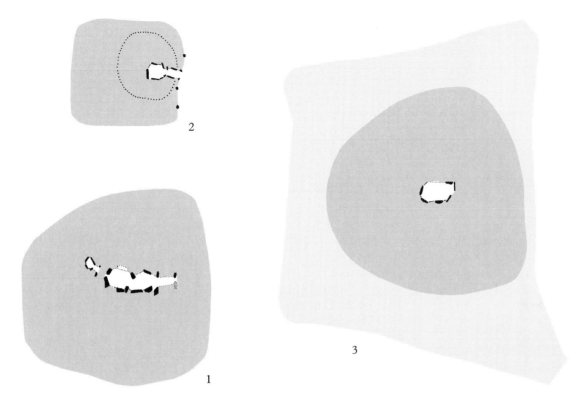

FIGURE 25. 1, King's Head Cairn, ROS 25. A large multi-period cairn, probably built in three phases, the last of which appears to have been heel-shaped. 2, Balvraid, INV 51. A small round cairn later enclosed by a square cairn. 3, Boath Short, ROS 11. A large cairn, probably heel-shaped in plan, which is surrounded by a trapezoidal platform.

PLATE 10. Boath Short (ROS 11), from the south. The platform is just visible between the figure and the ranging pole (scale in feet), photographed in 1957.

deeply concave forecourts and concave sides, formed by long oblique horns (though displaced cairn material may partly fill the forecourts to produce a nearly square plan). It is clear that at Boath Short, where the cairn and platform are distinct features and the latter has a wide level surface (apart from disturbance and stone dumping), the observed plan of the platform closely reflects the original plan, which is approaching a square in shape. The size of the cairn strongly suggests that it is an enlargement of the primary cairn and masks the original entrance which lies well within its apparent edge; certainly there was no access from the front of the platform.

5.13) Balvraid (INV 51), on the west side of the Central Highlands, is geographically an outlier of the group of Orkney-Cromarty cairns in the Western Isles. The cairn was already greatly reduced, and one side had been lost to erosion, before the excavations in 1965. The cairn is square, about 15 m across, and was edged by a wall-face of rounded boulders (figures 25, 2; 30). It was found that the chamber was surrounded by a small inner cairn about 9 m in diameter, which was faced by walling. The excavator did not interpret the inner cairn as a cairn core with a purely structural function because it seemed to be unnecessarily wide, especially for a chamber that was thought to have had a relatively low roof. The monument was therefore interpreted as a two-period structure, with the small chamber covered by an unusually small cairn, which was later enclosed by the square cairn. The axis of the square cairn differed from that of the chamber by 15°, and the passage continued to be accessible from the centre of one side. It was tentatively suggested that the square cairn had been no more than a platform surrounding the inner cairn. In the Hebrides there are certainly two, and possibly five, square cairns that may be compared with the Balvraid cairn. The closest parallel for the plan of both the cairn and the chamber, and for size, is Unival (UST 34) in North Uist. The question, whether the short horned and square cairns were built as platforms with round

cairns rising dome-like within them, is, because of the present state of the monuments, answerable only at Boath Short (ROS 11) which on several counts is an exceptional monument.

Long cairns

5.14) Throughout the province of the Orkney-Cromarty cairns the appearance of long cairns in relatively small numbers, but in variety, has posed some of the most intractable problems. The cairns range from seemingly simple featureless structures (such as ROS 39) to one of the largest and most complex in the whole of Scotland (INV 31). The only firm information, which in itself offers contrasts, comes from three excavations in Caithness and Orkney (see ¶ 10. 23–5). None of the eleven long cairns in the Central Highlands has seen even limited excavation, and thus only a superficial description of their present appearance is possible, and even this is often hampered by dense vegetation or dumped field-gathered stones.

5.15) The cairns, unless greatly reduced in height, appear as great mounds of loose stone, overgrown with turf and vegetation along the sides. All the cairns are wider at one end, the proximal end, and unless badly damaged, are also higher at this end. Wester Brae (ROS 39) is the smallest of the cairns, and also one of the least damaged (figure 26, 1). It is 28 m long, and relatively wide at 14 m across the proximal end. In plan both ends appear to be rounded, and the straight sides converge gently towards the rear, or distal, end. In long profile the cairn rises steeply at the proximal end to a height of 1.65 m, and slopes gently to a little lower near the distal end. Wester Lamington (ROS 40) is slightly larger, and rises steeply to 2 m high at the proximal end; its plan may well be similar to Wester Brae, but at the time of our visit it was impossible to record beneath felled trees. Woodhead Long (ROS 41) (figure 26, 2) is of longer narrower proportions. It is over 40 m long, and the proximal end is gently convex (the distal end is damaged), and the convergence of the straight sides is hardly perceptible. There

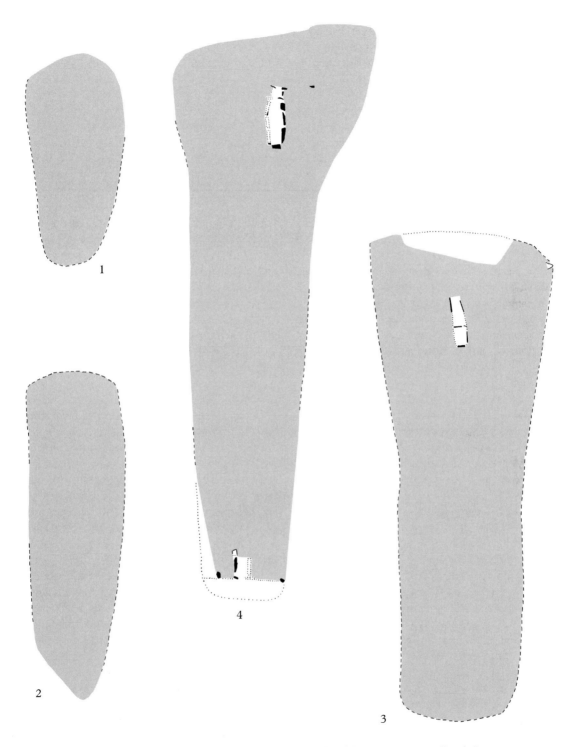

FIGURE 26. Long cairns. 1, Wester Brae, ROS 39; 2, Woodhead Long, ROS 41; 3, Boath Long, ROS 10; 4, Mid Brae, ROS 31.

has been much disturbance down the centre of
the cairn; it is about 2 m high midway along
the axis, and may well once have been as high
or higher near the proximal end. Morangie
Forest (ROS 45) is likely to have been of the
same size and plan before buildings were
inserted into one side; disturbed cairn material
remains to a height of 1.65 m. Apart from their
plans all four cairns appear to be featureless.
Little can be said of Cairnside (ROS 60) which
is so damaged that it was overlooked until an
early nineteenth-century map was studied and
the name of the nearby house drew attention
to its remains. It is at least 52 m long, and
appears to have a straight proximal end, parallel
sides for half its length, and converging sides
down the other half. Although the edges are
distinct except at the distal end, the plan may
have been affected by former ploughing.

5.16) Four cairns, besides being larger,
differ in that the edges are re-aligned midway
down their long sides (hardly detectable
without planning) and by other features, which
probably indicate a combination of separate
elements in the one cairn, and thus imply
multi-period construction. The range of
complexities that may be present in long cairns
can be appreciated more readily in the cairns
of Sutherland and Caithness (Henshall and
Ritchie 1995, 41–7; Davidson and Henshall
1991, 47–59).

5.17) At Boath Long (ROS 10) a rim of
cairn material remains undisturbed except
across the proximal end, and it preserves the
plan of the cairn (figure 26, 3). It is 67 m long,
and probably consisted of two parts. The
proximal half is trapezoid in plan, narowing
from about 26 to 16.5 m wide. It is likely that
the end was originally convex; the present
misleading appearance of a forecourt formed
by projecting horns is due to a later cultivation
plot which has impinged on the cairn. The
distal half of the cairn is parallel-sided, 16.5 m
wide, with a gently convex end. The two parts
evidently merged in the central area where
the cairn material has been totally removed. A
chamber has been exposed nearly in the centre
of the proximal part of the cairn, its axis slightly

skew to that of the long cairn. Around the
chamber the cairn is still 2.8 m high; the distal
half of the cairn (unfortunately virtually
destroyed) almost certainly would have been
lower and either level or diminishing in height
towards the distal end. Kinrive West (ROS 27)
is the same shape and size as Boath Long.
Although superficially disturbed, a substantial
amount of the cairn material remains, and it
probably roughly reflects the original profile of
the cairn. The maximum height, between 2
and 3 m, is in the centre of the proximal part,
and the distal part is mainly a metre or more
lower. Human bones were found in the cairn
in the later nineteenth century, but the circumstances are unknown. There is no sign of a
chamber, though it is possible that a roofless
chamber could be concealed where the cairn
material is deepest.

5.18) Mid Brae (ROS 31) is a larger, more
complex, but disastrously reduced and damaged
cairn. In 1872, when it was still an impressive
monument, it was depicted by officers of the
Ordnance Survey as a round mound, about
22 m in diameter, with a long tail attached,
and a total length of about 80 m (figures 26, 4;
27). We can be confident that the size, and the
striking contrast between the wider proximal
end and the long narrow 'tail', were correctly if
crudely recorded, and this was as much as was
then required. The plan of the cairn made in
1996 indicated a monument about 77 m long,
of which roughly three-quarters is the 'tail'.
The proximal end appears to be straight and
about 29 m wide, and the proximal part, which
may be heel-shaped, appears to be off-centre,
as indeed was shown in 1872. The 'tail' seems
to taper very gradually from about 18 m wide
to perhaps 12 m wide at the distal end, which,
like the opposite end, seems to have been
straight. There was a chamber at each end of
the cairn. The destroyed distal chamber
appears to have been aligned on the axis of the
'tail', and the proximal chamber is on an
almost parallel axis some 3.5 m to one side,
which presumably accounts for the lopsided
plan of the cairn. The two chambers must have
been about 47 m apart.

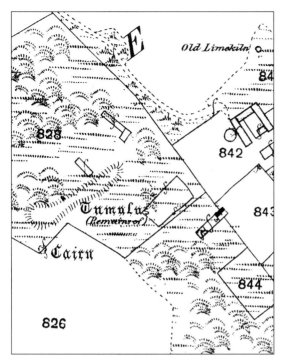

FIGURE 27. Mid Brae, ROS 31, depicted on the OS 25-inch map surveyed in 1872.

5.19) Edderton Hill (ROS 57), now almost totally destroyed, is 61 m long and unusually narrow. The proximal end is straight, and it was about 14 m across. The cairn narrows into a parallel-sided long central portion only about 7 m wide, and expands slightly at the distal end. There is no indication that it contained a chamber, even though the state of the proximal part, where the cairn material is deeper, is favourable to discovery and investigative hollows have been made into it. The only record of the Heights of Dochcarty cairn (ROS 58) gives (if correct) almost unbelievably long and narrow proportions, 79 by 6 m.

5.20) The spectacular cairn on Essich Moor (INV 31) is by far the largest of the long cairns, and also the most remarkable, because it has been relatively little damaged and four components can be identified. The total length of the monument is about 126 m (figure 28, the size has to be stressed because the plan is presented at a smaller scale than the other cairns). It occupies a ridge which rises at each end. On each rise there is an immense cairn, and shallow cairn material links them into one monument. Seen from a distance and enhanced by the topography, it presents a high saddle-shaped profile. One of the terminal cairns is heel-shaped with a straight front edge (which forms one end of the monument), straight sides, and a rounded back; the plan is clearer about a metre above ground level. The cairn is about 43 m long by 36 m wide, and about 2.6 m high (but appears much higher due to the slope of the ground). The other terminal cairn is oval, about 44 by 36 m, and probably about 2 m high. In each cairn part of a chamber is exposed, and these chambers are probably very much larger than the visible parts suggest. It is not possible to be precise about the orientation of the cairns, but it appears that their axes, and those of the chambers they contain, are slightly skew to the axis of the whole monument, and roughly parallel to each other. The two terminal cairns are about 38 m apart, and the space between them is filled by a clearly defined parallel-sided spread of cairn material about 18 m wide and 1 m high. Near one corner part of a small chamber can be seen, aligned almost transversely to the axis of the monument, and within the surrounding cairn material it is just possible to trace a small round cairn. This little chambered cairn is the fourth component of the monument, and clearly predates the centre part of the long cairn.

Forecourts and façades

5.21) Cairns of all forms were edged by a wall-face, which was the most vulnerable part of the whole building. The pressure from behind, the less than ideal building material, interference from outside, and weathering, all contributed to their inevitable collapse unless protected by later additional cairn material. Glimpses of these wall-faces, or their footings, whether of primary cairns or of enlargements, can occasionally be had (at ROS 36, 27, 31). Lower Lechanich South (ROS 30) is unique in the Central Highlands in that substantial spaced

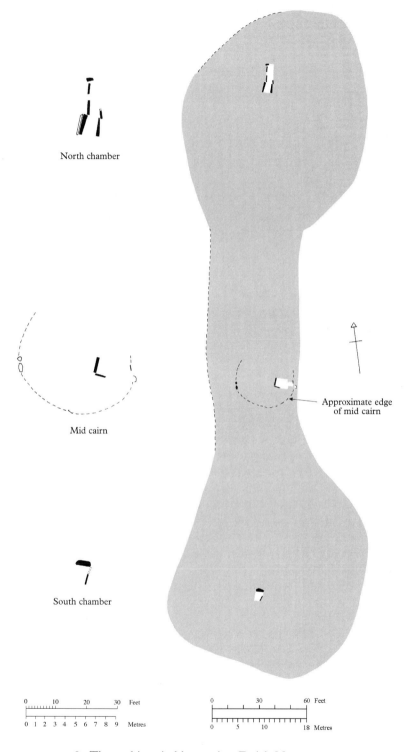

North chamber

Mid cairn

Approximate edge
of mid cairn

South chamber

```
0      10      20      30   Feet
                             
0 1 2 3 4 5 6 7 8 9  Metres
```

```
0              30        60  Feet
                             
0          5        10       18  Metres
```

FIGURE 28. The multi-period long cairn, Essich Moor, INV 31.

upright slabs stand round the edge, and they are all the more striking because the walling that presumably once linked them has disappeared. In parenthsis, it may be noted that a large block standing on the edge of the cairn at Balnaguie (ROS 6) is not a relic of such walling but appears to be a single stone; it is a curious feature, with only one known parallel, at Cnoc Chaornaidh North-west (SUT 69) in Sutherland.

5.22) At those round cairns that are considered to be single-period constructions, their small size, together with the height of the chambers that they covered, mean that the bounding wall-faces were probably built a metre or more high. The wall-faces at the entrances, because of the short passages, must have been higher, at least 2 m, in order to support the cairn material rising over the roofs of the chambers (and this observation indicates that the roofs of the outer compartments of bipartite chambers were, as generally supposed, lower than those of the inner compartments). Thus the entrances would have been handsomely defined by a pair of portal stones bearing a lintel, and by a wall-face increasing in height and continuing over the lintel. It seems likely that in the first phase of building, when the chamber and cairn core were standing without the casing, the passage was also in being and was backed by the core reaching as far as the portal stones, though probably of reduced thickness (figure 23). When the outer casing of the cairn was added, the line of its wall-face may have been adjusted at the front to merge with the outer end of the core and the portal stones. This arrangement would result in the flattened or slightly concave fronts which have been inferred at round cairns (¶ 5.6).

5.23) There is little doubt that the cairn at Kilcoy South (ROS 24) was essentially round, and probably quite small (figure 29). Limited investigations in 1997 on one side of the entrance exposed the basal course of the wall-face edging the cairn (plate 5). The wall-face consisted of virtually contiguous, rather irregular, upright boulders, the tallest 0.7 m high. If the front of the cairn is symmetrical,

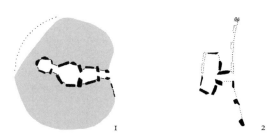

FIGURE 29. Façades. 1, Kilcoy South, ROS 24; 2, Belmaduthy, ROS 8.

the wall-face formed a slightly concave forecourt roughly 3.5 m across and 1 m deep. It is assumed that at the outer ends of the forecourt the wall-face turned to edge the cairn round the rest of the circuit, but tracing it was beyond the resources of the recent operation.

5.24) The distinction between a round cairn with a flat frontage and a heel-shaped cairn is hazy. The former plan seems appropriate at small cairns, but even at Kilcoy South (ROS 24) there is the possibility that the forecourt was wider, and its wall-face formed a sharp angle with the side of the cairn, a plan which would be similar on a smaller scale to that of the cairn at Houstry (CAT 29) in Caithness. At both heel-shaped and long cairns the interest in the area at the entrance to a chamber led to the provision of wide forecourts and imposing façades. It is only at large cairns that these features can be detected on surface examination (unless some façade orthostats can be seen), because collapsed walling and blocking material obscure the forecourt plans.

5.25) It is unknown how frequently façades were elaborated by the incorporation of spaced orthostats into the wall-face. On one side of the entrance at Belmaduthy (ROS 8) there are a portal stone and two orthostats, 1.4 m or more high, and from these it can be estimated that the forecourt was about 14.5 m wide by about 1.2 m deep (figure 29, plate 11). The cairn is so damaged that its plan is not known. The Balnaguie (ROS 6) cairn was round; the passage has been destroyed, but there are two substantial blocks, 5 m apart, close to where the entrance portal stones might be expected,

PLATE II. Belmaduthy (ROS 8) from south, showing the two façade stones and the low stone at the entrance to the passage.

and thus probably sited on the edge of the cairn before its hypothetical enlargement (figure 24, 3). It is tempting to interpret them as part of a former façade. More speculatively, a similar explanation might be considered for the detached stones near the entrances at Ballachnecore and Leachkin ROS 3, INV 38). At the square cairn at Balvraid (INV 51) (figures 25, 2; 30) the widely spaced orthostats in the straight façade had been removed, and it needed excavation to identify their sockets. There had been a central pair of portal stones, and two, or possibly three, orthostats on each side of them.

5.26) The ends of long cairns in the Central Highlands appear to be straight or convex in plan. The remains of an incomplete straight façade with orthostats seems to be present at the distal end of Mid Brae (ROS 31) (figure 26, 4). It is likely that, besides a pair of portal stones, originally there were two more orthostats on each side of them. There may have been a straight façade at the proximal end of the cairn also, but all that can be seen is the portal stones and one other orthostat in a convincing relationship to them. It may be that the prostrate stone at the corner of the proximal end of Boath Long (ROS 10) belonged to an orthostatic façade. The straight ends at long cairns, whether including façade stones or not, may belong to a phase that predates the building of the long cairn itself.

Cairns and chambers

5.27) Only about a third of the monuments included in the Inventory provide reasonably reliable information on both the cairn and the chamber, or chambers, that they covered. As might be expected, all types of chamber are found under round cairns, and there is little correlation between cairn size and chamber size; large chambers can be seen under relatively small cairns (ROS 48), and small chambers under very large cairns (ROS 12). Chambers are known to be present in only three out of the small number of long cairns, and the meagre evidence, for what it is worth, suggests that all the chambers are rectangular.

5.28) Much consideration has been given in this Section to the multi-period constructional history of many cairns, whether certain or inferred, but information is sparse regarding the chronological relationships of the parts of such cairns, or of one monument to another. Two chambers, which are so small that they have been referred to as cells, are primary to bipartite polygonal chambers, one of average size and the other unusually large (Scotsburn Wood East and King's Head Cairn, ROS 47, 25). In each the later chambers were built in relation to the earlier structures, and in the former case access was provided from one to the other. Continuity of tradition may be further demonstrated by the position of the detached

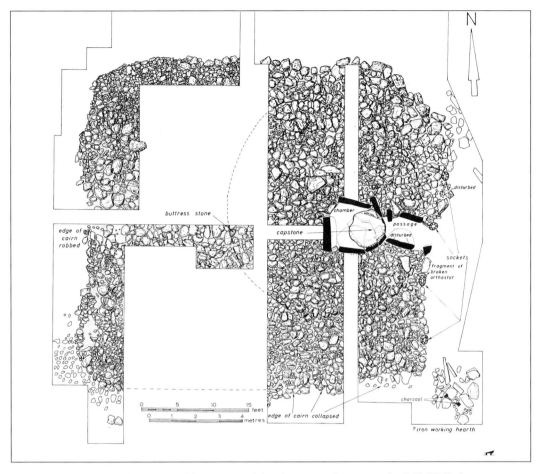

FIGURE 30. Balvraid, INV 51. Plan prepared for the excavation report by J. X. W. P. Corcoran.

cell at King's Head Cairn and the accessible cell at Kilcoy South (ROS 24), both lying obliquely to the main chamber behind the inner right hand corner; this gains in significance from the same positioning of cells at two chambers in Sutherland (SUT 37, 43), and perhaps of the standing stone on the perimeter of the cairns at Balnaguie and Cnoc Chaornaidh North-west (ROS 6, SUT 69). The expectation that small chambers, and in particular single-compartment chambers, are relatively early, receives further support at Balvraid (INV 51), where a small chamber under an unusually small cairn was the primary structure.

5.29) The relationship of polygonal and rectangular chambers is particularly obscure.

As has been noted already, the large round cairn at Heights of Brae (ROS 22) covered two chambers; one, probably the earlier, is rectangular but there is little of it to be seen, and the other is a polygonal bipartite chamber. There may have been a similar sequence at Balnacrae (ROS 4), but there are grave difficulties in interpreting the remains (¶ 4.48–51). It is reasonable to assume that small rectangular chambers are in general earlier than large ones. The roofing of rectangular chambers, except perhaps for the very smallest, depended on adaptation of the circular vault, and with increasing size the roofing was increasingly demanding; it follows that the large single-compartment rectangular chambers, such as that at Mid Brae (ROS 31), are likely to be among the latest built. Lacking structural evidence, it can only be surmised that the normal bipartite chamber at Tarradale (ROS 61) predates the larger atypical chamber.

5.30) Little can be deduced at present from the certain or probable enlargement of round and heel-shaped cairns, but a more informative sequence can be seen at Balvraid and Boath Short (INV 51, ROS 11). At the former a small round chambered cairn was later enhanced by a square cairn, or possibly a square platform, though access to the passage was retained. A similar sequence, on a much larger scale, is evident at Boath Short, where a large polygonal chamber is covered by a probably heel-shaped cairn that is so big that it is almost certainly an enlargement, and this cairn was surrounded by an almost square horned platform which allows little doubt that it sealed the entrance.

5.31) The larger and more complex of the long cairns consist of a large cairn at one end, or at both ends, joined to a narrower cairn which is either parallel-sided or slightly tapering. In four instances it is known that the large terminal cairns contain a chamber, aligned nearly but not quite on the long cairn axis; it is likely that all the expanded terminal cairns were, or are, chambered. Only at Boath Long and Mid Brae (ROS 10, 31) are the chamber plans known, and at the latter the chamber is exceptionally long. The large size of the terminal cairns suggests that they are themselves multi-period structures. One, and possibly another, is heel-shaped (INV 31, ROS 31), and the second terminal cairn at INV 31 is oval (see figure 28). The other component of these complex long cairns appears to be a simple long cairn without a chamber, similar to the independent long cairn at Woodhead Long (ROS 41). The small rectangular chamber with a small cairn in the parallel-sided part of Essich Moor (INV 31) can be seen to be engulfed by the long cairn, and clearly predates it. The slightly skew or off-set positioning of the rest of the chambers and their cairns strongly suggests that they are not contemporary with the long cairn element, but the sequence in which the parts were built is not clear. The whole arrangement and the very size of the Essich Moor long cairn have a contrived appearance. It is tempting to assume that the two terminal cairns were set on the knolls at each end of the ridge, and were later linked together, but this interpretation requires that three chambered cairns were already sited in a straight line, two of them facing in opposite directions, and the third at right angles.

6. The use and sealing of the chambers, and the history of the cairns of the Orkney-Cromarty group

The deposits in the chambers

6.1) From the small number of chambers which have been excavated in the Central Highlands, that at Kilcoy South (ROS 24) is alone in producing a meaningful stratigraphy, and four phases of activity can be detected. The disappointing results from the other three chambers were due to severe damage before the investigations, and probably also to the failure of unburnt bone to survive.

6.2) Only at Kilcoy South (ROS 24) is there any evidence, and very meagre evidence, of a chamber being used for burials. There were several patches of charcoal on the floor of both the ante-chamber and the main chamber, also a small deposit in a chink between two wall orthostats, and with the charcoal was a small amount of cremated bone (figure 31). The character of these deposits suggests that they may be the residue of more substantial remains which had either been cleared away or had decayed. Post-dating the floor deposits, the entry between the ante-chamber and the main chamber had been crudely blocked with large slabs, which, at the time of the excavation, were still in place below a large lintel. In crevices between the slabs, 0.6 m above the floor, were two small deposits of charcoal with burnt bone, and one deposit also contained a sherd. This lost sherd was said to be 'indistin-guishable' from the late neolithic impressed sherds found by the excavators in the nearby chamber at Carn Glas (ROS 12). Possibly the material in the blocking at Kilcoy South had been scooped up from the chamber floor.

Besides the deliberate blocking of the entry into the main chamber, other portions of the chamber may have been closed off. There was a sill-stone on the floor of the entry between the passage and ante-chamber, and a double sill at the entry to the inner compartment, and these may be the remains of similar, but neater, blocking.

6.3) After the main chamber had been closed off, the floor of the main chamber, inner passage and inner compartment was covered by a layer of clean sand. The sand was between 0.15 to 0.23 m thick in the main chamber, and increased to roughly 0.7 m thick in the inner compartment, but was absent from the ante-chamber and passage. The excavators thought that the sand had been blown into the chamber. It indicates that at this time the inner part of the chamber had lost its roof, while the roof of the passage and ante-chamber was presumably still intact. In the ante-chamber and overlying the sand in the main chamber was a filling of large slabs, which the excavators interpreted as collapsed walling (it is not pos-sible to comment on the shallow and disturbed filling of the passage and inner compartment). The difficulties in explaining the presence of the stony fillings of chambers have been highlighted by Barber and are discussed in ¶ 10.67. It now seems unlikely that the fillings represent ritual sealing of the burial deposits, an interpretation that has been favoured in recent years.

6.4) Beaker sherds certainly post-date the floor deposits. In the main chamber sherds in the style formerly described as bell beakers, and a large domestic beaker (figure 32, 1–6), were mostly in two groups lying on the sand layer (a single beaker sherd on the floor at the foot of an orthostat in the main chamber is assumed to have been displaced from above), but a few sherds (not now precisely indentifiable) were found up to 0.46 m above floor level, and thus seem to have been in the stony filling above. Sherds of a short-necked beaker (figure 32, 8), which contrasts markedly with the other beakers and is typologically later, were found in a discrete group just outside the entry to the

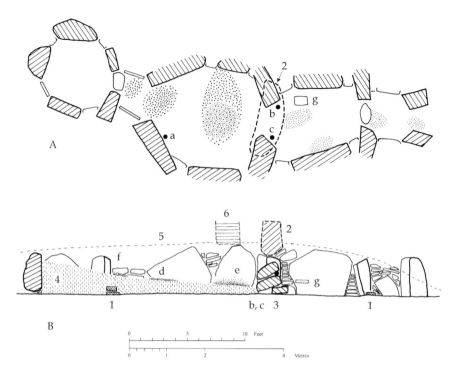

FIGURE 31. Kilcoy South, ROS 24.

A, plan of the deposits in the chamber as recorded by Woodham, 1958. Fine stipple, charcoal deposits on the floor; coarse stipple, deposits of beaker sherds on or above the sand layer.

B, reconstructed section through the chamber, based on Woodham, 1958, and the elevation drawn by MacGregor and Loney (1997).

Key: 1, sill-stones; 2, approximate position of the lintel; 3, blocking below the lintel; 4, layer of sand; 5, level of the chamber filling at the time of the excavation (in the ante-chamber and main chamber the filling was of large slabs deliberately introduced); 6, base of modern field wall. a, sherd of cord-decorated beaker on the floor; b, deposit of charcoal and bone; c, similar deposit with sherd; d, beaker sherds on the sand layer; e, beaker sherds on the sand layer and up to 0.46 m above the floor; f, sherds of beaker 8 on the sand layer or in the lower part of the filling above; g, quern low in the slab filling, the precise level not known.

inner compartment, either lying on the sand or in the stony filling above. All the beakers are incomplete, and range from the whole side of one to a single recognisable sherd of another, and some sherds are worn and some are scorched. It seems, then, that the beaker sherds were associated with the stony filling, their condition suggests that they were rubbish, and some groups of sherds had not been scattered suggesting that they had not been seriously displaced. These facts may indicate that the chamber filling, rather than being collapsed walling, had been thrown in to fill a dangerous hollow after the chamber had lost its roof. A saddle quern (figure 33), found inverted below a particularly large slab, was incorporated in the filling material of the ante-chamber (though if it were part of collapsed walling, as first suggested, it was contemporary with the chamber itself).

6. 5) There are, then, four phases in the history of the chamber: the period of its use for burials, of which virtually no evidence survived; the blocking of access to the main chamber, and possibly the blocking, too, of the entries to the inner compartment and the

ante-chamber, perhaps consecutively; the loss of the roof over the main chamber and inner compartment, followed by the deposit of a layer of sand; after an interval, and with the rest of the roof removed, the infilling of the whole structure, possibly in two stages, by the makers of beaker pottery.

6.6) Little can be said about the other three excavated chambers. Carn Glas (ROS 12) had been investigated in 1906, and by the time of the excavation in the mid 1950s it had been used for the burial of sheep carcasses. The floor of the passage and chamber were covered by a layer of sand 0.05 m deep, which was perhaps a similar feature to the layer of sand at Kilcoy South (ROS 24) less than 1 km away. The few artefacts were in the sand layer. A fine leaf-shaped arrowhead is appropriate to a pre-beaker phase of use of the chamber, and sherds of a late neolithic pot (a few pressed into the clay floor) were compared by the excavators to the sherd, mentioned above, found in the blocking at Kilcoy South. There was a sill-stone between the portal stones at the inner end of the passage, and another between the two compartments of the chamber. Sherds of a beaker, a barbed-and-tanged arrowhead, and a saddle quern presumably were associated with the chamber filling (figures 32, 33). There is a similarity in the findings from these two chambers, and at both there were some pieces of quartz.

6.7) No details of the chamber usage are available from the excavation at Balvraid (INV 51) because the chamber had been disturbed to ground level; there is no formal report of the work, and the finds are lost. They included a small leaf-shaped arrowhead, appropriate to the period when the chamber might be expected to have been used. The passage had been deliberately blocked and the outer end of the passage between the portal stones had been neatly closed by walling. In the blocking were some undecorated neolithic sherds. Sherds of an incomplete undecorated beaker (figure 32) were found above a fallen orthostat, but because the chamber had been ransacked this does not necessarily imply that the chamber was already partly ruined when the makers of this pottery were active at the cairn. Some lignite beads are likely to have been associated with the beaker. The chamber at Tomfat Plantation (INV 52) had been totally wrecked before its excavation. A few small sherds, probably of an undecorated beaker, and a few pieces of quartz, were the only finds.

6.8) Although the only direct evidence for the use of the chambers for burials may have been provided by the small amount of cremated bone at Kilcoy South (ROS 24), there is the possibility that unburnt bone may have totally decayed in the excavated chambers. There are nine instances of human bones having been found casually in cairns (presumably in the chambers) in the Central Highlands, mostly during their destruction, including the terrifying experience in 1826 of a youth at the Cairn of the Gallows (Cnoc Navie, ROS 18) where a skull fell out, and after running away he returned to see it vibrating (due to the presence of a field mouse). These vague pieces of information, and the presence of unburnt burials in chambers in other parts of the Orkney-Cromarty province, indicate that the chambers were probably used, and indeed designed, for inhumations.

6.9) The blocking of parts of the structure has been noted at Kilcoy South and Balvraid (ROS 24, INV 51), and the probably deliberate infilling of the chamber has been noted at the former chamber where the two activities were separated in time. Blocking material laid immediately outside the passage entrances has not been identified at the excavated cairns, but this may be due to degradation and interference; it has been inferred that a considerable amount of external blocking is probably present at some unexcavated monuments (¶ 5.5). Finally, the Kilcoy South chamber was ruinous at the time that the users of beaker pottery appeared at the site. They may even have been responsible for unroofing the chamber, and perhaps for its infilling. It may be suspected that the beaker sherds at the other three chambers signal similar activities.

The destruction of the cairns

6.10) It has been shown, as noted above, that some chambers of the Orkney-Cromarty group may have been unroofed by the end of the third millennium. In contrast, a few cairns survived with their chambers intact, or virtually so, into the nineteenth century. It may be assumed that cairns were continually at risk throughout this long period, either to stone robbing or to the investigations of the curious, but they were also protected by superstition. By far the greatest amount of destruction took place through the nineteenth century. This was the direct consequence of the radical changes in agricultural management at this time, coupled with the siting of cairns on or adjacent to the fertile land undergoing improvement. Stone was needed to build the walls of newly laid out fields and new farm buildings. Protection of monuments of any type was evidently not considered possible. In reply to a request that 'investigators ought in all cases to restore such monuments to the state in which they found them', it is distressing to read the response of the Secretary of the Society of Antiquaries of Scotland that investigations

> will frequently be only in slight anticipation of the march of agricultural improvement, which sweeps off such remains without preserving any record of their contents.... It does not appear reasonable that the systematic explorer... should be called on to re-edify these (often in partial ruin at the outset), merely that they may be wholly swept away a few years afterwards. (Stuart 1868, 307)

In an account of the parish of Rosskeen written in 1838 (NSA) it was noted that already many cairns (not necessarily chambered) had been greatly reduced or entirely removed, though there was great reluctance to destroy at least one which was thought to have plague buried beneath it. The earliest recorded robbing of an Orkney-Cromarty-type cairn for building-stone was at Woodhead Round

(ROS 42) in 1817. It is known, or can be reliably inferred, that thirteen or fourteen more were severely damaged or destroyed between 1824 and the late 1880s, and many more must have suffered, unrecorded, at this time.

6.11) In a few cases a little more of their history is known. The discovery in about 1856 of the large intact chamber in the King's Head Cairn (ROS 25) was kept secret, and for about fourteen years it was used as a whisky store, until the cairn was removed for building stone and the chamber was wrecked. Similarly the chamber at Boath Short (ROS 11) was evidently known, perhaps from the eighteenth century if the story of its use as a hide-away is to be believed, then seemingly lost to sight and later re-opened; unusually in this case the cairn was not seriously robbed. The cairns at Cnoc Navie, Carn nam Fiann and Carn Glas (ROS 18, 55, 12) were virtually intact until 1826, 1854, and 1882 respectively, and were totally or almost destroyed during the following years. The end of a less complete monument is also recorded: the orthostats of the large chamber, Clachan Biorach (ROS 14), stood free of cairn material at the end of the eighteenth century; only two stones remained standing in 1860 when they fell during a storm, and they were broken up and removed in the 1950s. The folklore relating to the orthostats at Heights of Brae (ROS 22) implies that the cairn had been removed and the chamber ruined well before the nineteenth century.

6.12) Once the first phase of agricultural improvements was over, most of the monuments have not been further damaged, or at worst have had field-gathered stones dumped on them, though there are, of course, exceptions (ROS 5, 12, 31, 57). Fourteen cairns are in conifer forests, and in the 1950s and 1960s these cairns were sometimes affected by deep ploughing over their edges, and occasionally right across them, and then by being planted over (although the remains of chambers were respected). Present management has removed these threats. On the other hand afforestation has had the effect of protection from casual interference. It is notable that the four least damaged long cairns are in areas that, because the land was very marginal, remained as common grazing into the second half of the nineteenth century, and then were afforested; in more fertile areas the cairns would have been plundered.

Cairn names and folklore

6.13) A number of cairns have specific names (the gaelic names are either discussed in Watson 1904, or translated for us by I. Fraser, School of Scottish Studies, University of Edinburgh). Some names are straightforwardly descriptive. Carn Liath (grey cairn) was applied frequently to cairns and other classes of monument throughout northern Scotland, and is recorded at three chambered cairns in the Central Highlands (ROS 10, 45, 51); Carn Glas (also grey cairn) occurs twice (ROS 12, INV 31). There is also Clachan More (the big stones), Clachan Corrach (the steep or rough stones), and Clachan Biorach (the pointed stones) (ROS 61, 3, 14). Other cairn names are clearly romantic and probably date from the eighteenth century. Carn Fian, Carn na Feinne, Carn nam Fiann, Carn Fionntairneach (ROS 7, 52, 54, 55, the exact meaning of the last is obscure) relate to the Fingalians. The Temple, The Druid's Circle, and Druidtemple (ROS 37, INV 17, 30) are similarly the result of antiquarian imagination. Clachan Gorach (the foolish stones) (ROS 22) was explained by the legend that the stones were people who had been turned to stone for dancing on the Sabbath. Likewise, The Priest's Sepulchre (ROS 35) perhaps reflects post-reformation attitudes and superstition about mysterious ancient structures. The Giant's Grave (INV 46) is a nickname applied after the reconstruction of the chamber in the early nineteenth century.

6.14) Other names need more consideration. Carn Urnan (ROS 13) is cognate with the parish name, Killearnan (the church of St Iturnan). It is instructive that in the mid nineteenth century an explanatory tradition was current that the cairn was the burial place of a spurious King Urnan. Similarly, the King's Head Cairn (ROS 25) was thought to be the burial place of a beheaded king, and that the nearby cairn (ROS 27) was the burial place of those slain with him. This myth must be relatively recent, and stems from the local placename Kinrive, an anglicized form which was mistakenly interpreted as the gaelic Ceann righ (the king's head); correctly the name is Ceann-ruigh (the head of the ridged slope). The name Carn na Croiche (ROS 18) (cairn of the gallows) appears uncomplicated, and there is a long and perhaps credible tale set in the seventeenth century which ends with the execution of thieves there. Preas Mairi (ROS 19) (St Mary's Grove) presumably refers to the enclosure later used for private burials rather than the remains of the neolithic chamber within it.

6.15) Cairns of all types were frequently explained as covering the bodies of those killed in battle, and Ballachnecore (ROS 3) was specifically connected with a skirmish in the fifteenth century. The story, possibly true, that Boath Short (ROS 11) was used as a refuge by eighteenth-century brigands has been mentioned above.

7. The artefacts from the cairns of both the Orkney-Cromarty and Clava groups

7.1) For no area in the present quartet of volumes have the artefacts made such an unsatisfactory assemblage, and they demonstrate most tellingly how systematically the chambers were cleared out in antiquity. Few monuments have been examined in ways that might have been expected to provide artefactual evidence from beneath the cairn or deposited, accidentally or otherwise, in the course of construction. From the cairns of Orkney-Cromarty type there are few potentially early finds; the excavator of Balvraid (INV 51) described sherds of undecorated neolithic pottery among the artefacts recovered, but as all these have now been lost, the attribution cannot be authenticated. The fragments of very friable sherds with impressed decoration from Carn Glas and Kilcoy South (ROS 12, 24) are presumably of late neolithic date.

7.2) The most consistent discovery is that of beaker pottery in a range of styles, but few vessels in contexts that are in any way helpful. There are sherds from Carn Glas (ROS 12), Kilcoy South (ROS 24), Balvraid (INV 51) and probably Tomfat Plantation (INV 52) (figure 32). Some are more diagnostic than others: from Kilcoy South there are certainly sherds from all-over-cord ornamented beakers, a vessel decorated by impressions, a comb-impressed vessel that may be described as a european bell beaker, and a vessel that would formerly have been described as a short-necked beaker.

7.3) The development of beaker pottery in Grampian as outlined by Shepherd (1986) offers a suitable methodology for placing the small number of vessels found in the cairns into the sort of sequence of steps suggested by Lanting and van der Waals (1972) using the data provided by Clarke (1970). Thus the all-over-cord and european bell beaker fragments from Kilcoy South (ROS 24) (vessels *1–5, 7*) fall into steps 1–2 as envisaged by Shepherd. With them were pieces of a large storage jar, of similar high quality with impressed decoration (*6*). Vessel *8*, a developed northern beaker (N 2 in Clarke's terminology) would fall within step 4. The fragments of vessel *4* from Carn Glas (ROS 12), would fall within steps 5–6, judging from the likely zonation of the decoration. What this means in chronological terms is uncertain, but the steps 1–2 vessels are indeed likely to be early, with the radiocarbon date from Sorisdale, Coll, within the third quarter of the third millennium BC offering a broad horizon (Ritchie and Crawford 1978), with later styles continuing into the second millennium.

7.4) Hanley and Sheridan (1994) have mapped the distribution of beaker pottery round the Black Isle and the Inverness area (including that from Carn Glas and Kilcoy South) in their discussion of a cist containing two such vessels at the edge of Balblair Wood, not far from the cairn INV 54. The deposition of beaker sherds in ROS 12 and 24 may mean very little about the usage of the chambers for burials, but may have had more significance to the users of this pottery than being merely rubbish (¶ 6.4–7). It may be noted that the field-walking exercises that have been undertaken in the Black Isle and on the Morayshire coast have failed to reveal further examples of this distinctive pottery.

7.5) The flint artefacts are hardly more informative. From Carn Glas (ROS 12) there is a leaf-shaped arrowhead and a barbed-and-tanged arrowhead. There was a small leaf-shaped arrowhead from Balvraid (INV 51), as well as a number of lignite beads, but nothing is known about their form. These finds offer no chronological precision beyond the later neolithic and early bronze age.

7.6) At two of the Kilcoy cairns (ROS 12, 24) Woodam discovered quern stones (figure 33), and these have been described and illustrated by Close-Brooks (1983). At Kilcoy South

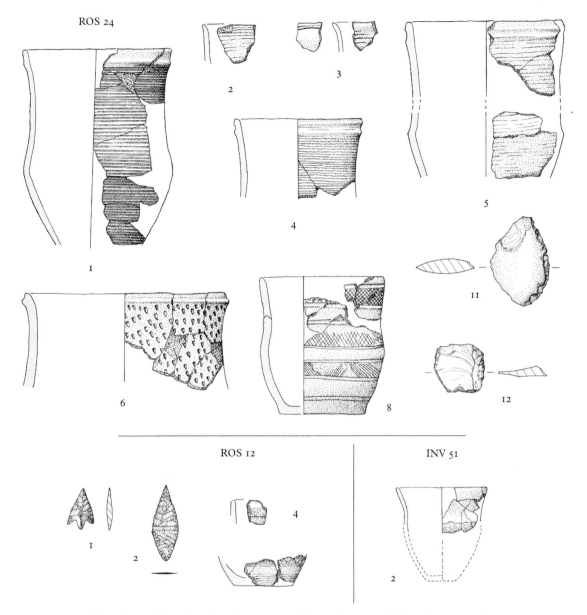

FIGURE 32. Finds from Kilcoy South, ROS 24, Carn Glas, ROS 12, and Balvraid, INV 51. Pottery 1:4, flints 1:2.

(ROS 24) the quern lay among the slabs filling the ante-chamber, and at Carn Glas (ROS 12) the quern was found above modern sheep burials in the filling of the chamber. They are saddle querns and are not readily datable.

7.7) Finds from cairns of Clava type are equally discouraging. The calcined pin from Corrimony (INV 17) is certainly a bone, but whether it should be elevated to the status of a pin is uncertain. The pottery found below the chamber floor of Balnuaran South-west (INV 10) in the course of excavation in the late

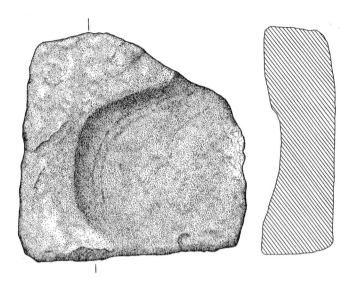

FIGURE 33. Querns, from Kilcoy South, ROS 24 (above), and Carn Glas, ROS 12 (below). Scale 1:8. From Close-Brooks 1983, drawn by M. O'Neill.

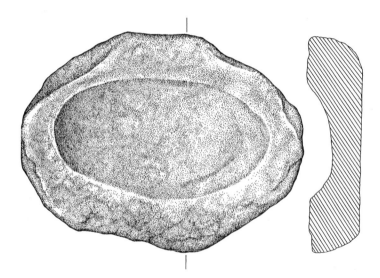

1820s is unfortunately lost, but the two vessels were quite fully described and illustrated by Lauder (figure 34). The pottery may reasonably be interpreted as flat-rimmed ware, and may be attributed to the later bronze age activities on the site, but the difficulties of dating this disparate class of vessel have been outlined by Coles and Taylor (1970, 96–8) and Piggott and Simpson (1971, 10–11).

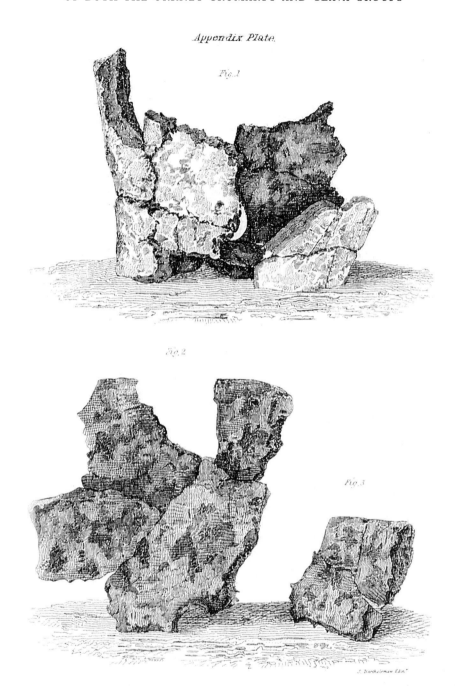

FIGURE 34. Balnuaran South-west, INV 10. The pottery, now lost, from Mrs Campbell's excavations in the 1820s. From T. D. Lauder 1830.

8. The passage-graves of the Clava group

8.1) As has been explained already (¶ 1.11), amongst the cairns with the distinctive traits which link them together as belonging to the Clava group, only the passage-graves are described in detail in this volume. There are certainly eleven passage-graves (INV 5, 9, 10, 16, 17, 18, 26, 30, 37, ROS 13, BAN 1), and two more monuments (INV 49, 55), the classification of which is not wholly certain, have also been included. All are within the boundaries of the region which we have called the Central Highlands, apart from Lagmore (BAN 1) in the lower Spey valley which has been included for completeness. New plane-table plans (except for Corrimony and Culdoich South, INV 17, 55) have been prepared with attention

to accuracy and detail, and are the basis for the following commentary.

The plans of the passage-graves and ring-cairns

8.2) The cairns are round, and are edged by a kerb of massive stones. The diameters of the passage-graves range from 9.5 m at Kinchyle of Dores (INV 37) to 17 m at Balnuaran of Clava North-east (INV 9). Within the kerbs, and contained by them, were steep-sided cairns which must have been 4 m or more high to enclose the chambers. At most of the passage-graves the cairns have been removed, or nearly so, leaving the kerbs as rings of substantial contiguous stones, but at three monuments, Balnuaran North-east and South-west and Corrimony (INV 9, 10, 17), the cairn material remains to a height of about 2.3 m. Centrally within the cairn at these three monuments is a circular chamber entered by a passage, with the lowest course of the walls built of boulders (plates 12, 13). The character of the Balnuaran cairns is evocatively captured in the colour photographs in Bradley 1996. At other cairns

PLATE 12. Balnuaran of Clava North-east (INV 9), view from south-west.

PLATE 13. Balnuaran of Clava South-west (INV 10), view from the west with stones 6, 7 and 8.

only the lowest course of the chambers and passages can be seen, or can be partially traced, or it may not be visible. The chambers vary between 3 and 3.8 m in diameter. Against the outer face of the kerbs at a number of cairns a low stony bank is clearly visible, and this was probably a standard feature. The cairns are surrounded by a circle of standing stones, between 18 and 32 m in diameter. The uniformity of the design of the cairns, the evident importance of their external appearance, the emphasis on circularity, the surrounding stone circles, the orientation of the entrances, the incorporation of cupmarked stones, and the absence of any hint of secondary alterations or additions, all distinguish them from the chambered cairns of Orkney-Cromarty type. It was only after our fieldwork had been almost completed that it was known that the Clava-type passage-graves were further distinguished by their unexpectedly late date.

8.3) Monuments that are certainly ring-cairns of Clava type are listed in Appendix 2, and the best preserved example (INV 8) is described with a plan in the Inventory. All the ring-cairns of Clava type have, or had, a ring of standing stones. The cairn kerbs are indistinguishable in appearance from those of the passage-graves; their diameters range from about 13 to 27 m, and thus there is some overlap with the kerb diameters of passage-graves. The internal diameters of ring-cairns range from about 5 to about 9 m, and these spans are too great to be roofed by corbelling; thus they can be distinguished from the foundations of chambers. At several ring-cairns it can be seen that there was no passage giving access through the kerb. It is clear that originally the cairns of ring-cairns were not appreciably higher than their kerbs, and were hollow in the centre like vast doughnuts, contrasting with the high pudding-like mounds covering the chambers of the passage-graves (plate 14). A number of monuments that are clearly remains

PLATE 14. Balnuaran of Clava Centre (INV 8) and Balnuaran of Clava South-west (INV 10) from the north-east.

of Clava-type cairns but which cannot be classified at present are listed in Appendix 3, 1.

The cairns of the passage-graves

8.4) The cairn kerbs have always been one of the most impressive features of Clava-type cairns. The kerbs were built of carefully selected boulders, and only occasionally was a split slab included, though this happened more commonly in Strathspey. The kerb-stones were placed touching, or nearly so, with the flattest faces to the outside and forming a regular curve. The appearance of the outer face of the kerb was evidently of great importance, so much so that in one instance a thin vertical stone of triangular cross-section was neatly inserted into a chink between kerb-stones (at INV 30); this stone is likely to be a rare survival, and similar care can be seen at a few ring-cairns (INV 29, 34). Irregularities in the shapes of the kerb-stones were largely hidden, of course, in the cairn material behind them. The great majority of the surviving kerb-stones are intact, and, while some have horizontal upper surfaces, it is clear that the rounded or pointed tops of most of the boulders gave the kerbs an uneven upper edge; possibly they were levelled by walling which has disappeared.

8.5) The massive character of the kerbs has to be emphasized because it is generally difficult to appreciate (see frontispiece). The lowest 0.5 m or so of the kerb-stones is likely to be hidden by the external bank and by the remaining cairn material; or, if they are deprived of this support, the kerb-stones (which were normally set on the old ground surface) are likely to have been displaced to lean outwards or to have fallen flat, and they are often partly concealed. At the two Balnuaran cairns (INV 9, 10) the largest kerb-stones were exposed during excavation, and at most of the other cairns the size of the largest stones can, with ingenuity, be measured or calculated. The tallest stones are on the south or south-west side of the monuments, near the entrance, though the kerb-stones which form the portal of the passage are always lower than their neighbours. At the Balnuaran cairns the kerb-stones are up to 1.4 m high; elsewhere the tallest stones vary between a little over 1 m high (for instance at INV 17 and 26) up to 1.65 or even 1.85 m high (at INV 5 and 18). The impact of the kerb at this last cairn, Croftcroy, would have been all the more striking because the cairn is one of the smallest. Many kerb-stones are very substantial blocks, from 0.3 to 0.6 m and exceptionally 1 m thick, and some can be as much as 1.7 m long. The gradual, but not entirely consistent, decrease in the heights of the kerb-stones towards the back of the cairn is a noticeable feature, a difference of between 0.4 and 0.6 m being usual. At several cairns, and notably at Balnuaran South-west and Druidtemple (INV 30), undisturbed kerb-stones often lean slightly inwards, and this is likely to be deliberate to counteract the pressure of the mass of the cairn; most of the vertical kerb-stones at the North-east cairn are known to have been been reset.

8.6) If the outer faces of the *in situ* kerb-stones were exposed to ground level the kerbs would appear more regular than at present, and this is particularly true of the rear of a number of cairns where only the tips of the shorter kerb-stones can be seen, and the kerb has a misleadingly insubstantial appearance (INV 5, 16, 49). Despite these handicaps the plans of the kerbs are more revealing than might be expected. In particular, when a drawn

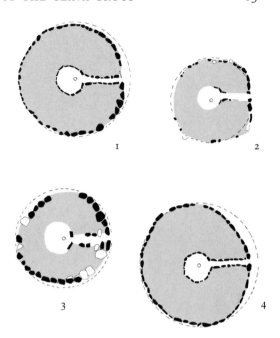

FIGURE 35. Cairns of Clava-type passage-graves. The kerbs are shown with the 'best-fit' circle dashed and its centre as an open circle. 1, Balnuaran South-west, INV 10; 2, Carn Daley, INV 16; 3, Druidtemple, INV 30; 4. Balnuaran North-east, INV 9.

circle is imposed on the plans, the precision of the layout of some, and anomalies at others, which are hardly noticeable on surface examination, become apparent.

8.7) The outer face of the kerbs of Dalcross Mains, Tullochgorm, Culdoich South and at Lagmore (INV 26, 49, 55, BAN 1) are set on fairly accurate circles. Balnuaran South-west (INV 10) is so nearly circular that subtle anomalies would seem insignificant if they were not repeated at several other cairns (figure 35, 1). The kerb is very slightly flattened, by less than 1 m, in the arc including the entrance, and there is also a tendency for short runs of kerb-stones to be set in almost straight lines. The flattening of the kerb beside the entrance is very obvious at Cairn Daley (INV 16), where two-thirds of the kerb (as far as it can be seen) is circular, but the straight front, consisting of the portal stones and four massive kerb-stones, is straight (figure 35, 2). At Avielochan (INV 5) the cairn is strictly circular apart from a very slight flattening across the entrance, and it is probable that the more damaged kerb at Croftcroy (INV 18) was similar. At Balnuaran North-east (INV 9), where many of the kerb-stones have been reset but almost in their original positions, about a third of the kerb on the south-west side follows a curve a little within the line of a true circle (the axial diameter is about 1.2 m less than the transverse diameter) (figure 35, 4). At other cairns, though the kerbs were built with great care, some kerb-stones at the side or back may run in straight lines. This is most noticeable at Druidtemple (INV 30) where the plan is considerably distorted (figure 35, 3), and is less pronounced at Kinchyle of Dores (INV 37) and Carn Urnan (ROS 13). In its present state the precise plan at Corrimony (INV 17) cannot be seen, but there appears to have been an irregularity on one side.

8.8) At the three monuments where a substantial part of the cairn survives, Balnuaran North-east and South-west and Corrimony (INV 9, 10, 17), the cairn material is rounded stones. A cutting made into the cairn at Balnuaran North-east showed that the lower part was built with large boulders which had been bonded with turf and topsoil to form a solid core around the chamber. During the excavation at Corrimony large boulders were observed behind the kerb-stones, but the cairn structure was not examined (plate 15).

8.9) A bank built against the foot of the kerb is an obvious feature at these three cairns and at Avielochan (INV 5), and, though less obvious due to disturbance or other factors, is certainly present at four more monuments (INV 16, 26, 49, BAN 1). At the Balnuaran cairns (INV 9, 10) the banks remain to a maximum height of 0.5 m, and they extend from the kerbs as flat platforms about 1.6 m wide, and have a total width of 3.5 to 4.5 m. They were shown on investigation to consist of a lower layer largely composed of slabs, with mainly rounded stones above this, and at the South-west cairn there were remnants of a top

PLATE 15. Corrimony (INV 17). Stuart Piggott's excavation of 1952 showing the kerb-stones leaning acutely outwards and the boulders immediately behind them (scale in feet).

surface of flat slabs which had the appearance of damaged paving. The bank around INV 10 is clearly visible at the top of plate 14. At Corrimony (INV 17) the bank is 2 m wide, and elsewhere the banks are up to 3 m wide; the heights of the banks are estimated as between 0.4 m at INV 26 and 1 m at INV 5. The excavations at Balnuaran showed, as had previously been assumed, that the banks were part of the original design (though there may have been an interval before they were added), and were needed to support the kerbs; the result of inadequate support is seen at Corrimony (INV 17) where the whole kerb has collapsed outwards (plate 15).

8.10) The bank at Avielochan (INV 5) clearly continues across the passage entrance, thus impeding if not preventing access when the passage was roofed. At the two Balnuaran cairns (INV 9 and 10) the banks at the entrances have been greatly worn down by visitors, but excavation at the North-east cairn seemed to show that the bank had always been continuous (Bradley 2000, 73, but see ¶ 9.2). Before the Corrimony excavations (INV 17) the bank here also appeared to be unbroken, but it was found that originally there had been a gap which later had been deliberately closed.

The passages and chambers

8.11) There are alternative designs for the entrances to the passages. The portal stones may be set circumferentially as part of the kerb, with the passage walls butting against their backs (as at INV 9, 10, 30, ROS 13); or the portal stones may be set radially and belong to the passage walls which pass through the kerb, with the outer ends of the portal stones either in line with the outer face of the kerb (as at INV 5, 16, 26), or projecting forward of the kerb and thus emphasising the entrance (as at INV 17, 18, and BAN 1). In all cases the portal stones are lower than the adjacent kerb-stones, generally by about 0.4 m, and at Balnuaran North-east it was shown that, in order to achieve the height adjustment, they were set in sockets 0.3 and 0.4 m deep. Presumably the portal stones were intended to bear a lintel with its upper edge roughly level with the tops of the adjacent kerb-stones. The well preserved projecting entrance at Lagmore (BAN 1) is built with substantial shapely blocks and retains a somewhat displaced lintel; the entry is 0.6 m wide and nearly 1 m high (figure 36). Other entrances, judging by the height of the portal stones, were at least 1 m high, and where they appear to be substantially less they may once have been heightened by walling. The widths of entrances are between 0.53 and 0.73 m.

8.12) The walls of the passages were built with a basal course of orthostats, and there are remains of an upper course of large horizontal flat slabs at the Balnuaran cairns, Corrimony, and formerly at Avielochan (INV 9, 10, 17, 5). Most of the passages increase very slightly in width from the entrance, and some may have increased slightly in height; the inner end of the two passages at Balnuaran were at least 1.23 m high, including some walling. The passage at Corrimony has unusual features. The tall portal stones were as high as the adjacent

FIGURE 36. Lagmore, BAN 1. General view and detail of the entrance, drawn by F. R. Coles, 1906.

kerb-stones; beyond them the passage walls are built normally of boulder orthostats supplemented with rough walling, but from half way along the walls are built with three courses of boulders laid flat, and at the time of excavation there were six lintels *in situ*. The roofing of the passage seems to have been at much the same level throughout, about 0.8 m above the floor (figure 37). The differences in the walling may reflect two stages in the construction of the cairn, the chamber with its supporting core followed by the outer casing. Because all the chambers are much the same size, the length of the passages was dictated by the size of the cairns; the passages (excluding the exceptionally planned INV 18) vary between 3.3 m long at INV 37 and about 7 m (or 8 m including the projection beyond the kerb) at INV 17. A curious feature at Lagmore (BAN 1) is the alignment of the passage, of which only the outer 1.7 m is visible, towards the side of the chamber.

8.13) The chambers are central within the cairns (though not always exactly so), and, with the exception of Croftcroy (INV 18) mentioned below, they are round in plan, and the similarity of the chambers is one of their notable features. They may not be precisely circular at ground level, perhaps due either to slight mismanagement or subsequent settlement. There is no reason to think that those chambers now reduced to only the basal course of close-set orthostats were not similar to the three that are more complete, Balnuaran North-east and South-west and Corrimony (INV 9, 10, 17) (plates 12, 13). It was a remarkable achievement for the builders to roof chambers of this size in stone, especially as the quality of the masonry is poor; the chambers are the same size as the very largest *circular* spaces to be roofed among the Orkney-Cromarty-type chambers, such as Brahan Wood, Skelpick Long or Tulloch of Assery A (ROS 53, SUT 53, CAT 69).

8.14) At each of the Balnuaran chambers (INV 9, 10) the basal course, as in the passages, was of contiguous orthostats. Both boulders and slabs, mostly with vertical sides and flat faces, were used, and they were set to form a smooth wall-face to the interior. At both chambers there are carefully selected quarried blocks, between 0.9 and 1.05 m high, on either side of the entrance. The rest of the orthostats decrease in height rather irregularly to about 0.6 m high at the rear. The orthostats at the entrance overlap the innermost orthostats of the passage wall, and above this at the North-east cairn the walling at the inner end of the passage is skew to the axis and merges into that of the chamber. The chamber walls survive to a height of 2 m with little oversailing, but illustrations of the North-east chamber in the mid nineteenth century show that there was then a further metre which oversailed considerably (figure 4). It has been calculated that the span to be roofed would be 2.5 m at a height of 3.5 m, which would need an enormous capstone, or perhaps two, but the span would be only 2 m at a height of 4.25 m (Bradley 2000, 46–7). Above the carefully constructed basal course the masonry has a crude appearance. It consists of large horizontal waterworn slabs in irregular courses supplemented by small slabs and rounded stones. At Balnuaran South-west, and less markedly at Balnuaran North-east, the large slabs are in vertical stacks, a feature already noted in 1830 (figure 3). This has produced irregular vertical joints running up the wall, which, with the rounded tops and varying heights of the stones of the basal course, presented the builders with problems of stability, and it is indeed remarkable that so much of the chamber structure has survived.

8.15) The Corrimony chamber (INV 17), standing 2 m high, was built with even less refinement. The basal course is of low boulders which are not graded in height, above which the wall is of boulders and cobbles, and the upper part (rebuilt after the excavation in 1952) was mainly built of relatively small slabs. The very rough appearance of the chamber walls has been emphasised by settlement, and it is difficult to assess how far this had increased the considerable oversailing of the upper part. There can be little doubt that a

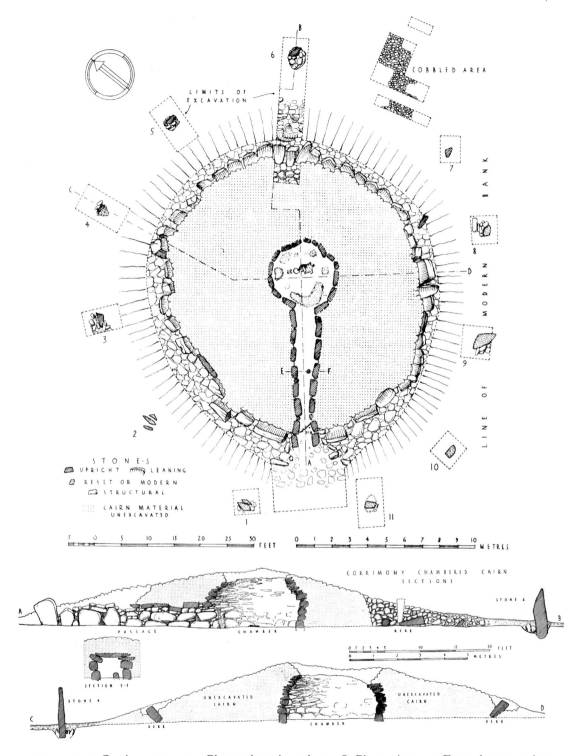

FIGURE 37. Corrimony, INV 17. Plan and sections drawn S. Piggott in 1952. From the excavation report.

huge flat block lying on the cairn is the cap-stone displaced from the centre of the roof.

8.16) As at the Balnuaran chambers, there is a pair of substantial rectangular blocks framing the entrance at both Druidtemple and Avielochan (INV 30, 5), and at the latter the stones of the basal course are graded and set in a smooth curve, and a few courses remain above. At Carn Urnan (ROS 13) care was taken to give a regular face to the basal course, but there is little difference in the heights of the stones, and the orthostats at the entrance were not specially selected. The entrances to chambers are between 0.95 m wide (at INV 10) and 0.64 m wide (at INV 30).

8.17) The exceptional chamber at Croftcroy (INV 18) is a small elongated space, about 2.8 m long and 0.72 m wide, now defined by a basal course of boulders; it is differentiated from the passage merely by a slight narrowing of the walls midway from the kerb.

The circles of standing stones

8.18) Before examining the design of the circles, it is necessary to appreciate the partic-ular difficulties arising from their mutilated condition. Some stones, mainly large boulders, survive in position and intact, but clearly many of the stones have been damaged, either deliberately or by weathering, and in other cases there is uncertainty about their condi-tion. Thus the original height of many stones is unknown, their shapes may have been affected, and sandstone slabs which suffer vertical cleavage may be drastically reduced in thick-ness without necessarily reducing their height. Most of the remaining fallen stones are intact, so their former height can be measured, but it is unknown how deeply they may have been set into stone-holes. Further difficulties have been introduced by the re-erection of fallen stones, which in some cases are not in their original positions. Finally, there are tantalising gaps from which stones may have been removed without record. In the following commentary the inner faces of the stones are taken as the diameter of each circle.

8.19) The bases of the standing stones at Corrimony (INV 17) were found, when exam-ined, to be set in stone-holes about 0.3 m deep, and packed around with cobbles. At Lagmore (BAN 1) deeper stone-holes with packing have been partly exposed by erosion. On the other hand it was surprising to find during the recent excavations at Balnuaran North-east (INV 9) that two large standing stones had not been set in stone-holes, but were supported merely by a modest amount of packing; this material had been augmented in recent times, so that, like most of the standing stones at the Balnuaran cairns, they are now surrounded by little cairns. It is even more surprising that the very tall standing stone, 2.2 m high, at the adjacent ring-cairn (INV 8) was set up in the same way. Thus the removal of standing stones from the Clava-type cairns would have been quite easy, especially if they had fallen, and there might be no trace of the stones even on excavation.

8.20) The circles were laid out in relation to the axis of the passage and chamber. Two stones were sited symmetrically in front of the entrance and on either side of the axis; these stones were particularly impressive, both for their overall size and their height, and often were regular in shape with vertical faces. The tallest of these stones still standing, 2.8 and 2 m high, are at the two Balnuaran cairns (INV 9, 10), and other notable stones in this position remain at Druidtemple and Carn Urnan (INV 30, ROS 13). There is a huge fallen stone, 3.5 m long, near the entrance at Lagmore (BAN 1), and formerly there was a pair of simi-lar size at Croftcroy (INV 18). There is certainly a tendency for the standing stones to be smaller towards the back of the circles, but it is not possible to comment in detail. The circles must have been very impressive when intact; other stones besides those near the entrance were over 2 m high (at BAN 1 and INV 9), and even the shortest stones were seldom less than 1.3 m high. The diameters of the circles are roughly proportionate to the diameters of the cairns, with the standing stones generally between 2 and 7 m from the cairn kerbs.

8.21) There are eight circles where enough stones survive to allow discussion of their arrangement, and at six of them the stones are placed accurately on the line of a circle. In four cases a standing stone was set behind the chamber on the projected axis. This layout, when the stones are more or less evenly spaced, requires an uneven number in the circle. At three circles (INV 9, 30, 37) the rear stone is not exactly on the axis, and another monument, Lagmore (BAN 1) lacks an obvious axis.

8.22) The plans of both the cairn and the circle at Carn Urnan (ROS 13) are relatively complete (figure 38, 1). Four upright stones are accurately placed in a circle centered on the chamber with one stone set on the axis at the rear. Three prostrate stones that have fallen outwards remain undisturbed, though two have been reduced in size. The original design of the circle is clear: there were nine stones, somewhat unevenly spaced, of which that on the west side of the entrance and another on the north-north-west side are missing. The stones are very substantial blocks with rounded tops, 1.95 to 1 m high.

8.23) The circles round the Balnuaran cairns (INV 9,10) are particularly impressive, both for their size which is appropriate to the large scale of the cairns, and the use of large rectangular sandstone slabs. However, many of the stones have been re-erected or re-sited. Thanks to Fraser's careful plans made in or before 1883, it is known that only four or five of the eleven stones in the South-west circle (INV 10), and six of the ten stones in the North-east circle (INV 9), are undisturbed.

8.24) There is no doubt that the circle at Balnuaran South-west (INV 10) was laid out in an accurate circle with a stone on the axis at the rear (figure 38, 2; plate 13). Three of the fallen stones have been re-erected in, or close to, their original positions, and it can be accepted that the spacing of the eight stones round more than half the circuit on the north-west side is approximately as designed, and it seems that they were set slightly closer together round the back. Two stones on the opposite side of the circle were moved in the

nineteenth century to allow widening a public road and building a wall along each side of it. These stones still stand on the circle, probably close to their original positions. The southern stone was merely re-aligned for convenience parallel with the verge (it can be seen in its original circumferential position in Stewart's painting of 1857, figure 4; see also Fraser's plan of 1883, figure 6). The other stone has been used as the terminal of the wall on the opposite side of the road. Between these stones is a steeply leaning boulder that has been incorporated into the base of the opposite wall. Although Jolly recorded that the boulder has been moved this may be doubted, because Fraser makes no such comment, and if it were restored to a vertical position it would stand virtually on the line of the circle. Between these three stones and that on the axis there is a wide gap, and the question arises whether it was filled by one or two stones. The care and effort expended on the construction of this handsome circle, only one stone of which was not a sandstone slab, suggest that symmetry would have been a consideration. From this it follows that there were thirteen stones in the circle, with two in the gap on the north-east side; these would be even more conveniently accommodated if the second of the reset stones had stood further south, projecting into the carriageway. The unlikely alternative, that there were twelve stones in the circle, requires that the stones to the east of the axis were spaced more widely than the complementary stones on the north side of the axis.

8.25) It seems that the circle around Balnuaran North-east (INV 9) was not constructed with quite the same care (figure 38, 3). There are ten stones, of which the four on the south-west side are sandstone blocks, and the rest are boulders some of which are irregular in shape (see frontispiece and plate 12). The stone behind the chamber is to the side of the axis, and the six undisturbed stones are not set precisely in a circle. Fraser recorded the three stones on the south-west side of the monument whilst they were still lying as they had fallen, and when he subsequently made his

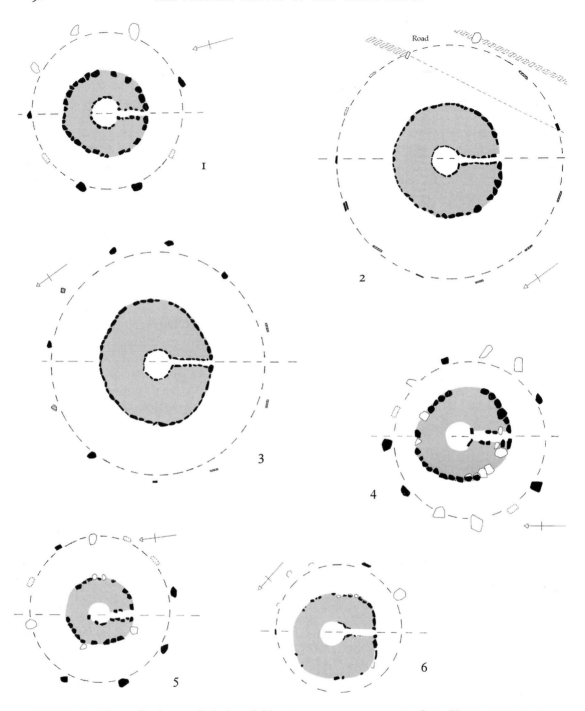

FIGURE 38. Plans of cairns and circles of Clava-type passage graves. 1, Carn Urnan, ROS 13; 2, Balnuaran South-west, INV 10; 3, Balnuaran North-east, INV 9; 4, Druidtemple, INV 30; 5, Kinchyle of Dores, INV 37; 6, Carn Daley, INV 16.

Key: stones *in situ*, black; stones known to have been re-set (and in the case of INV 9 shown in the positions proposed in ¶ 8.25), hatched; fallen stones, white; hypothetical stones, dotted.

plan he was surely correct in suggesting that at least one of them had been misplaced when re-erected. The very large rectangular stone to the west of the entrance has been set upside down where its head lay, thus distorting the circle by about 2.8 m. It is likely that the stones on either side of it were reset, not in their original positions, but in relation to this stone. It is known that there was once an eleventh stone in the circle, and its position is marked by a small boulder on the north side. The original number of stones is more likely to have been eleven than twelve, depending on whether or not a stone is missing from the gap on the west side. This gap would be slightly reduced if the stones on either side stood as claimed above, but it would still be a little more than the space between any of the other stones. On the other hand a stone placed in the gap would produce a spacing considerably closer than elsewhere in the circle.

8.26) At first sight the circle at Corrimony (INV 17) (plate 16) is nearly as impressive as those at Balnuaran, but excavation in 1952 showed that out of eleven stones, only four are original and undisturbed. A fifth stone, found to be loose in a stone-hole, may have been reset in its original position. The four undisturbed stones are in the north quarter of the circuit, fairly evenly spaced with one of them on the axis, but they are not set on the arc of a circle. The adjacent fifth stone greatly exaggerates the irregularity of both the alignment and the spacing, and there may be doubts that it is *in situ*. However, the early accounts of the monument supply enough information to indicate that the present setting roughly reproduces the original design. At the time of the first record in about 1860 there were nine standing stones, which are shown on an accompanying sketch plan evenly spaced apart from a wide gap on one side. A plan made about twenty years later again shows these nine stones, but only six are standing, two have fallen, and one has been moved to inside the circle, and the gap has been filled by two additional 'stones' (figure 39). This plan shows the wider spacing of the stones behind the chamber and so seems to be reasonably accurate. Subsequently one of the stones then standing and the three prostrate stones were reset where they remain on the south side of the circle. The two 'stones' added after 1860 are spurious composite arrangements which

PLATE 16. Corrimony (INV 17) from the north-east.

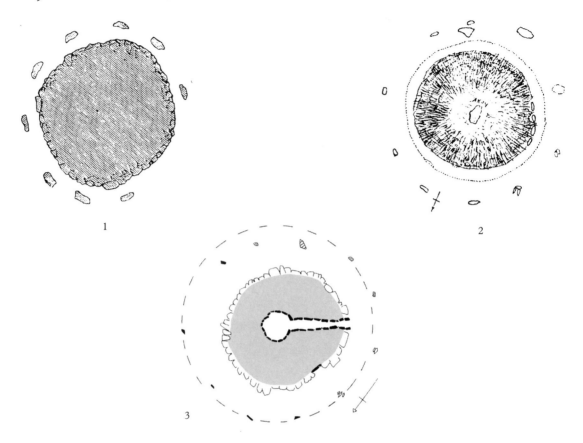

FIGURE 39. Plans of Corrimony, INV 17. 1, about 1860 (Mitchell); 2, about 1880 (Grant); 3, 1952 (Piggott, redrawn).

still exist, and perhaps were never intended to deceive. It can hardly be doubted that two stones once stood here on the west side of the entrance, bringing the original number in the circle to eleven. The excavator looked for, and failed to find, evidence for a twelfth stone in the wide gap on the north-east side (and if the fifth stone mentioned above is not *in situ* the gap may not have been as wide). There is no reason to doubt his conclusion, though unfortunately since the excavation a boulder has been placed in the gap. Investigation of this area revealed some cobbling which appeared to be an original feature (figure 37).

8.27) The circles at Kinchyle of Dores and Druidtemple (INV 37, 30) are similar to Carn Urnan (ROS 13) in size and appearance, and their surviving stones are placed on a regular circle, but they do not have a stone set on the axis at the rear, and they almost certainly consisted of an even number of stones. The Kinchyle of Dores circle probably had ten stones (figures 2, 1; 38, 5). Five stones remain upright, two more are prostrate, and two stones once stood in the wide gap on the south-east side; another stone (of which there is no record) is likely to have filled the gap behind the chamber. The stones seem to have been more widely spaced round the west than the east half of the circle. In the Druidtemple circle the spacing of the stones seems to have been closer than elsewhere, apart from an unusually wide gap in front of the entrance. Ten stones remain, of which five stand and five have fallen. There are two gaps (besides that at the entrance), which, if each had once contained a stone, would provide a regular spacing with a total of twelve stones (figures 5; 7; 38, 4).

8.28) The circle at Carn Daley (INV 16) is so damaged that any reconstruction must be tentative (figure 38, 6). There is the stump of a stone exactly on the axis, which implies that there was an uneven number of stones in the circle. A fallen stone lies to one side of the entrance, and the next stone is represented by a stump. It seems probable that three rather than two stones stood in the arc connecting the first two and the axial stones. It is clear that all three prostrate stones in this arc cannot be *in situ*. A design with three stones here would provide somewhat closer spacing of the stones round the back of the cairn (as at ROS 13 and INV 10), and would mean that all three prostrate stones belonged to the circle and that only the southern one is out of position. Assuming that there was approximate symmetry, this arrangement would give a circle of eleven stones with a wide space in front of the entrance (as at INV 30). The alternative, with two stones in the arc, would mean wide (but not exceptionally wide) spacing, that only one of the three prostrate stones is *in situ*, and that one of them did not belong to this side of the monument. The six surviving stones at Lagmore (BAN 1) are set accurately on a circle, and include some impressively tall stones even at the rear, but they are so unevenly spaced that the original number is uncertain.

8.29) Over the years the unitary design of Clava-type cairns, both passage-graves and ring-cairns, has been questioned, and this was one of the objectives of Bradley's excavations at Balnuaran (INV 8–10). He was able to demonstrate the structural unity of the ring-cairn, and the identical building methods and materials in all three cairns, but the structural unity of the North-east cairn fell short of absolute proof, though hardly to be doubted. Our new plans of four passage-graves show that they were laid out in a single operation, and there is no reason to think that it was otherwise at the other cairns, allowing that they were built in stages. At each monument it

may be assumed for practical reasons that the chamber and cairn were built before the circle was erected. The centres of the chamber, kerb and circle virtually coincide at Balnuaran South-west, Kinchyle of Dores, Carn Urnan and Lagmore (INV 10, 37, ROS 13, BAN 1). At other cairns the kerb is centered on the chamber, but either there is no circle of standing stones, as at Avielochan (INV 5), or the setting of standing stones is too incomplete or too irregular for comment, as at Dalcross Mains or Balnuaran North-east (INV 26, 9). The centre point of the kerb at Corrimony (INV 17) appears to have been at the side of the chamber, and no centre point can be identified for the standing stones. At Druidtemple (INV 30) the standing stones are in an accurate circle which is centered on the side of the chamber, and the same would have been so at Carn Daley (INV 16) if the setting of standing stones, now very incomplete, had been circular. In these two cases it may be suspected that the line of the proposed circle had been lost by the time it was to be built, and a convenient point on the top of the cairn was used as the new centre.

Cupmarks

8.30) Cupmarked stones have been used as building material in three of the passage-graves, the two Balnuaran cairns and Corrimony (INV 9, 10, 17), and the stones occur in all parts of the structure. Some of the cupmarks are easily seen on the smooth surfaces of sandstone slabs. For various reasons others are less easy to discern, and some are problematic due to weathering, unfavourable lighting conditions, their position hidden within the structure, or the type of surface (certainly some claimed in nineteenth-century publications to be present on conglomerate stones are most unlikely to be of human origin). There is one cupmarked stone in the kerb of each of the Balnuaran cairns; both stones are towards the back of the cairns, and not on the axis, and the lower parts of the designs are hidden by the bank. The boulder at INV 9 is entirely covered with cupmarks, one of which is ringed, and channels (plate 17); the slab at INV 10 bears a few cup-marks. In the passage of INV 9 and in the chamber wall beside the entrance of INV 10 there are similar handsome orthostats with a number of cupmarks, some ringed (plate 18). There are further cupmarked stones in the same chamber: two orthostats bear single cupmarks, on the face of one but below present ground level, and on the upper edge of the other, and three horizontal slabs used in the upper walling bear cupmarks on the upper surfaces, either singly or in a group, and virtually hidden. In the chamber of INV 9 one horizontal slab built into the wall has a cupmark. At Corrimony the

PLATE 17. Balnuaran of Clava North-east (INV 9), cup-and-ring marked kerb-stone.

PLATE 18. Balnuaran of Clava South-west (INV 10), cup-and-ring marked orthostat in the chamber.

PLATE 19. Corrimony (INV 17), cupmarked slab.

large block which was almost certainly the capstone bears over twenty cupmarks on its upper surface (plate 19). There are two or three cupmarks on the inner face of a standing stone on the west side of the circle at Balnuaran South-west, and three or four on the outer face of a monolith towards the rear of the stone circle at Corrimony. The cupmarks at these three cairns (INV 9, 10, 17) vary from elaborate and all-over decoration to single large cups, and to single or grouped small cups. The incorporation of cupmarked stones in the cairns, and their actual positioning, has been considered as highly significant by some writers (notably by Bradley 2000, 217).

9. The use and later history of the cairns of the Clava group

The deposits in the chambers

9.1) The interiors of the passage-graves, and also of the ring-cairns, have mostly been badly damaged, and consequently the results of modern investigations have been disappointing; the Corrimony passage-grave (INV 17) is the exception and is described below. Amongst the rest of the monuments, including ring-cairns, the evidence, as far as it goes, is consistent that there had been only one, or occasionally two, burials. When they were excavated in 1952 Druidtemple and Kinchyle of Dores (INV 30, 37) produced meagre amounts of cremated bone from their disturbed floors, in each case belonging to a single individual, and no artefacts. Nothing of significance was found at Avielochan (INV 5) during a rather casual investigation in 1909. It was particularly disappointing that the re-examination of the chambers at Balnuaran (INV 9, 10) in the mid 1990s showed that the original floors had been removed or greatly disturbed (Bradley 2000, 67). There had been much activity around and in these cairns in the late bronze age. It now seems that this was the date of the two flat-based pots (figure 34) and a considerable amount of cremated bone found in the South-west cairn in the late 1820s. In these unpropitious circumstances it is not surprising that there was no evidence at any of these five chambers that they or the passages had, or had not, been deliberately sealed.

9.2) In the well preserved chamber at Corrimony (INV 17), excavated in 1952, the lower part of its filling remained intact. The floor was sand, and in it thin layers of iron pan 'suggested that fresh sand had been strewn over the area at intervals, and consolidated by

trampling' (Piggott 1956, 183). The stain of a crouched inhumation, which had completely decayed, was detected in the sand in the centre of the chamber. This was the only burial; other stains around the edge of the chamber, though unexplained, were shown not to have derived from bones, and there was no burnt bone. The burial itself was covered by a layer of slabs, and the whole floor had been covered by a layer of waterworn stones. This layer of stones extended along the lintelled passage, and filled it for over half its height; the filling was considered to be deliberate. Midway down the passage, at one side, a rounded block 0.22 m high had been firmly set upright. The sole artefact, found at the mouth of the passage, was a badly decayed piece of bone, interpreted as a pin. Across the passage near its outer end there were the lower courses of rough walling, considered to be deliberate blocking. A gap in the bank surrounding the kerb had originally allowed unhindered access to the passage, but the gap was later filled in to complete the annular form of the bank. Excavation in front of the entrance of Balnuaran North-east (INV 9) produced no indication of a break in the material of the bank (which was, however, only 0.2 m thick), but the ground surface below was worn (which was attributed to building operations rather than subsequent usage) (Bradley 2000, 73). The question of chamber accessibility is perhaps still open. At Corrimony, in those parts of the cairn which were investigated, it was found that pieces of white quartz had been strewn deliberately during the construction of the monument. White quartz was also noted at Druidtemple (INV 30).

The destruction of the cairns

9.3) The South-west chamber at Balnuaran (INV 10), about a millennium after it was built, was re-used in the late bronze age, at a time of considerable activity in the area including the building of a round house (Clava South, see Appendix 3, 4). Presumably the chamber was still intact, and there had been little damage to any of the Balnuaran monuments. It is not until the eighteenth century that there are glimpses of the condition of the Clava-type cairns. As well as the Balnuaran and Corrimony passage-graves, at least some of the ring-cairns were still substantially complete. Towards the end of the century the situation changed. The 'druidical temples' (i.e. the cairns of Clava type and cognate monuments) to the east of Inverness were being attacked: 'they were blasted for the purpose of building farm houses and offices. Stones are scarce, and at a great distance, and the temples stood in cultivated and fertile fields' (OSA 1793, 631). Again, Anderson wrote of the same area 'ten or twelve stone circles and cairns may be counted, and many more are known to be destroyed' (1838, 449). More specifically, most of the passage-graves had been reduced to little more than concentric circles of upright or fallen stones before they were first recorded. The finding of part of a jet armlet above floor level in the passage at Avielochan (INV 5) might suggest that its passage was roofless by late prehistoric or early christian times; it is to be expected that the surviving passage-graves had suffered varying amounts of gradual degradation during the centuries. Kinchyle of Dores (INV 37) was in more or less its present condition by 1760, Druidtemple (INV 30) before 1824, and others (INV 16, 18, 26, 49) were recorded between 1869 and 1884. Since these dates there have been only minor changes to the monuments. Because there were no standing stones, Avielochan was not recognised until 1909 when the already reduced cairn was further robbed for ballast for the adjacent railway line.

9.4) The chambers of the three most complete cairns were opened for investigation, not destruction, and the monuments were respected by their landowners, even to re-erecting or replacing some of the surrounding standing stones (leading to subsequent confusion). The two Balnuaran chambers (INV 10, 9) were opened respectively in the late 1820s and some years later, and were evidently already without their capstones. By the 1920s there had been considerable deterioration of the cairns, and the monuments were taken into State Care. Exposure of the whole circuit of kerb-stones and consolidation of the main features was then undertaken. The other well preserved cairn, Corrimony (INV 17), was thought to be intact until excavated in 1952, when it was found to have been opened in the early part of the nineteenth century, at which time the roof may still have been complete. It is curious that the existence of the chamber does not seem to have been general knowledge when the monument was visited in about 1860. It was taken into State Care in 1954.

10. The passage-graves of northern Scotland: assessment and commentary

10.1) It has been inevitable that consideration of the passage-graves of northern Scotland has been dominated by the Orcadian cairns because of the quality and quantity of the monuments, the concentration of archaeological investigation there, and the presentation of the most remarkable of the cairns to the public. On a lesser scale there has been investigation and presentation of some fine cairns in Caithness. As has been constantly pointed out, the condition of the cairns in Orkney and Caithness is due to the quality and availability of the building stone, which has encouraged refinement of building techniques and exceptional stability for the structures. The four volumes (by Davidson, Henshall and Ritchie) which have now completed coverage of the northern mainland and Orkney have focused on the structure of the cairns. Since writing the first two volumes three important excavations have been published (Smith ed. 1994, 10–25; Barber 1997; Masters 1997), some smaller scale excavations have been reported, numerous papers of synthesis and speculation have appeared, and evidence has accumulated from our field work in the southern part of the region. With the completion of the project we are now in a position to take some steps towards a more balanced picture, and, particularly regarding the Orkney-Cromarty-type cairns, to offer insights into their design and original appearance.

10.2) In the northern mainland and Orkney there are certainly one hundred and eighty, and probably over two hundred, chambered cairns of Orkney-Cromarty type, to which can

be added at least twenty-eight in Argyll and the Western Isles. In contrast, twelve cairns cover chambers of Maes Howe type in Orkney, and eleven or possibly thirteen cairns cover chambers of Clava type in the most southerly part of the region. The three types of chamber are distinct and are considered separately, but their relationships are unclear and are still a matter for debate.

Cairn structure in the Orkney-Cromarty group

10.3) It is a general misconception that the northern passage-graves were covered by very large cairns and that the chambers were entered down long passages, but as far as the Orkney-Cromarty-type cairns are concerned this is not normally the case. It needs to be emphasised that the great majority of cairns covering Orkney-Cromarty-type chambers are round. On the mainland, on surface examination, 77% of the cairns are this shape, and 4% may be heel-shaped; 8% are short horned, and (predominately in Caithness) 11% are long, though it can hardly be doubted that many of the remaining twenty-nine long cairns cover or covered Orkney-Cromarty-type chambers. In Orkney the proportion of cairns of the round tradition is even more striking, 88% if ten rectangular close-fitting cairns (which are adaptations of the round format) are included; the one short horned cairn represents about 2% of the total and the long cairns about 10%.

10.4) Throughout the mainland well over half of the round cairns are of moderate size with diameters of 20 m or less (in most cases including slippage, so the diameter as built may be 2 or 3 m shorter), and there are rare examples as small as 10 m. In Orkney, where no round Orkney-Cromarty-type cairn exceeds 21 m in diameter, the small size of the round cairns is particularly notable. Because most of the cairns would have been at least 3 m high to enclose the chamber, the centre of the cairn must have consisted of a high stable structure, and it has become clear in recent years that the cairn core, long recognised to exist but not fully appreciated, is the essential element in the cairns.

10.5) It is now possible to recognise the basic design of Orkney-Cromarty-type cairns, as indicated in ¶ 5.4–6. The model consists of a chamber within a solid cairn core, which was enclosed and protected by a casing of generally looser cairn material to form a round cairn centered on the chamber and confined by a wall-face. The chamber and core were generally high, but the finished cairn was of modest or small diameter and the passage was short. It is apparent that the basic design of Orkney-Cromarty-type cairns was simple in concept, but needed considerable experience and skill to build.

10.6) It is of crucial importance to understand that the wall/roof of the chamber was dependant on the core, and that the two were built as a unit; the chamber and cairn core should be regarded as a single stable hollow structure, capable of standing unsupported, a concept that tends to be overlooked when the chamber wall (or more correctly, the wall-face) is visible and the outer wall-face of the core is hidden by the casing. A structure of this type need not be surprising; corbelled cells of the early christian period in the west, quite recent small huts in rural Italy and Iberia, and (on a larger scale) the prehistoric *nuraghi* of Sardinia, all demonstrate the practicality of unmortared stone buildings with false-corbelled vaults. In the case of the cairns, the core was constructed of densely-packed stones, and its outer wall-face was either vertical or complemented the vertical inward curve of the chamber walls. This curve was controlled by the precise amount that each layer of stones could oversail without collapse, and the height of the chamber was related to the span to be roofed, and was only affected by the size of the available capstone or lintels. The core was no thicker than was required for the stability of the chamber, and thus its size and plan were largely dictated by the chamber plan, and the core was as likely to be oval or rectangular as round. This method of construction applies to all Orkney-Cromarty-type chambers, whatever

their size, and whatever form of cairn eventually covered them.

10.7) The only detailed examination of a core structure was undertaken by Barber at Point of Cott in Orkney (ORK 41, a long cairn). The circumstances were unusual because of the remaining height of part of the core, and the opportunity to dismantle the whole monument, and further, this was a cairn where the builders' expertise in exploiting the slabby stone was most fully developed. The core was 2 m thick around a stalled chamber, which resulted in a rectangular core structure that had been at least 2.5 m high. The stability of the chamber wall-face was increased by the use of the horizontal arch principle; inward pressure served to jamb the stones together. Barber presented an illuminating analysis of the sophisticated design and technical expertise exhibited by this core structure, and demonstrated his conclusions by a partial reconstruction (Barber 1992, 16–23, figures 2.6, 2.7, 2.8; 1997, 9–13, 60–1). Doubtless most other Orcadian cairns, and also many in Caithness, were built with a similar refinement of technique, and with the character of the chamber walls constant from floor to roof (see, for instance, Camster Round, CAT 13, Davidson and Henshall 1991, figure 8, plate 7).

10.8) On most of the mainland including parts of Caithness, where the main building material is boulders and cobbles, the chamber walls and core cairns are more coarsely built and the construction differs slightly, but the principles are the same. The lower part of the chamber walls are partly or largely orthostatic with linking panels of fine walling, but the character of the oversailing upper part changes where large corbel stones form the vaulted roof. The lower part of the cairn core supported the wall and the lowest corbel stones, and above this it acted as a counterweight to the oversailing upper corbel stones. As in Orkney, the strength of a structure of slabs laid in a horizontal curve was well understood, and it was increased by laying the corbel stones with an outward and downward tilt (any settlement or pressure on their inner ends would tend to lock them together); tilting the stones also helped to keep the chamber dry. A fine example of a ring of corbel stones in a round vault was photographed by Corcoran at The Ord North (SUT 48, see Henshall and Ritchie 1995, plate 4), and horizontal arches must have been used for elongated vaults (the weakness of the roof at ROS 11, described in ¶ 4.21, is due to ignoring this principle).

10.9) Over the years cairn cores have been seen or glimpsed at many cairns, and have been variously described and often misunderstood. It is important to identify them for the clarification of other features within the cairns. Excavation at many Orcadian cairns, both round and rectangular, has consistently revealed that they are bounded by double wall-faces, the inner belonging to the core, the outer to the casing, here generally modified into a narrow band of masonry (in our 1989 volume the cores were referred to as 'cairns', and the casings as 'outer skins'). These cairns are familiar uncomplicated structures.

10.10) In Caithness excavation has been focused on exceptional monuments, to be discussed later, but in the multi-period cairns at Tulach an t-Sionnaich and Camster Long (CAT 58, 12) Corcoran exposed the lower parts of the cairn cores of small round primary cairns (figure 41, 1, 2). At the latter the two chambers may not have received casings (or they may have been removed, or may partly survive behind one chamber; the cores are referred to as round cairns in the publication, Masters 1997, 137, 139–40, 178–80, illustration 8), and at the former only a small part of the casing was exposed. Evidence regarding the structure of four round cairns CAT 31, 39, 62, 63) was found by Anderson excavating in the 1860s, but it is clear that his method of exposing only short stretches of wall-face led to misinterpretation of the diameters of both the cores and the cairns (e.g. at CAT 63, figure 40, 1). Short stretches of a wall-face were seen during conservation work behind the chamber at Camster Round (CAT 13), and also above the inner end of the passage, which is a reminder that the cairn cores passed over

the passages and that above this level the cores were uninterrupted. As is to be expected, the core diameter seems to be about 6 m, though probably somewhat more at ground level, and it reaches to a height of 3.5 m. Elsewhere the presence of core wall-faces may be indicated in passage walls by vertical joints, or by the rare presence of transversely-set orthostats. Further south, due to the nature of the cairn material and lack of excavation, only at the greatly destroyed Embo cairn (SUT 63) has part of a cairn core been observed, consisting of four layers of closely packed horizontal blocks.

10.11) It is the outer casing, centered on the highest part of the chamber roof and confined by a wall-face, that gives the cairns their round plan. In Ross-shire and Sutherland no outer wall-faces are visible, but at many of these cairns their size and shape are perfectly clear. It has been shown (in ¶ 5.6, 22–3, figure 24, 1) that in some Ross-shire cairns the entrance to the passage is recessed, giving the cairn a flat or slightly concave front, and it is suggested that the passage was not extended through the casing, but that the casing was narrowed at the front of the cairn to line up with the existing entrance through the core. If so, the length of the passage equates with the thickness of the core, and implies that the inward-sloping wall-face of the core was visible rising above the outermost passage lintel. The plan of the excavated primary cairn at Tulach an t-Sionnaich (CAT 58) seems to show just such a merging of core and casing, though without flattening the front of the cairn. At other cairns, and perhaps more commonly, as seen at most excavated Caithness and Orcadian cairns, the passages were lengthened (indicated by breaks in the walls) and the casing enclosed the whole core. It seems likely that cairns with recessed entrances gave rise to heel-shaped cairns.

10.12) When the unexcavated round cairns are surveyed it is evident that a considerable number, besides those of Ross-shire (¶ 5.5), are likely to be of the simple form that has been described, characterised by their relatively small size, the central position of the chamber,

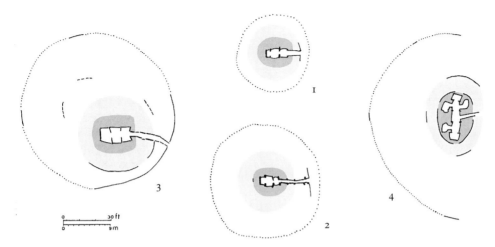

FIGURE 40. Simplified plans of excavated cairns of Orkney-Cromarty type illustrating their probable structure. 1, Warehouse North, CAT 63; 2, Camster Round, CAT 13; 3, Tulloch of Assery B, CAT 70; 4, Isbister, ORK 25 (based on Hedges 1983, frontispiece, and Smith 1989, illus. 1).
Key: dark stipple, cairn core; light stipple, cairn casing; dotted edge, the final extent of the cairn.

the shortness of the passage, and at a few by a tendency for the front edge to be flattened, and some cairns may indeed be heel-shaped. In Sutherland SUT 8, 36, and 70 may serve as examples, and at Strathseasgaich (SUT 73) there is a remarkably small cairn surrounding a large chamber. In Caithness CAT 23, 31 and 63 are examples, and at Houstry (CAT 29) the built concave front has been revealed by unofficial investigation, and is reflected in the outer edge of the cairn. In Orkney three excavated round cairns (ORK 2, 26, 27) have flat front edges, seemingly maintaining a trait which had a practical origin. (It will be found that a quick and often revealing check of the relationship of cairn edge, chamber and entrance can be made by overlaying the published plans with a series of concentric circles drawn on transparent film.)

10.13) It is clear that a minority of round cairns, and some that are approaching a heel shape, do not conform to the basic design. The criteria are their overall size, a considerable distance between the entrance and the edge of the cairn, and/or the excentric position of a chamber, and there may be more subtle

indications. Hidden within these cairns there may be smaller cairns of basic type, and the evidence that some Ross-shire cairns may have received secondary enlargements has been discussed in ¶ 5.7–10. Some cairns, such as ROS 12, 25, SUT 5, 6, 45, 54, CAT 1, and ORK 4, appear from superficial examination to have been enlarged simply, and sometimes extensively, though not to cover additional structures.

10.14) More information is available from four partly excavated cairns. Reasons were given in our 1995 publication for supposing that the outer end of the passage and the kerb at The Ord North (SUT 48) were additions to the primary cairn (p. 21, 38, though figure 15 could perhaps be ammended to suggest that the primary cairn was closer in plan to the later kerb with its flattened front). Camster Round (CAT 13) was seen as a simple round cairn until the straight façade was exposed in 1966. In 1991 we suggested that the outer part of the passage and the façade were additions (p. 54, figure 8). A more radical suggestion can now be made, that the primary cairn around the small chamber was of normal proportions, with a core about 6 m in diameter (¶ 10.10), and a casing about 13 m in diameter with a flattened front, the passage being 3 m long entered between the second pair of transverse slabs in the passage walls at the point of a slight kink in their alignment; if so, the addition to the front was probably part of an enlargement carried round the whole cairn (figure 40, 2). The surface appearance of SUT 26, 60, CAT 3 and 17, with the widening of the cairns across the front, perhaps indicates a somewhat similar development.

10.15) Other cairns are likely to incorporate structures apart from the recognised chamber. The immense cairn, Tulloch of Assery B (CAT 70), when partly excavated in 1961, produced a large chamber and passage occupying only the SE quadrant. The cairn core around them was not observed but it is to be expected that it was almost rectangular measuring about 10 by 8 m, and included the innermost part of the passage which is aligned on the chamber axis. To the south of the chamber a wall-face was exposed which formed one third of a circle with a diameter of 15 m centered on the centre of the chamber. It can hardly be doubted that this wall-face with its marked inward batter edged the casing around the core (in previous publications the casing has been referred to as the core), and that three other stretches of walling seen at a high level in cuttings were not (as assumed by the excavator) part of the cairn belonging to the chamber (figure 40, 3). It is easier to envisage the chamber and its cairn as the primary structure with its north edge a little north of the centre of the final cairn and with other structures built beside it, rather than vice versa. The unusual and unexplained feature of this putative primary cairn is the middle section of the long passage with its poorly built orthostatic walls aligned a little south of the chamber axis. The outer part of the passage, aligned further to the south, was presumably designed to be radial to the final kerb, rather than intentionally aligned on the centre of the final cairn as the excavator suggested. The entry through the outermost kerb, together with its masonry blocking, indicates that the final cairn was completed

within the neolithic period, and not for later single-grave burials. In the unexcavated cairns ROS 36, 42, SUT 29 and 45, the chambers may well share them with other structures.

10.16) The remains of another huge cairn have been partly excavated over the years at Isbister (ORK 25). Since our description (based on Hedges' report of 1983 and our observations, Davidson and Henshall 1989, 125), further investigations were made when the chamber was given a modern cover (Smith 1989). The cairn is D-shaped due to erosion, but it is assumed to have been round with a diameter of 31 m. Within it is a long chamber of an unusual design with side cells. Our proposed interpretation of the construction varies in some particulars from those of other writers (figure 40, 4). The casing was evidently oval, about 15 by 11 m, its wall-face and body solidly built of slabs and still 3 m high in one part. The core, its wall-face eventually traced round the whole circuit, was about 3 m thick from the chamber walls, but less than 1 m thick behind the cells and the ends of the chamber. There were also subsidiary wall-faces within both the core and the casing. The primary cairn was later enclosed, slightly off-centre, by a rubble mound edged by a wall (see further ¶ 10.51). Other features outside the cairn, which have been interpreted as the façade of a huge forecourt, have complicated the interpretation of the monument and are partly of natural origin and partly unexplained.

10.17) Throughout the province there are rare instances of round cairns covering two chambers. Huntersquoy and Taversoe Tuick (ORK 23, 49) are well known, and remarkable in that each contains two chambers one above the other entered from opposite directions on sloping sites, and they were certainly of unitary construction. In Caithness there are chambers back-to-back at Langwell (CAT 34) and side-by-side at Sithean Dubh (CAT 48). In each the paired chambers appear to be identical or nearly so, about 2 to 3 m apart, and physically so precisely related that it is hard to believe that each pair of chambers was not designed and built together. The short horned cairn, Tulloch of Assery A (CAT 69), when excavated, did not provide certain proof that the back-to-back chambers were contemporary in a single core, but the contrary argument is unconvincing (Corcoran 1972, 34). The question arises whether in other cairns the chambers may be sequential. Two round Ross-shire cairns, Heights of Brae and Tarradale (ROS 22, 61), contain chambers close together on parallel axes, but in each cairn the chamber designs differ (¶ 4.51, 5.7). It seems probable that one chamber is a replacement of the other (especially when the position of the passage entrance of the smaller chamber at ROS 22 is considered), but if so there was the difficulty of constructing the core of the later chamber even if the earlier chamber were partly dismantled, as has been tentatively suggested to explain the enigmatic remains at Balnacrae (ROS 4, ¶ 4. 48–51). The two dissimilar chambers at Embo (SUT 63), back-to-back with their axes slightly staggered, also seem unlikely to be contemporary, and at Calf of Eday Long (ORK 8) there is no doubt that the larger chamber succeeded the smaller. (In retrospect it seems unlikely that ORK 1, once thought to contain a second chamber, is other than a stalled chamber with a secondary structure built into the end of its rectangular cairn.) Unusually large cairns were not required, nevertheless CAT 48 (and its neighbour CAT 49 which almost certainly also covers two side-by-side chambers), ROS 22, 61 and 4 are very large cairns, and it is clear that the passage entrances were no longer accessible when the cairns took their final form.

10.18) The original appearance of the round cairns can now be considered. The exterior of the unenlarged cairns was edged by the wall-face of the casing, the height of which at the entrance had to be sufficient to retain the casing and/or the core rising to chamber roof level. The minimum height depended on the length of the passage and the height of the outer part of the chamber, and it is likely to have been between 1.5 and 2 m; probably the wall maintained the same height round the whole circuit. The quality of the masonry is impressive where it has been seen in those areas with ideal building material, sometimes built on a plinth, and occasionally treated decoratively (as at ORK 3 and 37, and modestly at CAT 26 and 69). Within the enlarged cairn at Isbister (ORK 25) part of the casing wall-face was preserved for its full height of nearly 3 m, standing vertical with the top curving inwards; presumably the casing either merged with or covered the top of the core and chamber roof. However, this cairn is atypical in several respects, and the external wall-face of at least some cairns, if not most, would certainly have been lower, particularly so where the building stone was less stable. Some outer wall-faces are likely to have been built with an inward batter, as at Tulloch of Assery B (CAT 70). Thus the cairns would have appeared as solid masonry drums, 2 to 3 m high, visually unbroken for the entrance which would normally have been filled with masonry, and with a gently domed top of casing material rising perhaps another metre or more. It may be speculated that the core structure sometimes protruded above the steeply rising upper surface of the casing, especially in areas lacking good building stone and when the cairn diameter was small in relation to the size of the chamber. The rectangular Orcadian cairns were an exceptional development, with the casing only a metre thick, and it has always been assumed that it formed a platform with the core rising behind it.

10.19) The rounded profile, generally thought of as normal for chambered cairns, was only acquired when the cairns were subsequently enlarged, or when they were in decay. In most cases the outer wall-face is likely to have partly collapsed quite soon, and the material outside it is probably simply displaced stone. Certainly at Camster Long (CAT 12) Masters' careful study of the extra-revetment material showed that it had all fallen from the upper part of the wall-face (1997, 142–5), and similarly at Point of Cott (ORK 41) there was no evidence that any material had been deliberately placed outside the wall-face to conceal it, as has sometimes been suggested was done at chambered cairns elsewhere (the evidence from Tulloch of Assery A, CAT 69, also carefully observed, was ambiguous).

10.20) If the heel-shaped plan developed from round cairns with flattened entrances it is to be expected that a heel-shaped plan may sometimes have been used for primary cairns. However, the relationship of heel-shaped cairns to cairns with other plans has only been demonstrated at Tulach an t-Sionnaich (CAT 58) where the heel-shaped cairn was an addition to a small round cairn, and was itself later incorporated into a long cairn (figure 41, 1). Here the heel-shaped façade was a solidly built platform sealing the entrance, but down the sides it merged with a substantial cairn which appears to be an enlargement of the primary cairn. Other heel-shaped cairns are evidently additions to round cairns, and at some their façade may seal the passage entrance, but at others, such as SUT 37 and 75, the passage continued to be accessible. Heel-shaped forecourts can be detected at some very large and presumably complex multi-period cairns, including long cairns, but their place in the building sequence is not known. Heel-shaped cairns are a small minority on the mainland (though there is difficulty in identifying them from surface inspection), they are unknown in Orkney, but, strangely, they are the commonest cairn plan in Shetland. The Shetland cairns are small versions of the mainland cairns, with both accessible and sealed entrances, and at Vementry (ZET 45) it can be clearly seen that a round cairn is surrounded and sealed by a secondary heel-shaped platform.

10.21) Short horned cairns are a rare and distinctive form, and, with one exception, they cover normal chambers. The casing of the cairns was edged by a double wall-face, with the entrance in the centre of the wider forecourt. In view of what has been said about simple round cairns, it may seem surprising that the evidence from two excavations leaves little doubt that short horned cairns are of unitary design. At Ormiegill (CAT 42), where the wall-face of the core and the double wall-face

of the casing are still partly visible, there is no room for a hypothetical earlier round casing. Any suggestion that it may have been demolished to build the more elaborate cairn can be countered by the probability that an earlier structure would merely have been enclosed. The excavation of Tulloch of Assery A (CAT 69) revealed two similar chambers back-to-back 4 m apart, and it was clear that the core structure of one of the chambers (and probably the core had included both) was integral with the horned casing. In short horned cairns the casing must have reduced in height along the horns, and it seems likely, as Corcoran suggested regarding CAT 69, that the main part of the casing resembled a high platform above which rose the dome-like core structure.

10.22) An extreme, and presumably late, version of this design can be seen at Boath Short (ROS 11, ¶ 5.12). The very impressive cairn, which is almost certainly an enlargement of an earlier cairn, rises above a very extensive platform. The plan of the platform is nearly square with stubby horns, it is clearly an addition to the cairn, and there is no question of there having been access to the passage from its forecourt. The wide low platform surrounding The Ord North (SUT 48) may have been a similar feature, though retaining the circular plan of the cairn. The excavator of the small square cairn at Balvraid (INV 51) considered that it too was an addition to a round cairn, and had probably been in the form of a platform, but in this case designed to allow continued access to the chamber (figures 25, 2; 30).

10.23) One important point about the long cairns has to be emphasised: they are frequently much less damaged than has been supposed. The long profile of some well preserved cairns is smooth, the height diminishing gently towards the distal end, and in the past there was a general assumption that this was once so at all long cairns. Variation in the height of parts of the cairn tended to be explained by severe robbing or other damage. Each cairn has to be high enough to contain the chamber within, generally at the proximal end, but the rest of the cairn may be considerably lower, and sometimes very low indeed. This contrast produces the familiar 'head-and-tail' profile, but where there is more than one chamber (or maybe some other large feature) the profile may seem disconcertingly irregular. Excavation has shown that the double-humped profile of Camster Long (CAT 12) is due to two chambers some distance apart, and that the transverse hollow behind the 'head' at Tulach an t-Sionnaich (CAT 58) indicates the junction of two components of the cairn. Further, the method of building some long cairns with seemingly random large vertical slabs, or with the 'empty box' device (see ¶ 10.25), gives, on partial collapse, an appearance of severe robbing. Also, cairns that have been almost entirely removed may retain their outline plan as a regular slight ridge of consolidated stone and turf or heather, and the plan may provide

subtle indications of the former components of the cairn.

10.24) Two modern excavations of long cairns (CAT 12, 58) have revealed their multi-period history, in both cases of three periods, but of different components and arranged differently within the long cairn which was the last addition (figure 41, 1–2). The evidence of multi-period construction at many other long cairns, the presence of a chamber which may or may not be on the axis (and occasionally one or even two more chambers), the variations in their external appearance including the presence or absence of horned forecourts, and entrances both accessible and sealed, has been reviewed in all four of our volumes. It is a reasonable assumption that chambers in small round cairns were the primary structures. Some of the long cairns are very large monuments, and some include immense mounds, and as we have stressed, these cairns are clearly complex

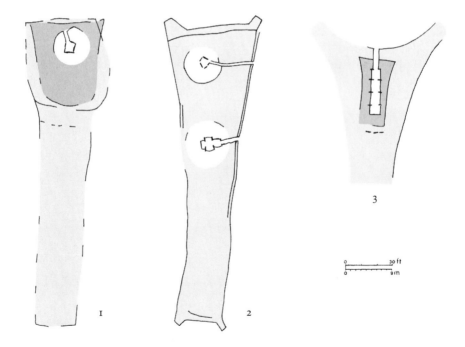

FIGURE 41. Simplified plans of excavated long cairns, 1, Tulach an t-Sionnaich, CAT 58 (primary cairn, white, heel-shaped cairn, dark stipple, long cairn, pale stipple); 2, Camster Long, CAT 12 (based on Masters 1997, illus. 4) primary cairns white; long cairn, pale stipple); 3, Point of Cott, ORK 41 (based on Barber 1997, figure 3) (cairn core, dark stipple).

structures which cannot be dissected, let alone understood, from the present data. Yet, though the diversity is bewildering, and seems individually idiosyncratic, an involved and inscrutable logic must lie behind the near identity of the pairs of large complex cairns at South Yarrows and Coille na Borgie (CAT 54, 55, SUT 22, 23) (figure 42; see Henshall and Ritchie 1995, 47). We can do no more than point out the problems in studying the long cairns, tentatively identify some of the components, and sometimes suggest a structural sequence.

10.25) On the other hand the horned chambered cairn at Point of Cott (ORK 41) has now been shown by Barber's excavation to be of unitary design though built in three phases (1997, 9–18, 60–5). A rectangular core containing a stalled chamber, built to the most sophisticated standard of Orcadian chambered cairns, had a rectangular structure added at the rear, and both were enclosed within a horned long cairn with a number of internal wall-faces along the sides. The rear end and much of one side of the cairn has been lost to erosion, but, on the assumption that its design was symmetrical, the long cairn was the same width as several in Caithness (figure 41, 3). The body of the long cairn behind the core had been a remarkable but ramshackle labour-saving structure comprising three rows of irregular empty roofed boxes made of a mixture of slabs and walling, in two layers, and together about 2 m high and 5 m wide. This structure had not butted against the back of the core, and the short gap between them had been filled in later. Both the method of construction and the gap between the two parts are reminiscent of the arrangements at Tulach an t-Sionnaich (CAT 58), arrangements which can be detected at some other mainland long

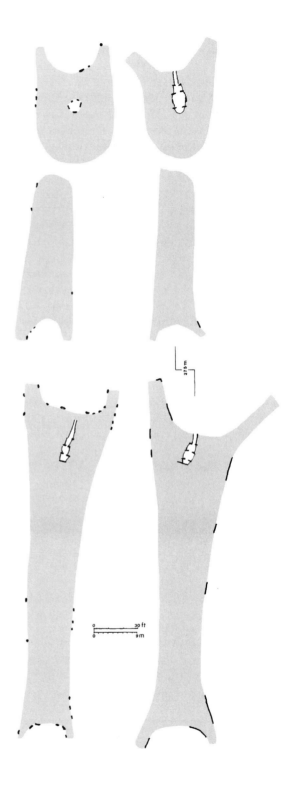

FIGURE 42. (opposite) The Coille na Borgie and South Yarrows cairns (SUT 22, 23, CAT 54, 55), from plans made in 1994 and 1985 and supplemented from Anderson 1886, 238. The Coille na Borgie cairns are shown in their correct relationship, the South Yarrows cairns are parallel 275 m apart.

cairns. At Point of Cott the long horned cairn encloses both the core and the rectangular box structure, and the passage entrance is in the centre of the crescentic façade. In long profile the cairn must have been nearly 3 m high over the chamber, and 2 m high for the rest of its length (a fragment of walling on top of the cairn led the excavator to suggest that it had been higher still). It may be suspected that Point of Cott is unique (as are many long cairns), in that it combines the components of such multi-period cairns as Tulach an t-Sionnaich into an architectural whole.

10.26) The building of a single-period long cairn with a horned forecourt is less surprising when the similarity of the forecourt plans of the unitary short horned cairns is recalled. The wall-faces of all these façades are double (though not necessarily all along the sides of long cairns) indicating that there was a step-like wall in front of the main wall-face. The façades with central entrances must have been very impressive, 2.5 m or more high and diminishing along the wide sweep of the horns. A shallow forecourt with a blind façade, originally 2.5 m high, has been excavated at Camster Long (CAT 12) (Masters 1997); it was fronted by a narrow platform which also formed the stubby horns. Deep horned fore-courts seem to be a speciality of Caithness and north Sutherland, in contrast with the absence of horned forecourts in Ross-shire and Inverness-shire where the façades are straight or slightly concave.

10.27) The cairns in the western part of the Orkney-Cromarty province (described in Henshall 1972, 124–43) differ in some respects from those in the rest of the province, though Loch Gleann na Feannag (UST 23), with its large chamber, small cairn and very short passage, epitomises the simple round cairn. The frequent use of spaced orthostats in the final wall-face of cairns is a distinctive feature in the west. The majority of cairns are large and round, generally with a short passage and recessed entrance. At least five large cairns, of which Rudh'an Dunain on Skye (SKY 7) is the smallest and best known, have unusual deeply recessed V-shaped forecourts, and the ortho-stats edging the whole cairn including the forecourt give these monuments a unitary appearance. Whether this is so awaits investi-gation. The western version of the short horned cairn is square, sometimes with stubby horns; Carn Liath Balgown and Unival (SKY 3, UST 34) provide close parallels for ROS 11 and INV 51. There are several long cairns with axial chambers, and at least one has a 'head-and-tail' profile (UST 7). Carinish long cairn (UST 10), with its horns and sides defined by orthostats, is significant because of its similarity to the only mainland long cairns treated in this way, Coille na Borgie North and South (SUT 22, 23) on the north coast of Sutherland.

10.28) The link between Carinish and the Coille na Borgie cairns (UST 10, SUT 22, 23) suggests the possibility that other uncommon features at cairns on the mainland and Orkney (besides the square cairns already mentioned) may be attributable to ideas coming from the Western Isles. In the south of the province the occasional inclusion of orthostats in façades, though not round the rest of the cairns (except at the puzzling ROS 30), presumably derived from the western cairns. The close connection already noted between the Coille na Borgie and South Yarrows paired cairns (CAT 54, 55) suggests that the stimulus to the development of wide horned forecourts in the north of the province may also have come from the west. Among the Hebridean cairns the interest in their external appearance, expressed in the use of orthostats and the elaboration of forecourts, may have had its distant origin in the Clyde cairns of south-west Scotland. Among the latter cairns the use of orthostats in wall-faces and façades is a common feature, as are impressive and sometimes deep forecourts. The Hebrides and north Argyll are the areas of interface between the cairns of Orkney-Cromarty and Clyde types, though admittedly the few Clyde cairns as far north as the Hebrides and west Sutherland (SUT 9) do not display external elaboration; these northern Clyde cairns may be seen as providing links rather than making a direct contribution to the external design of some of the Orkney-Cromarty-type cairns. The existence of links across northern Scotland is demonstrated by the similarities in pottery styles in Orkney and the Outer Hebrides, including sherds from the site beside the long cairn at Carinish (Armit in Crone 1993, 370–5, Armit 1996, 57–9).

10.29) In summary, it has been suggested that in the earliest phase of tomb-building a very large number of relatively small chambered cairns were built, austerely walled outside and with the entrance virtually disguised by the masonry inserted to seal it. External elaboration with forecourts, either with straight façades or deeply concave façades between horns, focused attention on the entrance, and this seems to indicate a shift in emphasis from activity concentrated inside the tomb to additional ceremonial developing outside the cairn. The provision of a forecourt may be part of the primary design, but often seems to have entailed enlargement of an existing cairn. Interest in the external appearance of cairns may have stimulated further enhancement, a stepped surround (double wall-faces are found almost exclusively on horned cairns now that it is realised that inner wall-faces at simple cairns are the facing of cores), the incorporation of orthostats, and decorative walling. Cairns were evidently enlarged for various reasons, sometimes for the addition of another chamber, sometimes by the addition of a long cairn (originating in a quite different monumental tradition), and often for reasons that are at present unknown, and which sometimes may be post-neolithic in date.

Chamber design in cairns of the Orkney-Cromarty group

10.30) When the architecture of the chambers covered in our four volumes is considered, the essential unity of the group is clear, based as it is on the same building techniques, and on the underlying design of a space entered between portal stones and divided by one or more pairs of transverse slabs. It is certain that there was a general development from small and simple to large and sophisticated chambers, but there is little hard evidence for detailed analysis if we are cautious about the status of their contents and uncertain about the helpfulness of the few relevant radiocarbon dates. The core-and-casing building method and its refinements were ingenious economic solutions to the problem of constructing a permanent chamber, and could not have evolved without experiment and experience with less ambitious structures. Thus small single-compartment chambers are likely to be early and significant. The identification of such chambers is difficult, but the few certain examples (CAT 12, 58, SUT 63, 74, ROS 25, INV 51) do seem to be widespread. Possibly other examples have been incorporated into larger chambers, such as ORK 21, ROS 24 and 47.

10.31) Chambers are mainly known to us by their two-dimensional plans, and it is important to envisage them in three dimensions. Their designs evidently developed in response to the local building stone, giving rise to a southern style and a northern style, and we should no longer think in terms of development from south to north. In the former style the emphasis is on round or polygonal compartments with an extensive use of orthostats in the walls, and roofing by round or oval vaults. The northern style is characterised by rectangular chambers with the side walls built entirely of masonry and subdivided into compartments, and by roofing with barrel vaults. A bipartite plan is normal among the southern style chambers; it is the almost exclusive form in Ross-shire, quite common in Sutherland, but a minority form in Caithness. The outer compartment may resemble an extension of the passage (and at such a chamber as Embo, SUT 63, figure 43, 1, it may indeed be the passage through the cairn core rather than an ante-chamber), or it may vary in relative size to be the equal of the inner compartment (figure 43, 2). In all these chambers the two compartments are separate entities connected through a portal formed by a pair of transverse stones bearing a low lintel. The chambers vary greatly in size with overall lengths between 2.6

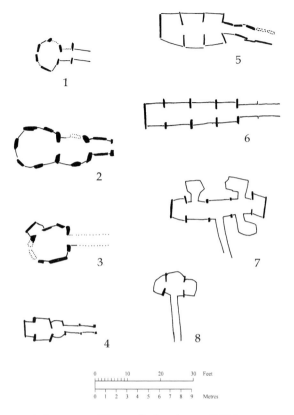

FIGURE 43. Plans of chambers of Orkney-Cromarty type. 1, Embo, SUT 63; 2 Skelpick Long, SUT 53; 3 Kyleoag, SUT 37; 4, Camster Round, CAT 13; 5, Tulloch of Assery B, CAT 70; 6, Point of Cott, ORK 41; 7, Isbister, ORK 25; 8 Huntersquoy, ORK 23.

and 6.7 m, and the largest vaulted spaces measure 3.5 by 3.25 m or 4.2 by 2.5 m and may use corbel stones weighing up to a ton. In Ross-shire some chambers with rectangular plans are clearly local variants, and presumably the rare large rectangular undivided chambers are an even more localised (and late) development (¶ 4.32–6, 42–3).

10.32) Cells, either pre-existing structures or integral with the chambers, are known occasionally among southern-style chambers (at ROS 24, 47, SUT 37, 43, CAT 31), opening off the side or a rear corner (figure 43, 3). Architecturally, cells become significant when they are placed axially and are approached through a low portal to produce a tripartite plan, which in turn led to further developments. There are four certain examples of Yarrows-type chambers with small low-roofed axial cells behind vaulted main chambers (CAT 23, 55, SUT 25, 33), but three Camster-type chambers have identical ground plans with the vault rising from the rear of the chamber, thus incorporating the cell area and leaving the portal stones as an internal division (CAT 12, 13, 64) (figure 43, 4). All seven chambers are small and in the southern style with (where known) low lintelled ante-chambers; indeed the intact chamber at Camster Round (CAT 13), which greatly impresses visitors, is in floor area one of the very smallest Orkney-Cromarty-type chambers. The importance of cells to their builders, whatever was their original usage, is also evident in Orkney, where two stalled chambers (ORK 21, 51) possess a cell, either axial or lateral, and the unique chamber at Isbister (ORK 25) has three lateral cells (figure 43, 7). This last chamber seems to be firmly rooted in the Orkney-Cromarty tradition with its divisional stones (even if hardly projecting into the floor area), and the shelved end compartments treated in the same way as at some other Orcadian chambers, yet the number of cells and other features seem to link it also with the Maes Howe-type chambers (see ¶ 10.51).

10.33) Caithness is the region where southern and northern style chambers are found together. There are a few more small unclassified tripartite chambers of Yarrows/Camster type, and two in the south of Orkney (ORK 67, 70). Tripartite chambers in the northern style account for less than half the Caithness chambers, but are quite common in Orkney. These chambers, the Assery type, are distinguished by division into compartments of roughly equal length and a continuous roof (figure 43, 5). Tripartite chambers of this form may be quite small (3.4 m long at ORK 47), two impressive chambers have been excavated (CAT 70, ORK 28, both about 5.4 by 2.7 m), and the largest of all appear to be nearly 8 m long (CAT 17, ORK 76) and so just overtake the largest of the southern style chambers. Once the restriction imposed by a circular vault had been broken the way was open to building stalled chambers with four compartments: two and probably two more are known in north-west Caithness, and there are more in Orkney (figure 43, 6). The possibilities of lengthening chambers were pushed to extremes in Orkney, but those with five or more compartments comprise only about 20 per cent of the total number of chambers. They are, however, very well known, the most extraordinary of all being nearly 27 m long with twelve or even fourteen compartments (ORK 31, 30). It is likely that some of the most extravagant chambers are the result of enlargements; there is some evidence that Midhowe (ORK 37) started as a five-compartment chamber and was twice extended (Davidson and Henshall 1989, 25).

10.34) The few tiny chambers of Bookan type are peculiar to Orkney, and with their clustered compartments, low slab roofs, and (with one exception) semi-subterranean construction, provide a striking contrast to all other chambers (figure 43, 8). The compartments are generally equipped with benches or shelves, thus replicating the arrangements in the terminal compartments of some Orcadian stalled chambers. At Huntersquoy (ORK 23) it had been felt desirable to provide simultaneously both a tripartite and a Bookan-type chamber. The purpose of these specialised end compartments and the Bookan-type chambers may perhaps have been for a ritual requirement that also gave rise to the cells mentioned above (¶ 10.32).

10.35) In the west of the province the chambers are built of boulders and slabs, understandably in that rocky landscape. They are simple in design, of a single round or oval compartment (with two exceptions), and vary from small to astonishingly large; the greatest spans are about 5 by 3.5 m or even 6 by 3.8 m at SKY 10 and UST 23, very considerably greater than the span of any compartment on the mainland. At the excavated cairn, Achnacreebeag (ARG 37, Ritchie 1970), the earliest structure, behind a chamber of average size,

was a tiny closed chamber, a sequence probably repeated at ARG 39, and perhaps to be compared with similar circumstances seen in Ross-shire (¶ 5.9). One puzzling anomalous cairn in Lewis has to be noted: within the stone circle at Calanais, and secondary to it, there is a very small bipartite chamber (LWS 3; Ashmore 1996, 73). It remains a puzzle, seemingly out of place both chronologically and architecturally.

10.36) This brief survey of the cairns and chambers is intended to indicate the likely development of their designs, but not to suggest a detailed chronology other than that on balance and within their own areas small chambers are likely to be earlier than large chambers. Differences in both the available building materials and the labour resources, and probably in some cases isolation, will have affected what was built. However, a few clues can take us a little further. In Orkney, a Bookan-type chamber is contemporary with a tripartite chamber at ORK 23, and is earlier than a stalled chamber at ORK 8; Bookan-type chambers cannot be regarded as 'degenerate' or late. At Camster Long (CAT 12) the small single-compartment chamber is probably earlier than the tripartite chamber, and the latter is so similar to the nearby chamber under a round cairn (CAT 13) that these two chambers must be virtually contemporary though treated differently in their later history (figures 41, 2; 40, 2). It can hardly be doubted that on The Ord the small ruined chamber was replaced by the nearby large almost intact chamber (SUT 49, 48); nor that the chambers in the three cairns at Loch Calder in Caithness, only 200 and 30 m apart, were built in sequence, one to replace the other: a small single-compartment chamber (CAT 58) followed by two bipartite southern-style chambers (CAT 69) followed by an Assery-type northern-style chamber (CAT 70). This tiny area at one end of the loch saw an extraordinary amount of building activity which spanned nearly the full gamut of cairn and chamber plans: probably four phases at Tulach an t-Sionnaich, a complex unitary cairn at Tulloch of Assery A, and a large chamber with extensive neolithic secondary structures at Tulloch of Assery B.

10.37) Long cairns appear to provide a chronological horizon, even if, in view of their variety, it is in soft focus. Because long cairns cover chambers of almost every type, and most are probably additions to the chambers they cover, long cairns might be seen simply as a phenomenon appearing almost at the end of a long period of chamber-building during which the wide variety of plans had gradually developed. But this seems not to have been the case if the six short horned cairns and the long cairn at Point of Cott (ORK 41) are all unitary structures (see ¶ 10.21, 25), and if their cairn design indicates that they are roughly contemporary (see ¶ 10.26), and particularly if Point of Cott is not even early among long cairns. It must follow that their chambers are also roughly contemporary, and the chambers in question are a large four-compartment stalled chamber (ORK 41), three bipartite chambers (CAT 69, 26), three southern-style tripartite chambers (CAT 42, SUT 25, 33), and possibly one quite large single-compartment chamber (SUT 2, if the horned cairn is primary). It is difficult to avoid the conclusion that the building of most primary cairns with their variety of chamber designs lasted a relatively short time; a period of energetic and creative activity, and of ambitious projects. The development and the maintenance of the skills required also implies that they must have been constructed at quite short intervals, but there are too many imponderables (the original number and distribution of cairns, the size of the communities involved in the operations) to calculate the time-span. The conclusion that single-period horned cairns were contemporary with a variety of chambers indicates that the secondary long cairns were generally added to primary cairns after no great length of time. Pertinent questions are why long cairns were added to a minority of chambered cairns, why these were selected, and why some continued to be accessible while others were not. This view of a relatively short time-scale for the building of the majority of Orkney-Cromarty-type

passage-graves and long cairns is difficult to reconcile with a long chronology for building these chambers, at least in Orkney, that is required to allow links with the cairns of Maes Howe type (¶ 10.51, 73, 74). It has to be assumed that cairn-building, particularly of those with large chambers, continued after long cairns were no longer being built.

The cairns of the Maes Howe group

10.38) Twelve cairns of Maes Howe type have been identified in Orkney, and a considerable amount is known about the structure of eight of them (described in Davidson and Henshall 1989, 37–51, with additional information on ORK 36, 66, 72 noted below). The chambers are rectangular or square and undivided, the passages approach at right angles to the axis, and between three and six (exceptionally fourteen) cells surround the chambers. The cell roofs are mostly corbelled, and are 1.5 to 2.7 m high. Besides the differences in design between chambers of the Maes Howe and Orkney-Cromarty types, some of the former also differ in their masonry, using long slabs which often stretch the whole length of the end walls, and sometimes having large blocks in the lower courses; tall vertical slabs were not used, except at Maes Howe itself and in a unique way as facings of buttresses.

10.39) The cairns are round with diameters of about 12 to 21 m, except for ORK 16 and 22 with their extraordinary long chambers. The cairns, like those of the Orkney-Cromarty group, were built with the chamber contained within a core, and the core was surrounded by a casing faced by good quality walling (except at Maes Howe and Howe, ORK 36, 66, discussed below), and the tops were domed with carefully laid capping (seen at ORK 12, 44, 54). It was clear to the excavators of Wideford Hill (ORK 54) and Pierowall (ORK 72) (Sharples 1984) that the stone lying outside the casing wall-face was displaced material from the cairn. At Quanterness and Quoyness (ORK 43, 44) the outer spread of stone has been interpreted as an additional casing designed to form a very large domical turf-covered mound, but at these cairns also the peripheral stone should be seen as collapsed cairn material (detailed discussion in Sharples 1984, 83–4, 115–6, and Davidson and Henshall 1989, 40–43). Thus in external appearance the cairns of both groups were probably orginally indistinguishable.

10.40) The three smallest cairns, ORK 12, 53, 54, are similar in size, and are unusual in that each chamber is recessed into a hillside to give it a level floor. When the cairn structure at Wideford Hill (ORK 54) was fully exposed during excavation (figure 44, 1) it was seen that the base of the core and the casing rise steeply from the front to be on a level with the chamber roof at the rear. It was concluded that the vertical outer wall-face had had a horizontal wall-head, and the wall-face must have stood about 3 m high at the front but was of negligible height at the back. There is an additional wall-face within the casing, as also at ORK 43 and 72. The original profile of Wideford Hill was not stepped as it appears today.

10.41) At Quoyness (ORK 44) the wall-face of the casing still rises vertically to a height of 2.7 m in one part of its circuit, and the upper surface of the casing and core reach a height of 4 m against the chamber in a continuous upward slope. The present appearance of the cairn is confusing, with the core projecting above the casing, the now unroofed outer part of the passage forming a deep walled trench, and a later neolithic platform and wall surrounding the primary cairn. At Quanterness (ORK 43) the core wall-face evidently passed just outside the cells, and is indicated by a break in the passage walls (Davidson and Henshall 1989, 40) (figure 44, 2). There is an additional refinement at this cairn in that the large rectangular cells were precisely designed, even to giving their outer walls a slightly concave plan reflecting the curve of the core wall-face. It need not cause surprise that in Orkney drum-like cairns could stand without support, nor that they should eventually collapse into featureless rounded mounds of greater diameter, much as happened to many brochs. Structural failure was probably the result of deterioration of the stone due to wet and frost, and to human interference.

10.42) The passages are notably long compared with those in Orkney-Cromarty-type cairns, but similar in width and height. The shortest, at Wideford Hill (ORK 54), is 5.3 m

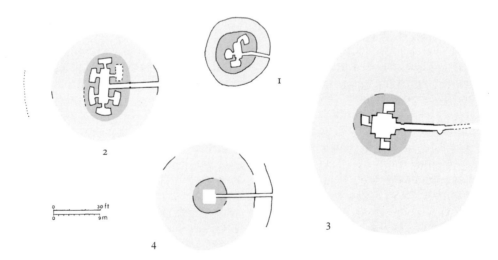

FIGURE 44. Simplified plans of excavated cairns of Maes Howe type. 1, Wideford Hill, ORK 54; 2, Quanterness, ORK 43; 3, Maes Howe, ORK 36; 4, Howe, ORK 66 (based on Smith ed. 1994, illus. 6). Key: dark stipple, cairn core; light stipple, cairn casing.

long, and at Quanterness (ORK 43) the passage is 9.4 m long. Approach to the chambers was very difficult: there was no concession by making the passages easier to negotiate, nor any attempt to shorten them by narrowing the casing at the front of the cairns. The masonry of the passage walls is known to be continuous from chamber to outer wall-face at three cairns (ORK 12, 44, 53), affirming the unity of the whole structure. Accepting that the cairns had vertical outer wall-faces resolves another uncertainty: the passages of all the cairns mentioned above were roofed for their full length, including those where the roofing now starts at the core with the core wall-face exposed above the present entrance. Two cairns not yet mentioned, Maes Howe and Howe (ORK 36, 66), have passages walled by masonry of outstanding quality, and both, as well as that at Quanterness, are floored by precisely fitting slabs on which the walls rest, another distinctive feature. At Maes Howe the inner passage from the chamber to the 'door checks' is 9.5 m long, and is relatively spacious at 1.35 m high and over 1 m wide; but there was a further 6.5 m reaching to the edge of the mound, of which only the inner part survives roofed lower and 0.7 m wide; the total length was therefore about 16 m, but it is not known how much of the outer end was roofed. Nearly as amazing is the length of the passage at Howe which led to a small chamber in a tiny core; the passage was 0.7 m wide and high (a single lintel survived), but it was 8 m long from the chamber to the casing wall-face, plus 3 m through the 'forework', giving a total unbroken length of 11 m.

10.43) Maes Howe and Howe (ORK 36, 66) (figure 44, 3, 4) are not strictly speaking cairns because, though the cores were built normally of horizontal slabs, the casing is of clay mixed with small stones, and the mounds were evidently designed to be rounded in profile, and grass-covered. Maes Howe is, of course, enormous; it is certainly 32 m in diameter and may have been as much as 38 m, and it was well over 7 m high. The casing, only examined in two cuttings in the 1950s, is not edged by walling,

but probably by a low bank of turves. Howe was very much smaller, 19 m in diameter, and was probably about 5 m high. Its construction was elaborate and unique. It was edged by a two-faced wall, 1.5 m high and probably never higher, which was continuous with walling backing the passage walls and encircling the core. Together, these walls provided an external revetment, and internally protection for the stone structure when the clay casing was added. The 'forework' (referred to as a 'platform' or 'façade' in the report, Haigh in Smith ed. 1994, 14–17, but its height and form are uncertain) was built against the front of the mound. Maes Howe and Howe are each surrounded by a shallow ditch which, apart from any cult significance, is likely to have been the source of the clay used in the mound. Investigations at Maes Howe in 1991 exposed a hole for a large standing stone on the platform near the back of the mound, which raised the possibility that the mound may once have been surrounded by a stone circle (Richards 1992, 448).

10.44) The exceptional standing of Maes Howe (ORK 36) is evident from the size of the mound; the elegance of the design, the astonishing quality of the internal structure, and the precision in handling the immense slabs in the passage, have frequently been described, and need not be repeated (Ashmore 1990; Davidson and Henshall 1989, 45–51, 142–5, both with references). The cairn core is 12 m in diameter, the absolute minimum size to enclose the chamber, and it remains 4.3 m high, with its wall-face stepped to follow the profile of the chamber wall. It is likely that there is a solid backing of walling between the passage walls and the casing, as at Howe (ORK 66).

10.45) Howe (ORK 66), now totally destroyed, certainly had features only paralleled at Maes Howe (ORK 36) (the clay casing, the quality of the passage masonry including the paving, the surrounding ditch), but Howe was little more than half the size, and it had other unique features such as the 'forework' mentioned above. The excavation was carried out under considerable difficulties, and it was found that the centre of the mound had been almost completely removed before it had been covered by a succession of iron age buildings (Smith ed. 1994). The cairn core was only 6.5 m in diameter, and so small that even the smallest Maes Howe-type chamber (ORK 53) would not fit within it. The surviving core material indicated that the destroyed chamber had been square, about 2.5 m across. The evidence for cells raised above floor level, similar to those at Maes Howe, is ambivalent, and the published plans are misleading because they show, instead of the putative chamber, a mysterious rectangular structure below floor level.

10.46) This structure had certainly been an earthhouse; it was found with its roof complete, and had been entered at its outer end (i.e. that farthest from the passage) from an iron age round house, the floor of which was on infill 1 m above the floor level of the passage (and presumably also that of the chamber). The contrast between the poor quality of the outer half of the earthhouse and the well built inner half indicated that it had probably been built in two stages. The positioning of the inner half precisely below the site of the chamber, the quality of the masonry, and the carefully constructed openings in each side wall and beneath the passage giving the appearance of openings to cells (which did not exist), led the excavator to suggest that the inner part of the earthhouse had originally been part of the chamber, and, though this seems improbable, it is difficult to disagree with the evidence for this conclusion. Interpretation of the structure is another matter. The excavator proposed that it had been a 'cell', 1 m high, below the chamber floor (his citing the two-storey Orkney-Cromarty-type chambers, ORK 23, 49, as parallels is hardly relevant). It remains an enigma.

10.47) Both Maes Howe and Howe (ORK 36, 66) were built, partly at least, on a clay platform overlying an earlier structure. In the case of Maes Howe its nature is unknown; in 1991 a small excavation in front of the entrance revealed a path of slabs roofing a drain, on almost the same alignment as the passage (Richards 1992, 447–8). At Howe the foundations of two buildings, each with a hearth, were exposed in front of, and partly beneath, the entrance, and aligned almost on the passage axis (Haigh in Smith ed. 1994, 10–14, 21–2). One of the buildings was misleadingly interpreted as a stalled cairn, but the internal width was 4 m, twice that of the widest stalled chamber, and the wall was only 2 m thick, so clearly the structure had not been roofed in stone. The proportions of the building are close to those of the houses at Knap of Howar, Papa Westray (A. Ritchie 1983), though it is unknown whether the building served a domestic or another purpose. The important point is the stratigraphic relationship of the burial mound and the building, the plan of which relates it to Orkney-Cromarty-type chambers.

10.48) A postulated sequence for the Maes Howe-type cairns largely depends on their perceived architectural development. The three smallest chambers with three or four cells (ORK 12, 53, 54) are likely to be early, followed by the larger six-cell chamber at Quoyness (ORK 44), followed by the similar but larger and more precisely planned chamber at Quanterness (ORK 43). The architectural qualities of Quanterness seem to foreshadow the meticulous design of the Maes Howe chamber and passage (ORK 36). The bizarre chambers at Holm of Papa Westray South, with its fourteen cells, and Eday Manse (ORK 22, 16), presumably lie centrally within any sequence and were presumably inspired by the excessively long chambers in the Orkney-Cromarty group.

10.49) Maes Howe (ORK 36) is significantly different from the other cairns, not only in size and external appearance, but in the contrast between the area of the core and that of the mound, and in the emphasis on the main chamber at the expense of the cells. Externally, the clay mound at Howe (ORK 66) seems to have been something of a compromise; it was edged by a relatively low wall, and was fronted by the wall-face of the 'forework', but the relative sizes of the core and the mound are similar to Maes Howe. The abandonment of solid stone vertical-sided cairns for rounded mounds at these two monuments suggests a change in perceptions and usage. This seems even more evident when the deliberate difficulty of reaching the chambers down the excessively long passages, and the exceptional (but different) chambers that were the goal, are considered. At Maes Howe extraordinary care and effort was spent on constructing the passage; the quarrying and setting of slabs of this immense size were operations which were otherwise only undertaken by the builders of the magnificent local stone circles. There was also the unique provision of a closing stone and a recess in the wall to house it. The chamber at Howe possessed a further mysterious feature, the cellar-like cavity which it is assumed was beneath the chamber floor. It may be speculated that these two monuments reflect radical changes, from a primary concern with burial and housing the bones of ancestors to a central position in other more diverse cult practices.

10.50) Some features that differentiate the Maes Howe-type cairns from those of Orkney-Cromarty type have been emphasised, and others may be added: there are no secondary enlargements of the former (apart from surrounding platforms) nor attempts to embellish the exteriors; stones decorated by pecking or scratching are only known in these chambers (Sharples 1984, 102–05; Davidson and Henshall 1989, 82–3, plates 24–7; Ashmore 1986; Bradley 1998; Bradley et. al. 1999), and perhaps most telling of all, the pottery deposited in the chambers is exclusively grooved ware contrasting with Unstan ware in chambers of the Orkney-Cromarty group. On the other hand the external appearance and the method of construction was the same for the cairns of both groups (apart from ORK 36 and 66). The unusual device of building chambers in a hollow excavated into a hillslope appears at a few cairns of Orkney-Cromarty type, mainly at Bookan chambers. This leads to consideration

of cells, diagnostic of Maes Howe-type chambers, and known rarely, singly and widespread among those of Orkney-Cromarty type, apart from the unique chamber at Isbister (ORK 25).

10.51) This chamber (ORK 25, figure 43, 7) provides one key to understanding the relationship of cairns of Orkney-Cromarty and Maes Howe types, and, by extension, of Unstan ware and grooved ware, and the house types with which they are associated. The chamber can be regarded as essentially of Orkney-Cromarty design (¶ 10.32), a perception endorsed by the large quantity of Unstan ware found in it. But the provision of three cells at a rectangular chamber (in which the transverse divisional slabs are minimised), the long lateral passage, and the oval cairn needed to accommodate them, are all suggestive of Maes Howe-type design. The Unstan chamber (ORK 51) is wholly characteristic of Orkney-Cromarty design though with a single cell, apart from a lateral passage and a round (rather than rectangular, in the Orcadian context) cairn. Isbister can be interpreted as either a hybrid monument (implying partial contemporaneity of two distinct designs of chambered cairns, and by implication, of two distinct communities, in Orkney), or as a transitional monument in a continuing architectural development (as suggested by Renfrew, 1979, 207–12). The primary cairn at Isbister was later covered with a mound of stones and clay edged by a wall, over 30 m in diameter, which can be compared with the casings at Maes Howe and Howe (ORK 36, 66). This indicates a continuing interest in the monument, and, significantly, the hoard of stone objects almost certainly sealed below the secondary mound are appropriate to late neolithic grooved ware or single-grave contexts (Davidson and Henshall 1989, 79). Parallel with the unresolved question of the relationship of the two types of chambered cairns in Orkney, current study of neolithic Orcadian pottery is suggesting that Unstan ware and round-based bowls may have evolved locally into grooved ware (MacSween 1992, full publication forthcoming).

The passage-graves of the Clava group

10.52) The distinctive nature of the monuments of the Clava group has been commented upon since serious studies of chambered cairn morphology began in Scotland, and the passage-graves have long been contrasted with the cairns of the Orkney-Cromarty group to the north (¶ 2.17, 38). Further, it is now known that the building of the two groups was separated by many centuries. Three dominant features of Clava-type passage-graves are immediately highlighted by this comparison: building with concentric circles of (generally massive) upright stones, a south-west orientation (¶ 10.62), and expressing this by grading the heights of the stones. As more architectural detail becomes available, the more the structural differences between the passage-graves of Clava and Orkney-Cromarty types become apparent, quite apart from the presence or absence of circles of standing stones. The basic design of the former is governed by the concept of building in a circular form; the design of the latter emerged from the practicalities of constructing a stone chamber, which might be round, polygonal or square, and without any indication of an ideological constraint or purpose. The Clava-type kerb of contiguous upright boulders makes a different statement from the walling which edged the cairns to the north. The differences in building methods of the two types of chamber are even more significant. The basal courses of the Clava-type chambers were, like the kerbs, built with contiguous boulders of varying height, and this in itself was an illogical foundation for constructing an ambitious corbelled roof. At Balnuaran (ORK 9, 10), where the upper walls are best preserved, the walling above the base course consists of large horizontal slabs placed in stacks, an arrangement that creates irregular vertical joints running up the wall, and introduces structural weakness (¶ 8.14). This suggests a lack of appreciation of the principles for constructing a corbelled roof, known to the builders of Orkney-Cromarty-type cairns and gained by experience from roofing small chambers; their

building methods are described in ¶ 10.6–8, but the avoidance of vertical joints is so normal, structurally sound, and convenient during building, that it is taken for granted. In a round vault of similar size to those of Clava-type chambers, and built of similar materials, there would have been large corbel stones running back, and sloping down, into the cairn.

10.53) There is no doubt that the passage-graves and ring-cairns are contemporary, and that those at Balnuaran (INV 8–10) are of unitary design, and it is assumed that this is true of all Clava-type cairns. The close siting of the three cairns now within the enclosure at Balnuaran, their carefully considered relationship, and their architectural similarities, all declare that the two types of monument have to be considered together (figure 45). The ring-cairns in the Central Highlands were revisited in the course of the present survey, and two are described in detail in our Inventory (INV 8, 23). The widespread ring-cairn tradition belongs to a family of monuments, and it is now evident that former thinking about these monuments was simplistic. In the last decade much information has become available from excavations outside the area with which we are primarily concerned, and this has shown that ring-cairns are likely to be only one element and one phase in complex monuments which were in use over very long periods, and with individual sequences of events (Barclay 1992, 78–9, 81–2; Rees 1997; Mercer and Midgley 1997; Bradley 2000, 218–20). The notion of encircling an area to create a central space for the deposition of burials, or for other purposes, is a natural one. It may be that the unusual feature of the Clava-type ring-cairns is that they are single-period monuments (though re-used for late bronze age burials), and they are certainly the most splendid examples of this kind of structure. Probably they should be thought of as a local development with only very generalised connection with apparently similar monuments in other areas. The small group of undated earthwork enclosures in the henge tradition at the neck of the Black Isle are clearly an example of the regionalisation of

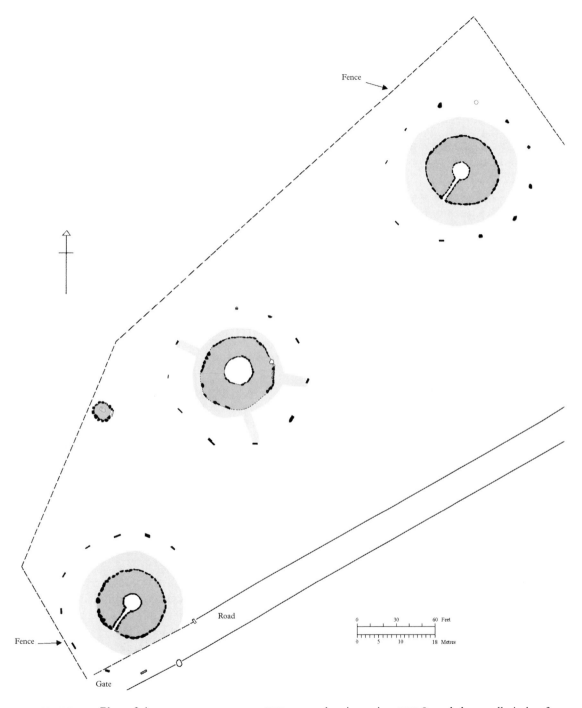

FIGURE 45. Plan of the two passage-graves, INV 9, 10, the ring-cairn, INV 8, and the small circle of stones, at Balnuaran of Clava, prepared in the field by RCAHMS in 1997.

monument distribution (Woodham 1953; Harding with Lee 1987, 362–3, 367–73; Bradley 2000, 212). There is no reason to think that the henge tradition affected the creation of Clava-type monuments except for tenuous notions about the enclosure of space.

10.54) Stone circles are an integral part of both forms of cairn, and at the passage-graves the number of stones varies between nine and thirteen (¶ 8.22–8). By 2000 BC stone circles had been long known in the north of Scotland, as the radiocarbon dates from The Stones of Stenness in Orkney demonstrate (Ritchie 1976, 50). It has long been recognised that the Clava-type cairns have a close relationship with the recumbent-stone-circles of Grampian because of the circles of standing stones, the grading of stones and the huge recumbent stones which emphasise the south-western arcs, and the frequent presence of poorly built ring-cairns. There is little new information about recumbent-stone-circles, and no firm dating of their construction period which is suspected to lie in the third millennium (Shepherd 1987, 124), but it is hoped that work currently in hand will change the situation.

10.55) The small ring beside the Balnuaran cairns has to be considered. It consists of stones laid flat, enclosing an area about 3.5 m in diameter, with a large boulder on the eastern side bearing a cup-and-ring and several cupmarks. There appears to have been no formal cairn material within the ring, but there was a covering of earth and stones about 0.3 m deep over a shallow pit (interpreted as a grave, but all traces of a body had vanished), and a scatter of quartz (Piggott 1956, 192, fig. 11). In 1972 this monument was linked to the newly identified class of kerb-cairns (Ritchie and MacLaren 1972, 8–10). Since then examples have been found in other parts of the country, and that at Claggan, Morvern, is dated to the late second or early first millennia BC (Ritchie et al 1975, 19–22, 33). There are now doubts about a close connection between the Balnuaran stone ring and kerb-cairns, partly because, unlike most kerb-cairns, the more regular faces of the stones are to the interior rather than

used to create a smooth outer face, and the date of this site is quite uncertain.

10.56) The presence of cupmarked stones at Balnuaran and Corrimony (INV 8–10, 17) has long been known, and that in two cases the cupmarks were partly hidden. One of the most intriguing recent discoveries at Balnuaran has been the cupmarked stones built into the walling of the chambers (¶ 8.30). The presence and actual positioning of the stones has been seen as highly significant by some writers, notably by Bradley, and he has suggested that there may have been an earlier structure or structures in the vicinity of which the stones were a part, and that the cairn-builders had a continuing interest in this form of decoration (2000, 121, 127). Alternatively, the distribution of the stones in the cairns can plausibly be regarded as random. It seems likely that large blocks and smooth boulders in the vicinity, already cupmarked, were used as convenient building material, and some blocks may even have been quarried from rock exposures bearing cupmarks. Around the Firthlands cupmarked stones have been found apart from monuments, on boulders, slabs and rockfaces (RCAHMS 1979a, 17–18; 1979b, 15; but Jolly 1882, 333–76 should be read with caution). Whether deliberate or opportunistic, the re-use of decorated stones is sometimes seen in the construction of burial cists, or casually in the fabric of cairns (Simpson and Thawley 1972). Balbirnie, Fife, provided examples of both occurrences, and it is likely that the cupmarked stones had come from an earlier feature on or near the site (Ritchie 1974, 2, 6–7).

10.57) The establishment of an early bronze age date for the cairns of Clava type means that they should be considered alongside other forms of burial. Cist burials were in use throughout the area, and are broadly contemporary. In modern archaeological terms the contrast is between burial monumentality and discretion. A good instance of this contrast is provided by the rich crouched burial in a cist at Culduthel, Inverness, which was accompanied by a beaker, barbed-and-tanged arrowheads, a wrist-guard with bronze rivets and with gold heads, an amber bead and a bone toggle; yet this burial had no apparent monument (Clarke et al. 1985, 267).

10.58) It is not easy to account for the appearance of a distinct class of monument, and with two different components (passage-graves and ring-cairns), in a relatively small area. The building of the passage-graves so long after the building of burial chambers had ceased is still difficult to explain. But, as Bradley has pointed out (2000, 221, 223), there was considerable interest in the chambered cairns to the north during the late neolithic and early bronze age, as witnessed by pottery and intrusive burials, and many of the chambers would still have been roofed and accessible. It was perfectly possible for the Clava cairn-builders to visit chambers in the northern part of the region in which they were living, though perhaps not understanding their purpose. Possibly this experience was linked with a remote tradition of providing access to the centre of circular structures, such as has been revealed by excavation at two complex sites to the south in Perthshire (Barclay 1992, 78–9). It may even be pondered whether the passage-graves were conceived primarily as burial places. Whatever the impetus, the Clava monuments are very remarkable both as structures and as expressions of their builders' thought-world. The cairns can be envisaged as a purely local phenomenon that flourished for a comparatively short time, created by adherents to a particular philosophy which involved an astronomical element in their thinking.

10.59) The Clava-type cairns of the Balnuaran-Culdoich group in Strathnairn have been regarded in the past as a cemetery of eight monuments (for instance in Henshall 1963, 20–21), but if only those that can be certainly so classified are considered, the total is reduced to six or seven including the newly discovered INV 55, and this is still a notable concentration. At Balnuaran there are four or five Clava-type cairns (INV 8–10, 41, ?40), presumably all broadly contemporary, as well as another mound of unknown type and date. In the late bronze age, after a gap of about a millennium, there was renewed activity; a round house was built (Bradley's Balnuaran of Clava South), one of the passage-graves was re-used for burial, and there was other evidence of disturbance. On our interpretation it is unlikely that any burial monuments were built at this time.

Orientations

10.60) In the Central Highlands there are thirty Orkney-Cromarty-type cairns where the state of preservation is such that the orientation of the passage may be measured with some degree of confidence (figure 46). All but two, the north chamber of INV 31, where the orientation may have been determined by that of the underlying ridge, and the larger chamber of ROS 31, fall within the quadrant centred on due east, with almost equal numbers falling north of east as south. There is a cluster of cairns where the entrance faces the narrower band between east-north-east and east-south-east. This wide range of orientations is found throughout the Orkney-Cromarty province and reflects no more than a broad preference rather than one designed with specific celestial movements in mind. An interest in the moon rather than the sun is sometimes suggested because of the changing position of moonrise in an eastern quadrant. The long cairns too seem to favour an axis with what may be inferred as the more important end to the east, with six out of nine favouring such an orientation; a notable exception is Mid Brae (ROS 31), with the appearance of being back to front. The orientations of some long cairns, such as INV 31, were clearly influenced by their actual sites.

10.61) It has long been known that Clava-type cairns are aligned towards the south-west quadrant, and this is certainly true at ten passage-graves, with an eleventh (INV 5) facing slightly east of south (figure 46). Burl has discussed in detail the orientation of both Clava passage-graves and ring-cairns (1981, 257–65), and a more recent summary is provided by Ruggles (1999, 130, 246, n. 78).

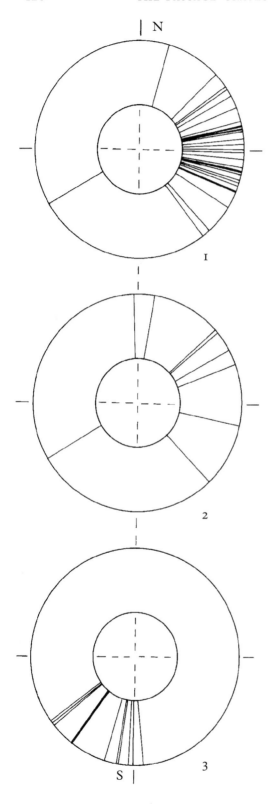

These alignments appear to be targeted on positions in the lunar cycle.

10.62) The two cairns at Balnuaran (INV 9, 10) were brought into the world of what is now thought of as archaeoastronomy as long ago as 1910 by Rear-Admiral Boyle Somerville, when, as a result of his survey work (not published until 1923) he asserted that 'The azimuth on which these alleys [passages] lie is precisely that of sunset on the day of the winter solstice', and 'There could scarcely be a more convincing proof of the existence of orientation than is contained in these facts and coincidences'. The passages of these cairns are on exactly the same axis, one behind the other (figure 45), and are remarkable for their precise solar orientation directed at the midwinter sunset. Observations undertaken in 1997 and 1998 during Bradley's examination of the monuments showed that on the winter solstice sunlight penetrates along the passage and into the chamber of the North-east cairn (the view from the South-west cairn is obstructed). The chamber was covered with tarpaulins, and he described how 'As the sun began to set, a narrow beam of light spread along the passage and across the chamber floor, striking the base of the rear wall.' His illustrations of direct light and penumbral light on the rear wall of both the passage-graves offer striking documentation of a phenomenon which can be observed for several days (Bradley 2000, 122–9, and see his dramatic frontispiece). Bradley believes that there was a wider relationship to the colours of the building stones and the cupmarked stones in the chambers as he explains at greater length (2000, 121, 126–8). It is perhaps surprising that the Balnuaran monuments did not initially receive the same attention as Maes Howe (ORK 36) in illustrating the relationship of field monuments to solsticial

FIGURE 46. (opposite) Orientations. 1, the axes of chambers of Orkney-Cromarty type; 2, the axes of long cairns; 3, the axes of chambers of Clava type. The heavy radial lines indicate two chambers with the same orientation.

regularity, perhaps because their chambers were unroofed. The alignment of Maes Howe on midwinter sunset has been convincingly demonstrated to be only a generalised one. The sun's rays in fact strike the rear wall of the chamber for as many as thirty-five days on either side of the moment of solstice, and in neolithic times it may even have been for a longer period (Ruggles and Barclay 2000, 67–8). These monuments are not alone in having a south-westerly orientation. The recumbent-stone-circles have been mentioned already (¶ 10.54). To the west there is the cairn at Kintraw, Argyll (Simpson 1967), and farther afield some circles and wedge tombs in southern and western Ireland. The relationships of these dispersed classes of monuments can only be guessed, but they do direct our attention westwards. The appearance of the Clava-type cairns at one end of a major through route, the Great Glen, has suggested in the past that it was from the west that their builders came, an idea that found some support from Newgrange in Co. Meath as the only other chambered cairn with a contemporary circle of standing stones. The early bronze age date of the Clava cairns means that links with Newgrange now have to be abandoned, and indeed the Clava cairns are less closely comparable with Newgrange than is often supposed.

The deposits in the chambers, and their closure

10.63) The contents of the chambers can be roughly divided into floor deposits with the material remains from the period of use, and the fillings above these deposits. Among the northern passage-graves most information comes from Orkney. It is a reasonable assumption that burial practices were much the same in all the cairns of Orkney-Cromarty type, and probably in those of Maes Howe type. The reports of burial deposits have been summarised, together with interpretations which now need rethinking, in Davidson and Henshall 1989, 52–6, 57–9; 1991, 60–5; Henshall and Ritchie 1995, 51–8, and ¶ 6.2–8

in this volume; the contents of the Clava-type passage-graves are described in ¶ 9.1–2 and are not mentioned again. Recurring features of the floor deposits are the broken, confused, and incomplete condition of the human and animal bone and of the pottery, and the presence of an earthy layer in which they may be embedded; a further puzzle has been the enormous variability in the quantity of material found in chambers, and indeed sometimes its total absence. Over the years elaborate explanations have been offered for these phenomena, and uncertain factors, such as the length of time a chamber may have been in use (either continuously or intermittently), and the possibility that there had been clearances (possibly incomplete) from a chamber, have to be borne in mind. The data from Orkney have been used by some scholars in attempts to reconstruct the burial rituals, and even the religious ideas and social organisation, of the communities who built the cairns. However, in the most recent investigation of a chamber and cairn (at Point of Cott, ORK 41) Barber has shown that much greater caution is needed in interpreting the observed phenomena, and consequently the unreliability of much of the former data. This is not an appropriate place to discuss Barber's findings in detail (see Barber 1988; 1997, 22–5, 66–71), or to attempt a thorough re-assessment of the evidence from other chambers, but his conclusions have radical implications.

10.64) Barber has argued convincingly that the incompleteness of skeletons, the variability in the condition of bones, and indeed the total loss of an unquantifiable amount of bone, are due, in general, to natural decay. (We would point out that in time dripping rainwater would have a localised but devastating effect.) At Point of Cott (ORK 41) a shallow earthy deposit over the floor contained a jumbled scatter of disarticulated bone. This deposit was shown to be the result of continuous animal activity, and this activity had obliterated any patterning or stratification of the humanly introduced material, i.e. the skeletons and artefacts. Barber believes that the earthy matrix was a natural formation, partly from disintegrating stonework, and partly from the organic parts of the human bodies, and, over a long period, of intrusive mammals and birds (including their prey, and droppings, both of which may include fish remains, and their bodies). A similar floor deposit at Quanterness (ORK 43) had previously been studied in pioneering detail by Renfrew (1979, 44–180), followed by that at Isbister (ORK 25) by Hedges (1983). Barber's observations at Point of Cott led him to question their findings, and in particular to conclude that there is no evidence at these three chambers for a burial rite that involved excarnation of corpses before interment; still less is there evidence from any other northern chamber.

10.65) If Barber is correct, three features of floor deposits can be simply explained: decay and not deliberate removal accounts for the absence of human bones, inhabitation and natural formation rather than deliberate introduction account for all or most of the animal bones and the earthy floor deposits (which may or may not incorporate human skeletal material and artefacts). Throughout its existence the voids in the Point of Cott cairn (ORK 41) were home to a range of mammals and birds, and Barber considers that they were the cause of the massive disturbance and breakage of the bones, both human and animal. The extent of animal activity in chambers has clearly been underestimated in the past. The view that the huge and bizarre range of animal remains recovered from Quanterness and Isbister (ORK 43, 25) was mostly introduced as part of ritual offerings has been hard to accept (Renfrew 1979, 153–6; Hedges 1983, 213–14, 226–30). Barber allows that some remains of food animals may have been brought into the chambers by man, but at Point of Cott it was not possible to identify them, and at these three chambers no butchery marks were to be seen; bones representing succulent food will have to be considered carefully in future investigations. Broken and incomplete pots remain unexplained, and there may be doubts that the large amounts of 'comminuted' bone found in

some Caithness chambers could have been produced solely by animal activity. Barber's hypotheses are attractive and convincing, and it remains to be seen whether they are upheld by future investigations. Sadly, they do imply that the evidence of probably complex activities, and probably spanning long periods, in many cases may have been lost.

10.66) It has always seemed probable that the normal burial practice was to bring intact bodies to the chambers, but the evidence has generally been destroyed by the processes described above. In a few chambers, notably at Midhowe (ORK 37), but also at ORK 43, 49, 51, CAT 38 and probably at ORK 21, 34, CAT 39, skeletons have been found in articulation, generally laid in a crouched position, sometimes back to a wall, and sometimes on a bench; benches (implying intact cadavers) are known at a number of other chambers, and there may well have been wooden benches elsewhere. Later, when the bones were in a skeletal condition, they were gathered together, and sometimes stored separately and with particular concern for crania, presumably to make space for more corpses. Clear evidence of this last procedure was found at ORK 37, 25, CAT 69, 70. There were, then, three phases of activity, sometimes running in parallel and probably repeated in cycles: the bringing in of corpses, of men, women and children; the clearing away of skeletons; and the formation of strata of jumbled bones generally embedded in an earthy matrix, and the last of these was a largely natural process. Sometimes burials continued to be added on top of an earthy layer. Rather unusually, the floor deposits in a group of chambers in east Caithness produced a considerable amount of cremated bone besides unburnt human bone, and a small amount of cremated bone was found at ROS 24 (¶ 6.2). Apart from the cremated bone, charcoal and burning have been noted sporadically in floor deposits.

10.67) Excavations have shown that passage entrances were often closed by walling, and indeed such closure was a practical necessity; also parts of chambers were sometimes closed off, as noted at Kilcoy South (ROS 24) (¶ 6.2–3). It is clear that many chambers were left empty above the floor deposits, and that later this space was often filled with stone fallen from the roof and walls. An unroofed chamber is a danger to stock, and infilling it by displacing the upper walling and corbel stones, or by dumping rubbish, is an obvious precaution whether in prehistoric or modern times. Inclusions of prehistoric material in the filling may contaminate and confuse study of the floor deposits. It has been suggested or claimed (by Henshall among others) that some chambers were deliberately filled, either partly or wholly, as a ritual act to seal the last burials. Recently this interpretation has been questioned (Barber 1997, 7–8, 65). Whereas fillings of collapsed material are relatively easy to recognise, it is much less easy to distinguish between casual and ritual fillings, and great caution is needed in re-interpreting old excavation reports (and until fifty years ago the latter interpretation was probably not considered). Ritual fillings of chambers may be considered 'not proven' for the time being. It should be noted that the smaller chamber at Camster Long (CAT 12) and the cell at South Yarrows South (CAT 55), both with intact roofs, were entirely filled with stones. At Holm of Papa Westray North (ORK 21) the cell had been deliberately filled in a number of layers (A. Ritchie 1995, 43), and the excavator of Corrimony (INV 17) believed that the layer of stones covering the burial and partly filling the passage had been deliberately laid.

10.68) Evidence for the deliberate filling of some passages is not easily dismissed. The roofing is intact and the passages are long at Maes Howe, Quanterness, Cuween Hill, and Camster Round (ORK 36, 43, 12, CAT 13), and it seems unlikely that either the rubble which partly or entirely filled them, or the apparently unscattered human bone at the last two, could have been introduced other than deliberately; at Holm of Papa Westay North and Embo (ORK 21, SUT 63) the roofing had gone, but the filling was clearly deliberate. The piling of slabs outside the passage entrances as an act of closure has been recognised at a number of excavated cairns on the mainland and was observed by Henshall during her excavation at Embo.

Chronology and dating

10.69). The only firm dating evidence for the construction phase of any of the passage-graves in the Central Highlands comes from five samples from the primary level at Balnuaran North-east (INV 9) obtained during Bradley's excavation in 1995. The dates are consistent, at about 2000 BC or slightly later. One sample from each of the ring-cairns at Balnuaran and Newton of Petty (INV 8, 45) gave a similar result. (The radiocarbon dates, including those relating to pre-cairn and late bronze age activity at Balnuaran, are detailed and discussed in Bradley 2000, 117–9, 156–8, 160–1, and the methodology for their calibration is given on illustration 106.) The similarity of all the Clava-type passage-graves and the ring-cairns (when strictly defined) strongly suggests that they are roughly contemporary. These cairns were therefore built at very least a millennium, and probably longer, after the last cairns of Orkney-Cromarty type were built, and probably several centuries after the latter had ceased to be used for neolithic burials. This chronological hiatus separates the two types of cairn architecturally, and their slightly overlapping distribution on either side of the Moray Firth (figure 11), which so exercised former writers, has no direct bearing on the present discussion. Yet the contrasting distribution of these two types of cairn is likely to indicate an underlying difference of traditions in these two areas, but one which is not marked in a way that is archaeologically discernible.

10.70) It is a much more difficult matter to establish the chronological span of the Orkney-Cromarty-type cairns, let alone any detail within it. In very general terms cairn-building and usage probably spans most of the fourth millennium BC. Although radiocarbon dating has been available to archaeologists for over thirty years, the ways in which the dates are handled have been changing. As explained in our volume on Sutherland (Henshall and Ritchie 1995, 75–6), there is an increasing insistence that multi-dated sequences are more reliable than single dates, and that dating based on a standard deviation of two sigma gives greater accuracy. With regard to the northern passage-graves, these controls discourage misleading precision and comparisons, and some of the earliest results should now be treated with caution, and the implications are discussed in our 1995 publication. The difficulty in obtaining grouped samples from construction phases has been a further disappointment. In 1995 a broad chronological framework was outlined in which it was shown that tombs in Sutherland (SUT 48) and Caithness (CAT 58, 69, 70) were in use in the second half of the fourth millennium BC, with a firm assumption that building the earliest cairns had started early in the millennium.

10.71) Since 1995 two excavation reports on chambered long cairns have been published, Camster Long (CAT 12) and Point of Cott (ORK 41). Three radiocarbon determinations from the former come from burnt areas beneath the cairn, associated with neolithic pottery, and they provide dates in the early centuries of the fourth millennium. The time lapse before the long cairn was built is uncertain, but the excavator felt that it was not significant, and concluded that the cairn was probably constructed in the second quarter of the fourth millennium (Masters 1997, 133, 177). At Point of Cott the material (including human bone) came from a range of contexts, and showed that the cairn was used for burials over a very long period, from the mid fourth millennium to the mid third millennium (Barber 1997, 58–60); the construction date of the long cairn is not known, but for design reasons it is unlikely to have been far removed from that of Camster Long.

10.72) Uncertainties continue regarding the relationship of early agriculture and early tomb-building. If the former is of late fifth/early fourth millennium date in calibrated terms, then a date early in the fourth millennium for the beginning of the Orkney-Cromarty tradition of tomb-building is probable, following the initial stage of establishing an agricultural economy. An indication of the time-span of chamber-building might have been expected from the stylistically late chamber at Isbister (ORK 25), but the dates from the foundation deposit and from the chamber contents are confusing, and keeping in mind reservations on the former handling of radiocarbon dates, it can only be said that the chamber was probably built early in the last quarter of the fourth millennium.

10.73) Turning to the architectural development of the tombs in an attempt to provide some detail within the chronological framework, it is not appropriate, of course, to think in terms of a linear progression. A simple tomb might have remained the focus for one community for a very long time, where a more complex tomb design may have evolved in another community at broadly the same period. Nonetheless there is no doubt that in all parts of the Orkney-Cromarty province there was increasing competence, confidence and ambition in the design of tombs, and this must be relevant to our enquiry. When the structural evidence was gathered in ¶ 10.36–7, the hypothesis was mooted that in Caithness and Orkney a variety of chamber designs (though excluding those that are perceived to be the latest) either predated or were contemporary with long horned cairns and short horned cairns. These distinctive forms of cairn are likely to have been built over a relatively short period, from which it would follow that all this activity would lie (on the evidence from Camster Long, CAT 12) in or before the second quarter of the fourth millennium, in a period of perhaps three hundred years or even less. This scenario may be expected to apply to other parts of the province, and it squares with the perception that, to maintain and develop the necessary building skills at a time of very short life expectancy, chambered cairns must have been constructed at fairly short intervals.

10.74) There is, however, a difficulty with this view, most acutely evident in Orkney, though it may be largely peculiar to the islands where chamber design was taken literally to extreme lengths and probably lasted longer than elsewhere. It is clear that the building of Orkney-Cromarty-type chambers overlapped the building of some chambers of Maes Howe type (¶ 10.50–1). Maes Howe itself (ORK 36), the last flaring of this tradition, is generally considered to date from about 3000 BC or a little later. There is, then, a gap of more than half a millennium between the proposed main building period of Orkney-Cromarty-type chambers and the building of Maes Howe. In Orkney there are over sixty cairns of Orkney-Cromarty type, and nineteen very long chambers can confidently be placed in the earlier part of this period, and eleven tombs of Maes Howe type in the later part, but even with the addition of a number of less remarkable Orkney-Cromarty-type chambers the total number of tombs is surprisingly small. Outside Orkney there is little indication how late chamber-building may have continued, though a few large chambers in Caithness invite comparison with some of the larger examples in Orkney, and a single radiocarbon date from before construction may indicate that the chamber at Tulloch of Assery B (CAT 70) was built no earlier than the middle of the fourth millennium. It is to be expected that further south the major tombs and their enlargements were built in the mid, or even perhaps in the later, fourth millennium, after the long cairn phase (at Mid Brae, ROS 31, there is no reason why the large typologically late chamber should not post-date its long cairn). In the Outer Hebrides the small tomb at Calanais (LWS 3) is certainly late; it is unique in being secondary to a remarkable setting of standing stones, and was probably built about 3000 BC (Ashmore 1996, 73). Four very late dates from Embo (SUT 63) are certainly puzzling. They should relate to the construction of this small bipartite chamber, and appear to indicate that it was built in the later third millennium, but they are also unsatisfactory in that they produced such a wide time-span; we should perhaps still be cautious about accepting their implication.

10.75) At least some of the Orkney-Cromarty-type chambers were in use for neolithic burials for a very long time. Three tombs and probably a fourth (ORK 21, 25, 41, ?CAT 70) have produced dates which indicate that burials continued into the third millennium, parallel with similar usage of chambers of the Maes Howe group. This is perhaps surprising considering that from a little before 3000 great changes were taking place in society, marked in Orkney by great ritual monuments, and the distinctive nucleated habitation sites of Barnhouse, Skara Brae and Links of Noltland. There is no information on the length of time that chambers in the south of the province continued in traditional use. Throughout the province excavation has shown that, in a ruined state, the cairns continued to attract attention through the bronze age, as attested by the beaker sherds at four sites in the Central Highlands, and elsewhere beakers, other types of pottery, and other artefacts, have been found, generally with single burials appropriate to their period. The cairns continued to have a powerful impact on local communities as objects of veneration and mystery, and as foci for burials. The cairn at Embo (SUT 63), which had never been impressive, testifies particularly clearly to the long-lasting significance of chambered cairns: after beaker interference it was opened for two food vessel cist burials, and used for cremations (which the inclusion of bronze razors indicates were of high status individuals) into the second quarter of the second millennium.

PART TWO

INVENTORY

ROS 1. ALCAIG MANSE
(Mulchaich)

See p. 241.

ROS 2. ARDVANIE

Parish Edderton
Location near the S shore of the Dornoch Firth,
8 km ESE of Bonar Bridge, 10.5 km WNW of Tain
Map reference NH 682874
NMRS number NH 68 NE 7
References RCAHMS 1943, 65–6; Childe 1944, 28,
30; Henshall 1963, 333, 335;
RCAHMS 1979a, 7, no. 1
Plan ASH and JNGR
Visited 15.6.56, 25.4.94

Description. The cairn is in a small patch of thin woodland, on the edge of a level terrace at 25 m OD, 200 m from the shore of the Firth. There is enclosed pasture to the E, rough pasture to the W, and the hillside which rises steeply a short distance to the S is afforested.

The centre of the cairn is bare cobbles, but the outer parts are covered with coarse grass and bracken. The cairn edge is difficult to trace exactly, particularly on the NW side where the ground falls away. The diameter is approximately 23 m, and the maximum height, to the N of the chamber, is 1.65 m. Several self-sown trees are growing on the cairn, and there is a large beech tree immediately W of the third orthostat described below. A track passes the E side of the cairn.

In the area of the chamber the cairn is hollowed, most deeply around a leaning orthostat on the N side. The chamber is SE of the apparent centre of the cairn, and has been entered from the E. On this side, about 4 m from the cairn

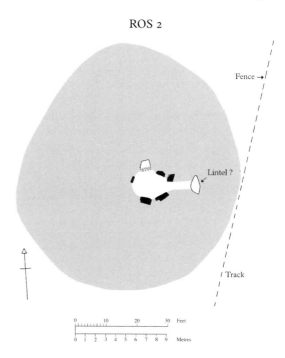

ROS 2

edge, is a flat slab measuring 1.8 m along the almost straight E edge by 1 m wide and 0.6 m deep. It appears to be a lintel, resting (as far as can be seen) on cairn material; it may be that the E edge was originally the lower surface and that the lintel has fallen to the W.

Large blocks of stone were used to build the chamber. About 1.8 m W of the lintel is an intact flat-topped rectangular orthostat set transversely to the chamber axis. It is over 0.7 m long (the N end is not visible), 0.6 m thick, and projects 0.25 m. Almost certainly it is a portal stone, and its partner to the S is either hidden or has been removed. Five more orthostats, set 0.38 to 1 m apart, belong to the walls of the chamber, and a sixth orthostat is probably missing from the wide gap on the SW side. The SE and S orthostats are 1.5 and 1.1 m long by about 0.56 m thick, and they project 0.55 and 0.7 m with probably intact upper surfaces. The latter orthostat is just taller than its neighbour, and is 0.76 m taller than the portal stone. The W orthostat has been reduced in size; it is over 0.6 m long (the N end is hidden) by 0.23 m thick, and hardly projects. The orthostat on the N side of the chamber is 1 m long by 0.35 m thick. It has a shattered top and leans to the N: if it were vertical it would project 0.53 m, with its base about 0.5 m in front of its recorded position. The NE orthostat is 1 m long by 0.3 m thick, and projects 0.43 m. It also has a shattered top, and was evidently taller than the portal stone. The chamber is 3.4 m long, and it was about 2.7 m wide.

ROS 3. BALLACHNECORE
(Bealach nan Core,
Clachan Corrach)

Parish Urray
Location 6 km WSW of Dingwall; 1.7 km S of Strathpeffer
Map reference NH 488565
NMRS number NH 45 NE 2
References Stuart 1868, 301; ONB 1873, No. 6, 74; Pitt Rivers 1885a, 152; Pitt Rivers 1885b, 12, 13; Childe 1944, 31–2; Henshall 1963, 334, 335
Plan ASH and JNGR
Visited 13.7.56, 22.10.95

Description. The cairn occupied a small level site on a hillside sloping down from E to W. The site is in a conifer wood, at 180 m OD, a little above the arable land. When seen in 1956 before re-planting the extensive views to the S and W could be appreciated.

Most of the orthostats of a chamber survive within the last remains of the cairn. The cairn is obscured by moss and forest litter, trees have been planted on it, and on the N side furrows have been driven into the edge. It is evident that the cairn was larger than the area, about 13.5 by 10 m, which can be detected on the surface, but on the N side the ground falls away quite steeply and thus it is clear that the cairn was never large. A stone beyond the apparent edge of the cairn on the SE side, and just protruding, may belong to the original edging of the cairn. The greatest depth of cairn material is inside the chamber, at maximum 0.7 m deep in the inner compartment.

The passage, which evidently approached the chamber from the E, has been destroyed. The chamber orthostats are intact boulders,

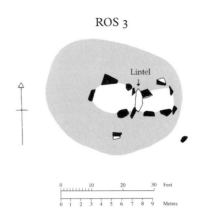

ROS 3

with two exceptions noted below which had been damaged 'quite recently' in 1885 (Pitt Rivers a). A pair of portal stones, 0.94 m apart, forms the entry into the chamber. They are 0.93 and 0.9 m long by about 0.4 m thick. The N stone is exposed for 0.6 m, almost its full height, and its partner, which is the same height, is exposed for 0.45 m. The outer compartment of the chamber has two orthostats on each side. On the S side they are 1.04 and 1.12 m long by 0.64 and 0.44 m thick, and project 0.65 and 0.7 m; the E orthostat is 0.3 m higher than the adjacent portal stone. The orthostats on the N side are displaced, but it is likely that originally they were more or less in line. The E orthostat is 1 m long by up to 0.4 m thick. It leans acutely to the N, and the exposed lower surface on the N side shows that when upright it was at least 1 m high. The W orthostat leans to the S and is a much larger stone than appears on the plan. The E end slopes down out of sight, and the W end is hidden below a lintel. The visible part is 1 m long by 0.7 m thick, and is exposed for 0.4 m on the N side. When the original positions of the leaning orthostats are considered, it seems clear that the compartment was roughly rectangular, nearly 3.5 m long and 1.63 to 1.8 m wide, and that all four orthostats were roughly the same height (and that it was not a passage as formerly described).

The entry to the inner compartment is between a well-matched pair of portal stones.

They are 1 m and over 0.73 m long (the S end of the N stone is obscured by an old tree stump) by 0.37 and 0.3 m thick, and they project 0.6 and 0.56 m. The lintel which rested on them is displaced to the E, and leans against the NE corner of the S inner portal stone. The lintel is 2.25 m long by 0.95 m wide by 0.3 m thick. The wider E face slopes down steeply to the E. Four orthostats of the inner compartment remain, and probably one or two have been removed from the wide gap on the SW side. The SE orthostat is 1.1 m long by 0.64 m thick, and projects 0.95 m; it is a pointed block 0.66 m taller than the adjacent portal stone. The back-slab is damaged; it is 1.15 m long by 0.4 m thick, and projects 0.9 m. The NW orthostat is an impressive pointed block, 1.6 m long by 0.95 m thick, and projects 1.75 m; its true height, measured from ground level on the E side of the monument, is 2 m, 0.3 m higher than the SE orthostat. The top of the NE orthostat has been broken off; the stone is 0.6 m long by 0.55 m thick, and projects 0.9 m. The compartment is 4.2 m long by 2.65 m wide. The chamber is about 7.8 m long.

Outside the chamber, 1.5 m S of the SE orthostat of the inner compartment, there is an intact regular boulder set on end and leaning to the S. It is 0.8 m long by 0.4 m thick, and measures 0.95 m down its sloping S face. The boulder appears to be *in situ* and to be part of the structure.

The monument is the un-named site visited by Stuart in 1867 on the same ridge as the fort of Knock Farril. His note that 'there was a cairn, of which two ruined chambers alone remain' suggests that the cairn had been removed fairly recently and that the chamber was in much the same condition as now. Certainly there has been no change since it was recorded and illustrated by Pitt Rivers and Tomkin in 1885 (figure 9).

The chamber 'is traditionally said to be the spot where a number of the followers of Brodie of Brodie were interred having been slain at "Loch na Pairc" in a conflict with the Macdonalls of Glengarry at the latter end of the 15th century' (ONB).

ROS 4. BALNACRAE

Parish Dingwall
Location in Strath Sgitheach, 5.5 km N of Dingwall
Map reference NH 533646
NMRS number NH 56 SW 1
References ONB 1875, No. 9, 49; RCAHMS 1943, 29–32; Childe 1944, 31; Henshall 1963, 334–5; RCAHMS 1979a, 7, no. 3
Plan ASH and JNGR
Visited 14.7.56, 17.5.95, 6.8.97

Description. The upper part of the strath, which formerly supported a scattered crofting community, is planted with conifer forest or left as rough grazing. The cairn is just beyond the inland limit of forestry, on a hillside sloping down from NW to SE, at nearly 250 m OD. The cairn has wide views over the strath, to its head and the high mountains beyond, and in the opposite direction down to the Cromarty Firth. Heights of Brae (ROS 22) is in sight on the sky-line 4 km to the SSW.

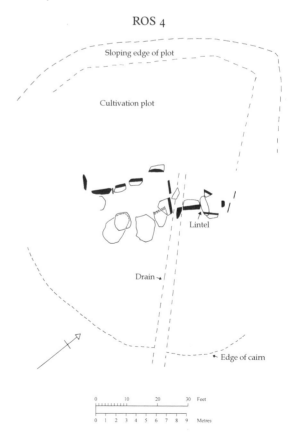

ROS 4

Sloping edge of plot

Cultivation plot

Lintel

Drain →

← Edge of cairn

0 — 10 — 20 — 30 Feet

0 1 2 3 4 5 6 7 8 9 Metres

The cairn material has been almost entirely removed, leaving exposed an impressive group of upright, leaning, and prone slabs (plate 9). There can be little doubt that the monument is a ruined chambered cairn, and that the chamber was of exceptional size, and was probably built in two phases. However, the remains are very perplexing, and no satisfactory interpretation of them can be offered (discussed in ¶ 4.48–51, figure 22).

The remains of the cairn are covered with turf. A rim of cairn material about 0.5 m high survives on the downhill SE side, and here the cairn edge is clear. Elsewhere there is little depth of cairn material except around the row of four orthostats where it is up to 0.7 m high. To the NW of them all the cairn material has been removed to make a cultivation plot. The NW edge of the plot probably coincided with the edge of the cairn, but only the former can be traced, indicted by a break in the slope of the hillside and a change from turf to heather. On the NE and SW sides the cairn merges into the ground and the cairn edge cannot be traced. The cairn diameter was probably about 30 m. A drainage ditch has been cut from the plot through the cairn from NW to SE.

The axis of the internal structure is roughly NE to SW. At the NE end is a pair of portal stones 0.66 m apart. They are 0.95 and 0.6 m long by 0.1 m thick, and their shattered tops hardly project. About 0.4 m SW of the SE stone, and almost parallel to it, is a block 0.6 m long by 0.3 m thick, with a broken top projecting 0.4 m. Two orthostats have evidently formed most of the SE wall of the NE part of the structure. They lean respectively to the SE and NW, but when upright they would probably have been more or less in line. They are 1.56 and 2 m long by 0.25 and 0.5 m thick, and over 1 and 1.5 m high. The opposite wall may be represented by an orthostat about 2.2 m SW of the NW portal stone. The orthostat is a rectangular pointed block which is probably intact, over 0.9 m long (the W end is not visible) by 0.26 m thick, and it projects 0.95 m. It leans to the S, and appears to have been slightly displaced. At this point the structure seems to have

been roughly 1.5 m wide, and a prone block lying across the axis is probably a displaced lintel. It is 1.8 m long by 0.2 m thick, and 0.6 m wide across the lower face. It slopes down to the N with the N edge in the ground and the S side supported by the two orthostats on the SE side of the structure.

Immediately SW of the second orthostat, exposed in the drainage ditch but seemingly *in situ*, is a transverse block, 1.07 m long by 0.5 to 0.25 m thick; it is 1 m or so lower than the orthostat and projects 0.4 m. North-west of it is a stone of similar size, which has probably been displaced when the drain was cut. These two stones, which seem to be intact, have the appearance (perhaps misleading) of a pair of low portal stones.

Only 0.4 m to the SW, and about 6 m from the first pair of stones described, is a pair of stones which look like unusually large and tall portal stones. They are 1.5 and 1.25 m long by 0.3 and 0.25 m thick. At their bases they are only 0.35 m apart, but the opposed sides diverge as they rise. The SE stone has been damaged on the NE face and down the SE side. If upright, its height would be a little over 1.75 m, but it leans steeply to the SW, supported by the almost prone slab on its S side. The NW stone is a regular rectangular slab which projects 1.2 m.

Two rows of orthostats extend south-westwards from the putative portal stones. The first orthostat of the SE row, on which the adjacent portal stone rests, leans acutely to the E with the tip only 0.9 m above ground level and its base only just embedded in the turf. It is clear that this orthostat stood almost at right angles to the portal stone, probably slightly to the ESE of the present position of its base. The orthostat is 1.2 m long by 0.3 m thick, and would be 2 m high when vertical. The next two orthostats are prone, and give the impression that they have fallen to the SE and the S, and then have remained undisturbed. They are irregular in shape, and the SW side of the first has been damaged. They are about 1.85 and 1.9 m wide (their presumed maximum length when upright) by 2.7 and 3.3 m long (their presumed former height), by up to 0.4 m thick. Alternatively, the last slab may have been set on its W edge and have fallen to the E, in which case it would have been about 3.3 m long above ground level by about 1.8 m high. A smaller damaged slab lies on this slab.

The NW row of four orthostats stretches to 7.6 m SW from the NW portal stone. They are spaced 0.9 to 0.3 m apart, and if upright they would form an almost straight line, though stepped slightly and progressively to the SE (this feature is exaggerated on the plan by the tilt of the stones). At the NE end of the row, and 0.8 m W of the portal stone, is an orthostat leaning acutely to the NW. It is 1.7 m long by 0.25 m thick, and projects 1.1 m, though a cavity against the NW face shows that its height is over 1.4 m and the base lies 0.2 m further to the SE than shown on the plan. The next two orthostats lean to the SE. They are 1.35 and 1.2 m long by 0.25 m thick, and project 1.2 m with damaged upper edges. The SW orthostat is an irregular slab 2 m long by 0.45 m thick, and projects 0.75 m with a probably intact upper edge. Between the last two orthostats and transversely to them the top of a damaged slab projects only 0.2 m; it is 0.6 m long by 0.1 m thick.

The most impressive of the standing stones is 0.58 m W of, and at right angles to, the last orthostat described. It is 1.5 m long by 0.3 m thick, and is exposed for 2 m, almost its full height. It is an intact regular slab with a rounded top, and leans slightly to the SW. It has the character of a back-slab of a chamber, yet it is outside the structure as defined by the existing orthostats.

Many prone slabs are partly exposed within and around the chamber.

The monument was in much its present condition well before 1875 (ONB).

ROS 5. BALNAGROTCHEN

Parish Alness
Location in the valley of the River Alness, 7.5 km WNW of Alness
Map reference NH 581735

NMRS number NH 57 SE 1
References Woodham 1956b, 24; Henshall 1963, 336
Plan EVWF and ASH, revised by ASH and JNGR
Visited 5.7.58, 15.5.95

Description. The cairn is on a wide terrace on the S side of the valley of the River Alness, in a level field at 210 m OD. The two Boath cairns (ROS 10, 11) are 220 and 380 m to the N and NNE, on the same terrace. Much of the valley is afforested, but in the vicinity of the cairns there are enclosed fields and rough pasture.

ROS 5

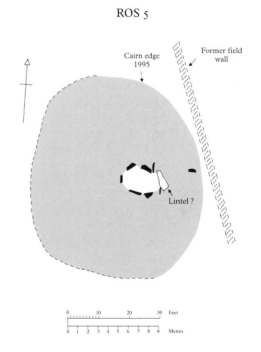

The cairn has been considerably damaged since it was recorded in 1958 (Henshall). At that time the E side was crossed by a field wall running NNW to SSE, and elsewhere the cairn edge was defined by the limit of ploughing. When visited in 1995 the edge round the W half appeared to be unchanged, but the wall had been removed, and on the NE side recent ploughing had evidently eaten into the cairn itself. The diameter N to S is 19 m (as it was in 1958), and E to W it is 17 m. The turf-covered surface is rather uneven, and is covered with many stones and boulders cleared from the field. The cairn remains 1 m high measured from the N side where the ground level is slightly lower.

In 1958 five slabs defined an oval chamber about 3 m long by about 2.2 m wide. The two orthostats on the S side are 1 and 1.3 m long by 0.4 and 0.26 m thick, and project 0.65 and 1.1 m. The back-slab is 0.62 long by 0.27 m thick, and projects 0.13 m. These orthostats are 0.2 and 1.25 m apart. The two orthostats on the N side, similar in size to those opposite, have been removed and there is a depression where they stood. The entry into the chamber was between a pair of long thin portal stones which barely projected (no longer to be seen). The stones were not opposite each other and were unusually far apart. Although they appeared to be *in situ*, it seems likely that the S stone had been displaced. East of the portal stones lay a stone which was probably a displaced lintel, about 2 m long. Several other large displaced slabs lay about the chamber. Some 3.3 m E of the N portal stone an orthostat (not now visible) may have belonged to the N wall of the passage.

An electricity pole stands 6.3 m N of the first orthostat described.

On the first edition of the OS 6-inch map the cairn was shown (beside a field wall and untitled) as an unploughed area of much the same shape and size as it was in 1958.

ROS 6. BALNAGUIE

Parish Knockbain
Location on the Black Isle, 8 km NNW of Inverness
Map reference NH 628547
NMRS number NH 65 SW 3
References Beaton 1882, 488–9; RCAHMS 1943, 3–6; Childe 1944, 28, 34–5; Woodham 1956a, 69, 71, 88; Henshall 1963, 336–7; RCAHMS 1979c, 7, no. 1
Plan ASH and JNGR
Visited 11.7.56, 2.5.96

Description. The cairn is on the south-facing slope of the central ridge of the Black Isle, at 100 m OD, in a region of mixed forestry and pasture. The actual site, in a small patch of thin woodland, slopes down gently from N to S, and there is a drop to a small burn on the W side.

The cairn has been almost entirely removed except for a rim of cairn material about 0.5 m high, which remains on the N and W sides. The edge of the cairn is clear round the NW quadrant, except for a break which was probably made for the access of carts during robbing. A stone stands just within the cairn edge on the NNW. The rectangular base of the stone measures 0.95 by 0.53 m, and it is 0.75 m high with an irregular top which appears to have been broken long ago. Round the S part of the cairn the edge is indistinct, and fades away round the E side. The diameter of the cairn is about 29 m. About 4.5 m within the projected E edge (its position confirmed by Beaton's plan of 1882) there are two stones, nearly 5 m apart, which were probably part of a façade beside the entrance to the chamber. The N stone is triangular in plan, about 1.26 m wide across the E face by about 0.7 m thick, and 1.15 m high, narrowing towards the top. The S stone is a similar block which leans to the W with the base partly exposed. It appears to be somewhat displaced.

The orthostats of the bipartite chamber are exposed for almost their full heights. There is a rectangular orthostat on each side of the outer compartment. The N orthostat, 1.55 by 0.75 m, and 0.8 m high, was formerly somewhat larger as the top and the W end have been smashed. The S orthostat is over 1.7 m long (the W end is not visible) by 0.43 m thick, but it was originally thicker as pieces 0.05 m thick have sheared off most of the N face; it is 0.9 m high, but the upper part has been damaged. A pair of portal stones 0.87 m apart forms the entry to the inner compartment. The N stone is a roughly rectangular block, 1.06 m long by up to 0.4 m thick, and 0.55 m high. It is damaged on the E face, though part of the flat original upper surface, which slopes down gently to the S, survives. Its partner is almost completely hidden by the roots of a large oak tree. This stone appears to be an intact boulder, about 0.9 m long, over 0.33 m thick, and over 0.47 m

ROS 6

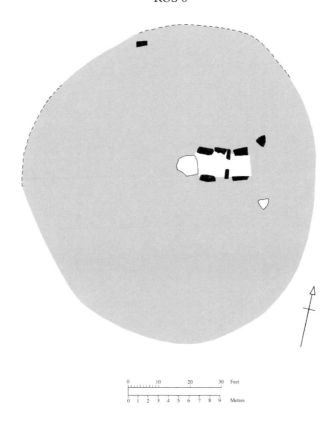

high. The outer compartment is 1.85 m wide and was at least 1.65 m long.

The N wall of the inner compartment consists of two orthostats. The eastern is an intact rather irregular boulder set on end, about 1.1 m wide by 0.6 m thick, and the pointed top is 1.24 m high. The W orthostat is a rectangular block, probably intact with an irregular top, 1.57 m long by 0.56 m thick, and 1.42 m high. The back-slab leans steeply to the W, and the E edge of the base is just exposed. This massive intact stone has a rectangular base, fairly flat faces, and a rather irregular top edge. It is 1.85 m long by 0.6 m thick, and when vertical it would have been 2.1 m high. One orthostat remains on the S side of the compartment, an impressive intact rectangular block, 1.46 m long by 0.5 m thick, with a pointed top 1.92 m high. The chamber orthostats are set close together, apart from a gap of 0.76 m between the last orthostat and the S portal stone, and it

is possible that it was originally filled by a narrow orthostat. The inner compartment was about 2.9 m long by 2.2 m wide, and the total length of the chamber was at least 5 m.

About 1880, when the cairn was first recorded, cairn material remained in places up to 1.3 m high. The outer part of the cairn survived as a circular bank only broken by a gap on the NW side, and the chamber itself and the putative façade stones were fully exposed within the bank (see Beaton's section, p. 489; our tentative interpretation of the plan in figure 24, 3). The cairn was in its present condition well before 1943 (RCAHMS).

ROS 7. BALVAIRD (Carn Fian)

Parish Urquhart and Logie Wester
Location at the W end of the Black Isle, 1.5 km NNE of Muir of Ord
Map reference NH 539519

NMRS number NH 55 SW 10
References OSA 5, 1793, 214; Brown 1816; ONB
1872–3, No. 31, 56; Woodham 1956a, 69, 71;
Henshall 1963, 337; RCAHMS 1979c, 7, no. 2
Plan ASH and JNGR
Visited 12.7.56, 20.10.95

ROS 7

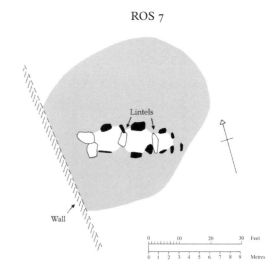

Description. The cairn is at the edge of a level field, at 100 m OD. An old field wall crosses the W side of the cairn, and to the W of it the ground drops away to the valley floor. There is a wide view from the site to the NW round to the SE, across the broad strath to distant hills and mountains. Bishop Kinkell and Muir of Conan (ROS 9, 34) are 850 m to the NNE and NE.

The cairn has been very greatly reduced, though on the NE an ill-defined edge may roughly indicate its original extent on this side. Most of the orthostats of the chamber remain, and in the outer compartment of the chamber cairn material is about 1.2 m high measured from the ESE edge of the cairn. The remains of the cairn are grass-covered, and an old rowan tree is growing in the inner compartment of the chamber. Large stones and boulders lie about the site, some of which are probably displaced constructional stones from the chamber.

The orthostats of the passage and chamber are all boulders (with one exception noted below), some of them rather irregular in shape, and all seemingly intact. On the ESE side of the monument two stones 0.72 m apart are evidently portal stones at the entry to the passage. They are 0.68 and 0.57 m long by 0.4 and 0.34 m thick, and are about the same height. Just in front of the S stone and parallel to it is an irregular boulder, which may be the S stone of an outer pair of portal stones, indicating that there may have been a short extension of the passage. This stone is 0.8 m long by over 0.26 m thick (the W face is not visible), and 0.3 m high above ground level to the E. The portal stones are taller, and project for 0.44 and 0.26 m. The passage is about 1.6 m wide. On each side there is an orthostat; these are 0.94 and 0.83 m long by 0.25 and 0.44 m

thick. They are about the same height, and a little taller than the portal stones; the S stone is exposed for 0.53 m on its S side.

Across the inner end of the passage there is a lintel. It is rather irregular in shape, 1.95 m long by 0.4 m wide, and 0.8 m deep down the E face. It appears to rest on the surface of the cairn, and leans against an upper corner of an orthostat to the W, but it is probably *in situ* supported by hidden portal stones. The lower surface of the lintel is about 0.9 m above ground level.

On the S side of the outer compartment of the chamber are two orthostats, 0.9 and 1.15 m long by 0.85 and 0.6 m thick. They are exposed on their S sides for 0.85 and 0.7 m. On the opposite side of the compartment is an orthostat 1.45 m long by 0.8 m thick; it is exposed for 0.9 m on the N side, but its height above ground level is nearer 1.6 m. It is only a little taller than the orthostats on the S side.

A second lintel remains more or less *in situ* spanning the entry to the inner compartment. The lintel is 1.6 m long by 0.8 m wide by over 0.4 m deep. Its N end rests on the end of a portal stone set skew to the chamber axis. The portal stone is 0.95 m long by 0.35 m thick, and projects 0.15 m; it has a horizontal upper surface 0.7 m lower than the orthostat to the E.

The inner compartment is defined by an orthostat on each side and a prone block at the inner end. On the S side the stump of a slab (not a boulder) can just be seen; it is 1.4 m long by about 0.15 m thick. On the N side is an orthostat with a flat upper surface sloping down to the W; it is 1.15 m long by 0.65 m thick, and projects 0.3 m. There is little depth of cairn material around the W end of the chamber, and there can be little doubt that the prone block was a tall end-stone which has fallen outwards. It is 1.75 m long (the original height) by 1.1 m wide and 0.5 m thick. South of it is another block, 1.5 by 0.9 m, and up to 0.56 m thick; it is triangular in cross-section with a ridge running N to S. The former function of this stone is unclear. The chamber was about 5.6 m long; both compartments are 2.06 m wide, and probably they were roughly the same length, about 2.6 m (see figure 13 for a reconstruction of the plan).

The monument was recorded as Carn Fian on Brown's survey of 1816, and was evidently in its present condition by 1873 (ONB). The chamber may have been investigated in the late 18th century, because, by direction of the landowner, one of several 'tumuli' in the district 'was lately laid open, when 3 stone coffins were found in it, ranged in line from east to west' (OSA). This description suggests that two compartments of a chamber and a passage were exposed. There is the possibility, however, that the reference is to nearby Muir of Conan (ROS 34), which is not recorded on Brown's survey.

ROS 8. BELMADUTHY

Parish Knockbain
Location on the Black Isle, 8 km W of Fortrose
Map reference NH 644559
NMRS number NH 65 NW 2
References Beaton 1882, 489–91; RCAHMS 1943, 1–2; Childe 1944, 34; Woodham 1956a, 71, 72, 88; Henshall 1963, 338, 339; RCAHMS 1979c, 7, no. 3
Plan ASH and JNGR
Visited 11.7.56, 2.5.96

Description. The cairn, at 135 m OD, is in a field, which slopes down gently from NW to SE. The site has a wide view to the S, and is fairly open in other directions.

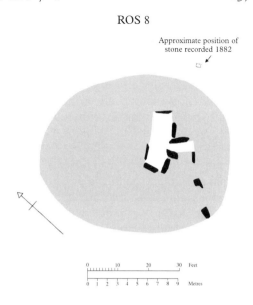

ROS 8

Approximate position of stone recorded 1882

The steep edge of the cairn has been formed by the limit of ploughing which has evidently distorted the plan. The cairn now measures 18.6 m SE to NW by 15 m transversely. It is less than 1 m high, turf-covered and fairly level, with some added field-gathered stones. On the SE side there has been a slightly concave façade of spaced orthostats, three of which survive on the SW arc (plate 11). The SW orthostat, a pointed block of conglomerate, is 1.03 m long by about 0.6 m thick, and on its SW side it is exposed for its full height of 1.4 m. The central orthostat is a sandstone slab with a flat face to the SE, and is probably intact; it is 0.9 m long by 0.55 m thick, and projects 0.95 m but is a little taller than the first orthostat. The NE orthostat is a thin block of conglomerate set transversely to the line of the passage. It is probably the stump of a much larger stone, and it leans to the SE; it measures 1.05 m long by 0.28 m thick, and projects 0.4 m. The orthostats are 2 m and 1.55 m apart.

The cairn was in the same condition when recorded by Beaton in 1882, except that he saw what was almost certainly a fourth orthostat of the façade. This stone, shown on his plan and section, stood roughly 7 m NE of the passage entrance, in approximately the position that the outermost orthostat on this side would be expected. The stone was about 0.6 m long by about 0.3 m wide, and projected about 0.9 m. The total length of the façade would have been about 14.5 m, probably consisting of a pair of portal stones and four façade stones (figure 29, 2). It is difficult, however, to accept the oval shape of the cairn shown on the 1882 plan.

The passage was evidently entered from the centre of the façade. The NE wall of the passage consists of a slab 2.04 m long by 0.4 m thick, which projects 0.73 m. Its irregular upper surface slopes down to the SE. The inner half of the SW wall is formed by a slab 1.17 m long by 0.6 m thick, which projects 0.66 m. It is not quite parallel to the NE slab, and is a little taller. The passage is 0.63 m wide at the inner end.

The axis of the rectangular chamber is at right angles to that of the passage. The chamber is 5 m long by 1.95 m wide. Five orthostats remain, presumably once linked by narrow panels of walling, and one or two orthostats are evidently missing from the NW side. As in the façade, both sandstone and conglomerate slabs were used, and the latter have greatly weathered uneven surfaces, and have probably been considerably reduced in size. The two orthostats forming the SE wall, both conglomerate, almost butt against the inner ends of the passage walls. The NE orthostat is 1.55 m long by 0.4 m thick, its pointed top projecting for 1.24 m, 0.6 m higher than the adjacent passage orthostat. The SW orthostat is 1.6 m long above ground level by 0.5 m thick, its rounded top projecting 1.27 m. Across the NE end of the chamber is a pointed block of conglomerate leaning to the NE; it is 1.64 m long by about 0.3 m thick, and projects 1 m. The NW wall is represented by an orthostat which has probably been reduced in thickness; it is 1.43 m long by 0.15 m thick, and projects 1 m. The SW end of the chamber is closed by an intact pointed slab, 1.45 m long above ground level, and 0.5 m thick. This impressive slab, projecting 1.45 m, has a true height of over 2 m, and is about 0.4 m higher than the other four orthostats of the chamber walls, all of which

are roughly the same height. A number of large slabs lie in the passage and around the chamber.

ROS 9. BISHOP KINKELL

Parish Urquhart and Logie Wester
Location on the W end of the Black Isle, 2.4 km NE of Muir of Ord
Map reference NH 541527
NMRS number NH 55 SW 3
References Henshall and Wallace 1956; Henshall 1963, 338, 339; RCAHMS 1979c, 7, no. 4
Plan ASH and JNGR
Visited 12.7.56, 25.10.95

Description. The last remains of the cairn are on the quite steep hillside that forms the SE side of the lower valley of the River Conon. It is 560 m NW of Muir of Conon (ROS 34) and 850 m NNE of Balvaird (ROS 7). The site is at 90 m OD, at the edge of a neglected area of mixed woodland with a field of pasture immediately to the NE. The cairn is partly in a strip through the woodland which has been cleared of trees to accommodate power lines, and the area of the chamber is heavily overgrown with bracken.

The chamber and passage, of which a number of orthostats survive, was aligned ENE to WSW along the contour. By comparing the ground level on either side of the field wall that crosses the NE edge of the monument, it is evident that cairn material remains up to 0.8 m deep in and around the passage and ante-chamber, but has been almost totally removed from in and around the main chamber. When seen in 1956 cairn material appeared to spread for about 9 m from the chamber on the S side. By 1995 a greater depth of forest litter made it impossible to trace the former extent of the cairn.

The easternmost pair of orthostats, set 0.7 m apart, are presumably portal stones at the entry to the passage. The N stone is incorporated into the field wall, and on the field side it is exposed for 0.8 m, nearly its full height; it is 0.85 m long by 0.6 m thick. This orthostat indicates the substantial size of the

ROS 9

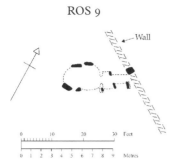

other four portal stones, which are evidently of similar dimensions; this could be appreciated more easily in 1956, when they were more visible, than in 1995, when only their tips could be seen. The S stone at the passage entrance (as presently exposed) is 0.7 m long by 0.2 m thick, and is 0.2 m shorter than its partner. A metre or so to the W a second pair of portal stones presumably formed the entry to an ante-chamber. They are 0.75 m apart, 0.55 and 0.46 m long by 0.2 and 0.23 m thick. The S member of a third pair of portal stones, about 1 m further W, was seen in 1956 to be about 0.8 m long, but only the very tip was visible in 1995. Its partner may well exist, totally hidden. All five portal stones are intact boulders with flat upper surfaces.

Four orthostats of the main chamber survive, and their irregular spacing suggests that at least two are missing. Clockwise from the S, the orthostats are 0.55, 1.05, 0.94 and 0.95 m long by 0.3 m or slightly more thick, and they project 0.45, 0.78, 0.85 and 0.6 m. The first and second orthostats are the same height as the orthostat in the wall, and the third orthostat is a little taller. There is no great difference in height between any of the orthostats, though those in the main chamber may once have been somewhat taller. The main chamber is 2.1 m wide and was about 3.7 m long.

ROS 10. BOATH LONG
(Carn Liatha)

Parish Alness
Location in the valley of the River Alness, 7 km WNW of Alness
Map reference NH 581738

NMRS number NH 57 SE 2
References Brown 1906, 20; Woodham 1956b, 24; Henshall 1963, 339, 341
Plan ASH and JNGR
Visited 3.5.57, 27.4.95

Description. The cairn is on a terrace above the River Alness, at 200 m OD. Boath Short and Balnagrotchen (ROS 11, 5) are on the same terrace, 170 m to the NE and 220 m to the S. The two Boath cairns are in an area of rough pasture, where traces of old enclosures and other walls indicate considerable agricultural activity in the past. The site of Boath Long is level.

The axis of the long cairn lies ENE to WSW, but for convenience it is described as lying E to W. The cairn was extensively robbed for building stone in the earlier part of the nineteenth century (Brown), but a rim remains largely undisturbed and generally about 1 m high. The edges of the cairn are clear except across the E end. The cairn is about 67 m long overall, by 26 m wide at the E end and 16.5 m wide at the W end. In plan the E half narrows gently from E to W, and the W half is almost parallel-sided. At the E end there appears to be a shallow forecourt formed by projecting horns, but it is ill-defined and probably is the result of former cultivation eating into the cairn. The foundations of a wall can be traced running E from each horn to enclose a roughly rectangular plot measuring about 20 m E to W by about 16.4 m N to S. At the SE corner of the cairn is a prone slab; it is over 1.25 m long with the NW end embedded in the cairn, 0.9 m wide, and 0.22 m thick.

The E part of the cairn, within the turf-covered rim, is of large bare cobbles, and it rises to a height of 2.8 m around the chamber, measured from the N side. Westwards from about 2 m W of the chamber there has been severe robbing. The cairn material has been totally removed from a rectangular area in the centre of the cairn by way of a gap through each side. Westwards of this is a similar rectangular area with a thin layer of stone below the turf, and low banks of bare cairn material remain around the deeply robbed areas.

ROS 10

Cultivation
plot

0   10   20   30   Feet

0   1   2   3   4   5   6   7   8   9   Metres

At the E end of the cairn, encased in cairn material, are six orthostats belonging to a passage and chamber, its axis slightly skew to that of the cairn. The orthostats are intact slabs, and, except for the taller back-slab, all are roughly the same height. A pair of slabs parallel to the axis has presumably belonged to the passage walls. The space between the slabs has been emptied and partly refilled with loose stones, misleadingly forming a rectangular hollow closed by cairn material at each end. The S slab leans slightly to the S, and the N slab leans more acutely to the S with an over-hang of 0.3 m. The slabs are 1.73 and 1.94 m long by 0.2 and 0.3 m thick. The full height of the S slab was only slightly more than the 1.2 m which can be measured down its N face, and the N slab was somewhat lower. The slabs diverge slightly westwards, and at maximum are 1.3 m apart.

About 1.8 m to the W the tops of a pair of portal stones can just be seen. The slabs are about 0.53 and 1.27 m long, and both are 0.13 m thick. These slabs are only 0.23 m apart, so one is likely to be slightly displaced. It is probable that these stones formed the entry from an outer compartment (of which nothing is visible) to an inner compartment. A slab forming most of the S side of the inner compartment is exposed in a hollow made against its S side. It is over 1.58 m long by 0.12 m thick, and a height of 1.1 m can be measured through the cairn material. The back-slab, which is about 0.4 m higher than the other orthostats and projects above the cairn material, is over 1.07 m long by 0.3 m thick. The inner compartment was about 2.5 m long. (See figure 15 for a reconstruction of the chamber plan.)

There are foundations of a small rectangular building close to the S side of the cairn near its E end.

ROS 11. BOATH SHORT
Parish Alness
Location in the valley of the River Alness, 7 km WNW of Alness
Map reference NH 583739

NMRS number NH 57 SE 3
References ONB 1875, No. 3, 17; Maclean 1888, 225; Brown 1906, 20; Woodham 1956b, 24–5; Henshall 1963, 340, 342
Plan ASH and JNGR
Visited 3.5.57, 26.4.95, 5.8.97

Description. The cairn is in rough pasture at 200 m OD, 170 m NE of Boath Long (ROS 10). Balnagrotchen (ROS 5) is in a field 380 m to the SSW.

This impressive monument consists of a turf-covered stone platform, trapezoidal in plan with slightly projecting horns at the corners (a very large version of the short horned cairn plan), within which rises a cairn, round in plan though flattened on the E side (plate 10). The platform mostly has well defined edges, though they are less clear along part of the E and N sides, and the NE horn has been almost obliterated by cattle trampling; the whole plan of the platform was clear in 1957. Where best preserved on the S side, the platform has a level surface about 1 m above the present ground level. Elsewhere some hollows have been made into the plat-form, and heaps of stones have been dumped (some probably derived from investigations in the cairn). The platform is 35 m from E to W, by about 50 m across the E side and 35 m across the W side. A fence runs just outside the E edge and crosses the SE horn.

The cairn of cobbles is mainly bare but with some turf cover. It is 3.3 m high above ground level, though a little more measured from the S side. The edge cannot be defined precisely as it has been distorted by robbing and by the investigations, and on the E side it merges into the platform. The diameters are roughly between 28 and 33 m. In the highest part in the centre of the cairn the top of the roofless chamber is exposed.

The chamber is now only accessible from above. It is partly filled with a variable depth of loose stones, though at the E end it is possible to reach down through them to what appears to be floor level. A pair of portal stones forms the entry, 0.7 m wide. The stones are regular

ROS 11

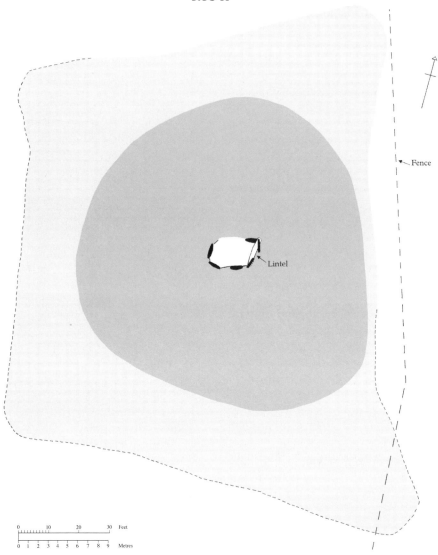

rectangular blocks of equal height, 1.15 and over 1.1 m long by 0.33 and about 0.27 m thick. They project only 0.8 and 0.5 m above the rubble on the floor, but their true height is 1.2 m or a little more. The portal stones bear a massive lintel set on its side and tilted to the W. It is over 2.85 m long by 0.4 m thick, and 1.63 m deep in the centre. To the E of the portal stones the structure is concealed by rubble.

The chamber is 4.2 m long by at least 2.5 m wide, and survives to a height of about 3.2 m above the floor. The lower part of the wall is built with spaced orthostats linked by walling. The orthostats are intact boulders with flat surfaces and rounded or pointed tops, except for one with a horizontal top. The walling reaches to the level of their shoulders. Above this, filling the spaces between the rounded tops of the orthostats and rising above them, the walls are built of layers of corbel stones, the uppermost flush with the top of the cairn. The corbel stones are either split slabs or flat boulders, generally about 0.2 m thick, and (where visible) up to 1 m long. The walls on the S side and W end of the chamber are fully visible except at the lowest level. The N wall of the chamber is largely hidden by corbel stones which have been displaced forwards and downwards, and which are in a highly precarious condition.

On the S side of the chamber there are two orthostats, 1.15 and 1.2 m long, and at the W end is an orthostat over 1.5 m long; all three are 0.3 m or more thick. The first orthostat is 0.28 m from the S portal stone, and the others are 0.95 and 0.33 m apart. The linking walling, best seen between the first and second orthostats, is of neatly laid split slabs with eight courses visible. The lower part of the N wall of the chamber is probably intact. At its W end part of a panel of neat walling running NE from the W orthostat can just be seen. At the E end, and butted against the N portal stone, there is an orthostat, 0.96 m long on the visible face (but longer behind) by 0.4 m thick. It is probable that one, or possibly two, orthostats are hidden behind the displaced corbel stones on the N side of the chamber. The tallest orthostat, at the W end of the chamber, can be calculated to be about 2.2 m high; the shortest orthostat, at the NE corner, is about 1.73 m high.

The upper parts of the walls on the S and W sides of the chamber consist of three or four layers of corbel stones which are more or less *in situ* (plate 3). Along the S side they oversail for 0.75 m, and across the W end only the uppermost layers oversail, but to such an extent that the edge of the top stone is only 2.45 m from the edge of the inward-tilted lintel. As already mentioned, the corbel stones along the N side of the chamber have all slumped inwards. At the SW corner the courses along the S and W sides are poorly bonded, and at the NW corner they appear not to have been bonded. The E wall of the chamber, above the portal stones, is formed by the lintel already described, its upper edge only 0.2 m below the top of the highest corbel stone at the W end (and when the lintel was vertical the top would have been slightly higher). At the SE corner of

the chamber the sides of the corbel stones lie against the face of the lintel, and at the NE corner the four somewhat displaced corbel stones that remain over the orthostat would similarly have butted against the lintel. The upper part of the chamber thus originally had a plan nearer rectangular than round, and the lack of adequate bonding at the corners has contributed to the instability of the corbelled part of the structure. Due to the inward movement of the N wall, which has been greater towards the W end, the plan of the top level is now triangular. It is likely that a layer of corbel stones is missing from the E part of each side wall, each of which is a little lower than the W part, but otherwise the walls appear to retain their original height. The chamber was probably roofed by three or four lintels at a height of 3.3 m.

The cairn was 'almost entire' in 1875 and the chamber does not seem to have been visible (ONB), but it had been exposed before 1900 (Brown). Maclean, in 1888, stated that the two cairns, Boath Long and Short, had been intact a century before, but 'within the last seventy years were removed for building houses and enclosures'. Evidently referring to the chamber in Boath Short, he says that it 'had a rude stair descending to the floor, and it had been the abode of a noted cateran from Lochaber', and relates his story.

The stone cist containing human remains found in 1863, recorded at Boath Short on the first edition of the OS 6-inch map, was (according to the ONB) in one of the small cairns in the immediate vicinity.

ROS 12. CARN GLAS, KILCOY

Parish Killearnan
Location on the Black Isle, 5 km ENE of Muir of Ord
Map reference NH 578520
NMRS number NH 55 SE 6
References Beaton 1882, 479; Donations 1925, 71; Woodham 1955; 1956a, 68, 71; 1956b, 23; Woodham and Woodham 1957a; Henshall 1963, 341, 342–3; RCAHMS 1979c, 7, no. 6; Close-Brooks 1983, 284–5

Plan chamber after Woodham and Woodham, cairn
ASH and JNGR
Excavation Woodham and Woodham 1955, 1956
Visited 11.7.56, 23.10.95

Description. Carn Glas is at 125 m OD in agricultural land sloping gently down from NW to SE. Its position provides extensive views across the Beauly Firth and to the hills beyond. Kilcoy North and South (ROS 23, 24) lie 900 m to the WSW and SW, and there are two bronze age cairns 170 and 200 m to the SSW.

The cairn was very large. In 1882 it seems to have been still virtually intact. The height was recorded as 6.4 m, and it covered 'a base of 1340 square yards' (Beaton), which gives a diameter of about 36 m. There is no reason to suggest that these measurements are not approximately correct. By 1906, when a barbed-and-tanged arrowhead and beaker sherds were found, the cairn had been greatly reduced, and at least part of the chamber had been exposed (Donations). At the time of the excavation in the 1950s, and when visited in 1995, the cairn was about 1 m high around the chamber. The uneven surface of the cairn is covered with grass but is extensively overgrown with gorse and other vegetation. Observation is also impeded by field-gathered stones which have been dumped around and on top of the remains of the cairn.

The cairn diameter appears to be roughly 35 m, but nowhere can the edge be identified with any confidence. The limit of ploughing defines the S and E sides, and the cairn merges into a spread of field-gathered stones on the NE and SW sides. A field-wall, the last in a

ROS 12

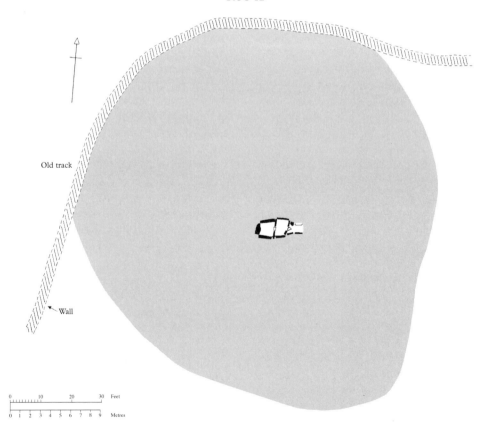

Old track

Wall

0   10   20   30   Feet

0 1 2 3 4 5 6 7 8 9   Metres

sequence of walls, curves round the NW side; the first edition 25-inch OS map surveyed in 1872 shows what is probably an earlier wall on this side. Investigation by Woodham and Woodham in the N quadrant of the cairn exposed the base of another wall, or bank, partly concentric with the existing wall and close to its S side (p. 109, 112, figure 3). This last wall was two-faced and infilled with rubble (only a short stretch of the last vestiges of this wall could be seen in 1995). The excavators suggested that it was the original retaining wall of the cairn, but it is almost unknown for retaining walls to be constructed in this way. Even if it were a later feature such as the edging of an early track, it probably indicates the original limit of the cairn on this side, and implies that the cairn diameter was indeed about 35 m.

In the centre of the cairn there is a small chamber (figure 16), only about 2.6 m long, which is approached by a passage facing E. The following description of the structure is taken from the excavation report (Woodham and Woodham), with some additional observations, as most of the structure can still be seen. It is built of close-fitting regular sandstone slabs (with one exception), all apparently intact, and mostly with horizontal upper surfaces. The excavators found that the outer part of the passage had been removed (though this may have been no more than a pair of portal stones at the entrance). Two orthostats remain on the S side of the passage, the inner set at an angle and so widening the inner part. The orthostats are 0.75 and 0.6 m long by about 0.15 m thick, and 0.44 and 0.53 m high. On the opposite side of the passage a flat slab was probably the lowest course of a stretch of walling, followed by a boulder orthostat 0.3 m long and 0.53 m high. The existing passage is about 1.2 m long by about 0.7 m wide at the E end.

A pair of portal stones, 0.45 m apart, forms the entry into the two-compartment chamber. They are 0.33 and 0.6 m long by about 0.14 m thick, and are about the same height as the adjacent passage orthostats. The S stone is markedly skew to the chamber axis. Between

them, let into the floor, was a triangular sill-stone nearly 0.1 m thick. At the inner end of the compartment was a second pair of portal stones, about 0.46 m apart, also with a sill-stone between them (the N portal stone has been removed and the entry is blocked by an upright slab). The stones were over 0.67 and 0.66 m long by 0.17 m thick. Each side of the outer compartment is composed of a large slab, 0.96 and 1.2 m long by about 0.2 m thick. On the S side a narrow gap between the side-slab and the S inner portal stone is filled by walling made of small stones. The N side-slab fits its allotted space neatly, but it has split vertically lengthwise, and by 1995 part of it was displaced. The compartment is about 1.2 m long by 1.45 m wide. A large flat triangular slab, 2 by 0.76 by 0.22 m, formerly lay across the NE corner of the compartment; the excavators had to move the slab to its present position outside the chamber on the N side.

The inner compartment is about 1.2 m long by 1.3 m wide. The back-slab is an impressive pointed block, leaning slightly to the W. It is 1.2 m long by 0.4 m thick. At 1.6 m high it is 0.73 m, or slightly more, taller than the side-slabs of the chamber which are all roughly the same height and a little taller than the passage orthostats. The side-slabs of the inner compartment fit closely corner-to-corner with the back-slab. The N side-slab is 1.55 m long by 0.2 m thick; the S side slab is a little lower and shorter, and rounded at the base. A panel of walling extends beneath the E end, and links the side-slab with the S inner portal stone.

At the time of the excavation the passage and chamber had a modern filling of loose stones. The clay floor was covered throughout by a layer of sand, 0.05 m deep, in which were occasional fragments of charcoal. The few finds were in this layer. There were a number of pieces of quartz in the passage. A tiny piece of burnt bone was found in the outer compartment. A leaf-shaped arrowhead, a flint flake, and neolithic and beaker sherds in separate deposits, were in the inner compartment. The N side of the inner compartment had been disturbed by a pit containing modern sheep burials. A barbed-and-tanged arrowhead and three sherds of a beaker had been recovered from the chamber in 1906.

FINDS
Artefacts. In the Royal Museum of Scotland (figures 32, 33).
1. Barbed-and-tanged arrowhead, speckled buff flint (EQ 345).
2. Leaf-shaped arrowhead, very finely worked, similar flint (EO 962).
3. Chip of similar flint, 25 mm long (EO 963).
4. Seven sherds from the rim, body and base of a beaker; decorated with zones of lattice and horizontal lines made by fine comb impressions; rather sandy black fabric, fine brown-buff surface (EO 961).
5. Many small rusticated sherds, probably all from one large pot; decorated with random finger-nail impressions and faint impressions of either a broken stick or twisted cord; friable heavily-gritted fabric, the walls over 25 mm thick but with the outer and inner surfaces broken apart, buff outside, black inside (EO 958–60).
6. Saddle quern, 620 by 470 mm, 130 mm thick (fully described in Close-Brooks) (EO 1116).
2–5 came from the sand layer in the inner compartment of the chamber, and some sherds of *5* were pressed into the clay floor; *6* was amongst the disturbed filling in the chamber. *1* and three sherds of *4* were found in 1906, but no details are recorded (the finding of these sherds is noted in the museum catalogue).
3, 5, not illustrated (but *5* is illustrated in Woodham and Woodham plate VIII, 1).

Bone. A tiny fragment of burnt bone (not certainly human) was found in the SW corner of the outer compartment.

ROS 13. CARN URNAN
(Carn Inenan, Cairn Irenan)

Parish Killearnan
Location at the W end of the Black Isle, 4 km ENE of Muir of Ord
Map reference NH 566522
NMRS number NH 55 SE 10
References Stuart 1868, 301; ONB 1872–3, No. 15, 6; Beaton 1882, 477–9; Childe 1944, 37–8; Woodham 1956a, 66, 68, 70; RCAHMS 1979c, 7, no. 5; Henshall 1963, 341, 343

Plan ASH and JNGR
Visited 28.4.97

Description. Located in an upland area of flat agricultural land at 160 m OD, there are wide views from the cairn in all directions. The Cairnside long cairn (ROS 60) is 650 m to the WNW, and Kilcoy North (ROS 23) is the same distance to the SE. The actual site of Carn Urnan is in an uncultivated corner of the garden of a croft house.

The cairn material has been almost entirely removed, leaving the kerb of the cairn, and the basal course of the passage and chamber walls, almost complete and nearly fully exposed. They are built of boulders of sandstone, or occasionally of conglomerate or schist. The cairn is surrounded by a stone circle. The whole area within the circle is covered with tussocky grass, and several bushes and small trees are growing between the circle and the cairn kerb.

The kerb is between 12 and 12.5 m in diameter. The relatively flat outer faces of the kerb-stones were carefully aligned to produce a regular outer face to the kerb, and they seem to have been set in a number of flattened arcs rather than in an accurate circle. The tops of the stones are irregular, but all appear to be undamaged. There are five gaps where a stone is missing, and on the W side one stone lies where it has fallen outwards. The boulders round the S half of the circuit are of an impressive size. The entrance faces SSW, between kerb-stones 0.67 and 0.6 m high, and 0.65 m apart. There are larger kerb-stones round the SE quadrant of the kerb; they measure up to 1.3 m long and up to 1 m thick, and the tallest on the SSE projects for 1 m. In the SW quadrant the kerb-stones are only slightly smaller, and the tallest is 0.8 m high. The stones diminish in size round the N half of the kerb, and the smallest of all behind the chamber measure about 0.43 by 0.45 m, and are about 0.4 m high.

The passage is about 4.5 m long, including the kerb-stones at the entrance, and at the inner end the passage is 0.83 m wide. It is filled

ROS 13

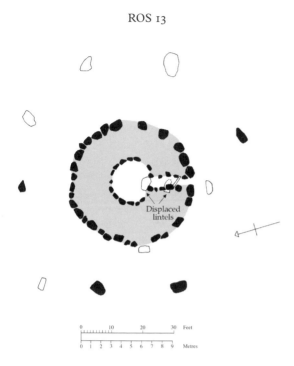

Displaced
lintels

| 0 | 10 | 20 | 30 | Feet |

| 0 | 1 | 2 | 3 | 4 | 5 | 6 | 7 | 8 | 9 | Metres |

with grass-covered stones, and the boulders forming the basal course are more visible on their outer sides where cairn material has been removed. The boulders are smaller than those used in the kerb; the tallest stone, on the E side, projects 0.52 m. Outside the entrance is a prone slab, 1.4 m long by 0.6 m wide and 0.4 m thick, which is likely to have been a lintel. A displaced and partly hidden lintel lies obliquely across the passage, and a third displaced lintel has its E end buried in the passage filling. A fourth lintel has been tumbled into the chamber from the inner end of the passage, and rests against the stones that form the entrance to the chamber. All four lintels are of similar size.

The chamber is about 3.8 m in diameter. The basal course of the wall consists of boulders arranged to give a fairly regular inner face, and not differing greatly in size. At most, they appear to be 0.6 m high, but they project less than this and some of them are almost hidden.

Seven stones of the surrounding stone circle remain, three of them fallen. To the SSE of the entrance is a fine almost rectangular stone with a rounded top. It is 1.55 m long by 0.8 m thick, and 1.95 m high. Clockwise, the next stone is an intact boulder which leans towards the kerb. It is approximately rectangular in plan with a rounded top, 1.65 m long above ground level by 0.9 m thick, and when upright it would be 1.45 m high. The third stone is a rather irregular block which may have been damaged long ago; it is 1.3 m long by 1.1 m thick, and 1.55 m high. The NNE stone is an intact almost triangular boulder with a flat face set towards the kerb, and a rounded pointed top; it is 1.05 m long by 0.6 m thick, and 1 m high. The three stones round the E side have evidently fallen outwards. The first is 1.65 m long and 0.9 m wide by 0.45 m thick, and it has probably been damaged down the SE side and at the SW end. The next stone is irregular in plan, and has almost certainly been damaged along the S side; it was over 1.9 m long and 1.0 m wide by over 0.3 m thick. The last stone is an irregular block, 2.3 m long and 1.3 m wide by 0.8 m thick. The upright stones are between 5.1 and 3.9 m from the kerb. Even allowing for the probability that there was originally a stone in each of the wider gaps on the SW and NNW, the spacing of the stones was evidently irregular (figure 38, 1). An intact but relatively small block lying outside the circle on the NW side is unlikely to have been a standing stone.

The cairn had evidently been denuded well before 1866 (un-named in Stuart), and by 1873 the monument was in its present condition, with the stone circle consisting of four upright and three fallen stones (ONB).

ROS 14. CLACHAN BIORACH

Parish Kiltearn
Location on the NW side of the Cromarty Firth, 3 km NNE of Dingwall
Map reference NH 562617
NMRS number NH 56 SE 4
References OSA I, 1791, 291–2; NSA 1845, 321; ONB 1875, No. I, 97; Maclean 1889, 304; Henshall 1963, 344; RCAHMS 1979a, 7, no. 6
Visited 16.5.95

Description. The site of this destroyed monument is in the cultivated land which rises from the NW shore of the firth. The monument was on a low knoll at 169 m OD, from which there are wide views over the firth and the Black Isle.

There can be little doubt that the monument described in 1791 was a denuded chambered cairn. It 'consists of a single row of twelve large stones, placed upright, and so disposed as to form two ovals, which are joined to each other. The areas of these ovals are equal; they are 13 ft [4 m] from east to west, and 10 ft [3 m] in the middle from north to south. At the west end of one of them is a stone, which rises 8 ft [2.4 m] above the surface of the earth; the other stones are from 4 to 6 ft [1.2 to 1.8 m] long. There is also, in the middle of this oval, a flat stone. . . . These ovals are situated on the top of an eminence, round which are marked out three concentric circles; one at the bottom, another 28 paces above the former, and the third 12 paces higher, immediately surrounding the ovals. The circumference of the first is 80, of the second 50, and of the third, or highest circle, 35 paces' (OSA, repeated by Maclean). The monument was almost entirely removed in the late 1830s (NSA).

Two stones were recorded in 1875 (ONB, and plotted on the first edition OS 6-inch map). 'The stones fell during a storm in 1860, when one of them was smashed. The unbroken one is large and in form is an isosceles triangle being very sharp at the apex. The other stone was of the same shape before it was broken – it is now a shapeless boulder. The name signifies "Sharp pointed Stones" which was quite descriptive when the stones were standing, pointed ends upwards.' The stones measured 3.6 by 2 m and 2 m square.

In 1995 the farmer told the writers that the stones were broken up and removed about 1950.

ROS 15. CNOC CHAORNAIDH NORTH-WEST

Now re-numbered SUT 69, and included in Henshall and Ritchie 1995, 142–3. This change was due to local government reorganisation in 1975, when the parish of Kincardine and Croick became part of Sutherland District.

ROS 16. CNOC CHAORNAIDH CENTRE

Not now considered to be a chambered cairn, but described with the chambered cairns of Sutherland in Henshall and Ritchie 1995, 153. Inclusion with the Sutherland cairns was due to local government reorganisation in 1975, when the parish of Kincardine and Croick became part of Sutherland District.

ROS 17. CNOC CHAORNAIDH SOUTH-EAST

Now re-numbered SUT 70, and included in Henshall and Ritchie 1995, 143–4. This change was due to local government reorganisation in 1975, when the parish of Kincardine and Croick became part of Sutherland District.

ROS 18. CNOC NAVIE
(Knocknavie, Carn na Croiche)

Parish Rosskeen
Location 2.5 km N of Alness
Map reference NH 656722
NMRS number NH 67 SE 11
References NSA 1845, 271; Maclean 1886, 331–2; Henshall 1963, 345, 347; RCAHMS 1979a, 7, no. 7
Plan ASH and JNGR
Visited 2.7.58, 26.5.94

Description. The cairn is just below the summit of Cnoc Navie, a steep flat-topped hill covered by conifer forest. The site of the cairn is level, at 235 m OD. If free of trees, the cairn would command extensive views in all directions except to the NE.

The large cairn, said to have been 6 m high, was almost totally demolished for dyke-building in 1826 (Maclean). A little depth of cairn material remains, and in the recent past it was ploughed through and planted. The trees have been felled and the surface of the cairn has

ROS 18

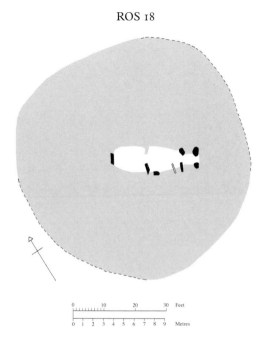

```
0        10        20        30   Feet
|||||||||||
0  1  2  3  4  5  6  7  8  9   Metres
```

been left uneven, and by 1994 it was thickly covered with blaeberries and moss. The surviving rim of cairn material is at most 1 m high on the NE and W sides, and the cairn edge can be traced for about half its circuit. The diameter of the cairn is between 22 and 23 m.

Seven orthostats belonging to a passage and chamber just project above the vegetation, and beside most of them holes have been dug down to near the old ground surface. Five metres within the SE edge of the cairn is a pair of portal stones which presumably formed the entrance to the passage. They are intact unshapely rounded granitic boulders set about 0.6 m apart. The stones are 0.55 and over 0.92 m long by 0.45 and 0.6 m thick, and 0.48 and 0.55 m high. A second pair of portal stones formed the entrance to the chamber. The SW stone is a sandstone slab and the NE stone is an intact boulder. They are 0.7 m apart, 0.93 and 0.75 m long by 0.3 and 0.55 m thick, and 0.55 and 0.8 m high. The passage, including both pairs of portal stones, was about 1.8 m long.

Although little of the chamber survives, there is enough to show that it was large, and similar in size and proportions to the bipartite chamber in the King's Head Cairn (ROS 25) 5 km to the ENE. The Cnoc Navie chamber was 6.6 m long, and the comparison indicates that it was probably divided into two compartments each slightly over 3 m long. The three remaining orthostats are sandstone slabs, certainly or probably with broken tops. A side-slab on the SW side of the outer compartment is 0.6 m long (it was visible for a length of over 1 m in 1958) by 0.4 m thick, and the shattered top is 0.6 m high. An orthostat set nearly transversely to the chamber axis 0.45 m to the NW is the SW member of a pair of inner portal stones. It is 1.1 m long by 0.3 m thick and 0.9 m high. The back-slab is set across the axis and leans to the NW; it is 1.1 m long by 0.3 m thick, and 0.75 m high, and it is 0.36 m taller than the NE stone at the passage entrance. In the outer compartment a thin vertical slab parallel with the SW outer portal stone does not appear to be *in situ* though its base is near the old ground level. (See figure 13 for a tentative reconstruction of the plan.)

The folk-tale regarding the name of the cairn (Cairn of the Gallows) is given in NSA. Human bones including a skull were found in the cairn (not necessarily in the chamber) in 1826, and were thought to be the remains of executed men buried in the cairn in the 17th century (Maclean).

ROS 19. CONTIN MAINS
(Pris Maree, Preas Mairi)

Parish Contin
Location in Strathconon, 2.3 km SW of Strathpeffer, on the edge of the village of Contin
Map reference NH 460558
NMRS number NH 45 NE 5
References ONB 1876, No. 6, 43; Pitt Rivers 1885a, 137–9; RCAHMS 1943, 41–2; Childe 1944, 32–3; Henshall 1963, 346, 347
Plan ASH and JNGR
Visited 13.7.56, 21.10.96

Description. In the agricultural land on the NE side of the strath, a little above the flat valley floor at 40 m OD, on a slight rise, are the orthostats of a large chamber. It is within a private burial-ground, which formerly was well maintained but is now becoming overgrown.

The burial-ground is rectangular with the long axis aligned E to W. Within the high boundary wall was a narrow border and a path which edged the raised rectangular plot where the burials were made. The chamber is at the SE corner of the plot, with the interior of the chamber at the same level as the path which edges it on the E and S sides, and with the higher ground, 0.7 m above the path, enclosing it on the N and W sides. It is likely that the raised area is partly composed of cairn material. A prostrate slab, about 2 m long and presumably derived from the chamber, has been used to revet the burial plot 1.4 m N of the chamber.

The chamber was in its present condition when first recorded in 1875 (ONB), and presumably had been so for a long time. Seven orthostats of the chamber survive, all of them seemingly intact and exposed for nearly their full heights. The chamber was entered from the ESE between a pair of well-matched pillar-like portal stones 0.7 m apart. Both stones lean slightly to the E. The S stone is 0.43 m long by 0.3 m thick, and 0.9 m high; its partner is similar and slightly shorter. On their W side is a thin slab, 0.7 m long, set on edge to form a sill only 0.14 m high. The outer compartment is 2.1 m long, and is divided from the inner compartment by a second pair of portal stones set 0.8 m apart. They are 0.8 and 0.7 m long by up to 0.3 and 0.22 m thick, and 0.84 and 0.7 m high; they have horizontal upper surfaces. Between them is a flat sill-stone, its upper surface flush with the ground. The N side of the outer compartment is almost entirely filled by a large rectangular block of stone, 1.76 m long by 0.36 m thick, and 0.83 m high. The top surface is horizontal, and three basins (formerly recorded as cup-marks) have been made into it long ago and are now considerably weathered. They vary between about 0.3 to 0.25 m in diameter, and 0.05 to 0.14 m deep.

Each side of the inner compartment is formed by a large block. That on the S side is particularly massive, and is even longer above

ROS 19

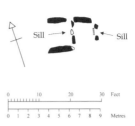

ground level; it may have tilted slightly to the S. The blocks are 2.25 and 1.9 m long by 0.5 and 0.4 m thick, and 1 and 0.67 m high. The inner compartment is 2.3 m wide, and it was probably approximately square in plan, but it lacks the back-slab. The chamber was at least 4.6 m long. (See figure 15 for a reconstruction of the chamber plan.)

In 1876 a cist was observed 'adjacent' to the chamber (ONB). It was 1 m long by 0.45 to 0.3 m wide, made of three thin slabs, their upper edges flush with the ground. Childe saw two thin slabs exposed 9 m W of the chamber, which he thought might have been part of a cist, but no such slabs could be seen below the undergrowth in 1996.

ROS 20. CROFTCRUNIE

See pp. 241–2.

ROS 21. EASTER ALNESSFERRY

See p. 238.

ROS 22. HEIGHTS OF BRAE
(Clachan Gorach)

Parish Fodderty
Location 3.5 km NW of Dingwall
Map reference NH 514615
NMRS number NH 56 SW 2
References NSA 1845, 253; Perrott 1858, 394; ONB 1875, No. 9, 64; Pitt Rivers 1885a, 146–7; RCAHMS 1943, 35–8; Childe 1944, 31; Henshall 1963, 346–7; RCAHMS 1979a, 8, no. 10
Plan ASH and JNGR
Visited 13.7.56, 16.5.95

Description. The cairn is on the top of the ridge that divides Strath Peffer and Strath Sgitheach, at 244 m OD. The site is a little above the fields on the S side of the ridge, in undulating rough grazing which extends down the N side of the ridge and across Strath Sgitheach and beyond. There are magnificent views in all directions, though the steepness of the ridge means that the floors of the straths are not visible. Balnacrae (ROS 4) is in view 4 km to the NNE.

The cairn occupies a prominent knoll, and, like the surrounding ground, it is covered by turf and heather and bears some juniper and gorse. The cairn has been greatly reduced and the surface in the centre is uneven, but mostly the cairn material is a metre or more deep. The edge of the cairn is difficult to trace as it merges into the slope of the knoll, but a slight break in slope indicates approximate diameters of 30 m from NNW to SSE by 25.5 m transversely. There are two chambers in the cairn,

to the N and S of the centre; both are aligned E to W and are less than 2 m apart.

Eleven orthostats relate to the more complete S chamber and its passage. The entrance to the passage is marked by a pair of portal stones about 7.5 m within the ESE edge of the cairn. They are 0.9 and 0.7 m long by 0.23 and 0.18 m thick. The S stone leans to the E, and if upright it would be about 0.6 m high, and about the same height as the N stone though this projects only 0.33 m. A second pair of portal stones forms the entry to the outer compartment. They are 0.7 and 1.03 m long by 0.5 and 0.13 m thick, and project 0.55 m, though the S stone is the taller by 0.2 m. In both cases the entries between the stones are 0.73 m wide. The passage was about 1.4 m long.

The outer compartment is roughly 2 m long, extending to a third pair of portal stones. They are 0.56 m apart, 0.9 and 0.65 m long by 0.45 and 0.33 m thick; the S stone projects

ROS 22

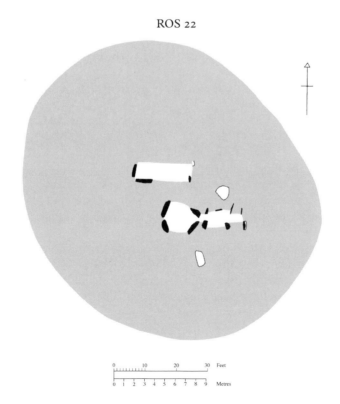

| 0 | | 10 | | 20 | | 30 | Feet |

| 0 | 1 | 2 | 3 | 4 | 5 | 6 | 7 | 8 | 9 | Metres |

0.8 m and is 0.16 m taller than its partner. These stones and the S outer portal stone are intact boulders. The N wall of the outer compartment is indicated by a slab which hardly projects; it is over 0.7 m long (the W end is not visible) by 0.14 m thick.

The polygonal inner compartment is about 3.25 m long. It retains four orthostats, which are large weathered blocks with flat faces (plate 2). Presumably the gaps of 1.8 and 2.0 m on the S and N sides were once filled with two more orthostats. The SE orthostat leans slightly to the SE, and is set 0.26 m from the adjacent portal stone. The NE orthostat leans considerably to the SW, and this displacement has reduced the entry to only 0.37 m wide. The SW orthostat leans to the NE; the upright NW orthostat is the tallest stone in the cairn. Clockwise from the SE, the orthostats are 1.6, 1.25, 1.75 and 1.22 m long, and they are 0.4 to 0.55 m thick. The tallest orthostat projects 1.57 m; the tops of the stones on the S side of the inner compartment are 0.65 m lower, and the NE stone is 1 m lower. The top of the N inner portal stone is 1.6 m lower than the tallest orthostat, and the N outer and N entrance portal stones (which may have been reduced in height) are 0.4 m lower still. It follows that the true height of the tallest orthostat is well over 2 m.

The rectangular N chamber is represented by four orthostats. On the E side the tips of a pair of portal stones hardly project. They are 1 m apart, 0.6 and over 0.43 m long, and the N stone leans acutely to the E. The back-slab, 5.35 m W of the S portal stone, is 1.25 m long by 0.33 m thick. Its broken top projects 0.7 m, 0.5 m above the intact horizontal upper surface of the side-slab. The latter is 1.6 m long by 0.4 m thick.

A large elongated slab, 1.6 by 0.7 by 0.4 m, lies to the S of the S chamber, and a less regular slab, 1.4 by 1.17 by 0.4 m, lies to the N of the outer compartment.

The cairn was already in its present condition in 1838 (NSA). The folklore, that the orthostats are human beings turned to stone for dancing on the sabbath, which is said to explain the gaelic name (translated as The Foolish Stones), is given by Perrott.

ROS 23. KILCOY NORTH
(Kilcoy IV)

Parish Killearnan
Location on the Black Isle, 4 km ENE of Muir of Ord
Map reference NH 570517
NMRS number NH 55 SE 2
References Woodham 1956a, 86; Henshall 1963, 347–8; RCAHMS 1979c, 8, no. 12
Plan ASH and JNGR
Visited 11.7.56, 23.10.95

Description. The cairn is at 130 m OD, in a field which slopes down gently from N to S. Kilcoy South (ROS 24) is 115 m to the S and Carn Glas (ROS 12) is 900 m to the ENE. There are wide views from the site to the Beauly Firth and beyond.

The cairn has been reduced in height, allowing some orthostats of a chamber to protrude; also field-gathered stones have been added to the cairn in recent times. The edge of the cairn is defined by the limit of ploughing, and its original size and shape are uncertain. As it now exists it is oval, 21.5 m NW to SE by 15 m transversely, with the fairly flat centre part about 1.5 m high measured from the lower SE edge. The orthostats are SE of the centre. Most of the surface of the cairn is covered with coarse herbage.

The group of six or seven orthostats appears to belong to a chamber with an E to W axis, probably consisting of two compartments, and rather irregular in plan. On the NE side of the group are two orthostats, which probably belong to the N side of an outer compartment. The E orthostat (possibly a portal stone) is an intact rounded boulder, 0.6 m long by over 0.5 m thick, projecting 0.5 m. To the W is the stump of a granite block, 0.64 by 0.27 m, projecting 0.44 m. Opposite them is a flat slab sloping down from S to N. It is 0.75 m wide by 0.25 m thick, and is exposed for 0.7 m. It may have fallen outwards from an upright position about 2.1 m from the last orthostat, and at

ROS 23

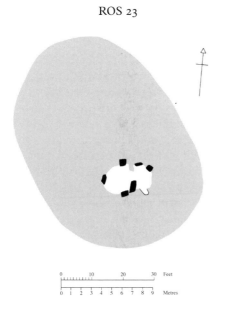

0   10   20   30 Feet

0 1 2 3 4 5 6 7 8 9 Metres

Map reference NH 570515
NMRS number NH 55 SE 3
References Woodham 1955; 1956a, 86; 1956b, 23–4;
1958; Woodham and Woodham 1957b; 1958;
Henshall 1963, 348–9; RCAHMS 1979c, 8, no. 13;
Close-Brooks 1983, 284–5; MacGregor and Loney
1997
Plan Woodham and Woodham, revised by ASH and
JNGR (also figures 18 and 29, 1)
Excavation Woodham and Woodham 1956, 1957,
1958; MacGregor and Loney 1997
Visited 11.7.56, 24.10.95, 5–8.8.97

Description. The cairn is at 125 m OD in agricultural land which slopes down gently from N to S. Kilcoy North (ROS 23) is 115 m to the N, and Carn Glas (ROS 12) is 950 m to the ENE. There are wide views to the S over the Beauly Firth and to the hills beyond.

Before the excavation of the remains of the cairn in the 1950s, the tops of two orthostats bearing a lintel could be seen, an arrangement that suggested a passage entrance which appeared to be at the centre of a deep horned forecourt (Woodham 1956a). Between 1956 and 1958 the chamber was excavated by A. A. and M. F. Woodham, and the area outside the entrance was partly investigated. Only brief accounts of this work were published, and subsequently the chamber was partly re-filled with debris. In order to provide a more detailed account of the monument the passage and chamber were re-opened in 1997, and limited excavation was undertaken in the forecourt area. The chamber and the excavation were filled in by the excavators, and the part of a field wall, which crosses the cairn and chamber (dismantled in 1957), was rebuilt, with the consequence that little of the structure is now visible. The following account has been compiled from Woodham's records and conversations with him, from MacGregor and Loney's report, and from personal observations in 1995 and during the work in 1997. The axis of the main part of the chamber lies ESE to WNW, but for ease of description it is assumed to lie E to W.

The cairn has been greatly reduced and disturbed, remaining at most 1.4 m high

right angles to the orthostat next described. This is an intact block with a wide horizontal upper surface, set transversely to the axis and lower than the other orthostats. It is 1.2 m long by 0.5 m thick, and projects 0.53 m. There can be little doubt that it is the S stone of a pair of portal stones, of which the N stone is missing.

The three orthostats to the W belong to the walls of an inner compartment. On the S side, and almost touching the portal stone, is a block which has shattered down its W side; it is now 0.77 m long by 0.4 m thick, and projects 0.65 m. Opposite is a square block which may be intact, 0.6 by 0.6 m and projecting 1 m. At the W end of the chamber is a pointed boulder, 1 m long by 0.4 m thick, which projects 1 m. It is probable that a missing orthostat once filled the gaps of 1.8 and 1.55 m on either side of the W orthostat. The compartment is 2.5 m long and wide. (See figure 14 for a tentative reconstruction of the plan.)

ROS 24. KILCOY SOUTH
(Kilcoy West, Kilcoy V)

Parish Killearnan
Location on the Black Isle, 4 km ENE of Muir of Ord

ROS 24

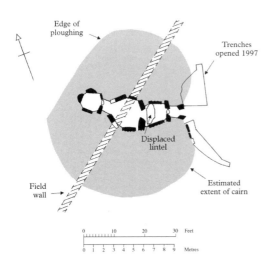

Edge of
ploughing

Trenches
opened 1997

Displaced
lintel

Field
wall

Estimated
extent of cairn

0   10   20   30 Feet

0 1 2 3 4 5 6 7 8 9 Metres

around the main part of the chamber. A field wall running from NE to SW rises over the centre of the cairn. Many slabs of moderate size, presumably from the upper part of the chamber, lie about the cairn and were removed from its E side during the excavations. On the NW side the cairn has been clipped by ploughing which has left a clear artificial edge. Elsewhere the edge is obscured by disturbance and by dumped field-gathered stones, as well as by the rank vegetation which covers the whole area. In 1997 a trench opened on the SE side of the cairn revealed that the front of the cairn was only slightly concave (plate 5). Three kerb-stones run southwards for 2.5 m from the portal stone on the S side of the entrance. The kerb-stones are rather irregular boulders set on end, the tallest 0.7 m high, and the small gaps between them are roughly packed with slabs. A fourth kerb-stone may be missing from a wider gap beside the portal stone. The southernmost kerb-stone leans outwards, and beyond this any continuation of the kerb is hidden below rubble. On the N side of the entrance the edge of the cairn is hidden behind banked rubble. It is probable that the rest of the cairn was round in plan, with a diameter of roughly 16 m (the profile of the field wall which runs level on either side of the cairn gives the best indication

of its size). A short distance from the front of the cairn the ground level drops away.

The area in front of the entrance, which formerly appeared to be a deep forecourt defined by projecting horns, was investigated in 1958. A considerable depth of unstructured stone was removed from this area, and on the S side a curved line of stones was exposed which was interpreted as the NE face of the SE horn. The 1958 trench which ran along the foot of the supposed horn was re-opened in 1997, and it was seen that these stones rest on a layer of root-filled loam 0.05 m thick, clearly a turf-line of no great age, and this in turn rested on the sandy subsoil. Thus it was evident that the supposed horn consisted of dumped field-gathered stones. A second trench was opened in 1997 in the N part of the forecourt area, but was only partly excavated when it was revealed that the bank of stony material, which had been regarded as the NE horn, is largely composed of field-gathered stones and has a ragged face curving to the NE. In front of the cairn, in the parts of the forecourt area examined in 1997, there remained only a thin spread of cobbles and small stones on the subsoil, and, on the N side, several small patches of charcoal. In 1958 a trench had been dug eastwards from the portal stones, and a patch of charcoal was found which stretched 2.5 m E from the portal stones by 3 m across. Presumably the field stones partly overlie some tumbled cairn material, but if there had been any formal blocking material in front of the entrance to the passage, this would have been found.

The orthostats of the passage and chamber are impressive blocks, generally rectangular in plan, with flat faces, and most of them are intact. There are four pairs of portal stones, all about 1 m high, which have horizontal, or nearly horizontal, upper surfaces. The walls of the ante-chamber and main chamber are built almost entirely with orthostats, and the small gaps between them are filled with narrow panels of fine dry walling. These orthostats are 0.3 m or so thick on their exposed upper surfaces, and probably considerably more at a lower level (thicknesses of individual orthostats are only given when they can be seen to be significantly over 0.3 m). In height the wall orthostats vary between 1.1 and 1.4 m; the shortest and tallest are on the S side of the main chamber. Behind the main chamber is an inner compartment, similarly built, but somewhat smaller in scale. Unexpectedly, four of the chamber orthostats were not firmly set on flat bases. In the case of two portal stones it seems that the overriding requirement was a horizontal upper surface to carry the end of a lintel; possibly the reason was the same for two orthostats at the inner end of the main chamber. Equally unexpectedly, the back-slab of the inner compartment was insecurely seated just above ground level (plates 5, 6, 7; figure 18).

The entry to the passage is 0.55 m wide between a well-matched pair of portal stones. They are almost square in plan with vertical sides, about 0.5 m across, and are set diagonally to form a splayed entrance. The passage walls are only about 0.6 m long. The lower part of each wall consists of an upright stone stretching almost its full length, a boulder on the S side, and a slab on the N side. Above the boulder there are a few rounded stones of the original walling, and the slab opposite is neatly packed around with tiny slabs. The passage is 1.2 m wide.

The entry to the ante-chamber is 0.68 m wide between the second pair of portal stones. Over them was a slightly displaced lintel which was removed during the original excavation. The portal stones are over 0.7 m long (their outer ends are hidden) by 0.5 and 0.4 m thick. Between them, embedded in the floor, was a flat sill-stone covering a shallow hollow containing blackened stones and charcoal. The ante-chamber is 2 m long, and it expands slightly westwards to a maximum width of 1.7 m. The orthostat on the S side is 1.5 m long, and that on the N side is slightly longer, but less at ground level. At each end of each orthostat there are panels of neat walling, mostly of thin horizontal slabs, and mostly of exactly the required length. The triangular gap between the N portal stone and the N orthostat is particularly carefully filled with a stack of

eight slabs. The panels of walling at the NW and SW corners have a substantial stone as the lowest course, and the panels remain to their original height of nearly 0.9 m, each topped by a corbel stone.

The entry into the main chamber is 0.65 m wide between the third pair of portal stones, of similar size to the second pair. The top of the S stone is horizontal, but the base slopes up to the S and only the N part rests on the ground. The stone is supported along each side by chock stones which extend beneath it. The portal stones carried a lintel, but about 1960 it was displaced to lie across the W end of the ante-chamber. (When the chamber was re-opened in 1997 it was not possible for safety reasons to expose the lintel fully; the top surface, originally the W face, was entirely visible, the E and W sides, originally the top and bottom surfaces, were partly visible, and the lower surface, originally the E face, was hidden.) The lintel is a massive rather irregular boulder 2 m long, and in the centre it was about 0.9 m deep and about 0.75 m wide. It tapers towards each end, and the original lower surface and W face were flat for most of their length. Above the N portal stone the uneven lower surface of the lintel was steadied by an eke-stone. The entry below the lintel was found blocked with large flat slabs, and in crevices amongst these were pockets of charcoal, burnt bone, and a sherd (Woodham 1956b, 24).

The main chamber is 3 m long by 2.4 m wide at the E end. There are two orthostats on each side, the eastern pair parallel with the chamber axis and the western pair placed skew to form an entry in the NW corner. On the S side of the chamber the E orthostat has an almost rectangular face, and is 1.5 m long above ground level. The adjacent orthostat is curious in that it has a nearly triangular face, with the horizontal top 1.44 m long and the vertical NW end 1.4 m high, and the lower edge so curved that less than half of it rests on the ground. The SE part of the stone is underpinned by small horizontal slabs which merge into the walling linking the orthostat to its neighbour. On the N side of the chamber the E orthostat has a maximum length of 1.1 m, and it contracts towards the base and to a pointed top. The crevice between it and the portal stone is filled with walling, and between it and the W orthostat walling survives to about 1 m high. The W orthostat (now leaning to the SE) is an angular block with a flat ripple-marked surface. Its total length is 1.6 m, but only a part of the lower edge rests on the ground. The SW part of the upper edge appears to have been broken, and possibly the orthostat once matched more nearly that on the SW side of the entry.

In the ante-chamber and main chamber, on either side of the third pair of portal stones, several corbel stones survive at roughly 1 m above floor level, and overhang the walling below by up to 0.2 m.

To the W of the main chamber there is less depth of cairn material, and the structure is more damaged. The axis of this part of the chamber differs by about 18° from that of the outer part. Access is between the orthostats at the W end of the main chamber, 0.7 m apart at the narrowest point above ground level. A very short, but wide, passage leads to the innermost compartment. On the S side of the passage an upright slab, which stretches almost the full length of the wall, forms the lowest course. The better preserved N wall, which remains 0.7 m high, consists of a similar slab, together with a little additional walling above it and also running eastwards under the sloping lower edge of the adjacent orthostat.

The inner compartment is almost circular, about 1.7 m in diameter. It is entered between a pair of portal stones, which, like the third pair, are set skew to the axis to continue the curve of the walls. The S portal stone is 0.8 m long by 0.45 m thick at the S end. It is 0.9 m high with a horizontal upper surface, and the pointed base penetrates the subsoil at the S end. The N portal stone (which in 1997 was found lying across the floor of the compartment) is a rectangular block, which was 0.57 m long and 1 m high when in place. In 1997 the recess occupied by this stone was precisely defined by walling which had butted against each side, and by the cobbles which had been closely

packed against its E face. The entry between the portal stones narrowed slightly to about 0.4 m wide at the top. On the floor between the portal stones were two stones, laid horizontally one above the other, and exactly fitting the space; possibly they were the remains of blocking.

The orthostat on the S side of the compartment (by 1997 leaning to the N) is 0.9 m long and was 0.85 m high. The N orthostat is about 1.1 m long and up to 0.5 m thick, and is 1.08 m high. It and the back-slab are unusual in being rounded boulders, though with a flat face set facing the chamber. The back-slab (which by 1997 had fallen westwards into an almost prone position) is 0.9 m long by 0.5 m thick. It was 1 m high when upright, but the jagged top indicates that it had been damaged long ago. The base, which is slightly pointed, had been set on small stones 0.1 m above ground level. The five orthostats of the inner compartment are linked by two or more courses of thin slabs, except on the SW side where there is one thin upright slab.

On the floor of the passage, ante-chamber and main chamber there were several patches of charcoal, which, with the exception of the two in the passage, also contained cremated bone (figure 31). Some charcoal and bones were also found in the gap between the orthostats in the SE corner of the main chamber (the only gap in which there was no walling), and a single beaker sherd lay immediately in front of the SW orthostat.

As mentioned above, the blocking between the ante-chamber and the main chamber contained two pockets of charcoal and burnt bone about 0.6 m above the floor, and one of them also contained a sherd of coarse pottery. Over the floor deposits in the main chamber, the inner passage and inner compartment, but not in the ante-chamber or passage, was a layer of clean sand. It was between 0.15 to 0.23 m deep in the main chamber and increased in depth in the inner passage, and filled the inner compartment almost to the tops of the orthostats. There were sherds of several beakers on the sand, in the centre of the main chamber and at the entry to the inner passage. Sherds of a single distinctive beaker (*8*) lay on the sand, or in the lower part of the stony filling above, at the inner end of the inner passage.

The ante-chamber, and above the sand in the main chamber, were filled with large slabs, which included a saddle quern. Some beaker sherds in the centre of the main chamber, about 0.46 m above the floor, were presumably also in the slab filling. (See ¶ 6.2–5 and figure 31 for discussion of the deposits in the chamber.)

FINDS
Artefacts. In the Royal Museum of Scotland (except *9, 14*) (figures 32, 33).
1. Sherds of a beaker, reconstructed to give a complete profile but lacking the base; a cordon below the rim; decorated with comb impressions; hard, dark fabric, burnished red outer surface (EO 1046).
2. Rim sherd and wall sherd of a beaker; decorated with cord impressions; worn sandy buff-pink fabric (EO 1047).
3. Two rim sherds probably from the same beaker; decorated with cord impressions, including two lines inside the rim; one sherd with fine buff-pink surface, the other greatly worn, gritty buff fabric (EO 1048).
4. Sherds of a beaker, mainly from the rim and neck, two from the shoulder angle, but none from the base; two cordons below the rim; decorated with fine cord impressions; hard red fabric, burnished outside, a few sherds scorched (EO 1049).
5. Sherds of a beaker, from the rim, neck, and shoulder, and one including the basal angle; decoration and fabric similar to *4*, but the cord-impressed lines are more widely spaced and the walls are thicker (EO 1050).
6. Sherds from the rim and neck of a large beaker; a cordon below the rim; decorated with deep random impressions; hard fabric similar to that of *5*, vestiges of burnishing outside and on the rim, the dark surface mainly scorched buff-pink (EO 1051).
7. Wall sherd of a beaker, evidently from immediately above the base; undecorated. It may come from *2* or *3*, or from a pot not otherwise represented.
8. Sherds of a beaker, sufficient surviving to reconstruct the profile; three slight cordons between paired grooves on the neck; decorated with three zones of lattice or chevrons and

horizontal lines, executed by incised lines, though some horizontal lines appear to be made with a fine comb; buff surface, heavily tempered friable dark fabric with fine grits, the base scorched (EO 1052).
9. Sherd of coarse pottery, 'indistinguishable from that found at Carn Glas' (ROS 12).
10. Quern, somewhat irregular in shape but seemingly complete, with a concave grinding surface off-centre, 520 by 490 mm, 160 mm thick (fully described by Close-Brooks) (EO 1115).
11. Scraper made on a flake of mottled buff flint retaining the cortex on one face.
12. Scraper made on a flake of brown flint.
13. Flake of speckled pale grey flint, 14 by 9 mm.
14. Flint flake.
1–6 came from the main chamber, lying on the sand layer; *8* was in the inner passage, probably in the stone filling just above the sand layer; *9* was in the blocking between the ante-chamber and the main chamber; *10* was in the slab filling of the ante-chamber; *14* was between the entrance portal stones. *7, 11–13*, also eight small sherds (belonging to *3, 4*, and *5*, or unattributable), were unstratified, found in 1997.
7, 9, 13, 14 not illustrated.
Human remains. Cremated bone, assumed to be human, with charcoal, was found on the floor in the ante-chamber and the main chamber, also in two crevices in the blocking between the ante-chamber and the main chamber (see ¶ 6.2).

ROS 25. KING'S HEAD CAIRN

Parish Kilmuir Easter
Location 7 km NE of Alness
Map reference NH 697751
NMRS number NH 67 NE 3
References NSA 1845, 305; Maclean 1886, 335–6; ISSFC 1899b, 363; Davidson 1946, 30–31; Henshall 1963, 349, 350; 1972, 563; RCAHMS 1979a, 8, no. 11
Plan ASH and JNGR
Visited 14.7.56, 24.5.94

Description. The cairn is in a birch wood, at 160 m OD on a hillside that faces SE, just above the agricultural land of Kinrive. If free of trees, the view to the E and S would be very extensive over the Cromarty Firth and the Black Isle to the mountains beyond. A long cairn, Kinrive West (ROS 27), is a little higher on the same hillside 250 m to the NE.

The last remains of the cairn are covered with grass and bracken (plate 4). A rim of cairn material surviving on the S and WNW sides is nowhere more than 0.6 m high, but it allows segments of the edge of the cairn to be traced. On the NW side the edge is overlain by the foundations of an old wall, and elsewhere the position of the edge is vague. The diameter of the cairn was about 28 m. The interior of the cairn is uneven, with scattered stones showing through the grass, and in places it has been robbed to ground level. A fence crosses the cairn SE of the chamber.

On the E side of the cairn, and about 5 m within the edge, a pair of portal stones formed the entrance to the passage. They are intact granitic boulders set 0.7 m apart. The S stone has fallen to the E; it is 1.18 m long by about 0.3 m thick, and would be over 0.7 m high if vertical. Its partner is 0.8 m long by 0.5 m

thick, and projects 0.45 m. About 2.15 m to the W is a pair of outer portal stones at the entrance to the chamber. These sandstone slabs are beginning to break up due to vertical cracks in the stone. They are 1.3 m apart, and are 1.4 and 0.8 m long by 0.55 and 0.25 m thick; they project 0.65 and 0.5 m (though their shattered tops are about the same height) and are 0.5 m taller than the entrance portal stones.

The chamber is unusually large with a total length of about 6.7 m, and it is built of massive orthostats, either sandstone blocks or boulders. Unfortunately the orthostats are largely obscured by the bewildering mass of stones which fills the chamber; the stones lie at all angles, and many of them are large and are clearly displaced corbel stones. The outer compartment is about 3.65 m long on the S side by 2.56 m wide. The S wall is formed by

ROS 25

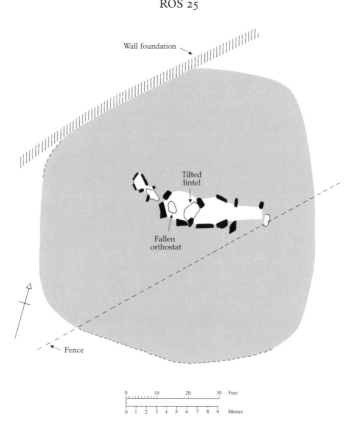

Wall foundation

Tilted lintel

Fallen orthostat

Fence

0   10   20   30 Feet

0 1 2 3 4 5 6 7 8 9   Metres

two orthostats, both leaning somewhat to the S. The E orthostat has probably been reduced in height and is shorter than its neighbour; the impressive W orthostat is an intact regular block which is almost fully exposed on the S side. They are 1.1 and 1.75 m long by 0.65 and 0.4 m thick, and 0.9 and 1.7 m high. On the N side of the compartment is a sandstone boulder, 1.15 m long by 0.34 m thick, and exposed for 0.8 m on the outside; it is probably intact and is slightly shorter than the orthostat on the opposite side of the compartment. The gap of 1.45 m to the W of the N orthostat was presumably filled by a missing orthostat. The inner portal stones are intact granitic boulders set 1.35 m apart, though with the N stone skew to the chamber axis. They are 0.9 and 1 m long by 0.45 and 0.65 m thick, and project 0.6 and 0.4 m. The S stone is somewhat taller than the N stone, and they are both considerably taller than the outer portal stones. A lintel, which has tilted to the W, is just supported by the inner portal stones. The straight E edge of the lintel was clearly the original lower surface which rested on the portal stones, and the sloping faces were originally vertical. The lintel is 2.2 m long by 0.45 m thick, and the upper sloping face measures 1.2 m from E to W.

The inner compartment retains three orthostats, and there are gaps for three more. The SE orthostat is 1.22 m long and 1.1 m high, with an irregular pointed top which may be broken, and the N face is splitting away. The intact W orthostat is the most impressive of all. It leans slightly to the W; it is 1.3 m long expanding to 1.45 m above ground level, and it is exposed for almost its full height of 2.05 m. The NW orthostat is probably intact; it is 0.78 m long and 1.1 m high. These three stones are 0.65 to 0.8 m thick. There are gaps of 1.0 and 0.35 m between them. In front of the W orthostat there lies a block that is likely to have occupied the gap on the S side; it is 1.35 m long by 0.73 m wide and 0.25 m thick. Various large slabs, which may be corbel stones or parts of orthostats, lie outside the chamber. (See figure 13 for a reconstruction of the chamber plan.)

North-west of the rear of the chamber is a group of relatively small sandstone slabs which appear to belong to a small chamber and passage (figure 19). This chamber (formerly regarded as a cist) is rather irregular in plan, measuring about 1.4 by about 0.95 m, and is walled by four orthostats. These, clockwise from the S, are 0.43, 0.76, 0.8 and 1.17 m long, and vary from 0.15 to 0.3 m thick. The floor is flat and almost at ground level, and the orthostats are 0.5, 0.7, 0.97 and 0.75 m high. On the S and W sides, in each of the gaps between the orthostats, there is a small horizontal rectangular slab, probably the lowest course of linking walling. The entrance, to the SE, is 0.4 m wide. A pair of stones 0.5 m E of the entrance may belong to a passage. They are set 0.64 m apart, but of the N stone, a boulder, only the S tip is visible. On this interpretation the passage, including these portal stones, was 0.97 m long, and its outer end was just over 1 m from the back of the bipartite chamber. The putative portal stones are 0.8 and over 0.3 m long by 0.33 and over 0.25 m thick. The S stone is the same height as the SE slab of the small chamber and the N stone is a little shorter. Between the two chambers is a large displaced slab, 1.67 by 0.9 m and 0.3 m thick, which slopes down from NW to SE, resting on the S portal stone and on the ground. This slab may have been a capstone or lintel of the NW structure, but is more likely to have been a corbel stone belonging to the bipartite chamber.

Maclean gave an account of the discovery of the chamber (1886). The cairn was said to have been about 4.5 m high. It was intact until about 1856 when two crofters broke into one compartment of the chamber from above, but the discovery was kept secret. Their only find was 'a layer of black earth'. The compartment 'had side walls of large flagstones, five feet (1.5 m) high, the roof formed of flagstones corbelling inwards and finishing with large flags closing in both sides at a height of about eight feet (2.4 m) from the floor'. About 1870 the cairn was partly robbed for dyke-building, and four years later more stones were removed to build a house, and the same part of the chamber was exposed to view. By the time of

Maclean's visit the cairn was in much the same condition as at present, and the two cists mentioned by him may be the small chamber described above, and part of the passage.

Davidson's reference to a human skull having been found is an error due to confusing this cairn with nearby Kinrive West (ROS 27).

The folklore regarding the building of the cairn is given in NSA; the story recounted there is of a great battle, in which a king was slain and his head struck off and buried beneath this cairn. This myth is linked to the placename Kinrive, mistakenly interpreted as King's Head (see ¶ 6.14).

ROS 26. KINRIVE EAST

See p. 238.

ROS 27. KINRIVE WEST

Parish Kilmuir Easter
Location 7 km NE of Alness
Map reference NH 699753
NMRS number NH 67 NE 2
References Maclean 1886, 336; ISSFC 1899b, 363; RCAHMS 1943, 81–2; Childe 1944, 28, 30–31; Henshall 1963, 350; 1972, 564, 565; RCAHMS 1979a, 8, no. 13
Plan ASH and JCW, revised by ASH and JNGR
Visited 14.7.56, 4.7.67, 24.5.94, 25.4.95

Description. The cairn is on a hillside sloping down from NW to SE, at 175 m OD. It is just above the enclosed fields of Kinrive, and below the Forestry Commission's Kinrive Wood. The land between the fields and the wood was formerly heather moor with a few scattered trees, but by 1994 it had been improved into pasture. The views from the cairn are extensive, over the Cromarty Firth and across the Black Isle. The King's Head Cairn (ROS 25) is 250 m to the SW, at a slightly lower level.

The cairn remains as a long mound of bare angular stones, aligned along the contour. A number of hollows have been made into the cairn and clearly it has been considerably disturbed in the past. There are several trees growing on it. When the cairn was planned in 1967 its size and shape were evident in general terms, but the edges were difficult to define, either because they were overgrown or (at the NE end) were overlaid by the foundations of a wall. In 1994 the edges of the cairn along the NW side and across the NE end were found to be obscured by stones and large boulders which had been dragged down from the improved ground. The SE side of the cairn had not been affected, and it was felt that the edge (seen before the growth of bracken) could be traced more accurately than in 1967. The following description and plan are the result of observations made on four visits spanning thirty-nine years.

The cairn is roughly 65 m long by about 21 m wide at the NE end. At about 19 m from the NE end the cairn is about 14 m wide, and appears to be parallel-sided until near the SW end where the width seems to increase slightly to about 16 m. These dimensions tally with those recorded by Maclean in 1886 except that he did not note the (perhaps doubtful) slight expansion towards the SW end. He considered that 'no portion of [the cairn] has been removed' and gave the average height as about 2.4 m. At present, the cairn rises from the NE end for about 8 m to its maximum height of 1.5 m measured from the NW side, and 5 m measured from the SE side. Westwards, this height is maintained for about 6 m, and then diminishes to an average of 1 m or so.

In 1967 the NE edge appeared to be straight in plan, and the E corner was clearly visible; the corner could still be identified in 1994 though it has been reduced by fence-building and the trampling of cattle. Because of the hill-slope the ground on the SE side is lower, and viewed from here the cairn is still an impressive monument. It rises steeply all along this side, with the lower part overgrown with grass and bracken. The edge can be traced for 26 m from the NE end, the centre stretch is overlain with stone from ancient disturbance, but the edge becomes clearer to the SW, and the last 9 m and the S corner are quite well defined. Running from near the NE end of the cairn, parallel to and about 2.7 m within the SE

ROS 27

Fence

0   10   20   30 Feet

0 1 2 3 4 5 6 7 8 9 Metres

edge, is a row of six closely-spaced boulders stretching for 4 m; they may be the base of a built edging. In 1967 the edge across the SW end and along the NW side was overgrown with heather and ill-defined. By 1994, as mentioned above, the NW side was almost entirely obscured beneath boulders.

FINDS
Human remains. Bones including a skull were found in the cairn before 1899 (ISSFC). Fragments of the skull were given to the Inverness Museum and Art Gallery by Dr (later Professor) W. J. Watson before 1917 (accession number INVMG 1978.036).

ROS 28. LOCH AILSH

Now re-numbered SUT 71, and included in Henshall and Ritchie 1995, 144. This change was due to local government reorganisation in 1975, when the parish of Kincardine and Croick became part of Sutherland District.

ROS 29. LOWER LECHANICH NORTH (Leachonich)

Parish Edderton
Location above the S side of the Dornoch Firth, 10 km WNW of Tain
Map reference NH 684859
NMRS number NH 68 NE 8
References RCAHMS 1943, 57–9; Childe 1944, 28–9, 30; Henshall 1963, 351; RCAHMS 1979a, 8, no. 15
Plan ASH and JNGR
Visited 15.7.56, 23.4.94

Description. The cairn, at 83 m OD, is on a hillside of heather moorland, which slopes down fairly steeply from NW to SE. To the E and S the cairn overlooks the outer part of the Firth, which is about 3 km away, and a small shallow valley which drains into it. The lower part of the valley and the land along the shore are cultivated, but the surrounding higher ground is moorland. Lower Lechanich South (ROS 30) is 120 m to the SSE at a lower level on the hillside, and Red Burn (ROS 36) is in view 5 km to the SE.

The cairn has been considerably robbed and disturbed. On the NW side the cairn material of loose angular and rounded stones is exposed, but on the SE side it is overgrown with heather. The edge of the cairn is clear, though the NNW or uphill side has been slightly clipped and straightened, probably by an old drain; the cairn diameter is about 17.5 m. The highest part of the cairn, to the N of the outer compartment of the chamber, is 1.3 m above ground level. Parts of the passage and chamber can be seen in a central hollow, which is partly filled with loose stones including several squarish slabs.

On the E side of the cairn, and 3.6 m within the edge, a pair of entrance portal stones marks the outer end of the passage. The S stone is a substantial rectangular block with a horizontal upper surface, 1 m long by 0.4 m thick, and projecting for 0.6 m at the S end where it must be almost fully exposed. The N stone is 0.55 m long by over 0.13 m thick; only the tip protrudes but it is level with the top of its partner. The stones are 0.53 m apart. Almost 0.9 m to the W, and only just visible beneath a lintel, is a pair of outer portal stones which forms the entrance to the chamber. The stones are 0.7 m apart, over 0.24 and over 0.3 m long by 0.2 and 0.25 m thick, and they project only 0.2 m. The portal stones support the lintel which slopes down slightly to the W, with its lower surface 0.25 m higher than the entrance portal stones. The lintel is 1.35 m long, 0.65 m wide and 0.23 m thick. The passage, including both pairs of portal stones, is about 1.5 m long.

Part of the outer compartment could be seen in 1943 (RCAHMS; Childe). On the S side there was a straight stretch of walling extending about 2 m westwards from the S outer portal stone. At the W end there could just be seen the E face of a stone which projected to the N for at least 0.3 m. This stone was evidently the S member of a pair of inner portal stones. The walling and portal stone were no longer visible in 1956 (Henshall). Three orthostats belonging to the wall of the inner compartment can still be seen. The back-slab is a shapely pointed intact block, 0.7 m long by 0.23 m thick, and projects 1 m; it is slightly taller than the other

ROS 29

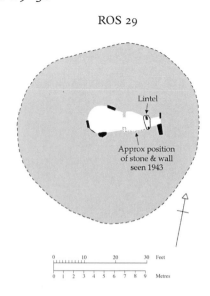

Lintel

Approx position
of stone & wall
seen 1943

orthostats. The S side-slab is intact with a rounded top, 0.85 m long by 0.42 m thick in the centre, and exposed for 0.3 m. A wall-face curves between these two orthostats for 0.7 m. Four courses 0.36 m high can be seen, with the uppermost course 0.4 m below the top of the back-slab, but in 1943 the walling was somewhat higher with the upper courses oversailing. The N side-slab is 0.82 m long by 0.2 m thick, and projects 0.45 m. The side-slabs are 1 and 2.2 m from the back-slab. The chamber is about 5.7 m long, and the inner compartment is 2.2 m wide between the side-slabs. Following Childe's measurements, the outer compartment may be estimated as about 2.1 m long and the inner compartment as about 3.3 m long.

ROS 30. LOWER LECHANICH SOUTH (Leachonich)

Parish Edderton
Location above the S side of the Dornoch Firth, 10 km WNW of Tain
Map reference NH 684858
NMRS number NH 68 NE 9
References ONB 1875, No.10, 12; RCAHMS 1943, 58–9; Childe 1944, 27–8, 30; Henshall 1963, 351, 353; RCAHMS 1979a, 8, no. 16
Plan ASH and JNGR
Visited 15.7.56, 23.4.94

Description. The cairn is 120 m SSE of Lower Lechanich North (ROS 29) which is in view 15 m higher on the same hillside of rough pasture. The South cairn is at 69 m OD.

The cairn is unusually sited on the steep side of an elongated knoll. The edge of the cairn on the NW side is almost level with the top of the knoll and over 5 m above the edge on the SE side. The cairn is also unusual in that the axis of the chamber (of which little can be seen) appears to be skew to the slope of the ground, and the chamber seems to be somewhat S of the centre of the cairn. To a modern observer the flat top of the knoll seems to offer a much preferable place for building a chambered cairn.

The cairn, mainly composed of angular stones, has been considerably robbed and disturbed. It is overgrown with gorse, broom, juniper, briars and bracken, and, except on the less densely-covered SE side, much of it was found to be impenetrable in 1994 and consequently most of the cairn edge could not be planned. The diameter is roughly 21 m, and there appears to be a considerable depth of cairn material remaining in the centre of the cairn.

A number of kerb-stones, rectangular in plan and some of an impressive size, can be seen on or just within the edge of the cairn. On the ENE side there are two blocks 2.1 m apart; the S block is 0.7 by 0.4 m and 0.7 m high with a rather pointed top, and the N stone is 0.7 by 0.3 m and 0.85 m high with a shattered top. On the NNE edge of the cairn two kerb-stones 1.06 m apart are 0.66 and 1 m long by 0.3 m thick, and 0.22 and 0.5 m high. They are at almost the highest part of the cairn edge and there is little depth of cairn material in this area. Three kerb-stones, 1.4 and 1.6 m apart, can be glimpsed in the undergrowth on the NW side of the cairn (not shown on the plan). The edge of the cairn on this side is confused by vestiges of an old wall. There are two more kerb-stones 1 m apart on the SW side of the cairn; the S stone is a shapely pointed block 0.5 by 0.25 m and 0.7 m high. (These stones and the cairn edge on the SW side are shown on the

ROS 30

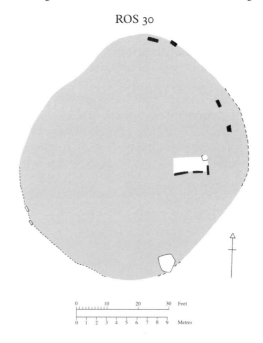

plan, but their position is only approximate having been taken from the 1956 plan in Henshall.) On the S edge of the cairn a large flat slab sloping down to the S is likely to be a displaced capstone or orthostat from the chamber rather than a fallen kerb-stone. It measures 1.65 m N to S by 1.6 m transversely by 0.35 m thick, and its S tip is broken.

At the lowest part of the cairn, about 4 m within the E edge, and about 2.5 m within the extended arc of the kerb-stones, is a pair of portal stones 0.52 m apart. The S stone is 0.9 m long, 0.23 m thick, and projects 0.8 m with an intact upper edge. Its partner has fallen to the W; it is 0.55 m long, 0.1 m thick, and over 0.5 m from E to W. Two orthostats, 0.4 m apart and almost in alignment, stretch W from the S portal stone. The orthostats are 1.1 and 1.38 m long, 0.22 and 0.2 m thick, and project 0.7 and 0.85 m. The former has an intact horizontal upper edge the same height as the adjacent portal stone; the latter, though shattered, is 0.3 m higher. The orthostats have been exposed by removal of cairn material from their S sides. The N side of the structure is hidden below cairn material which rises from the N sides of the orthostats until it flattens off to be level with the top of the knoll. Several interpretations of the orthostats are considered in ¶ 4.46. It is very unlikely that they were all part of a long passage, as was formerly thought to be the case by Childe and Henshall.

The condition of the cairn is unchanged since it was recorded by Childe in 1943, except that the overgrowth has continued unhindered since that time.

Human remains were found in the cairn in 1839 (ONB).

ROS 31. MID BRAE (Easter Brae)

Parish Resolis
Location on the Black Isle, 9 km NW of Fortrose
Map reference NH 661628
NMRS number NH 66 SE 4
References ONB 1872, No. 27, 56; RCAHMS 1943, 15–7; Childe 1944, 33–4; Woodham 1956a, 71, 76–7, 87, 88; Henshall 1963, 352, 353; RCAHMS 1979c, 8, no. 9
Plan ASH and JNGR
Visited 9.7.56, 29.4.96, 30.9.96

Description. The cairn is on the N side of the central ridge of the Black Isle, at 145 m OD. It is at the edge of a field of pasture near the upper limit of the enclosed land which slopes down to the Cromarty Firth. There are wide views from the cairn northwards over the Firth and Easter Ross to distant mountains to the N and W.

The long cairn, which had a chamber at each end, lies along the contour, and there is a slight downward slope from S to N across the site. The cairn axis is from WSW to ENE, but for convenience it will be described as lying W to E. The cairn has been greatly reduced and damaged, in the past by adjacent crofts (shown on the map, figure 27), later for the nearby farm buildings, road building, and recently by the extension of the steading (including a silage pit) and consequent movement of stock and other activities. The surface of the cairn is undulating and covered with broken turf, and has been much disturbed by the trampling of cattle. A metre or more of cairn material

remains over most of the cairn, but there is about half this amount around the W chamber, and the depth of cairn material also decreases towards the E end. In its present condition there are considerable difficulties in interpreting the remains of the cairn, and this was already the case in 1943. The 1996 plan of the cairn was made before the 1st edition OS map, surveyed in 1872, had been consulted. The map confirms that the plan records the shape and size of the cairn reasonably accurately despite recent disturbance.

The cairn is depicted clearly on the map, where it is shown as a mound about 80 m long, with a wide rounded W end about 22 m across, and, extending to the E, a narrower tail about 12 m across (figure 27). In the ONB it was recorded that 'a portion of the tumulus has been removed, for building purposes', but the chambers were not mentioned. This implies that the large W chamber had not been exposed. When Childe visited the cairn in 1943 he was told that the cairn had been robbed by road contractors 'within the last fifty years'. He found the W chamber was partly exposed, and he tentatively suggested that it had been within a round cairn (RCAHMS 1943). Woodham, equally tentatively, suggested that the monument was a long cairn, and an unsatisfactory plan was made in 1956 (Henshall 1963).

The cairn, according to the 1996 survey, is about 74.5 m long, but it was about 77 m long before the E end was curtailed. The cairn is about 29 m across the W end, and appears to narrow fairly rapidly to about 18 m wide at roughly 21 m to the E, from which point the eastern part of the cairn narrows very gradually to the E end, but the exact width there is uncertain.

The W end of the cairn appears to have been straight. The edge can be identified as an indefinite stony rise, about 4 m to the W of the negligible remains of an old wall, which crossed this end of the cairn (a more obvious feature in 1956). Around the NW corner and along the W part of the N side of the cairn the edge is similarly indefinite and much overgrown with gorse. Eastwards of this the

ROS 31

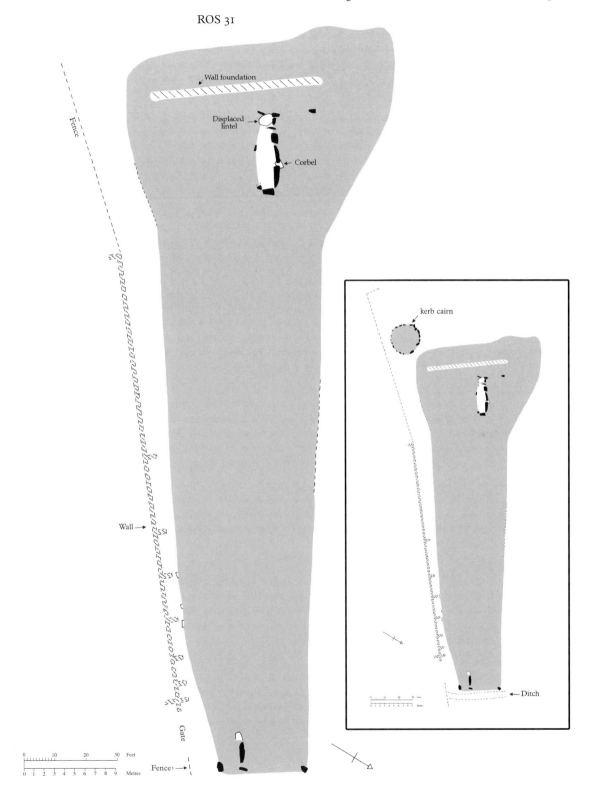

Wall foundation

Displaced
lintel

Corbel

Fence

Wall

Gate

Fence

0   10   20   30 Feet
0 1 2 3 4 5 6 7 8 9 Metres

kerb cairn

Ditch

precise position of the edge is unclear, due to the displacement of cairn stones outwards and downwards, and to field-gathered stones which have been heaped along the side, though among the jumble of large stones several may well be substantial kerb-stones. Even so, about midway along this side the cairn edge can be identified with reasonable confidence for about 12 m. The edge has been obliterated for the last 14 m up to a substantial boulder at the E end, which is probably part of the cairn structure (see below). The S edge of the cairn is even more difficult to define. The SW corner can be traced approximately, and to the E of this the edge can be picked up for about 7 m. A modern wall (the N wall of a silage pit) runs close to the presumed position of the cairn edge continuing eastwards. The space between the wall and cairn has been filled in and the turf surface between the two is level. The line of the cairn edge near its E end may be indicated by three substantial rectangular boulders which have the appearance of kerb-stones. They are spaced over 5.8 m; the easternmost and largest is 0.88 m long by 0.3 m thick, and projects for 0.16 m. The wall ends at a gate, and a fence continues its line eastwards. Cattle, moving through the gate and either NW across the cairn or around its SE corner, have virtually obliterated a section across the cairn and the corner, but a little cairn material survives at the extreme E end of the cairn.

The cairn has been truncated at the E end by a deep ditch which drains slurry from the farmyard, and cairn material dug from the ditch is piled along its E side. On the W edge of the ditch there are three boulders in line from N to S, evidently part of a modest façade across the E end of the cairn and about 2.5 m within the former eastward spread of cairn material (as indicated on the 1956 plan). The N boulder, already mentioned, probably marks the N end of the façade; the boulder measures 0.8 by 0.75 m and projects 0.55 m. The central boulder appears to be a portal stone. It is over 0.9 m long by over 0.3 m thick (only the E face is exposed), and projects 0.35 m. The S boulder, though it stands at the present SE corner of the

cairn, is only 1.75 m from the portal stone, and its position was probably midway along the S half of the façade; the SE corner of the cairn has probably been eroded by the passage of cattle. The S boulder measures diagonally 1.3 by over 0.6 m, and is exposed for its full height of 0.5 m. (See figure 26, 4 for our interpretation of the cairn plan.)

To the W of the portal stone is a slab that presumably formed the S wall of a passage, though it is unusually large for this function. It is 2 m long by 0.5 m thick; it projects 0.85 m in the centre, and the W part has been reduced in height long ago. Immediately to the W is a prone slab which measures 0.8 by over 0.6 m (its E side is hidden), and over 0.2 m thick. It is likely that this slab also was part of the S side of the structure, possibly a second portal stone. The structure appears to have been aligned on the cairn axis. There is no sign of the putative eastern chamber, which would have been in the most seriously damaged part of the cairn.

At the W end of the cairn there is a chamber aligned parallel with, but N of, the axis of the cairn. About 7 m within the W edge of the cairn is a pair of portal stones set 0.73 m apart, which form the entry to the passage. A stone in line with the portal stones and 3.4 m to the N may be a large kerb-stone in a façade across the W end of the cairn. The stone is 0.7 m long by 0.42 m thick, and projects 0.17 m. The N portal stone is an intact boulder, over 0.86 m long by 0.46 m thick, with the upper surface sloping down to the N. Its partner is a slab, over 0.9 m long by over 0.25 m thick. The N wall of the passage is formed by an orthostat 0.6 m long by 0.38 m thick. About 1 m E of the first portal stone is a portal stone at the entry into the chamber. This stone is a slab over 1.03 m long by 0.13 m thick, with an intact upper edge. Lying in the passage is a displaced lintel, rather irregular in plan though fairly flat; it is 1.62 m long by 1.08 m wide, and 0.3 m thick, and slopes down slightly to the E.

The rectangular chamber is filled with rubble, which is higher at the inner end, and is overgrown with gorse. Three large orthostats form the N wall. They are 1.05, 1.8 and 2.3 m long, and between 0.6 to 0.33 m thick. The outer slab projects 0.4 m and the two inner slabs, which have intact upper edges, project 0.7 and 0.8 m, all measured on the N side, but their true height is considerably more. A displaced corbel stone, 0.95 m wide by 0.75 m along its downward-sloping N face, and 0.3 m thick, overlies the junction of the two inner slabs and rests on the E slab. The S wall of the chamber is represented by a flat-sided intact boulder, over 0.7 m long (the E end is hidden) by 0.3 m thick, which projects 0.45 m. Formerly the E end of an orthostat could be seen at the inner end of the S wall (Henshall), but it and the rest of the N side of the chamber were hidden beneath dense gorse in 1996. The back-slab of the chamber is 1.45 m long by 0.68 m thick, and its irregular top projects 1.2 m measured on the outside. The passage and chamber orthostats are roughly the same height, except that the inner N orthostat is 0.35 m higher and the back-slab is 0.4 m higher still. A vertical stone, 0.46 m long, which butts against the W end of the central orthostat on the N side, was formerly thought to be a divisional stone of the chamber, but in 1996 it was found not to be earthfast; it may be a part of the structure which has been loosened, or it may be a fortuitously placed stone. The chamber is 6 m long by 1.8 m wide near the W end, and slightly narrower at the E end (see figure 20 for a reconstruction of the chamber plan).

Close to the SW corner of the cairn is a kerb-cairn. It is 7 m in diameter and 0.5 m high, with the turfed interior more or less level with the tops of the kerb-stones.

ROS 32. MILLCRAIG

Parish Rosskeen
Location on the N side of the Cromarty Firth, 1 km N of Alness
Map reference NH 658710
NMRS number NH 67 SE 24
References ONB 1874–5, No. 2, 56; Maclean 1886, 331; RCAHMS 1943, 79; Childe 1944, 31; Henshall 1963, 352, 353; RCAHMS 1979a, 8, no. 18

Plan ASH and JNGR
Visited 15.7.56, 24.4.95

Description. The cairn is at 70 m OD, in the cultivated land which rises from the N shore of the firth. The cairn, in the corner of a field, is within the remains of a circular wall about 50 m in diameter, which was built to enclose a small plantation of trees. The site slopes down from N to S.

The cairn, which is about 31 m in diameter, was partially removed for dyke-building in 1854 (ONB). Its outer limits survive as a substantial bank, generally about 0.7 m high, although more when seen from the lower S side. In the interior only a small and uneven depth of cairn material has been left. A gap through the bank on the W side was presumably to allow access during the destruction, and there is a smaller gap on the NNE side. The whole area within the enclosing wall is covered with coarse grass. Trees were once planted over the cairn, and some remain on its rim. The edge of the cairn is fairly clear on the N and S sides; there has been some quarrying into the ESE side.

North-east of the centre of the cairn is a group of six slabs, some of which are the orthostats of a chamber of uncertain plan. The westernmost, the most prominent feature of the cairn, is a huge slab aligned nearly E to W and leaning to the S with a maximum overhang of 0.9 m. It has a weathered surface on the N side, but the S face has been split away relatively recently (probably during the robbing of the cairn). The slab is 2.85 m long, and is now 0.15 to 0.2 m thick, and at the centre it measures 2.12 m down its sloping S face, virtually its full former height. Immediately to the E and at right angles to it is a slab with a shattered top. It is 1.22 m long by up to 0.53 m thick, and projects 0.52 m; it is 0.8 m lower than its neighbour. These two stones probably formed the N wall and part of the E wall of a large chamber.

The function of the remaining three upright slabs is unclear, and though they appear to be undisturbed it is difficult to suppose that they are all *in situ*. The W and S slabs are similar

ROS 32

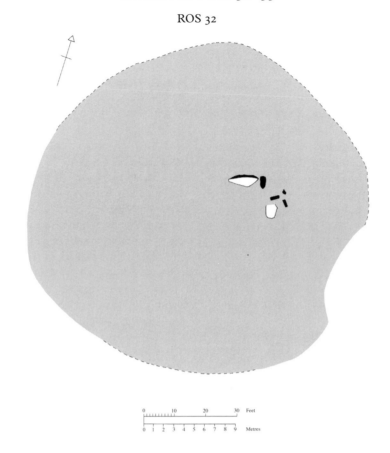

```
0          10        20        30   Feet
|‖‖‖‖‖‖‖‖‖‖|          |          |
0  1  2  3  4  5  6  7  8  9   Metres
```

rectangular blocks with horizontal upper surfaces. They are 1.0 and 0.67 m long by 0.26
and 0.33 m thick, and project 0.23 and 0.46 m.
The third slab, 0.42 m long by 0.33 m thick
and projecting 0.55 m, is more irregular. The
last two stones are exposed in the inner side of
the bank of cairn material. The sixth slab is
prone, sloping down to the N with the N end
buried. It is over 1.3 m long by 0.97 m wide
and 0.43 m thick.

'Human remains' were found in the cairn in
1854 (ONB).

ROS 33. MUIR OF
ALLANGRANGE

Parish Urquhart and Logie Wester
Location on the W end of the Black Isle, 2.7 km NE
of Muir of Ord
Map reference NH 550525

NMRS number NH 55 SE 7
References Woodham 1956a, 73; Henshall 1963, 352;
RCAHMS 1979c, 8, no. 14
Visited 12.7.56, 25.10.95

Description. The remains of the cairn are at
the edge of a field, in flat agricultural land, at
120 m OD. The cairn is 400 m ENE of Muir of
Conan (ROS 34).

The surface of the cairn is grass-covered
and uneven, in general about 0.6 m high. The
diameter is roughly 22 m, but the edges cannot
be traced precisely. The SE side of the cairn is
edged by a fence, the curved N side is defined
by the limit of ploughing, and on the SW side
the cairn merges into an area of field-gathered
stones. In the centre of the cairn there is a very
large upright sandstone slab. It is rectangular
in plan, and is aligned NW to SE. It has cracked
vertically near the SE end, and the upper edge

is shattered. The slab is 1.72 m long by 0.3 m thick. It projects 0.75 m, but its true height is well over 1 m (its top is about 1.8 m above ground level on the N side of the cairn), and when intact it was even taller. The size of this slab indicates the former presence of a chamber rather than a cist.

ROS 34. MUIR OF CONAN

Parish Urquhart and Logie Wester
Location at the W end of the Black Isle, 2.5 km NE of Muir of Ord
Map reference NH 546524
NMRS number NH 55 SW 9
References OSA 5, 1793, 214; ONB 1872–3, No. 31, 56; Woodham 1956a, 69, 71; Henshall 1963, 354, 355; RCAHMS 1979c, 8, no. 15
Plan ASH and JNGR
Visited 12.7.56, 3.5.96

ROS 34

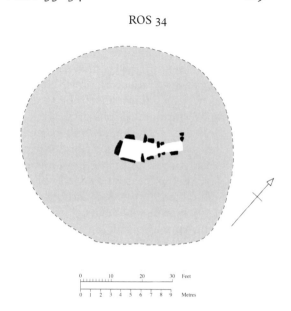

Description. The cairn is at the edge of a level field of pasture in flat agricultural land, at 120 m OD. The cairn is 400 m WSW of Muir of Allangrange (ROS 33), and 560 m SE of Bishop Kinkell (ROS 9). The site is heavily overgrown with broom and brambles, otherwise there would be wide views especially to the N.

The cairn has been reduced to between 0.5 and 1 m high. When it was visited in 1956 the edge could be traced (which was not possible in 1996 due to almost impenetrable vegetation), and the diameter was 18 to 20 m. Most of the orthostats of a passage and chamber are partly exposed near the centre of the cairn. There is more stone debris inside the chamber than outside it, and it is highest in the ante-chamber where it is flush with the tops of the orthostats; vertical measurements have been taken on the outside. With one exception, the orthostats of the passage and ante-chamber are intact rounded boulders; the three orthostats of the main chamber and one orthostat in the passage are slabs.

The passage faces NE. It is 2.2 m long between the portal stones on its NW side, and is 0.74 m wide at the inner end. At the outer end the low portal stone hardly projects; it is about 0.57 m long by 0.4 m thick. A kerb-stone

is exposed on its NW side. At the inner end of the passage the portal stone, set transversely to the axis, is 0.65 m long by 0.4 m thick, and projects 0.37 m. Beside it is a stone, 0.3 m square and hardly projecting, which belongs to the NW wall of the passage. The opposite wall is represented by three stones. At the outer end is a slab, 0.96 m long by 0.36 m thick, the SW end of which rises to a point projecting 0.66 m. The low second stone is 0.44 m long by 0.2 m thick. The third stone, set transversely, is over 0.46 m long (the SE end is not visible) by 0.32 m thick, and projects 0.27 m. It can be regarded as a portal stone, although, unlike its partner, it does not narrow the passage. The entry into the chamber is 0.52 m wide. The axis of the passage is skew to that of the chamber.

The ante-chamber is roughly 1.3 m long and wide, with an orthostat on each side. The SE orthostat is over 0.8 m long (neither end is visible) by 0.3 m thick, and projects 0.23 m; the opposite orthostat is 0.73 m long by 0.4 m thick, and hardly projects. The entry to the main chamber is between a well-matched pair of portal stones set 1 m apart. They are slabs with intact horizontal upper surfaces, 0.85 and 0.75 m long by 0.37 and 0.45 m thick, and they project 0.25 m. The almost square main chamber, defined by three orthostats, is 2 m long by 1.87 m wide. The orthostats have irregular upper surfaces, possibly damaged long ago. The side slabs are 1.62 and 1.1 m long by 0.22 and 0.5 m thick, and they project 0.57 and 0.45 m. The back-slab, the largest of the orthostats, is 1.5 m long by 0.6 m thick, and projects 0.87 m. The total length of the chamber is 3.5 m. The side orthostats of the ante-chamber, the portal stones between it and the main chamber, and the NW portal stone at the inner end of the passage are all about the same height; the other boulder orthostats are slightly shorter, and the four slab orthostats are considerably taller.

The monument was not recognised as the remains of a cairn in 1876, but was recorded in the ONB as a circle of four stones (presumably the four tallest orthostats of the chamber). The implication is that the cairn had been reduced to its present level well before this date. Either this chamber, or that at Balvaird (ROS 7), was investigated for the landowner in the late eighteenth century (OSA).

ROS 35. THE PRIEST'S SEPULCHRE

Parish Kiltearn
Location on the NW side of the Cromarty Firth, on the W outskirts of Evanton
Map reference about NH 6065
NMRS number NH 66 NW 9
References OSA I, 1791, 293; Pococke 1887, 177; Henshall 1963, 354; RCAHMS 1979a, 8, no. 19
Visited 24.4.95

Description. This lost monument was evidently on the W side of the village of Evanton, near the River Sgitheach. The site is either covered by recently built houses or is in the field to the W of them. The monument had been destroyed by the time of the survey for the first edition of the 6-inch OS maps in 1875.

The description of 1791 reads: 'On the north side of the River Skiack, and nearly opposite to the village of Drummond, a grave of oblong form, lined with stone in the same

manner as those above described [short cists]: it is called the Priest's Sepulchre, and is 7 ft. long, 3 ft. broad, and 3½ ft. deep [about 2 m long, 0.9 m wide, and 1 m deep].' It is highly probable that this structure was a chamber of a chambered cairn. Thirty-one years earlier, in July 1760, Pococke was journeying N from Foulis Castle, and he may have visited the same monument, then in a more complete state. 'A little beyond [the castle] to the North East is a Kern with two stones set up before it; in a cell there made by five stones, they found some bones. I went beyond it to the Burn [the Allt Graad/River Glass]'.

ROS 36. RED BURN

Parish Edderton
Location above the S side of the Dornoch Firth, 5 km WNW of Tain
Map reference NH 727834
NMRS number NH 78 SW 5
References ONB 1874, No. 10, 61; RCAHMS 1943, 61–2; Childe 1944, 30; Henshall 1963, 354, 355; RCAHMS 1979a, 9, no. 20
Plan ASH and JNGR
Visited 15.7.56, 24.4.94

Description. The cairn is in a relatively flat area on the steep side of Edderton Hill which slopes down to the S shore of the Firth. The cairn is on the edge of a large forest which has been planted and extended through the twentieth century; the area on the E side of the Red Burn was only planted in the early 1990s with the cairn left free of trees, and the land on the W side of the burn remains as pasture. The actual site of the cairn is a slight rise, 25 m E of the Red Burn, at 122 m OD. The cairn has extensive views to the N, and overlooks the whole Dornoch Firth. The Lower Lechanich cairns (ROS 29, 30) can be seen 5 km to the NW, and several chambered cairns can be seen in Sutherland on the N side of the Firth, but Edderton Hill (ROS 57) only 700 m to the E is not in view.

The cairn is still impressive in spite of several deep hollows that have been made into it and considerable robbing of the E side. Cairn material of boulders and cobbles is exposed over much of the surface; turf grows over the edges, and coarse grass covers the N to NW side and the robbed area on the E side. The site slopes down from S to N. The cairn rises steeply from a well-defined edge on the lower N and NW sides. Here, at ground level, there can be seen a number of stones which evidently belong to a wall-face revetting the cairn. On the N side three spaced stones, two boulders and a slab, 0.3 to 0.6 m long, lean acutely outwards; originally they were probably vertical and 0.4 m or more high, and set somewhat S of their present positions. About 2.2 m S of the centre stone there is exposed what appears to be a short length of an inner wall-face. Two substantial flat stones, one above the other and sloping down into the cairn, are probably two courses of the wall-face. Both stones are 0.45 m long and together they are 0.4 m high; the lower stone is 0.45 m from back to front and is about 1 m above ground level. On the NW side of the cairn a row of five relatively

small stones evidently belong to the base of the outer wall-face. The cairn edge on the SW side is overlaid by field-gathered stones, but the edge can be traced round the S side. On the E side, where the cairn has been robbed, the edge is obscured by field-gathered stones and by two rectangular pits which impinge upon it. At the junction of this badly disturbed area and the NE edge there is a large boulder. The cairn diameter is about 23.5 m. The height of the centre of the cairn taken from the E side is 3 m, and taken from the N side is 5 m.

Part of a chamber is exposed in a hollow on the ESE slope of the cairn. Two orthostats aligned E to W are 1.5 m apart. The S orthostat is a sandstone slab 0.66 m long and of unknown thickness. The N orthostat is 0.7 m long by 0.13 m thick. Immediately W of them is a lintel that slopes down to the W. It is 1.65 m long, 0.35 m thick, and over 0.8 m from front to back. The lower surface of the lintel on the E side is about 1 m above ground level, and the clearance below it is 0.2 m. Both the orthostats

ROS 36

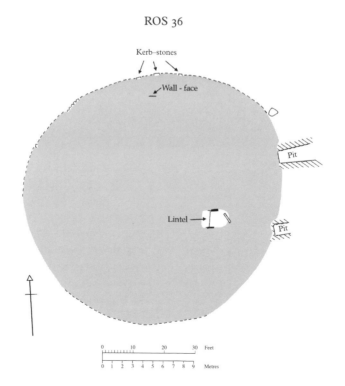

are the same height and rise about 0.1 m above the lower edge of the lintel, but the lower W part of the S orthostat extends 0.24 m beneath it. The lintel does not rest directly on the orthostat but on an intervening cobble, and the W part of the lintel rests on cairn material. It is evident that the lintel is not *in situ*; possibly it was originally set vertically on its long W edge and it has fallen towards the E. The cairn rises steeply from the W side of the lintel, and the hidden inner part of the chamber may still exist largely intact. In 1943 Childe noted that near the top of the cairn, where stones had been pulled away, the edges of flat slabs suitable for corbels could just be seen under the rounded stones covering the surface (RCAHMS, 62). It seems that the chamber was somewhat SE of the centre of the cairn. To the E of the orthostats the cairn has been very severely robbed and presumably the passage has been destroyed. An upright slab in this area is aligned NW to SE; it is 1.04 m long by 0.15 m thick in the centre, and projects 0.56 m. Although firmly set, it is unlikely to be part of the chamber structure. (For our interpretation of the cairn structure see ¶ 5.8 and figure 24, 2.)

In 1824 'Mr G Ross of Edderton took some of the stones while building a wall near this Cairn where he discovered a stone cist containing a [sic] urn which crumbled to pieces as soon as exposed to the Air' (ONB).

ROS 37. THE TEMPLE, TORE

Parish Killearnan
Location on the Black Isle, 8 km NW of Inverness
Map reference NH 617526
NMRS number NH 65 SW 2
References ONB 1871–3, No. 17, 25; Beaton 1882, 487–8; Childe 1944, 35–6; Woodham 1956a, 71, 72, 93; Henshall 1963, 354, 355; RCAHMS 1979c, 9, no. 17
Plan ASH and JNGR
Visited 10.7.56, 3.5.96

Description. The cairn is on the crest of a gentle ridge, in agricultural land, at 90 m OD. There are wide views to the S and E. The cairn

ROS 37

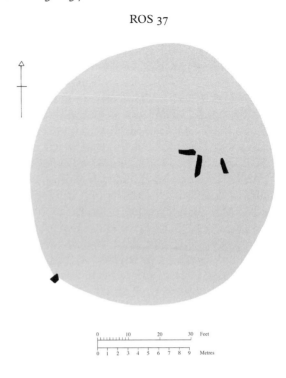

is within a small plantation of trees, once surrounded by a wall, and is covered by lush vegetation. Field-gathered stones have been added on the S and E sides.

The edge of the cairn is difficult to define precisely, but the diameter appears to be 24 to 25 m, and the height is about 1.65 m measured from the N side. The surface is uneven, several large slabs lie about, and the centre of the cairn is known to have been dug into. On the SW side a regular upright block is exposed for 0.83 m, almost its full height, and may be a kerb-stone.

To the E of the centre of the cairn the upper parts of two large orthostats are exposed, set at right angles and almost touching. There can be little doubt that they formed two sides of a compartment of a chamber. The N stone is 1.6 m long by 0.6 m thick at the E end, and the upper surface is rather irregular. The adjacent stone is 2.2 m long by 0.6 m thick, with an almost horizontal upper surface. The stones project 0.75 and 0.95 m from a hollow beside their E and N ends, and the true height of the taller stone is about 2 m. A third orthostat projects about 2 m to the E of, and not quite parallel to, the second orthostat. This last stone is over 1.7 m long (the S end is not visible) by 0.4 m thick, and is considerably lower than its neighbour, projecting 0.4 m. The last two stones, and probably also the first, are intact. The plan of the chamber is not evident.

The cairn had been robbed for building-stone before 1873 (ONB). In 1882 Beaton recorded that the centre had been left with a hollow, about 6 m in diameter and about 1.2 m deep, which was 'much encumbered by stones', and the first two orthostats described above stood on its NE edge. There were casual investigations some time before 1955, during which a whetstone was found (Woodham).

FINDS
Artefact. Whetstone, 50 by 10 mm, perforated at the wider end (cast in The Royal Museum of Scotland AL 203). Presumably unconnected with the neolithic phase of the cairn.
Not illustrated.

ROS 38. USSIE

Parish Fodderty
Location 2.7 km SW of Dingwall
Map reference NH 530565
NMRS number NH 56 NW 9
References ONB 1873, No. 9, 102; Childe 1944, 33; Henshall 1963, 356, 357; RCAHMS 1979a, 9, no. 27
Plan ASH and JNGR
Visited 23.6.51, 22.10.95

Description. The remains of the cairn are at the top corner of a field which slopes down quite steeply from W to E. Immediately to the S, beyond a field wall, where the ground slopes down more steeply, is conifer woodland. The site is at 95 m OD. There is a wide view across the extensive fertile land around the Cromarty Firth.

The cairn material has been almost totally removed, but some orthostats of the chamber survive. The area around the orthostats has been left unploughed with several trees growing on it. Seven orthostats, upright or leaning, and some large prone slabs, appear to belong to a

ROS 38

chamber of two compartments. The monument was already in this condition by 1873 (ONB).

The axis of the monument appears to have been roughly ESE to WNW. The eastern four orthostats are split boulders, set with the flat split faces to the chamber. These orthostats form the walls of an oval compartment about 2.3 m long by 1.85 m wide. The two contiguous orthostats on the S side are 1.43 and 1.2 m long by up to 0.55 m thick. The E orthostat projects 0.9 m and has a shattered top; the W orthostat projects 1.3 m, and only the tip is damaged. On the N side of the compartment the E orthostat is a shattered stump, 0.56 by 0.6 m, which projects 0.33 m. The W orthostat leans acutely to the S and the top has been reduced. It is 1.1 m long by about 0.4 m thick, and would be over 0.5 m high if upright.

A pair of stones forms the portal leading to the W compartment. The S stone is an intact boulder, 0.6 by 0.5 m and 0.77 m high. The displacement of its partner, which leans to the SSW and is supported by the S stone, has reduced the width of the entry to only 0.18 m. The N stone is 0.6 m long expanding to 0.8 m near the top, by 0.6 m thick; if upright it would be 1.03 m high, and slightly more before it was damaged. Only one orthostat of the W compartment remains *in situ*, on the NE side. It is 1.1 m long by 0.47 m thick and projects 0.6 m. Immediately to the W a large pointed block leans acutely to the S and rests on a prone slab. The former may have stood on the N side of the compartment. If so, the side of the block that would have been the base is about 0.9 m long and expands to 1.6 m higher up, and the thickness is about 0.55 m. From N to S the block measures 1.8 m, which would be the height if it were upright in the position suggested. On the upper surface there is a horizontal row of four evenly-spaced small hollows, with a vertical row of three below; these are almost certainly incomplete drill-holes for breaking up the stone, and not cupmarks. To the W of this block are two prone blocks, 1.55 and 1.2 m long and both 0.9 m wide. Besides other substantial blocks lying near the chamber, there is one of notable size, 2.35 by 1.3 m and up to 0.6 m thick.

ROS 39. WESTER BRAE

Parish Resolis
Location on the Black Isle, 8.4 km NW of Fortrose
Map reference NH 656613
NMRS number NH 66 SE 6
References RCAHMS 1943, 13; Childe 1944, 34; Woodham 1956a, 78; Henshall 1963, 356; 1972, 564, 565; RCAHMS 1979c, 9, no. 18
Plan ASH and JNGR
Visited 9.7.56, 21.9.67, 30.9.96

Description. The cairn is on the central ridge of the Black Isle, on land sloping down gently to the NW, above the present limit of agriculture, at 175 m OD. The area was formerly moorland covered with many small cairns, but it is now part of an extensive Forestry Commission forest. The site is near the NW edge of the forest, in a plantation of Scots pines. Woodhead Long and Round (ROS 41, 42) are 670 m to the SSW and SW respectively.

The actual site slopes down slightly from S to N. The cairn is overgrown with heather, moss and blaeberries, and old tree stumps indicate that it was once planted over. The forest trees have been planted up to the very edge of the cairn, but it has not been ploughed into. The axis of the cairn is ENE to WSW, though it is described here as lying E to W. The edge round the E end has been disturbed by tree planting and it can be traced only approximately. Apart from a small amount of quarrying into the S side, the edge round the rest of the cairn is fairly well defined, and especially so along the N side. The cairn is about 28 m long by about 14 m wide at the E end, and it narrows to a rounded W end. The cairn appears to be largely undisturbed, except for a hollow some 5 m in width made just W of the centre and extending towards the S edge. In long profile the cairn rises steeply at the E end, and from the highest part, about 6 m from this end, it appears to have sloped down very gently towards the W. At its maximum the cairn is 1.65 m high, and it is only a little less near the W end.

ROS 39

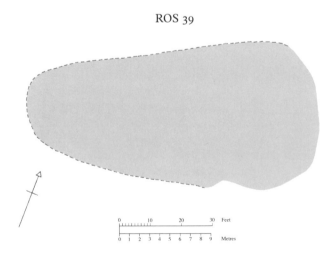

ROS 40. WESTER LAMINGTON

Parish Logie Easter
Location 5 km SW of Tain
Map reference NH 747780
NMRS number NH 77 NW 2
References RCAHMS 1943, 81; Childe 1944, 30;
Henshall 1963, 356; 1972, 564, 567; RCAHMS
1979a, 9, no. 28
Plan ASH and JCW
Visited 6.7.58, 5.7.67, 23.5.94

Description. The cairn is in a clearing deep in a conifer forest, at 152 m OD on a hillside sloping down gently from NW to SE. When visited in 1943 the trees had recently been felled and the location was described as 'the highest point on a broad moor . . . commanding a wide view to the Firth and the Sutors of Cromarty' (RCAHMS 1943).

The cairn is overgrown with blaeberries and heather, except along the top where the cairn material of cobbles and boulders is bare. The cairn is an impressive mound, its longer axis running SE to NW, and it seems to have suffered only superficial disturbance on the top and at the NW end. Although the sides of the cairn rise steeply, in every place where the cairn could be inspected the edges and plan were difficult to define. This is partly because the cairn has probably been built on a slight rise with which it merges, and partly because the sides of the cairn are overgrown. In 1994 the sides were overlaid with the remains of felled trees and it was found to be impossible to improve on the plan of 1967. The highest part of the cairn, towards the SE end and NE of the axis, is 2 m high measured from the SE end, and it appears to be 3 m high measured from what is probably a natural hollow along the SW side. In long profile the cairn rises steeply from the SE end, is level for two-thirds of its length, and slopes down gradually to the NW end. The cairn is about 32 m long by about 17 m wide across the centre.

ROS 41. WOODHEAD LONG

Parish Resolis
Location on the Black Isle, 8.3 km NW of Fortrose
Map reference NH 653607
NMRS number NH 66 SE 2
References RCAHMS 1943, 13; Childe 1944, 34;
Woodham 1956a, 78; Henshall 1963, 356; RCAHMS
1979c, 9, no. 19
Plan ASH and JNGR
Visited 9.7.56, 21.9.67, 30.9.96

Description. The cairn is on the north-facing slope of the central ridge of the Black Isle, at 185 m OD. It is situated a little beyond the

ROS 40

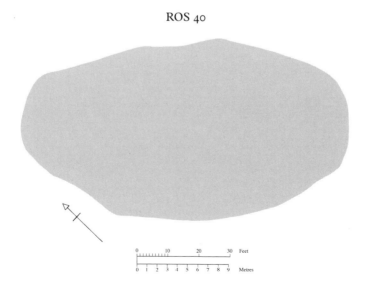

0   10   20   30   Feet

0 1 2 3 4 5 6 7 8 9   Metres

present limit of cultivation, in an area that was formerly moorland scattered with small cairns, but which is now part of an extensive Forestry Commission forest. Woodhead Round (ROS 42), 300 m to the NW, would be just visible if there were no intervening trees (RCAHMS 1943), and Wester Brae (ROS 39), 670 m to the NNE, would probably be visible at a slightly lower level on the hillside.

The almost level site is in a clearing in the forest. The cairn of boulders is covered by coarse grass, heather and moss. The trees that were planted on the cairn before 1955, and which had totally obscured it by 1967, have been removed. Forestry ploughing has come up to, and sometimes well within, the edge of the cairn.

The axis of the cairn is E to W. The edge, though not exactly definable due to the vegetation, is fairly clear except at the W end. The E end is slightly rounded in plan. Along the N side the cairn rises steeply, apart from a stretch which has been disturbed. Near the W end the cairn has been cut obliquely by a deep drainage ditch, the upcast from which is piled along its NW side. Because cairn material can be seen in the upcast and in the exposed section, it is evident that the cairn extended W of the ditch, but the end is hidden by the spread of the upcast. The cairn is over 40 m

long, and is probably nearer 44 m long. It is about 13 m wide at the E end, and narrows slightly to about 11 m wide at the westernmost point that can be measured. There has been considerable disturbance down the centre which has been left with a series of linked hollows; a particularly large hollow midway along extends to the N edge, and dumped material beyond the edge distorts this stretch of the N side. The height of the cairn increases from the E end to about 2 m at about 23 m to the W, and decreases to about 1 m on the E side of the ditch.

ROS 42.   WOODHEAD ROUND

Parish Resolis
Location on the Black Isle, 8.7 km NW of Fortrose
Map reference NH 650610
NMRS number NH 66 SE 1
References NSA 1845, 45; ONB 1871–5, No. 27, 61–2; RCAHMS 1943, 25–7; Childe 1944, 34, 35; Woodham 1956a, 71, 72, 88; Henshall 1963, 357; 1972, 564; RCAHMS 1979c, 9, no. 20
Plan ASH and JNGR
Visited 9.7.56, 21.9.67, 30.4.96

Description. The cairn is on the N side of the central ridge of the Black Isle, at 185 m OD. There are wide views to the N and round to the W, across agricultural land to the distant

ROS 41

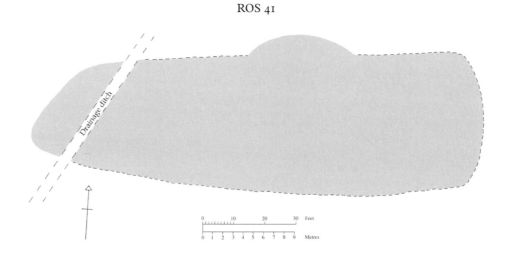

Drainage ditch

0 10 20 30 Feet
0 1 2 3 4 5 6 7 8 9 Metres

mountains beyond the Cromarty Firth. The cairn is in a corner of an arable field and immediately outside the very extensive Forestry Commission forest that covers the highest part of the ridge. The site slopes down gently from S to N, and the ground drops away more steeply from the N side of the cairn. Woodhead Long (ROS 41) lies 300 m to the SE.

The cairn was partly demolished by the landowner, Sir Alexander Mackenzie of Avoch, in about 1817 to build a farmhouse, and the chamber was exposed and investigated (NSA, ONB). The remains of the cairn are as much as 2 m high to the S of the chamber, and the stones are largely covered with turf. The edge of the cairn round the S side is clear. Round the NW side a rim of cairn material survives, though with an indefinite edge, and within this rim most of the cairn material has been removed. The edge on the NE side has been obliterated and an amorphous spread of stones extends well beyond the presumed original limits of the cairn. On the SE side a track running NE to SW passes close to the cairn. The diameter of the cairn was probably about 23 m judging by the curve of the surviving segment of the edge.

Near the centre of the spread of cairn material and field-gathered stones, but near the NE edge of a round cairn of the size suggested, a compartment of a large chamber is exposed, aligned NE to SW. At the NE end is a pair of portal stones set 0.9 m apart and skew to the chamber axis. The stones are the same height and retain their original nearly horizontal upper edges. They are 1.2 and 1.5 m long, 0.33 and 0.15 m thick, and project 0.36 and 0.9 m.

On each side of the compartment there are two orthostats separated by a gap of 1 m. The first orthostat on the SE side is over 1.1 m long (the NE end is not visible) by 0.12 m thick, and projects 0.6 m. The top is irregular and was probably shattered by the fall of the lintel described below. This orthostat was probably thicker in its original state, as a slab adjacent to

ROS 42

0   10   20   30 Feet

0 1 2 3 4 5 6 7 8 9   Metres

its NW face appears to be a portion that has sheared from it. The orthostat on the opposite side of the chamber is 2 m long by 0.25 m thick, and projects 1 m, and part of the original upper edge survives. The two orthostats at the inner end of the compartment are probably intact; they have pointed tops and flat inner surfaces, and are about the same height. They are 1 and 1.18 m long by 0.44 and 0.3 m thick, and project 1.06 and 0.97 m. In spite of the stones that choke the chamber, all four orthostats can be measured from close to floor level. The gap between the orthostats on the SE side is filled by a short length of walling, of which a stack of three small slabs is visible, and by a small upright stone 0.46 m long and 0.9 m shorter than the orthostat to the SW. In the gap between the orthostats on the NW side of the chamber there is a horizontal slab, 0.8 m by about 1 m and 0.14 m thick, its NW end overlain by two more flat slabs; possibly these are a small orthostat and corbel stones which have fallen outwards. The compartment is 1.86 m wide at the NE end narrowing to 1.12 m wide at the SW end, and the length was at least 3.7 m.

A number of corbel stones remain more or less *in situ*. Two are over the E orthostat, sloping down to the SE, one over the other (though the upper has moved outwards) and together 0.7 m thick. The lower corbel stone measures about 1.15 m wide by over 1 m from front to back, and 0.36 m thick; the other corbel stones are of similar size. Two more corbel stones rest side by side above the walling and on the shoulder of the S orthostat; the latter corbel stone overhangs the chamber wall by 0.23 m. A very large lintel, which evidently once rested on the portal stones, has been tipped over to the SW and now lies on its side. It only just rests on each portal stone, and is mainly borne by the N chamber orthostat and the lower of the corbel stones above the E orthostat. The lintel is 2.4 m long by about 1 m thick in the centre, and 1.2 m wide (the original height). The horizontal upper surface (which originally faced NE) is flat, and the lower surface (which originally faced SW into the chamber) descends to a point which almost reaches floor level and so now

completely blocks the entry into the chamber. The shape of the present NE side of the lintel, with two shallow arcs, would roughly accommodate the slight inward and downward slope of the tops of the portal stones.

Across the SW end of the compartment there is a slab leaning steeply to the NE. It was formerly assumed to be the back-slab of a single-compartment chamber, but it seems too slight for this role, and it is highly probable that there was a second compartment to the SW.

In deeper cairn material, on the chamber axis and nearly 4 m from the inner end of the exposed compartment, there projects the intact flat top of a large roughly rectangular block. It measures 1.17 by 0.6 m (the SW side is hidden), and although it projects 0.4 m at most, its true height is at least 1.5 m. This block is probably the back-slab of the chamber. There is no sign of either the side walls or the portal stones of the inner compartment. Such an interpretation would mean that the total length of the chamber was 7.55 m, and the unusually large bipartite plan can be matched at Ballachnecore (ROS 3).

Three lintel-like slabs lie across the inner compartment, at a level below the tops of the orthostats of the outer compartment and evidently not *in situ*. The NE slab is 1.65 m long by 0.76 m wide and 0.35 m thick; the other two appear to be smaller but are not fully exposed. A 'covered passage' which approached the chamber from the W is mentioned in the ONB, and may be an interpretation of these three slabs.

To the NE of the chamber, 2.7 m in front of the portal stones, and at the edge of the supposed round cairn, is a prone slab that may be a lintel. The tip of an upright stone, hardly visible below its N edge, may possibly indicate the outer end of the passage. The slab measures 1.76 by 1.12 m, and the upright stone appears to be positioned in front of the NW portal stone and at right angles to the axis of the monument. However, the prone slab is only one of many large slabs lying about the cairn, all of which are presumably corbel stones or lintels displaced from the chamber.

When the chamber was opened about 1817 it was found to contain 'a quantity of human bones of immense size' (NSA).

ROS 43. ALLT EILEAG

Now re-numbered SUT 72, and included in Henshall and Ritchie 1995, 144–5. This change was due to local government reorganisation in 1975, when the parish of Kincardine and Croick became part of Sutherland District.

ROS 44. BALDOON

Parish Rosskeen
Location 6 km N of Alness
Map reference NH 633759
NMRS number NH 67 NW 3
References Maclean 1886, 334–5; Ordnance Survey Record Card; Henshall 1972, 566–8; RCAHMS 1979a, 7, no. 2
Plan ASH and JNGR
Visited 5.10.63, 27.5.94

Description. The cairn was built on a level site on a hillside facing S, at about 285 m OD. The cairn is in Strathy Wood, a conifer forest first planted before 1875, and is a little above the cultivated land in the small valley of the Strathy Burn.

The cairn had been almost entirely removed long before it was mentioned by Maclean, leaving a group of orthostats exposed. When seen in 1963 the wood had recently been cleared and replanted, and the last vestiges of the cairn appeared to be round with a diameter of about 16 m (Ordnance Survey Record Card). By 1994 the cairn was in a small clearing surrounded by mature trees. The clearing is covered with turf and moss from which the orthostats of a passage and chamber project, with a tree growing immediately to the S of the passage. The edge of the cairn is not detectable except for a low bank of cairn material 4 m W of the prone back-slab of the chamber.

The passage and chamber were built of large boulders, some of them with flat faces and some less regular in shape. With two exceptions (noted below), all are probably intact, and the

upright orthostats are exposed for almost their full heights. The passage faces ESE, and the ground drops gently from in front of the entrance. There is a pair of portal stones set 0.68 m apart at the outer end of the passage.

ROS 44

The S stone, with a rounded top, leans to the E, and its partner, with a flat top, leans less acutely to the W. They are 0.8 and 0.7 m long by over 0.3 and 0.4 m thick, and would be about 0.8 m high when vertical. At the inner end of the passage there is a second pair of portal stones set 0.6 m apart. They are 1.33 and 0.8 m long by 0.75 and 0.33 m thick, and both are 0.75 m high with irregular upper surfaces. The passage is about 2.2 m long including both pairs of portal stones. Just E of the last portal stone is a substantial horizontal slab, 0.4 m long and 0.25 m thick, which appears to be part of the N wall of the passage (two slabs were visible here in 1963). A displaced lintel lies askew between the entrance portal stones, and presumably it once rested on them. It is a regular block 1.63 m long, with a rectangular cross-section measuring 0.5 by 0.45 m. Immediately to the W a second displaced lintel, less regular in shape, lies across the passage; probably it had rested on the second pair of portal stones. It is 1.7 m long, with a face 0.9 m wide tilted down to the W, and 0.4 m thick.

The outer compartment of the chamber is about 2 m long, and it evidently had two orthostats on each side. The orthostats on the N side are 0.5 and 1.1 m long by 0.45 and 0.3 m thick; they are about 1 m high, but because there is rather more cairn material in the outer compartment they project only 0.7

and 0.75 m. The first is a rectangular block with a horizontal top and the other is pointed. On the S side the E orthostat butts against the adjacent portal stone and leans acutely to the S; clearly it had stood almost parallel to the chamber axis. It is 0.75 m long by 0.3 m thick, and was over 1.3 m high when it was upright; the tip is broken. To the W there is a gap where an orthostat is missing; a prone slab here, only partly visible and of unknown size, may be the missing orthostat or part of it. A notably substantial pair of inner portal stones, set 0.68 m apart, divides the outer compartment from the inner compartment. The stones are both 1.3 m long by 0.65 and 0.5 m thick, and both are 1.15 m high. The S stone leans slightly to the W, and the flat top slopes down to the S; the flat top of the N stone is nearly horizontal.

The inner compartment was walled with five closely-set orthostats, but only the SE orthostat remains upright. It is 0.9 m long by 0.53 m thick and 1.3 m high. The other four orthostats are prone, but appear to have been hardly disturbed since falling. The SW orthostat is about 0.83 m wide by 0.3 m thick, and is over 1.6 m long; the outer end (or top) has been damaged and the inner end (or base) is hidden. The original position of the back-slab can be calculated exactly. When vertical, this orthostat was 1.3 m long with a broad flat base, by 0.45 m thick, and 1.75 m high; its E face was 0.4 m E of its present E end. The stone tapered to a horizontal upper edge, and it was the tallest orthostat in the chamber. The N orthostat is rather irregular in shape, and it is unclear exactly how it originally stood. It measures about 1 by 1.3 m and 0.4 m thick. The NE orthostat appears to have fallen inwards; it is 1.7 m long by 0.7 m wide, and 0.55 m thick. The inner compartment was about 2 m long, and the total length of the chamber was about 4.55 m. In 1886 ten orthostats, excluding the entrance portal stones and the inner portal stones, were still standing (Maclean). Outside the chamber to the N is a stone, 0.77 m long, which is likely to be a displaced corbel stone; between the inner portal stones another probable corbel stone is partly exposed tilted up to the E (not shown on the plan). (See figure 15 for a reconstruction of the chamber plan.)

A 'Stone Cist containing Human Remains found A.D. 1883' is recorded in the cairn on the OS 6-inch map revised in 1904. The 'cist' may be a compartment of the chamber rather than a later short cist.

ROS 45. MORANGIE FOREST
(Carn Liath)

Parish Tain
Location 5 km WSW of Tain
Map reference NH 729798
NMRS number NH 77 NW 10
References Stuart 1868, 301; Henshall 1972, 567, 568; RCAHMS 1979a, 7, no. 5
Plan ASH and JNGR
Visited 20.9.67, 24.4.94

Description. The cairn is on the steep S side of Beinn nan Gearran, at 180 m OD. It overlooks the watershed of a minor narrow pass through the hills, the Lairgs of Tain. The cairn is in a small unplanted area in the southern part of the Forestry Commission's Morangie Forest. The cairn was noted in passing by Stuart in 1866 (1868), at which time it was in open moorland in an area then known as the Hill of Tain.

The axis of the long cairn is slightly skew to the slope of the hill, with the wider end of the cairn uphill; the difference in the ground level between one end and the other is 8.25 m. The cairn of angular stones is bare except for coarse grass and bracken growing over the edges. Many hollows have been made into the cairn, including a deep hollow near the NE end, but only large boulders have been exposed in the body of the cairn. The edge along the straight NW side and across the NE end is fairly well defined. The edge along the SE side is difficult to trace. Clearly it has been distorted and spread for two-thirds of its length from the NE end due to a rectangular building and other ephemeral structures that have been built into this part of the cairn. The remaining third of this side shows no sign of disturbance, but the cairn merges imperceptibly

ROS 45

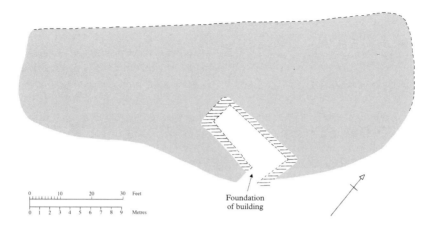

0   10   20   30   Feet
0 1 2 3 4 5 6 7 8 9 Metres

Foundation
of building

into the ground and the exact position of the edge is not clear. The SW end of the cairn has been disturbed, though the approximate position of the edge is evident. The length of the cairn is about 38 m, the width of the SW part is 9 to 11 m, but the width of the NE end before interference is uncertain. The height of the cairn, taken from the NW side, is 1.5 m near the SW end, and 1.65 m at 7.5 m from the NE end. The impression that the cairn is considerably higher at the upper NE end is largely due to the slope of the ground.

ROS 46. SCOTSBURN HOUSE

Parish Logie Easter
Location 8 km SW of Tain
Map reference NH 715761
NMRS number NH 77 NW 7
References ONB 1872, No. 25, 21; ISSFC 1899b, 362; Henshall 1972, 567, 568; RCAHMS 1979a, 9, no. 21
Plan ASH and JNGR
Visited 22.9.67, 23.5.94

Description. The last remains of this chambered cairn are in a field of pasture at 130 m OD. To the N the rising hillside is rough pasture scattered with self-sown trees, and to the S there is a wide view over agricultural land and areas of forestry, across the Cromarty Firth, the Black Isle and beyond. Scotsburn Wood East and West (ROS 47, 48) are higher on the same hillside, the latter 900 m to the ENE. The Scotsburn House cairn is overlooked by a steep knoll crowned by a dun, only 50 m to the SW. Both monuments are close to but above the Strathrory River which at this point runs in a gorge. The site of the cairn is level, on the top of a low knoll.

In 1872 the monument was recorded as 'a cairn of stones where human remains were found A.D. 1865' (ONB). In 1899 it was described as 'an indistinct circle' about 10.5 m in diameter, and it was not recognised as the remains of a cairn (ISSFC).

The last traces of the cairn are grass-covered, and at the maximum (between the last two orthostats to be mentioned) it is barely 0.5 m high. Around the edges the cairn material merges imperceptibly into the ground, and the former size and shape of the cairn are uncertain. Its present area is roughly 18.5 m ESE to WNW by 13.5 m transversely.

Five orthostats remain in the centre of the cairn. On the ESE side is a pair of portal stones. They are intact well-matched substantial granitic boulders set 0.86 m apart. They are 0.8 and 1 m long by about 0.7 m thick. The S stone leans to the E and would be 0.7 m high if upright; its partner is 0.73 m high. The ground drops away in front of them, so it is probable that they formed the entrance to the passage. The other three orthostats are sandstone slabs.

ROS 46

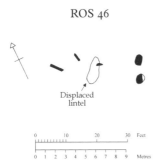

Displaced
lintel

0   10   20   30 Feet

0 1 2 3 4 5 6 7 8 9 Metres

About 3.2 m W of the N portal stone, and parallel to the probable axis of the chamber, is an orthostat 0.57 m long by 0.2 m thick, and protruding 0.6 m. An elongated intact boulder, which has the appearance of a displaced lintel, lies across the chamber axis. It slopes down from N to S, its N end resting on the orthostat and its S end resting on the ground. It is 2.7 m long by 1.08 m wide near the S end, and 0.8 m thick. To the W there are two more orthostats, both skew to the axis. The larger is over 7 m from the portal stones; it is 1.45 m long and projects 0.57 m. The plan of the chamber is not evident, and it is probable that one or more of the sandstone slabs is not *in situ*.

ROS 47. SCOTSBURN WOOD EAST

Parish Easter Logie
Location 7.2 km SW of Tain, 8.3 km NNE of Invergordon
Map reference NH 726768
NMRS number NH 77 NW 5 D
References Henshall 1972, 567, 568–9; RCAHMS 1979a, 9, no. 22
Plan ASH and JNGR
Visited 20.9.67, 25.4.94

Description. The cairn is on the S slope of Beinn an Lochain, at 205 m OD. It is 500 m ENE of the West cairn (SUT 48), and 25 m higher on the same hillside. These cairns overlook the most fertile part of the valley of the Balnagown River, and, if free of trees, they would have very extensive views to the S across the Cromarty Firth and the Black Isle. The site of the East cairn, in a clearing in a conifer forest, slopes down from N to S.

The cairn of cobbles and boulders is partly bare and partly overgrown with moss and heather, and it has been considerably disturbed and was formerly planted over. The edge of the cairn is well defined, and on the lower S side the cairn material rises steeply from the edge. The diameter from NW to SE is 16.5 m and transversely is 13 m. The height measured from the S side is about 2 m, and measured from the W side it is 0.8 m.

Within the cairn there are substantial remains of a chamber, and it is clear that it was thoroughly explored long ago. The surrounding cairn material is roughly level with the existing top of its wall. The interior of the chamber has been infilled with large stones (presumably lintels and corbel stones) and cairn material, and it is also partly overgrown, making it difficult to examine. The chamber orthostats are all intact shapely boulders set with flat faces towards the interior, and, in spite of the infilling, it is possible to take the heights of several of them from fairly close to the old floor level. The axis of the structure is ESE to WNW, but for clarity the structure will be described as lying E to W.

The easternmost orthostat is evidently the S member of a pair of portal stones at the entry to the chamber. The stone is 0.64 m long by 0.25 m thick, and projects 0.4 m. Its partner may well exist below piled cairn material. The outer compartment of the chamber is about 1.95 m long by about 1.22 m wide. There is an orthostat on each side at the inner end. The S side-slab is over 0.6 m long, but in 1994 it was almost entirely hidden. The N side-slab is 0.63 m long, over 0.1 m thick, and projects for 0.4 m, with a corbel stone in place above it. Westwards, walling links each side-slab with one of the portal stones forming the entrance to the centre compartment. A stone that appears to be a displaced lintel, probably from over the entrance to the chamber, lies across the compartment amongst the large stones that fill it. The stone is 1.4 m long by 0.38 m wide by 0.28 m thick.

The portal stones forming the entry to the

ROS 47

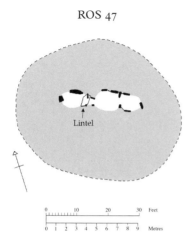

Lintel

0   10   20   30   Feet

0 1 2 3 4 5 6 7 8 9   Metres

centre compartment are 0.6 m apart, and are 0.3 and 0.6 m long, 0.23 and 0.2 m thick, and are the same height, about 0.6 m, and 0.18 m taller than the side-slab to the E. The compartment is 2.4 m long, but the width is uncertain because the S wall is hidden. On the N side there are two orthostats 0.3 m apart; they are linked by a short length of walling above which there are two corbel stones oversailing one above the other. The E side-slab is 0.82 m long, 0.25 m thick, and 0.3 m higher than the portal stones though it projects only 0.45 m. The top of the W side-slab can just be seen; it is over 0.5 m long (the W end is hidden), over 0.18 m thick, and almost the same height as the adjacent side-slab. A displaced lintel-like stone, over 1 m long, 0.45 m wide, and 0.2 m thick, lies across the middle of the compartment resting against the E side-slab and sloping down to the SW. It may originally have spanned the entry between the outer and centre compartments.

The entry to the inner compartment is by a narrow passage about 0.9 m long and 0.6 m wide. At the E end is a pair of stones which are not transversely-set portal stones. They are 0.26 and 0.5 m long by 0.2 and 0.12 m thick, and both project about 0.3 m. Immediately E of these stones is a displaced horizontal slab, over 0.9 m long N to S, 0.18 m thick, and 0.5 m wide on its sloping W face. This slab is likely to be a lintel fallen from over the entry. To the W

of the paired stones there are two portal stones. The N stone is over 0.5 m long by 0.16 m thick, and projects 0.3 m; the S stone is of similar thickness, but it is barely visible, though it is slightly taller than its partner. The portal stones support the E side of a lintel 0.3 m above the chamber filling. The lintel is a flat boulder, rather irregular in shape, which seems to be more or less *in situ*. Its maximum length, skew to the chamber axis, is 1.04 m; it is 0.6 m wide by 0.2 m thick.

The inner compartment, represented by two substantial orthostats, was formerly interpreted as the entrance passage (Henshall, RCAHMS). It is about 2.6 m long; the width is unknown as the S wall cannot be seen, and a number of relatively small slabs in this area are probably from collapsed walling. On the N side is an orthostat 1.3 m long by 0.36 m thick which projects 0.55 m, with a wide almost horizontal top which is slightly higher than the upper surface of the lintel. The back-slab is 0.64 m long by 0.4 m thick, with a flat top sloping down to the S. Though it only just projects above the rubble, it is 0.15 m higher than the adjacent orthostat, and a height of 0.8 m can be measured down its W face. The total length of the chamber is 7.6 m.

The rather limited observations suggest that the chamber may be of two periods, the W compartment probably predating the centre and E compartments (discussed further in ¶ 4.39; see figure 24, 4).

ROS 48. SCOTSBURN WOOD WEST

Parish Easter Logie
Location 7.5 km SW of Tain, 8.3 km N of Invergordon
Map reference NH 721767
NMRS number NH 77 NW 5 E
References Henshall 1972, 569, 571; RCAHMS 1979a, 9, no. 23
Plan ASH and JNGR
Visited 5.7.67, 25.4.94

Description. The cairn is on the same afforested hillside as Scotsburn Wood East

(ROS 47). The latter is 500 m to the ENE at a higher level, and the Scotsburn House chamber (ROS 46) is 900 m to the SW at a lower level. The site of Scotsburn Wood West, at 180 m OD, slopes down gently from N to S.

In 1872 the cairn was in a conifer wood and was sufficiently intact for it to be titled 'Cairn' on the first edition 6-inch OS map, and for its extent to be clearly shown. Since then the cairn material has been largely removed. Well before 1963 the remains of the cairn were deep-ploughed and were planted over, though the chamber area was respected. By 1994 the cairn had been cleared and left unplanted, and moss and heather have grown over its surface. A rim of cairn material remains, at the maximum no more than 0.5 m high above the present ground level, but a hole dug into the chamber shows that cairn material in the centre remains to a depth of 0.8 m above the old ground surface. The edge of the cairn is fairly clear, and the diameter is between 18 and 20 m.

Most of the large and intact orthostats of a passage and chamber remain. Both split slabs and boulders have been used. About 4.5 m within the cairn edge on the SE side is a pair of portal stones which has formed the entrance to the passage. The stones are 0.6 m apart; they are 0.76 and 0.6 m long by 0.15 and 0.23 m thick, and project 0.46 and 0.48 m. They have rounded upper surfaces sloping down away from the passage. A second pair of portal stones, 0.7 m apart, forms the entrance to the chamber. They are 1.33 and 1.3 m long by 0.2 and 0.4 m thick, and project 0.45 and 0.66 m. Both have fairly flat upper surfaces, and the NE stone is somewhat taller than its partner. The true heights of the N stones at the passage entrance and chamber entrance can be calculated as 0.8 and 1.05 m above the old ground surface exposed in the chamber. The passage is 1.3 m long between the two pairs of portal stones. Most of its NE wall is provided by an orthostat 0.7 m long by over 0.2 m thick, which projects 0.6 m.

On the SW side of the outer compartment of the chamber there is an orthostat over 1.74 m

ROS 48

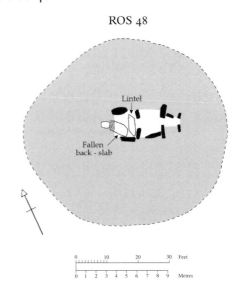

long by 0.36 m thick and projecting 0.4 m; the NW end is not visible, and the SE end butts against the adjacent outer portal stone. The opposite side of the outer compartment has been removed. The entry to the inner compartment is between a pair of inner portal stones set 0.94 m apart. They are 1.0 and over 0.85 m long by 0.33 and 0.3 m thick, and both project 0.17 m; the true height of the N stone is about 0.83 m. Their level upper surfaces are rounded in cross-section. A fallen lintel, which clearly once rested on the inner portal stones, lies to the NW of them. It is 2.45 m long, and is 0.7 m deep across the straight E edge (originally the lower surface), and 0.65 m wide (originally deep).

There is an orthostat on each side of the inner compartment. They are over 1.5 and 1.6 m long by 0.3 and 0.55 m thick, and project 0.5 and 0.8 m. In the inner part of the chamber, NW of the lintel, a hole has been dug down to the old ground surface. It shows that the filling in the inner compartment is 0.5 to 0.7 m deep, and the true heights of the side-slabs are 1 and 1.5 m. The hole has caused the back-slab to fall to the SE. It rests on the SW side-slab and on a large displaced stone on the chamber floor, and it slopes down to the NW with the base exposed above its original position. The back-slab is an impressive block, 0.9 m long at the base and slightly more higher up, 0.45 m thick, and it would be 2 m high when upright, the tallest stone in the chamber. The vertical face of the cairn core exposed behind the back-slab has the appearance of rough walling, and is topped by a large flat slab on a level with the existing cairn material (shown on the plan).

The chamber was about 4.4 m long when the back-slab was in place. The outer compartment is about 2 m long, and the inner compartment was only slightly longer and is 2.1 m wide.

ROS 49. STITTENHAM

Parish Rosskeen
Location 4.5 km N of Alness
Map reference NH 649743
NMRS number NH 67 SW 1
References Maclean 1886, 339; Henshall 1972, 570, 571; RCAHMS 1979a, 9, no. 24
Plan ASH and JNGR
Visited 22.9.67, 25.5.94

Description. The cairn is at 170 m OD on a hillside sloping down from N to S, overlooking the valley of the River Alness. The site is at the junction of the conifer forest on the upper parts of the hillside and the cultivated land of the lower parts. There is a fairly open view south-westwards across and up the valley, and southwards there is a glimpse of the Cromarty Firth and the Black Isle. The cairn is close beside the old route (now the main road A836) linking the Cromarty Firth with the inner part of the Dornoch Firth.

Evidently most of the cairn had been removed well before 1886 when it was described as a 'Druidical' circle, implying that the chamber orthostats were the only obvious feature (Maclean). When the cairn was visited in 1967 it was in a small plantation of pines, and the cairn, but not the chamber, had been planted over (Henshall). The trees were felled in the mid 1980s, and in 1994 the area was covered in rank grass, heather and gorse. Little more than the base layer of the cairn remains, and the surface is uneven and covered by grass; at most the cairn material is about 1 m

high to the NE of the chamber. The edge of the cairn can be traced round the SW half of the circumference. On the NW side it is clipped by a bank which edged an abandoned stretch of the road. The E side of the cairn has been almost completely removed, and the edge here, confused by tree stumps, cannot be identified. The diameter of the cairn is about 16 m.

On the SE side of the cairn, about 3 m within the edge, a pair of portal stones marks the outer end of the passage. They are intact granitic boulders 0.9 m apart, with their flattish upper surfaces sloping down away from the entrance.

ROS 49

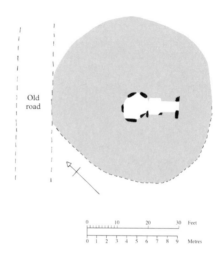

They are over 0.75 and over 0.5 m long, and both are 0.35 m thick, and they project 0.3 and 0.35 m, though the SW stone is 0.25 m lower than the NE stone. About 1.6 m NW of the former a similar boulder just projects; it is probably the SW portal stone at the entrance to the chamber. The boulder is over 0.48 m long by 0.22 m thick. A stone, thought to be its partner, was seen to the NE in 1967, but was not visible in 1994.

The orthostats of the chamber are split slabs, with the exception of the last orthostat to be described. The ante-chamber was just over 1 m long, but its walls do not survive. It was divided from the main chamber by a pair of portal stones. The SW stone is over 0.7 m long by

0.23 m thick; it is probably intact and is exposed for 0.6 m, which is almost its full height. In 1967 there could be seen the upper part of a stone leaning steeply to the NW which may have been its partner, with its base still more or less *in situ*; in 1994 this stone lay displaced in the centre of the main chamber. The main chamber has been dug out to about the old ground surface. It is about 2.45 m in diameter, built with five orthostats in the walls. Clockwise from the S they are 0.7, 1.05, 0.8, 0.98 and 0.85 m long, by 0.2 to 0.3 m thick. The first two and the last (a boulder) are exposed for 0.47, 0.95 and 0.8 m, almost their full heights; the third projects 0.55 m and the fourth, the tallest, for 0.73 m. The true height of the fourth orthostat is about 1.2 m, and it can be calculated that the true height of the NE entrance portal stone is about 0.5 m.

ROS 50. STRATHSHEASGAICH

Now re-numbered SUT 73, and included in Henshall and Ritchie 1995, 145–6. This change was due to local government reorganisation in 1975, when the parish of Kincardine and Croick became part of Sutherland District.

ROS 51. UPPER PARK (Carn Liath)

Parish Kiltearn
Location on the NW side of the Cromarty Firth, 1.3 km W of Evanton
Map reference NH 589665
NMRS number NH 56 NE 6
References Stuart 1868, 302; ONB 1874–5, No. 1, 59; Henshall 1972, 570–71; RCAHMS 1979a, 9, no. 26
Plan ASH and JNGR
Visited 22.9.67, 18.5.95

Description. The cairn is on the ridge that separates the lower parts of Glen Glass and Strath Sgitheach. The cairn, at nearly 120 m OD, is in a field at the upper edge of the cultivated land which extends along the S side of the ridge. N of the cairn the ground drops very steeply to the River Glass. There are wide views from the cairn over the Cromarty Firth and the Black Isle. The site slopes down from N to S.

The diameter of the cairn is 25 m. It has a fairly well defined edge for a short stretch of the E side, and especially so round the NW side where it rises undisturbed over a distance of 4.5 m. Elsewhere the cairn has suffered much interference. The cairn material of rounded stones is exposed in places, and otherwise it is covered with vegetation. There is a level rim around the main chamber, which is partly filled with stones and large slabs lying at various angles. The highest part of the cairn, to the SW of the chamber, is 1.2 m above ground level on the N side, and 3 m above ground level on the lower S side. In the nineteenth century the cairn was surrounded by a wall which can still be traced, and was planted with trees.

About 3 m within the E edge of the cairn the top of a boulder projects 0.3 m. It is 0.8 m long by 0.3 m thick, and appears to be an intact transversely-set portal stone, presumably at the entrance to the passage. About 3.2 m to the W is an almost parallel slab. It has a notably flat W face, and a shattered upper edge. It is 1.83 m long by 0.4 m thick, and projects 0.7 m above a considerable depth of cairn material. Its height implies that it is part of the outer compartment of the chamber. Both these stones are on the N side of the axis of the monument.

The inner compartment is 2.75 m further W. The curved NE side is defined by an orthostat and three corbel stones. The orthostat is 0.5 m long by up to 0.42 m thick, and projects 0.45 m. On its W side is a corbel stone, its upper surface 0.25 m below that of the orthostat; on its SE side are two corbel stones, set sloping down into the cairn. The corbel stones are 0.55 to 1.15 m wide along the wall-face, and the first is only 0.52 m from front to back and 0.1 m thick. On the S side of the main chamber is an orthostat, 1.7 m long by 0.25 m thick, projecting 1.3 m. It is 1.65 m taller than the first orthostat described (which indicates a true height of over 2 m), and it is a little taller than the other two orthostats. The width of the inner compartment is slightly over 3 m. Of the large displaced slabs which lie in and around the chamber, the largest, on the NW side,

ROS 51

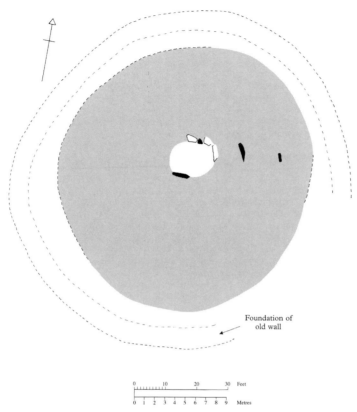

Foundation of
old wall

0   10   20   30 Feet

0 1 2 3 4 5 6 7 8 9 Metres

measures 1.9 by 1.05 by 0.3 m. (See figure 13 for a tentative reconstruction of the plan.)

This cairn is probably the monument mentioned by Stuart (1868): 'At Park is a circle of erect stones, 15 feet (4.5 m) in diameter, from which run eastward two rows 9 feet (2.7 m) in length and 6 feet (1.8 m) apart'. Stuart did not see all the monuments included in his report and had he visited Upper Park he would almost certainly have recognised it as a chambered cairn.

ROS 52. MAINS OF ARDROSS
(Carn na Feinne)

Parish Rosskeen
Location in the valley of the River Alness, 6 km NW of Alness
Map reference NH 615747

NMRS number NH 67 SW 6
References NSA 1845, 271; ONB 1875, No. 2, 18; Maclean 1886, 334; Henshall 1972, 572; RCAHMS 1979a, 8, no. 17
Plan ASH
Visited 18.4.68, 26.5.94

Description. The gaelic name of the monument indicates the former existence of a cairn, but only the orthostats of the chamber survive. The site is in a field on the N side of the valley at 200 m OD. The hillside slopes down from N to S, but the site itself slopes down gently from W to E towards a tributary of the River Alness.

The cairn had been removed long before the OS survey in 1875 (and probably before 1845, see below). The ONB records that the chamber was then in much the same condition as at present, except that all the orthostats were upright. When it was visited in 1994 the field had recently been ploughed and no vestiges of the cairn could be seen.

The chamber was built with slabs of impressive size, all but one of which are sandstone. They are rectangular in plan with smooth faces, and all are exposed for their full height, or nearly so. The axis of the chamber is slightly N of E and S of W. There are two slabs on each side, and a prone slab has clearly fallen outwards from the W end of the chamber. The SE orthostat is 2.6 m long (though 0.25 m less at ground level) by 0.46 m thick, and it is 0.8 m high with an intact horizontal upper surface. The opposite orthostat leans to the N. It is a thin slab of schist, 2.15 m long by 0.15 m thick, and it would be 0.95 m high when vertical. The SW orthostat is 2.6 m long by 0.3 to 0.35 m thick, and is 1.1 m high with an irregular upper surface. The orthostat opposite it leans acutely into the chamber with its base partly exposed. The slab is 3.1 m long by 0.25 m thick, and it would be 1.6 m high when vertical. The orthostats on the N side of the chamber are contiguous at ground level, and those on the S side have a gap of 0.55 m between them. The back-slab would have fitted neatly between the adjacent side-slabs. It is 1.4 m wide (the original length) by 0.35 m thick, and 2.15 m long (the original height, making it considerably taller than the other orthostats). The chamber is 5.6 m long by 1.5 m wide at the W end. Across the E end there lies a slab, 1.76 by 0.85 m and 0.13 m thick, which is obviously displaced. It rests on the field-gathered stones which partly fill the chamber, and is tilted down to the E.

The remains of the chamber evidently puzzled the 1875 surveyors. Maclean, who at the time was living at the Mains of Ardross, gave an account of investigations which they initiated. 'At the request of an officer of the Royal Engineers . . . it was carefully opened by digging a longitudinal trench, when it was discovered that two bodies were buried, the one at the foot of the other, in graves each about 7 feet [2.1 m] long, by 2 feet [0.6 m] broad, and only about 2 feet deep from the surface to the bottom. There are side walls

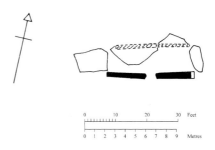

about a foot [0.3 m] high, and a division of a foot between the two bodies. The bodies were probably covered with flags, as disintegrated clayey slates were turned out in digging. The only remains found were a few teeth where the heads lay, and a thin layer of bituminous like matter, the whole length of the graves.' It is recorded in ONB 'a few teeth and small bones were found at the west end, and at the centre of the Grave at a depth of 2 feet below the surface from which it is inferred that two were buried in it, the one at the feet of the other.'

The chamber is almost certainly the unnamed 'small enclosure' mentioned (with inaccuracies) in the NSA. It was 'of an oblong form, about twelve or fourteen feet [3.6 to 4.26 m] long, and two or three feet [0.3 to 0.6 m] in breadth. It consists of a large and massive flat stone placed upright at the head, – while on either side, there are three or four similar stones placed in a line, but none at the foot. It was, we believe, originally roofed over, the entrance being at the open end; but it was, several years ago, considerably injured by some masons, who wished to obtain the stones for building a house in the vicinity.'

ROS 53. BRAHAN WOOD

Parish Urray
Location in Strathconon, 5.3 km SW of Dingwall
Map reference NH 504552
NMRS number NH 55 NW 2
References ONB 1873, No. 6, 63; RCAHMS 1979a, 7, no. 4
Plan ASH and JNGR
Visited 2.6.71, 21.10.95

Description. The cairn was built on a steep irregular south-facing hillside, at 155 m OD. The hill is covered with thick conifer forest, but if free of trees there would be extensive views from the site across the wide cultivated lands to the S.

The monument was used as a landmark for a corner of the boundary between the parishes of Urray and Fodderty, but it was ruined long before it was mapped in 1875. At that time it was recorded as 'some megalithic remains . . . and consists of several stones only three of which are erect, about 2 ft 6 in [0.76 m] above ground', and it was titled 'Stone Circle (Remains of)' (ONB). (An entry in RCAHMS 1943, 43, records a visit to a nearby knoll, mistaken for the 'stone circle').

The cairn material has been removed and only some orthostats of the chamber remain. The actual site of the cairn is a small level area, and its size indicates that the cairn is unlikely to have been more than 14 or 15 m in diameter. Several trees stand on the site which is covered with moss, bracken and brash. Forest debris may be up to 1 m deep in and around the chamber.

Eight orthostats define a large chamber of two compartments with the axis lying SSW to NNE (for ease of description it is described as lying S to N). There is no clear evidence whether the passage approached from the S or the N, but an entrance facing S seems the more likely. Three very substantial and seemingly intact blocks belong to the walls of the S compartment. On the W side there are two orthostats 0.75 m apart. They are 0.95 and 1.36 m long by 0.4 and 0.6 m thick, and project 0.75 and 0.8 m. An orthostat on the E side is 0.85 m long by 0.7 m thick, and projects 0.65 m. A 2 m gap to the N was presumably once filled by another orthostat. The N end of the compartment is marked by a portal stone set transversely to, and E of, the chamber axis. The visible part of the stone is 0.68 m long, but it slopes down to the W and is evidently longer. It is 0.2 m thick, and the broken upper surface projects 0.2 m. The width of the compartment is roughly 3 m, and the length (as

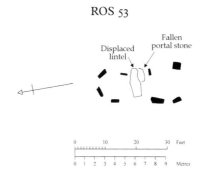

ROS 53

Displaced lintel

Fallen portal stone

it remains) is about the same, though it was probably somewhat longer if there was originally a pair of portal stones at the S end.

The N compartment retains four orthostats. At the N end are two intact boulders with rounded tops, 0.8 m apart. They are 1.15 and 0.91 m long by 0.35 and 0.38 m thick, and they project 0.95 and 0.53 m. The W orthostat is the tallest in the chamber. On the E side of the compartment is the stump of a rectangular slab, over 0.75 m long by 0.2 m thick, which projects 0.28 m. It is likely that a missing orthostat once filled the 1.5 m gap between this stone and that to the N. On the opposite side of the compartment is an orthostat of almost the same size, and probably another orthostat is missing from the gap between it and the lintel described below. The width of the compartment between these stones is 2.5 m, but its length is uncertain because the arrangements for linking the compartments are not entirely clear. The overall length of the chamber is 7.85 m, and when it was intact it was slightly more.

There is a gap of over 2 m between the compartments as they are now visible. In this gap is a displaced lintel and a leaning slab which appears to be a second portal stone on the E side of the axis. The lintel is 2.66 m long, 0.94 m wide, and 0.3 to 0.4 m thick. The wider upper surface is tilted down slightly to the N, and it seems that the almost vertical S side was the lower edge when the lintel was in place. The portal stone, just to the S and leaning to the S, is 1.2 m long by 0.25 m thick. If vertical, it would be over 0.33 m high with an intact horizontal top edge, and it would stand immediately S of the lintel. There can be little doubt that the lintel once rested on the portal stone (and its missing partner), and has been toppled to the N. An arrangement with two parallel pairs of portal stones nearly 1 m apart in the centre of a chamber is very unusual (discussed in ¶ 4.24, 41; see figure 19 for a tentative reconstruction of the plan).

ROS 54. CARN FIONNTAIRNEACH

Parish Rosskeen
Location in the valley of the Alness River, about 6 km NW of Alness
Map reference NH 6074
NMRS number NH 67 SW 4
Reference Maclean 1886, 334; RCAHMS 1979a, II, no. 41

Description. The only account of this destroyed monument, the precise location of which is not known, is given by Maclean. 'In 1848, a large cairn, "Carn Fionntairneach", on the farm of Ardross, similar to the one at Millcraig, was wholly removed. As well as the central cist, there were several others in the body of the cairn, proving after burials. A number of bones in good preservation were found, and a few flint arrow heads'. The comparison with the cairn at Millcraig (ROS 32) suggests that Carn Fionntairneach may have covered a chamber.

ROS 55. CARN NAM FIANN
(Glaick)

Parish Rosskeen
Location 5 km N of Alness
Map reference NH 635744
NMRS number NH 67 SW 10
References NSA 1845, 271; ONB 1875, No. 2, 14; Maclean 1886, 333–4; Ordnance Survey Record Card; RCAHMS 1979a, 7, no. 9
Visited 25.5.94

Description. The site of this destroyed cairn is at 300 m OD on a hillside which slopes down steeply from N to S. The site is in Stittenham

Wood, which was first planted before 1875, and now belongs to the Forestry Commission. When visited in 1994 the part of the wood containing the cairn was found to have been cleared.

The cairn was evidently fairly intact in 1845 (NSA). There can be little doubt that 'a large unopened cairn on the face of Knockfionn above Easter Ardross' refers to this monument (Maclean, who was using information gathered many years before publication in 1886). The cairn is shown with a diameter of 18 m on the OS 25-inch map surveyed in 1875. The supporting note in ONB reads: 'the site of this cairn can just be traced, but no more, the stones which composed it having been removed for building the adjoining dikes. So far as is known no interesting discoveries were made when it was being taken away'. In 1975 it was reported that 'all that survives are the slightest traces of a rim indicating a diameter of *c.* 18 m, and two earthfast stones which are probably the remains of a chamber and passage...' (Ordnance Survey Record Card). In 1994 deep heather covered the site and no sign of the cairn was detected.

The two upright stones mentioned above remain. One was just E of the centre of the cairn as seen in 1975. It is a regular rectangular block facing E and W, and is 0.8 m long by 0.4 m thick, and 1 m high. The second stone is 6 m to the E; it is a rough boulder facing N and S, 1.1 m long by 0.5 m thick and 0.6 m high. A loose boulder 0.8 m long lies beside it, and other boulders lie nearby on the hillside. Although the first stone described is suggestive of a chamber orthostat, there is insufficient evidence for this cairn to be firmly classified as a chambered cairn.

ROS 56. CNOC RAVOCH

Parish Kiltearn
Location 2 km NNE of Dingwall
Map reference NH 557612
NMRS number NH 56 SE 8
References OSA I, 1791, 292; W. C. Joass 1865, 5–6; Simpson 1866, 46–7; RCAHMS 1979a, II, no. 46
Visited 3.5.96

Description. On the S side of Cnoc Ravoch, at 190 m OD, are the last remains of a structure which was probably a cairn. It seems to have contained bronze age cists, but the remaining large slabs (and a nineteenth-century reference) suggest that possibly it also covered a chamber. The site is a small almost level platform on the steep hillside, and from it there are magnificent views in all directions except to the N. The upper part of the hill is pasture, and below this arable land stretches down to the shore of the Cromarty Firth. In the nineteenth century the hilltop, including the site, was covered by trees. The site of Clachan Biorach (ROS 14) is 700 m to the NE.

Near the centre of the platform is an upright slab of schist banded with quartzite, aligned N to S. It is 1.95 m long by 0.35 m thick, and 0.9 m high. The top has been shattered, and clearly the slab was once taller. An intact prone slab lies 2.1 m to the E. It is triangular, with a short straight side opposite and parallel to the vertical slab, and a pointed end to the E. The prone slab gives the impression that it once stood facing the vertical slab and has fallen to the E. It is 1.54 m across the W side, 2.36 m from W to E, and 0.4 m thick at the W end. A smaller slab lies to the S of the prone slab and other large slabs lie about the platform. In 1996 no cairn material could be detected below the turf.

Some support for considering that there was once a cairn on the site comes from a passing reference in the late eighteenth century (OSA). A 'circular cairn, in diameter about 30 paces' was located '800 paces W' of Clachan Biorach (ROS 14). The distance is approximately correct, but the direction of the site is to the SW; no cairn is known to the W of Clachan Biorach. In the centre of the cairn was 'a grave 3 feet 6 inches long, 18 inches broad, and 14 inches deep [1 by 0.45 by 0.36 m], neatly lined with four flat stones, and covered by another. There are also at the circumference three graves of the same dimensions, on the east, south, and west, but they are in a more ruinous condition than the central one'. This description seems to indicate that four short cists had been

exposed in the cairn. Over seventy years later Joass (quoted by Simpson) may have noted the same structure: 'a megalithic circle, most of the stones in situ' on the SW shoulder of Cnoc Ravoch. This implies that by the 1860s the cairn had been very severely robbed, and the term 'megalithic circle' suggests that some orthostats of a chamber may have been exposed (see ¶ 2.33 for ruined chambers being so called). Alternatively, but perhaps less likely, the existing upright slab and large prone slab may have been the side and capstone of a very large cist.

ROS 57. EDDERTON HILL

Parish Tain
Location above the S side of the Dornoch Firth, 4.5 km WNW of Tain
Map reference NH 734834
NMRS number NH 78 SW 14
Reference RCAHMS 1979a, 7, no. 8
Plan ASH and JNGR
Visited 24.4.94

Description. The cairn is on the fairly steep N side of Edderton Hill, 120 m above the S shore of the Firth. There is a wide view from the site northwards across the whole of the Firth and much of S Sutherland, and several chambered cairns are probably in view. The cairn is 700 m E of Red Burn (ROS 36), which is on almost the same contour, but is just out of sight. Both cairns are within the Forestry Commission's Morangie Forest.

The Edderton Hill cairn is aligned ESE to WNW along the contour, and there is a considerable drop in ground level from SSW to NNE across the cairn. When it was identified in 1971 the first planting of trees had been felled, and the cairn, already disturbed and robbed, was covered with coarse grass and heather (RCAHMS). The cairn measured 61 m long, 14 m wide across the straight E end, narrowing to 7 m wide near the centre, and about 10 m wide at the W end.

When the re-planting of this part of the forest was undertaken in the mid-1980s the cairn was severely mutilated. Deep transverse furrows were ploughed across the cairn at 4 m

---

ROS 57

```
0      10     20    30 Feet
0 1 2 3 4 5 6 7 8 9 Metres
```

intervals, except near the E end. The ploughing has exposed the cairn material of cobbles, boulders and slabs, and has dragged it down the slope to the N. Thus the edges at the ends of the cairn, and especially round the SE corner, are reasonably well defined, but the edges along the sides can be traced only very approximately. Despite the damage, the plan made in 1994 produced dimensions close to those recorded in 1971. It is still apparent that the cairn was wider and higher at the E end. Cairn material remains over 1 m deep for about 21 m from this end, but there is little depth of cairn material in the W part of the cairn. A deep hollow made long ago into the centre of the cairn near the E end was still an obvious feature in 1994.

ROS 58. HEIGHTS OF DOCHCARTY

Parish Fodderty
Location about 3 km NNW of Dingwall
Map reference NH 5261
Reference NSA 14, 1845, 252–3
Visited 16.5.95

Description. The site of this destroyed long cairn was near the top of the steep ridge that separates Strath Peffer from Strath Sgitheach, but its exact location is uncertain (see Appendix 4). The cairn was on the same ridge as the Heights of Brae (ROS 22) which was 1 km or so to the NW or W.

The only description of the long cairn was written in 1838 (NSA): 'Of the sepulchral remains [in the parish] called cairns, there is an excellent specimen on the heights of the property of Hilton, which measures 260 feet by 20 feet (79 by 6 m). It is situated on a little rising ground, having at the east end a standing-stone. Its height has, of late years, been much diminished by removal of the stones for the building of enclosures or fences. A number of bones have been discovered in it'. The cairn had been totally destroyed by 1876 (it is not mentioned in the ONB).

It is probable that there was a third neolithic cairn in the neighbourhood. The 1838 account of the long cairn is followed by a reference to two 'Druidical circles' (the usual appellation of ruined chambered cairns in the NSA). 'Of the one which lies due north of the cairn, there are only three stones remaining, the rest having been blasted and used in building.' The other is certainly Heights of Brae (ROS 22).

ROS 59. SWORDALE

Parish Kiltearn
Location on the NW side of the Cromarty Firth, 2.5 km W of Evanton
Map reference NH 578661
NMRS number NH 56 NE 8
Reference RCAHMS 1979a, 9, no. 25
Plan ASH and JNGR
Visited 25.4.95

Description. Near the top of the narrow ridge that separates the lower ends of Glen Glass and Strath Sgitheach, at 165 m OD, there is an enigmatic structure which may be the last remains of a chambered cairn. It is just above the cultivated land, in an area of pasture scattered with house foundations and long-abandoned rectangular cultivation plots.

ROS 59

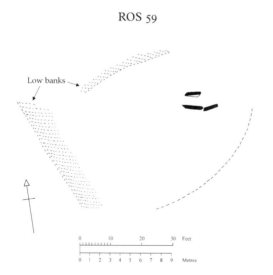

Three substantial slabs, all 0.3 m thick and exposed for nearly their full heights, may have formed part of the walls of a rectangular chamber aligned E to W. At the W end are two nearly parallel slabs, 1.27 to 1.05 m apart. The N slab is 1.52 m long; it would be 0.96 m high if vertical but it leans to the S with an overhang of 0.3 m. The S slab is 2.1 m long and 0.76 m high. Immediately to the E of the latter, but not quite in line with it, the third slab is 1.43 m long and 0.7 m high.

In an arc beginning N of the structure and extending in front of its E end small irregular mounds of stones show through the turf. To the SE these merge with a turf-covered stony spread which has a definable edge reaching to 9.5 m SW of the structure. It is doubtful whether these features are remains of a cairn. The area to the W of the chamber is at a slightly lower level and almost free of stones. To the W and N of this, where the edge of a cairn might be expected, any traces are obscured by low banks which edge former cultivation plots.

An outcrop of rock 20 m SSW of the chamber bears a group of cupmarks.

ROS 60. CAIRNSIDE

Parish Killearnan
Location at the W end of the Black Isle, 3.5 km NE of Muir of Ord
Map reference NH 560525
NMRS number NH 55 SE 73
Reference Brown, 1816
Plan ASH and JNGR
Visited 23.5.97

Description. The cairn is at the side of a field in flat agricultural land. It is at 140 m OD, and has wide views. Carn Urnan (ROS 13) is 650 m to the ESE.

The cairn is aligned N to S, with the wider end to the N. It is evident that the cairn has been reduced in height, and it has been used as a dump for field-gathered stones. It remains as a low, untidy, and much disturbed rise, with the N half overgrown with gorse, and the S part mainly covered with coarse grass. A track, with an old wall and fence along its E side, runs beside the E edge of the cairn for much of its length. The straight N end and the W side can

ROS 60

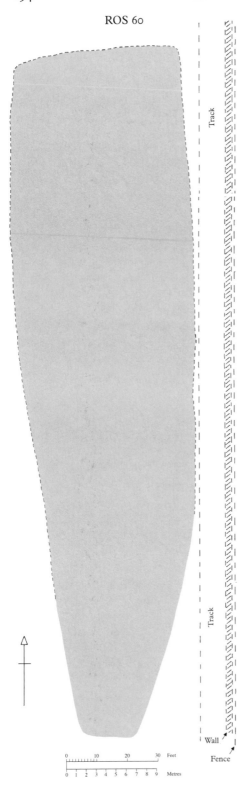

Track

Track

Wall

Fence

0   10   20   30 Feet

0 1 2 3 4 5 6 7 8 9 Metres

be traced a little within the present limit of ploughing. The cairn fades away to the S, and its southern extent is uncertain. The cairn was at least 52 m long, and may have been as much as 65 m long. The N half is almost parallel-sided, 16.5 m wide at the N end and slightly wider further S; the S half gradually narrows to about 13 m wide at the last definable point. From the N end the cairn rises for about 13 m to a maximum height of a little over 1 m, which height it retains for about 16 m, and then it gradually dwindles towards the S end.

The cairn is indicated on a survey of 1816 by a row of four dots, and is titled 'Grey Cairn'. The nearby house is named Cairnside. However, the cairn was not recorded on the 1st edition of the 6-inch OS map surveyed in 1872–3, implying that by then it had been severely reduced. (We are grateful to Dr D. Alston, Curator, Cromarty Courthouse, for drawing our attention to this cairn.)

ROS 61. TARRADALE
(Clachan more na Taradin)

Parish Killearnan
Location 2 km E of Muir of Ord
Map reference NH 549497
NMRS number NH 54 NW 123
References Logan 1831; 1834
Plan ASH and JNGR
Visited 1.7.99, 20.7.99

Description. The cairn is situated a little above the flat cultivated land bordering the Beauly Firth, on an undulating hillside, at 40 m OD. The cairn is on a knoll in a conifer wood.

The cairn, composed of cobbles, has been reduced to its lowest level, presumably to build a nearby field wall. Near the centre of the cairn there project the orthostats of two chambers, and many displaced slabs and large blocks lie about on the NE half of the cairn (which is furthest from the field wall). The orthostats appear to be undamaged (except for three mentioned below), as are most of the large displaced stones. The cairn is covered with forest litter and coarse grass, and a number of trees are growing on it and even within the chambers. The surface of the cairn is uneven, and the edge can be traced only approximately. Four kerb-stones, two of them slightly displaced, survive close together on the E side, roughly on the projected axis of the S chamber. The diameter of the cairn is about 25 m. It is unlikely that the depth of cairn material is anywhere more than 1 m, though it appears to be more when viewed from the edge because of the rising ground beneath it. The chambers are only 2 m apart. Both were entered from the ESE, but for ease of description the axes are treated as lying E to W.

The passage to the N chamber is represented by a single orthostat, at the W end of the N side. The orthostat is about 0.6 m square, and projects 0.45 m. The entry from the passage to the chamber is 0.6 m wide between a pair of transversely set portal stones. The stones are similar in size (about 0.9 by 0.4 m) and in shape, with almost horizontal upper surfaces. They project 0.5 and 0.6 m, and the N stone is a little taller than the adjacent passage orthostat. To the E of the S portal stone is a displaced block, 1.2 m long, 0.5 m wide and 0.35 m thick, which is likely to have been the lintel that once rested on the portal stones. East of it, and lying across the projected axis of the chamber, is another lintel-like block, possibly displaced from over the destroyed passage entrance.

One orthostat remains on each side of the outer compartment of the chamber. The stone at the outer end of the S wall is roughly 0.6 m square, and is a little taller than the adjacent portal stones. The other orthostat, at the inner end of the N wall, is 0.85 m long by 0.4 m thick. These stones are about the same height, and project 0.6 and 0.56 m. The compartment is about 2.55 m long, and was roughly rectangular, about 1.7 m wide.

The circular inner compartment is entered between a pair of portal stones only 0.22 m apart. They are 1.05 and 1.22 m long by 0.6 m thick, and they project 0.55 m with gently rounded upper surfaces. All the orthostats described above are rounded boulders.

ROS 61

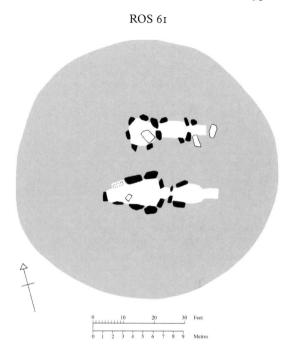

```
0          10         20         30   Feet
|││││││││││││││││││││││││││││││││││││
0  1  2  3  4  5  6  7  8  9   Metres
```

The five orthostats forming the wall of the inner compartment are irregularly spaced, with a wide gap of 0.83 m on the S side. They are similar in size, between 0.76 and 0.93 m long and between 0.45 and 0.6 m thick. The two E orthostats are boulders, and the three at the back of the compartment are rather angular blocks with pointed tops. It is noticeable that all the orthostats, together with those of the outer compartment, are set with their flattest faces to the interior. The orthostats and the portal stones do not vary greatly in height. The tips of the NW and W orthostats have been broken, and the former is the tallest stone, 0.37 m higher than the portal stones, and on the outside it is exposed for a height of 1.07 m. The compartment is between 2.4 and 2.55 m in diameter.

Lying horizontally inside the inner compartment is a displaced flat block, probably a capstone, measuring about 1.25 m by 0.96 m and 0.3 m thick. A displaced corbel stone rests against two orthostats on the W side. Other corbel stones lie outside the chamber on the cairn material, having been dragged from their places in the upper part of the wall. An arc of four such stones round the SE side of the inner compartment is particularly noticeable. The corbel stones are flat boulders, generally measuring about 0.8 m by 0.6 m.

At the S chamber the passage and the outer part of the outer compartment have been destroyed. Two substantial orthostats forming the inner end of the compartment converge slightly to the W. The width of the compartment at their E ends is 1.75 m. The orthostats are 1.13 m and 1.33 m long by 0.6 and 0.4 m thick. The S stone is a rectangular block with a rather uneven upper surface; the N stone is a more irregular boulder with the top edge sloping down to the E. The S stone projects 1.3 m measured on the S side where the cairn material is lower, and the opposite stone is about 0.4 m less in height. Between these two orthostats there lies a large displaced slab, 1.14 m long, and two more similar slabs lie further to the E.

A pair of low portal stones form an entry 0.37 m wide into the inner part of the chamber. The S stone is 0.85 m long by 0.34 m thick, with a horizontal upper surface 0.45 m lower than the adjacent orthostat to the E. The N stone is smaller and slightly lower. There are gaps of 0.4 and 0.6 m between the portal stones and a pair of orthostats to the W. The gap on the S side is filled by a displaced stone lying lengthwise.

The inner part of the chamber is wedge-shaped in plan, 2.7 m wide across the E end by 5.45 m long. The pair of orthostats mentioned above, set skew to the axis and 0.77 m apart, form the E wall. They are 0.93 and 0.88 m long by 0.55 and 0.46 m thick. The S stone has a nearly horizontal upper surface and its partner has a pointed top; they are the same height and a little taller than the S stone of the outer compartment.

The converging almost straight N and S walls each consisted of three orthostats, but the innermost on the N side (shown prostrate on Logan's plan, plate I) is missing. The E and centre orthostats on the S side and the W orthostat on the N side are massive blocks, the most conspicuous features of the monument. The first of these is exposed to near its base on the outside and stands 1.67 m high (and 0.5 m above the orthostat to the NE); the true height of all three is about 2 m. The two on the S side lean slightly to the S. The first of these is a boulder, about 1.1 m long by 0.65 m thick, with a rounded top. Its neighbour to the W is more irregular with a pointed top, though with a flat face to the interior, 1.48 m long by 0.55 m thick. The largest of these orthostats is that on the N side, a rectangular block 1.8 m long by 0.7 m thick, with a narrow horizontal top. The E orthostat on the N side is about 0.45 m lower than that to the W, and is the same height as that to the SE; it has an irregular pointed profile. The W orthostat on the S side is relatively slight, over 1.15 m long (the E end is hidden beneath a tree) by at most 0.3 m thick, and projecting 0.7 m. The back-slab is also relatively small, 0.96 m long by 0.43 m thick and 0.8 m high with a shattered top.

The inner part of the chamber may have been divided. Between the centre and W orthostats on the S side a low rectangular stone projects into the chamber skew to the axis. It leans slightly to the SE, its horizontal top 0.7 m below the top of the centre orthostat and about level with that of the W orthostat. The transverse stone is 0.64 m long by 0.4 m thick. It has the appearance of being a portal stone, the N end of which has been displaced eastwards.

The plan made by Logan in 1831 shows the monument in virtually its present condition (plate I, our reconstruction of the plan in figure 21). He recorded its name as Clachan more na Taradin. (We are grateful to Dr A. Robb for identifying the cairn.)

INV 1–4.

See pp. 241–2.

INV 5. AVIELOCHAN

Parish Duthil and Rothiemurchus
Location in Strathspey, 3.5 km NNE of Aviemore

Map reference NH 909167
NMRS number NH 91 NW 3
References Cash 1910, 197–203; Henshall 1963,
359–60
Plan ASH and JNGR
Excavation Cash, 1909
Visited 20.4.58, 1.5.97

INV 5

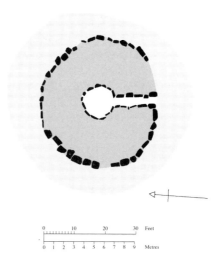

Description. The cairn is in the corner of a field, at the edge of a quite restricted area of cultivation on the valley floor. To the W and N the land is afforested, to the E and S it is rough grazing with scattered trees. The actual location, at 240 m OD, is a slight rise which is left unploughed and bears a few trees, and several birches are growing on the cairn itself. The site is 120 m from the NE shore of Avie Lochan, and is only 30 m W of the main railway line from Perth to Inverness.

Before 1909 the cairn was overgrown with grass and heather, and the upper parts of eleven kerb-stones could be seen round the S and W sides. In that year it was robbed to provide ballast for the railway, and this activity led to the excavation of the passage and chamber. Both are still fully visible (and this allows the true heights of the outer parts of the monument to be measured from the chamber floor).

The cairn is edged by a heavy kerb which is almost complete. Within it the remaining cairn material is mainly turfed over, fairly level, and less than 1 m high. Against the outside of the kerb is a turf-covered bank. The kerb is built of boulders and a few split slabs, and all are intact. Ten of the kerb-stones lean outwards, and one leans inwards, all with their hidden bases *in situ*. Round the N and E sides the outer faces of most of the kerb-stones are completely hidden by the external bank, but the inner faces have been exposed by the removal of the cairn material. The kerb now appears rather irregular, but it is clear that the outer faces of the kerb-stones, if fully exposed, would form a more regular curve. The diameter of the kerb is about 12.5 m.

The kerb-stones in the SW quadrant are the most impressive. The largest kerb-stone of all is immediately W of the passage entrance. It is 1.13 m long by 0.5 m thick, and projects 0.56 m,

but its true height is 1.65 m. The following eleven kerb-stones are only a little smaller; all are closely set (except for a gap where a stone is missing), and most have horizontal upper surfaces. The heights of the stones diminish gradually, though not consistently, towards the rear of the cairn. The kerb-stones behind the chamber, which hardly project, are quite substantial stones 1 m high. On the E side, apart from the penultimate SE kerb-stone, only the upper parts of the inner surfaces of the kerb-stones can be seen, though their thicknesses can be roughly estimated. A number of kerb-stones are missing on the E side of the entrance.

The outer edge of the bank outside the kerb is clearly defined, except round the northern third of the circuit where it merges into the slope of the ground. The bank is composed of small rounded stones, and is undisturbed apart from some superficial robbing on the NNE side. There is no break where it crosses the entrance to the passage. The bank appears to be about 2.4 to 3 m wide and 0.5 m high, but its actual width must be more, and against the kerb-stones its true height is 1.0 to 1.3 m. When the monument was intact the overall diameter was about 20 m, with the upper parts of the kerb-stones probably visible on the S side, but barely visible or hidden on the N side; all round the NE half of the circuit the bank is flush with, or just higher than, the tops of the kerb-stones (except where there has been disturbance).

The passage, facing S, is about 4 m long. It is entered between a well-matched pair of boulders set 0.66 m apart. The W orthostat is 0.7 m long by 0.47 m thick; it is 0.8 m high, and is 0.5 m lower than the adjacent kerb-stone. Four more contiguous stones on each side form the base course of the passage walls, with an additional small vertical slab filling a gap on the W side. All but one are split slabs with flat faces and nearly horizontal upper surfaces; they are lower than the boulders at the entrance and the smallest is only 0.3 m high. At the time of the excavation there was a second course consisting of horizontal slabs. The width of the passage varies between 0.54 and 0.93 m.

The chamber is almost circular, 3 by 2.8 m. The wall stands up to 0.6 m high, roughly built of split slabs and occasional small boulders. At the entrance a pair of orthostats 0.43 m high and 0.86 m apart overlap the ends of the passage walls. On the opposite side of the chamber the stones of the base course are only 0.15 m high. Above the base course, except on the NW side, two to three more courses survive, and a few more stones were in place in 1909.

Due to the removal of much of the cairn material within the kerb, and the exposure of the chamber and passage to ground level, the present appearance of the monument is curious and perhaps misleading. The relatively high level of the top of the bank, which largely conceals the outer face of the kerb, gives the impression that the chamber and passage were built in a hollow on the top of a small knoll.

There is no indication whether or not the cairn was ever surrounded by a circle of standing stones.

The excavator found the passage and chamber filled with loose stones covered by peaty earth, indicating that the upper part of the structure had been removed long ago. At the outer end of the passage were some fragments of charcoal, and here and in the chamber some scraps of bone (not certainly human) were found. In the passage, above floor level, was a segment of a 'jet' armlet.

FINDS
Artefact. In the Royal Museum of Scotland. Part of an armlet of cannel coal, iron age or later in date (EQ 310).
Not illustrated.

INV 6. AVIEMORE

Ring-cairn, see Appendix 2

INV 7.

See p. 241.

INV 8.   BALNUARAN OF CLAVA CENTRE (Ring-cairn)

Parish Croy and Dalcross
Location in Strathnairn, 8 km E of Inverness
Map reference NH 757444
NMRS number NH 74 SE 3
References Jolly 1882, 305–9; Fraser 1884, 347–50; Piggott 1956, 188–90; Henshall 1963, 361–2, 363; Barclay 1990, 17, 20, 21; Bradley 1996; 2000, 18–23, 48–59, 83–6
Plan ASH and JNGR
Excavation Piggott 1953, Bradley 1994
Visited 15.4.57, many times until 11.8.98

Description. This ring-cairn is situated between the two passage-graves, Balnuaran of Clava North-east and South-west (INV 9, 10). For a description of the location and previous investigations, see Balnuaran of Clava North-east, INV 9.

The ring-cairn of Balnuaran of Clava Centre consists of an outer kerb of substantial stones with a bank against their outer faces, an inner kerb edging an empty central area, and a surrounding circle of standing stones, three (or just possibly four) of which are linked to the outer kerb by low banks or 'rays' (plate 14).

The cairn kerb is almost complete for two-thirds of the circuit, but round the S third most of the kerb-stones are missing. The kerb is somewhat irregular in plan, though the irregularities may have been exaggerated by disturbance. In places the stones run in almost straight lines, which is most noticeable on the W and E sides. The diameter of the kerb is between 17 and 18 m. The kerb-stones are intact boulders with occasional slabs (which are breaking up). Mostly the stones are substantial, set touching, with flat faces to the outside, and leaning slightly inwards. They are taller than they appear because the lowest 0.2 m or more is hidden by the external bank.

The tallest surviving kerb-stone is on the SSW side. It is a regular block, 1 m long by 0.45 m thick, and projects 1.4 m. Many of the stones project about 0.9 m, and on the E side, where the stones have been displaced to lean steeply inwards, one stone can be seen to have had a true height of 1.3 m. The kerb-stones round the N side are markedly smaller and are set upright, and they project only 0.33 m or so. A stone on the E side bears at least one cupmark, so positioned that it was formerly

hidden by the bank. Elevations of the outer and inner kerbs, and a record of the types of stone used, are given in Bradley 2000, illustration 17.

The bank outside the kerb has been robbed and disturbed, and its indefinite outer edge merges into the ground. The bank appears to be about 1.5 to 2 m wide, and at most is 0.3 m high against the kerb-stones. A small part in front of the largest kerb-stones on the SSW side was excavated in 1953, and the bank was sectioned on the E and ESE sides during the excavations in 1994 (see below).

The cairn of bare cobbles, confined between the outer and inner kerbs, is 1 m or a little more in height, and has been restored to a nearly flat surface level with the tops of all but the tallest kerb-stones. The composition of the cairn was investigated in 1994 by a radial cutting on the E side, 4 m wide. The core of the cairn, up to 0.5 m thick, was made up of very large blocks, and the space between the core and the inner kerb was filled with smaller

INV 8

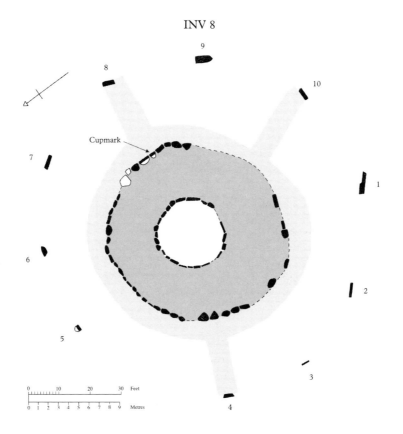

rubble. Above this the cairn material was a mixture of rounded stones and blocks. Through this layer a radial break was detected by a slight difference in the character of the cairn material; the break was aligned on one of the rays and standing stone *8* (see below). The uppermost 0.4 m of the cairn consisted of loose stones, probably redeposited from the clearance of the central area (Bradley 2000, 52–3, illustration 56, 130).

The inner kerb is set on an almost exact circle 6.3 m in diameter, but it is not central to the outer kerb. The inner kerb is complete apart from two small gaps (now filled with walling), and the inner faces of the kerb-stones are virtually fully exposed. The stones, a mixture of slabs and boulders, have flat faces and vertical or nearly vertical sides, and fit together closely. The tops of the boulders are rather irregular, and the tops of the slabs are damaged. The tallest stone, on the SSE side, is 1.1 m high, and the shortest stones, on the N side, are 0.6 m high.

When first recorded, the central area was partly filled with stones (Jolly, 305; Fraser, fig. 14). By the time it was excavated in 1953 it was empty, and the floor was found to have been disturbed. Two small upright stones 'suggested that some form of cist or stone setting had been destroyed', and the floor 'was blackened by charcoal, and there was a sparse scatter of cremated human bone' (Piggott).

There are nine standing stones and a barely visible stump of a tenth stone in the circle around the cairn. The stones are fairly evenly spaced except for a wider space on the NNW side, and this suggests that originally there were eleven stones in the circle. The existing stones are described clockwise from that on the SSW side, which was probably the largest before it was broken. Six of the stones are slabs, rectangular in plan with flat faces, and these have been damaged by lengthwise vertical cleavage. The rest of the stones are boulders or blocks of conglomerate. According to Fraser, stones *1, 2, 7* and *10* were lying prone until they were re-erected in the later 1870s.

Stone *1* is the stump of a shattered slab, 2.2 m long by 0.5 m thick, and 0.6 m high. Stone *2*, which has lost some stone from both faces, has a jagged pointed top; it is 1.55 m long by 0.33 m thick, and 2.5 m high. Stone *3*, a slab which has broken off flush with the ground, is 0.8 m long by 0.17 m thick. Stone *4* is a weathered slab, 1 m long by 0.4 m thick, and 1.66 m high. Stone *5* has broken, and leans steeply to the N; the stump of this block is 0.65 m long by 0.26 m thick, and would be 0.56 m high if upright. Stone *6* is an intact rather irregular boulder with a rounded top, 1 m by about 0.57 m, and 1.45 m high. Stone *7* is the stump of a slab, 1.45 m long by about 0.4 m thick; it has split so that the W part is 0.37 m high and the E part is level with the turf.

Stone *8* is a block which is rectangular at the base, but the sides and the top have been damaged; it is 1.17 long by 0.47 m thick, and 1.34 m high. Stone *9* is a boulder 1.7 by 0.74 m, and 2.2 m high; it is rectangular in plan with a pointed top, which, with the sides, has probably been damaged. Stone *10* is a slab 1.15 m long by 0.5 m thick, and 1.52 m high. The surface has sheared off the N face, and the top is damaged. An upright stone outside the circle on the ESE side is not shown on early plans, and is assumed to be a modern addition.

Three of the standing stones, *4, 8* and *10*, are linked to the cairn by low narrow banks, or rays, of carefully packed small stones. They were first noticed when the vegetation around the cairns was removed in the 1870s, and they are a clearly-defined feature of the monument. They are about 2 m wide and 0.2 to 0.3 m high. At one end they merge with the bank outside the cairn kerb, and at the other end they merge with the mound of packing around the base of each standing stone. Stones *8* and *10* are not quite central to the axes of the rays leading to them. It has been suggested that there is a fourth ray linking the kerb with standing stone *7* (Bradley 2000, 19, 20, illustration 14), but this awaits confirmation by excavation. The outer end of the S ray was examined in 1953, and the E ray was examined in 1994 as part of a long cutting through the cairn, the external bank, and extending to the packing around stone *8*. The bank and ray consisted of a layer of flat slabs mixed with rounded stones, with stones more common in the upper part. The base of the standing stone was in a hollow, only 0.15 m deep, which may have been formed by the weight of the stone, and it was surrounded and supported by a small cairn of packing material. It was demonstrated in the excavation that the bank, ray, and packing cairn were of the same materials and merged together, from which it was concluded that the whole monument was of unitary design.

The area between the E and S rays, including standing stone *9*, was also excavated in 1994. Stone *9* was found to be set in a substantial socket, 0.4 m deep, with stone packing material, and more packing, partly modern, rose above ground level. A large area of the old ground surface was examined, but the only discoveries were many pieces of worked flint and quartz near the S ray, and remains of a burial of the first millennium AD. This consisted of a small rectangular setting of flat slabs, below and around which was a concentration of cremated bone and pieces of charcoal.

There are several cupmarked stones, all indicated on Bradley's plan, 2000, illustration 14:

1. Stone in the outer kerb on the E side, facing standing stone *8*. Several cupmarks, the lower ones hidden (Jolly no. 3, fig 3a; Bradley 2000, illustration 50 G).
2. The adjacent kerb-stone to the S. The visible markings are unconvincing, but cupmarks have been recorded in positions that are now below ground level (Jolly no. 4, fig. 4; Bradley 2000, illustration 50 F).
3. Kerb-stone facing stone *9*. One cupmark, not seen by us.
4. Stone in the inner kerb on the SW side. One cupmark.
5. Standing stone *9*, outer face. One cupmark (Jolly no. 2, fig. 3; Bradley 2000, illustration 18).
6. Standing stone *9*, inner face. One possible faint cupmark.

(Cupmarks claimed on the inner face of standing stone *4*, Jolly no. 5, fig. 5, are natural.)

FINDS
Artefacts. Museum not yet allocated.
Flakes and chips of flint and quartz, sixty-five pieces in total, were found in 1994, on the old ground surface to the E of the S ray (detailed in Bradley 2000, 83–6); some flint flakes were recovered from the central area in 1953. Not illustrated.
Radiocarbon dates. See ¶ 10.69.

INV 9. BALNUARAN OF CLAVA NORTH-EAST

Parish Croy and Dalcross
Location in Strathnairn, 8 km E of Inverness
Map reference NH 757444
NMRS number NH 74 SE 1
References Anderson 1834, 446–51; Stewart 1857; Joass 1858; Innes 1860, 49, pl. VII; Jolly 1882, 303–5; Fraser 1884, 345, 346, 348; Somerville 1923, 218–22; Kennedy 1931; Piggott 1956, 195; Henshall 1963, 362–4; Thom 1967, 62; Thom, Thom and Burl 1980, 246–7; Barclay 1990, 19–29; Bradley 1996; 2000, 32–8, 69–88
Plan ASH and JNGR
Excavation Kennedy 1931; Bradley 1995
Visited 15.4.57, many times until 11.8.98

Description. Three large cairns stand only 50 and 70 m apart on a level site on the flood plain of the River Nairn. They are about 200 m from the river, at 105 m OD. In the mid nineteenth century the area was treeless stony rough grazing covered with gorse and heather, and scattered with many large boulders (Jolly, 302). At that time the remarkable number and variety of prehistoric structures in the neighbourhood was well known. Agricultural improvements in the later nineteenth century caused extensive damage or destruction to the monuments. The sides and floor of the valley are now mainly enclosed pasture with some arable fields. The Balnuaran cairns are protected within an enclosure, one side of which is formed by a minor public road, and they are surrounded by beech trees which provide a pleasantly secluded atmosphere.

The three bare cairns, each surrounded by a circle of standing stones, are in a nearly straight line from NE to SW. The NE and SW cairns are passage-graves (INV 9 and 10), and between them is a ring-cairn (INV 8); additionally, there is an inconspicuous small kerb-cairn close to the NW boundary of the enclosure (figure 45). Many indistinct features can be detected beneath the turf in the rest of the enclosure. Near the NE end there is certainly a small cairn, and what appears to be a roadway between two low banks of stone running to the NE; one of the banks may veer and link with the remains of a wall running E from the outer side of the E standing stone of the ring-cairn (but see Bradley 2000, 15, illustration 11, for a more detailed interpretation).

Investigation and recording of the two passage-graves took place spasmodically through the nineteenth century. The chamber of the South-west cairn was revealed in the late 1820s, and that of the North-east cairn somewhat later. Some of the fallen stones of the surrounding circles were re-erected by the landowner in the later 1870s (ISSFC 1880a, 32 fn). From about that time, until the cairns were taken into State Care in 1925, a series of illustrations shows that the condition of the cairns, particularly of the North-east cairn, had deteriorated badly. Work was undertaken on all three cairns in 1930 and 1931 to clear vegetation and displaced cairn material, followed by the exposure and re-instatement of the cairn kerbs, and excavation of a portion of each chamber floor (the work was supervised by M. K. Kennedy and published by Barclay in 1990). The three cairns were the subject of detailed examination and limited excavation between 1994 and 1996 as part of a wide-ranging study by Bradley.

The Balnuaran of Clava North-east cairn contains a chamber and passage fully exposed to view, and is edged by a kerb of boulders, outside which is a low bank, and the whole is surrounded by a ring of standing stones (frontispiece, plate 12). The cairn was restored to a regular profile in 1931, mainly by replacing fallen cairn material. It remains about 2.3 m high, and the diameters of the kerb are between 16 and 17.5 m.

The kerb, of massive boulders with one quarried slab, is complete apart from two breaks, each for a single missing kerb-stone, on the E and SE sides. When restoration work was undertaken in 1931 it was found that nineteen of the kerb-stones had fallen outwards, but not necessarily to a prone position, and some of them were buried beneath stony debris (clockwise from the entrance, stones *4–6, 10, 11, 15, 18–24, 29, 31, 33–35, 38*). All of them were restored to their original positions. In three places a large slab was found lying behind or above the kerb-stones. In 1995 two more kerb-stones were found and replaced (*40–1*).

As the cairn is now presented, the inner faces of the kerb-stones are hidden by the cairn material that they support, and the lower 0.5 m or so of their outer faces is concealed by the external bank. However, in most cases it is possible to record the thicknesses of the stones, either across the top surfaces or in gaps along the sides. Generally they are 0.3 to 0.5 m thick, and occasionally as much as 0.6 m thick. Almost all the kerb-stones have flat vertical outer surfaces, and they are generally placed to form a regular curve. Most of the stones are touching, sometimes above ground level, but occasionally they are as much as 0.37 m apart.

The larger and more shapely kerb-stones, many of them with horizontal upper edges, are in the SW arc, and project 1 m or so above the external bank. The kerb on this side is interrupted by the entrance to the passage. It is 0.53 m wide between two large kerb-stones of equal height, though they are not as high as some of the stones in this arc. The excavations in 1995 revealed that the tallest kerb-stones stand 1.3 to 1.5 m high above the old ground surface, and the four kerb-stones beside the entrance are set in sockets 0.22 and 0.4 m deep. The total height of the tallest kerb-stone is therefore nearly 1.7 m. Round the rest of the cairn most of the of the kerb-stones have rounded or pointed tops. The stones diminish in size towards the rear, and the smallest project only 0.38 m above the bank, but it is evident that their true height is nearer 1 m, and that they are much more substantial stones

INV 9

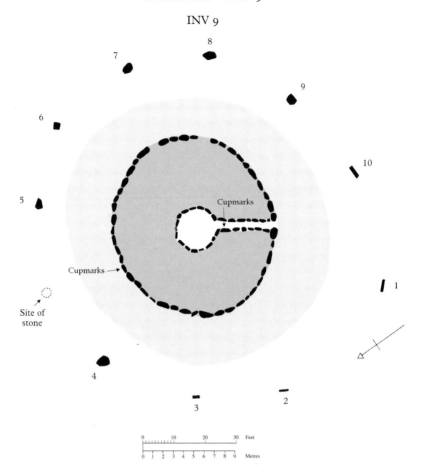

than they now appear. The graduation in size is not regular; a notable a stone on the E side is 1.45 m long by 0.6 m thick and projects 0.83 m. Elevations of the kerb, passage and chamber wall, and a record of the types of stone used, are given in Bradley 2000, illustrations 35–7.

On the N side of the kerb, the outer face of stone *20* is covered with cupmarks, one of which is ringed, and with a number of channels (plate 17). The stone had fallen outwards and was discovered in 1931.

A small cutting was made into the SSE side of the cairn in 1995. In the limited area that could be observed the core of the cairn consisted of large stones mixed with turf or topsoil containing lenses of charcoal. The core seemed to have been designed as a stable structure to support the chamber, and had probably not

extended as far as the kerb. It had been capped by a layer of smaller stones reaching to the kerb-stones.

The passage is 6 m long. The basal course of the walls consists of close-set orthostats, six on the NW side, and seven on the SE side. The two outermost are 0.62 and 0.4 m high (the latter is unusually small), and they increase in height to 1 and 0.85 m at the inner end. The orthostats are boulders, except for the innermost on each side which are regular quarried slabs with horizontal top edges and notably flat faces; that on the NW side is cupmarked. On both sides of the passage a number of quite large horizontal flat slabs resting on the orthostats are the remains of an original course of rough walling. These slabs, first noted by Jolly, indicate that the passage was roofed at a height of at least 1.23 m at the inner end, where it is 0.72 m wide.

The chamber is about 3.8 m in diameter. The basal course consists of sixteen orthostats, a mixture of slabs and boulders. On each side of the entrance is a slab orthostat, 1.14 and 0.9 m high, which overlaps the end of the adjacent passage orthostat. Round the NE side of the chamber the orthostats are a little lower, and those opposite the entrance are 0.6 m high.

Above the orthostats the walling is rough, in irregular courses, incorporating large horizontal slabs, with smaller stones filling the gaps around the orthostats and between the large slabs. Apart from a few small pinnings, the walling is original. On each side of the entrance a horizontal slab rests, skew to the axis, on the innermost passage orthostat and the adjacent chamber orthostat, and merges with the chamber walling. On the NW side the wall remains to a height of 2 m, and to a little less on the NE side, with some slight oversailing in the upper part. Beside the entrance the wall is reduced to 1.55 m high. It can be calculated from the earliest illustrations that the NE side stood about 3 m high in the mid nineteenth century with considerable oversailing in the upper part (Innes, Stewart, Joass) (figure 4). Though less marked a feature than in the South-west chamber, the large slabs on the NW and SE sides of the chamber tend to be placed in vertical stacks.

The chamber was 'cleared out' about 1853 by 'the late Mr. Forbes of Culloden, . . . when a few bones were found in it' (Fraser, 348). Excavation in 1931 revealed a layer of black soil with stones below (Barclay, 22). In the light of work in the South-west cairn in 1994, it is likely that these features were of natural origin, and that the original floor had been removed (Bradley 2000, 70).

The bank built against the outside of the kerb now appears to be about 0.45 m high against the kerb-stones, and between 3.5 to 4.5 m wide, extending as a level platform for roughly 1.6 m from the kerb, beyond which it slopes down to the present ground level. These dimensions were shown to be approximately correct when a small part of the bank on the S and SW side was examined in 1995. It was found to consist of an unstructured mass of slabs, with mainly small rounded stones above (Bradley 2000, illustrations 33, 77). The bank continued without a break across the entrance to the passage. The outer part of this substantial bank sloped down to become a thin layer of scattered slabs (probably displaced material, though the excavator considered that the platform extended as a deliberate feature as far as the ring of standing stones, see Bradley 2000, 73, illustrations 80, 81). Two standing stones, 9 and 10 (the latter re-erected in the 1870s), were within the excavated area. Neither was set in a stone hole, but they were supported by small mounds of stones.

There are ten standing stones surrounding the cairn. The spacing of the stones is rather irregular, and a stone may be missing from the large gaps on the WSW and N sides. In the centre of the latter is a hollow in which a small boulder has been set up, almost certainly to mark the site of a missing stone (Jolly knew that there were once eleven stones in the circle, and Fraser showed the hollow as an open circle on his plan of 1883). It is possible, but doubtful, that there was originally a stone in the gap on the WSW side (see ¶ 8.25). A small stone opposite the entrance to the passage is a glacial erratic and is not part of the circle. Thus it seems probable that there were originally eleven stones in the circle.

The standing stones are described clockwise from the tallest, that to the SW of the entrance. The stones that have not been re-erected are between 6.7 and 7.6 m from the cairn kerb, and are set fairly accurately in a circle. Stones 1, 2, and 10 lay radially to the kerb until they were re-erected in the 1870s (see Fraser's plan). Stone 1 is 11.2 m from the kerb, which supports Fraser's suggestion that this huge rectangular slab was re-erected upside down where its top edge lay. It is possible that stone 2 also has been wrongly positioned, and that stone 10 has been set at an oblique angle to the line of the circle (though in approximately its original position). The provision of a visual link between the misplaced stone *1* and the rest of the circle may have influenced the placement of these two stones. A fourth stone, *6*, was re-erected before 1880 (Jolly, 303).

The first three stones and the last stone in the circle are quarried sandstone blocks, rectangular in plan with flat faces, and the vertical bedding planes are causing lengthwise splitting. All the stones are supported by packing material forming small 'cairns' which rise 0.2 m or so above the turf, and are presumably largely modern; the heights of the stones are given to the present ground level. Stone *1* is a huge thin slab, rectangular in elevation, 1.24 m long by 0.24 m thick, and 2.8 m high. Stone *2* is a shattered stump, broken before 1881; it is 0.9 m long by 0.23 m thick, and 0.85 m high. Stone *3* is 0.77 m long by 0.32 m thick, and 2 m high; its upper part is severely damaged and pointed. Stone *4* is an intact boulder with a rounded top and narrowing slightly towards the base, about 1.15 by about 1 m, and 1.55 m high. Stones *5* to *9* are boulders, and are probably intact, varying between 1.2 and 1.75 m high, the last stone being the tallest. Stones *5* and *7* are irregular in shape, roughly 1.2 long by 0.7 m thick; stones *6*, *8*, and *9* are more shapely with fairly vertical faces, about 0.62, 1.4 and 0.95 m long by about 0.58, 0.8, and 0.86 m thick. Stone *10* is a rectangular block, 1.2 m long by 0.36 m thick, and 1.72 m high.

There are cupmarks on several stones.

1. Kerb-stone *20*, found in 1931 (plate 17). Cupmarks (one ringed) and channels (Barclay 21–2; Piggott, plate XLI, a; Bradley 2000, illustration 34, 50 D).

2. A second cupmarked stone was found in 1931; the find-spot is uncertain, and it is implied that it was not a kerb-stone (Barclay, 21–2).

3. The innermost orthostat on the NW side of the passage. Several cupmarks, one ringed (Jolly no. 1, fig. 1; Bradley 2000, 33).

4. The fourth orthostat from the entrance on the NW side of the passage. Faint cupmarks (Bradley 2000, 33), but they look suspiciously natural.

5. A horizontal slab built into the chamber wall high on the NW side (indicated on Bradley 2000, illustration 37).

6. A small slab with one cupmark found unstratified in the cairn in 1995 (Bradley 2000, 87, illustration 88, 11).

FINDS
Artefacts. Museum not yet allocated
Over 100 flakes and pieces of flint and quartz from the surface levels of the platform and beyond; all probably of late bronze age date (Bradley 2000, 83–7).

Human remains. A few fragments of cremated bone were found scattered on the bank, probably of late bronze age date (Bradley 2000, 88). A few bones were found in the chamber about 1853.

Radiocarbon dates. See ¶ 10.69.

INV 10. BALNUARAN OF CLAVA SOUTH-WEST

Parish Croy and Dalcross
Location in Strathnairn, 8 km E of Inverness
Map reference NH 756443
NMRS number NH 74 SE 4
References Lauder 1830, 15, 418–19, plate in Appendix; Stewart 1857; Innes 1860, 49, pl. VI; ISSFC 1880a, 31–2; Jolly 1882, 303; 309–13; Fraser 1884, 341–4; Somerville 1923, 218–22; Kennedy 1931; Piggott 1956, 195; Henshall 1963, 364–6; Thom, Thom and Burl 1980, 246–7; Barclay 1990, 19–30; Bradley 1996; 2000, 24–31, 63–9, 83, 85–8
Plan ASH and JNGR
Excavation Kennedy 1930, 1931; Bradley 1994, 1995
Visited 15.4.57, many times until 11.8.98

Description. The cairn is within the same enclosure as the North-east passage-grave (INV 9) and the ring-cairn (INV 8) at Balnuaran (figure 45). The siting and history of the South-west cairn is similar to that of the North-east cairn, *q.v.*, except that the chamber was investigated earlier, about 1828 (Lauder), and the monument has been affected by a public road which crosses one side.

In design the Balnuaran of Clava South-west cairn is very similar to the North-east cairn. It is edged by a kerb of large boulders, outside which is a low bank, and the whole is surrounded by a ring of standing stones (plate 13). The chamber and passage are fully exposed to view and are aligned exactly on the same axis as the North-east monument. The South-west cairn, which by 1925 had been robbed and disturbed by road-menders, has been restored to a regular shape, mainly by replacing fallen cairn material. The cairn is at most 2.3 m high, and the diameter of the kerb is about 15.5 m.

Much of the kerb was visible before the monument was taken into State Care, and work in 1931 exposed the remaining kerb-stones, only three of which had to be re-erected from a prone position (stones 7, 8 and 41 clockwise from the entrance). The kerb is complete except at the entrance, and for a gap for a single stone on the W side, and for the possibility that another stone is missing on this side where the rather wide spacing of the restored stones may indicate that stone 7 has been wrongly set. Two cuttings made through the external bank in 1994 and 1995 showed that it conceals about 0.6 m of the lower part of the kerb-stones, which are thus very considerably taller than they appear. They are set on the old ground surface, not in sockets. The largest stones on the SW side of the kerb are particularly impressive; they project almost 1 m above the bank, and their full height above the old ground surface is about 1.6 m. The stone forming the NW side of the entrance is a little shorter than its neighbour, with its full height estimated as about 1.3 m. The missing kerb-stone on the SE side of the entrance has been replaced by a long low slab set somewhat skew to the curve of the kerb, and the kerb-stone beside it appears to have been reduced in height. Round the NE half of the circuit the kerb-stones diminish in height with the smallest at the rear of the chamber. Even these are substantial stones about 1 m high from the old ground surface, though they only project between 0.5 to 0.25 m above the bank.

Most of the kerb-stones lean slightly inwards, which seems to be a deliberate feature. They were carefully set so that their outer faces formed a regular curve, though with a tendency for short runs to be set in almost straight lines, most obvious on the W and NE sides. Mostly the stones are contiguous, but there are small gaps between some of them round the NE side, though their hidden lower parts may be closer. Stone 31 on the E side is the only quarried slab in the kerb. It is 0.95 m long and its true height is about 0.9 m. It bears cupmarks on the outer surface, partly hidden by the bank. Elevations of the kerb, passage and chamber, and a record of the types of stone used, are given in Bradley 2000, illustrations 25, 26, 28.

On a plan made in 1910 Somerville shows a pair of stones aligned as a continuation of the passage walls outside the kerb, but as this is the only record of them it is clear that they were not substantial, and they could not have stood in the relationship to the kerb that he shows (redrawn in Bradley 2000, illustration 132, and see pp. 24, 164). It is very doubtful if the stones were part of the original structure.

The bank surrounding the kerb is about 3.5 to 4 m wide. It has a flat surface, 0.2 to 0.5 m above the present slightly undulating ground level (clearly visible on plate 14, and Bradley 2000, illustration 131). The edge is sharply defined round two-thirds of the circuit, but is less distinct in front of the entrance, and has been lost on the SE side where it is cut by the road. There is no break in the bank in front of the entrance (as was shown during the restoration work in 1931, see Barclay, illustration 2, section C–D), though the surface here is slightly depressed by wear. The edge of the bank is clearly depicted on the nineteenth-century plans, though its surface was then largely hidden below fallen cairn material; this was removed from the more compacted material of the bank during the restoration work in 1931. Bradley made two cuttings through the bank on the WSW and N sides. He found that the bank is about 0.6 m high, made of slabs and rounded stones, with more slabs in the lower part and more rounded stones in the upper part. In the N cutting it seemed that some of the original upper surface of horizontal small slabs had survived, and this had the appearance

INV 10

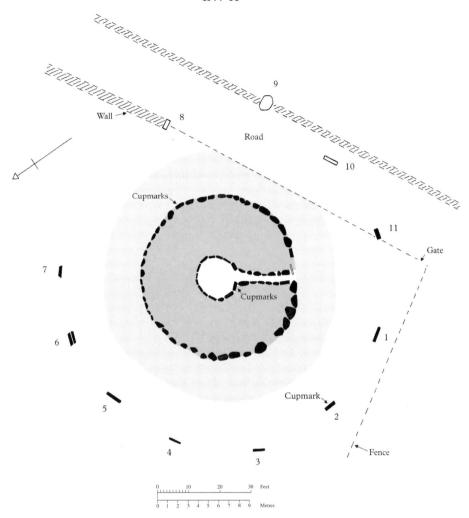

of damaged paving. A few fragments of worked quartz were found in and on the bank, and in 1931 deposits of seashells were found.

The passage is 0.6 m wide between the two outermost stones, and increases in width towards the inner end; it is 5.8 m long. The basal courses of the walls consist of six close-set orthostats on each side, 0.6 to 0.8 m in height, with an additional slim upright stone filling a gap between the first two on the SE side. The first orthostat on the NW side is a slab which has been shattered, but otherwise the orthostats are intact boulders, and stones of various sizes fill the irregularities between their shoulders. A little walling remains above the orthostats, and at least some of it appears to be original, particularly a slab laid transversely to the wall above the first orthostat on the NW side, and several large horizontal slabs on the opposite side where the walling reaches a height of 1.2 m.

The chamber is 3.8 m in diameter. The basal course of the chamber wall consists of fourteen orthostats, either boulders or slabs, selected for their flat faces and mainly vertical sides, and they are close-set to form a smoothly curved wall-face. The entrance is 0.95 m wide between a notable pair of quarried slabs

probably split from one block. The NW slab is
0.9 m long by 0.4 m thick, and 1.05 m high,
with a flat rectangular face which bears a
number of cupmarks, several surrounded by a
ring (plate 18). Most of the surface of the
similar slab on the SE side has split away. The
tops of the rest of the orthostats are rounded
or pointed, and the stones decrease in height
rather irregularly to about 0.6 m high on the
NE side, though with a conspicuous exception
1.14 high on the E side. Excavation in 1931
showed that the bases of the first four orthostats
from the SE side of the entrance were at different levels (Barclay 19, illustration 2), and
excavation in 1994 showed that the orthostats
must have been set in sockets; in particular
the socket of the largest orthostat beside the
entrance must have been over 0.6 m deep.

The chamber wall survives to a height of
2 m on the NE side, which is only about 0.3 m
lower than in 1883 (Fraser), and there is a little
oversailing in the upper part. The walling above
the basal course is rough in appearance, with
no indications of modern rebuilding. It consists of large horizontal waterworn slabs up to
1.2 m long, with the spaces around and above
them made up with small slabs and rounded
stones. The large slabs are in vertical stacks,
which result in irregular vertical joints through
the wall-face. The height of the wall decreases
to the SW, and no walling survives above the
orthostats forming the entrance.

In addition to the cupmarked orthostat
already mentioned, Bradley has identified more
stones in the chamber that bear cupmarks on
unexposed surfaces. It is just possible to see
that three horizontal slabs built into the back
walling are cupmarked on their upper surfaces,
and there is a cupmark on the top edge of one
of the orthostats (Bradley 2000, illustration 28).

The passage and chamber, evidently already
roofless, were opened in the late 1820s by the
direction of the landowner (Lauder). In the
past there has been uncertainty about which
chamber was opened at this time due to an
error on the first edition of the 6-inch OS map,
but Lauder's drawing (our figure 3) is an
accurate depiction of the SW chamber, passage,

and the kerb on the E side of the entrance.
Cremated bone and parts of two flat-based
pots were found in the centre of the chamber.
In 1931 an area on the S side of the floor was
investigated, but the results were misunderstood (Barclay, 19–21). When a small part of
the floor was re-examined in 1994 it was found
that the original floor had been removed, and
had been replaced in the late bronze age by a
layer of soil rich with charcoal (and the lowest
strata recorded in 1931 were recognised as
natural gravel and clay) (Bradley 2000, 66–7).
Two tiny fragments of cremated bone were
found.

There are ten standing stones surrounding
the cairn, and one nearly prostrate block. A
wide gap on the ENE side suggests that one, or
more likely two, stones are missing, and that
originally there were probably thirteen stones
in the circle (see ¶ 8.24, figure 38, 2). They are
described clockwise from that to the SW of the
entrance. All the stones, with the exception of
the boulder (stone 9), are quarried blocks of
sandstone, rectangular in plan. Vertical breaks
run lengthwise through the stones, and an
unknown amount has sheared off the flat
faces of most of them. The remains of the split
slab (stone 6) give an indication of how much
may have been lost.

Only four of the stones (4, 6, 7 and 11) have
not been re-erected or moved in the later
nineteenth century. According to Fraser's
record (figure 6), stones 1 and 2 had fallen
outwards, and stone 3 had fallen inwards, and
they were re-erected in the late 1870s; stone 5
was 'restored'. Fraser noted that stones 8 and
10 were moved in connection with the road-
making, but are presumably close to their
original positions; on one of Stewart's drawings of 1857 (figure 4) the latter stone is shown
before it was moved. According to Jolly, stone
9 was moved for the same reason, but on the
same drawing it is shown already in its present
position even before the wall was built over it.
The stones are fairly evenly spaced, and, apart
from stones 3 and 9, stand almost exactly in a
circle; they are 7.6 to 8.8 m outside the cairn
kerb. Some stone packing can be seen around

the base of most of the stones, probably dating from the nineteenth century or later.

Stone *1* has been greatly damaged by vertical splitting; pieces have broken away from both faces, and almost certainly it was once much taller. It is 1.5 m long by 0.24 m thick, and 1.5 m high. Stone *2* is a fine slab with rectangular faces, and is probably intact; it is 1.25 m long by 0.34 m thick, and 2.2 m high. There are two possible cupmarks on the E face. Stones *3* and *4* have been reduced in thickness; stone *3* probably retains its full height with the original sloping top edge, but stone *4* is broken. They are 1.2 and 1.27 m long by 0.25 and 0.2 m thick and 1.7 and 1.47 m high. Stone *5* is 1.6 m long by 0.4 m thick, and 1.96 m high; though reduced by weathering, it probably retains its top edge. A parallel thin upright slab 0.13 m from the SE face (shown on early plans) appears to be part of the packing inserted when the stone was re-erected. Stone *6* has split in two, with the S part leaning inwards more steeply than the N part, though it retains its sloping top edge. It is 1.17 m long by 0.6 m thick, and 1.6 m high. Stone *7* is on the axis and leans to the NE; only a stump remains, 1.23 m long, at least 0.26 m thick, and 0.3 m high.

Stone *8*, which has been placed to form the end of the wall on the NW side of the road, is 1 m long by 0.42 m thick, and 1.22 m high, with a rounded and probably intact top. Stone *9* is a large irregular boulder which leans steeply outwards to the SE. It is crossed by the wall running along the side of the road, and is difficult to measure. It is roughly 1.2 m long by 1.2 m thick, and would be about 2 m high if upright. Stone *10*, which has been reset on the verge parallel with the road, is much weathered with an irregular rounded top; it is 1.57 m long by 0.33 m thick, and 1.7 m high. Stone *11* is 1.04 m long by 0.33 m thick, and 2 m high with a damaged top edge.

There are a number of cupmarked stones.
1. Kerb-stone on the E side. This stone was fully exposed in 1931, and bears cupmarks almost to the base, but the lower part is now hidden by the bank. (Barclay, illustration 15; Bradley 2000, illustration 30, 50 C).

2. Orthostat in the chamber on the NW side of the entrance. There are several cupmarks, some surrounded by rings (Jolly no. 6, fig. 7; Bradley 2000, illustration 24, 50 A) (plate 18).
3. The fourth orthostat in the chamber wall, NW side. One cupmark below floor level (Bradley 2000, illustration 50 B).
4. On the top edge of the ninth orthostat, on the NE side of the chamber. One large cupmark (Bradley 2000, 26).
5. On the upper surface of three horizontal slabs built into the chamber wall on the NE side, a total of eleven cupmarks (Bradley 2000, 26, illustration 28).
6. Standing stone *2*, E face. Two or three cupmarks; the rest of those recorded by Jolly are unconvincing (Jolly no. 11, fig. 11; Bradley 2000, 27).
Jolly claimed that other stones bore cupmarks: standing stone *5*, outer face (his fig. 12), no cupmarks are visible, but there has been some flaking of the surface; standing stone *11*, S face (fig. 10), all the hollows are natural; third passage orthostat on the SE side (fig. 8), all the hollows are probably natural; orthostat in the chamber on the SE side of the entrance (Jolly no. 8), the surface has flaked off; a large loose stone formerly lying in the chamber, now lost (fig. 9), said to have borne two cupmarks.

FINDS
Artefacts. *1* lost, *2* museum not yet allocated.
1. An almost complete, but broken, flat-based pot. 'The clay is of the coarsest kind . . . The bottom is flat, the inside very black, from having been burned, the outside red; across the exterior of the bottom it measures 6½ inches [150 mm], and across the interior exactly 5 inches [127 mm], and the height, in its fractured state is 4½ inches [115 mm]. There were also two pieces of a second similar pot.' Found below the chamber floor. (Lauder, 418–19, plate in Appendix; our figure 34).
2. Twelve fragments of worked quartz. Found in the bank, associated with the layer of horizontal slabs, and unstratified (Bradley 2000, 83, 85–6).
Human remains. Cremated bone in some quantity was found in and around the pots discovered during the first investigation of the chamber (Lauder, 418). Two fragments of burnt

bone were found unstratified in 1994 (Bradley 2000, 87–8).

Radiocarbon dates. See ¶ 10.69.

INV 11.

See p. 241.

INV 12.   BELLADRUM SOUTH
(Belladrum Home Farm)

Parish Kiltarlity and Convinth
Location near the junction of Strath Glass and Glen Convinth, 4 km S of Beauly
Map reference NH 515415
NMRS number NH 54 SW 8
References ONB 1872, No. 49, 21; RCAHMS 1943, 109; Henshall 1963, 366, 367; RCAHMS 1979b, 8, no. 7; Thom, Thom and Burl 1980, 262, 263
Plan ASH and JNGR
Visited 13.4.57, 1.10.96

Description. The lower end of Glen Convinth is a mixture of cultivated fields and woodland. The site of the ruined cairn is in a field, a little below the crest of a gently rounded ridge, at 46 m OD.

INV 12

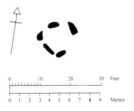

There is no surviving cairn material, but there remain five close-set orthostats which evidently formed most of the wall of a polygonal chamber. In 1872 these were recorded as 'a very small circle composed of five stones, one of which is lying, the others being two feet high' (ONB). It seems, then, that one of the existing stones has been re-set, which should be borne in mind when reading the description below.

The chamber is about 2.5 m in diameter.

Ploughing has reached almost to the bases of the orthostats, so that they are exposed for nearly their full heights on the outside, but the interior of the chamber is partly filled with loose stones. The orthostats are 0.18 to 1 m apart, except on the E side where there is a gap of 1.6 m which probably indicates the position of the entrance. The orthostats are boulders, except for a slab on the SW side, and all are set with flat faces to the interior. They are between 1.1 and 1.44 m long by 0.3 and 0.55 m thick, and clockwise from the SE they project 1.06, 1.08, 0.72, 0.95 and 1 m. The last two stones have retained their top edges. The fourth stone is the tallest of all, and 0.15 m taller than the fifth stone. Recently the fourth stone has split diagonally upwards from ground level on the E side, and the upper part has shifted slightly. The fifth stone was damaged long ago down its S side. The first and third stones lean slightly outwards.

INV 13.

See p. 241.

INV 14.   BRUIACH

Ring-cairn, see Appendix 2.

INV 15.

See p. 241.

INV 16.   CARN DALEY
(Balnagrantach, Gartalie)

Parish Urquhart and Glenmoriston
Location in Glen Urquhart, 2 km NW of Drumnadrochit
Map reference NH 494314
NMRS number NH 43 SE 1
References Grant 1883, 145; RCAHMS 1943, 157–8; Childe 1944, 38; Henshall 1963, 367–8, 369
Plan ASH and JNGR, additions from Henshall 1963
Visited 15.4.57, 22.10.96

Description. The cairn is high above the steep N side of Glen Urquhart, on the W side of the valley of a tributary. The hillside on which the cairn is located slopes down from NW to SE. The cairn, at 230 m OD, is at the upper limit of enclosed pasture before it gives way to rough grazing.

The site is level, but the ground drops away from the SE side. The cairn, and the circle of stones outside it, appears to stand on a platform, which is 1 m high at its maximum on the SE. The platform has been largely formed by relatively recent activity. Round the SE half of the site the edge of the platform has been formed by ploughing up to the line of the stone circle, and the edge fades away to the NE. On the NW side the platform is composed of field-gathered stones, and its straight edge has formed against the remains of a wall which bounded the SE end of a former garden. On the SW side the platform appears as a bank only 0.5 m wide against the feet of the kerbstones of the cairn, and the bank may be, at least in part, an original feature. The edge of the bank at each end swings sharply to the W and to the S to join the edge of the platform.

The cairn is edged by a boulder kerb. It has a diameter of about 12 m, though it is flattened in plan on the SW side. The entrance is in the centre of this side, between a pair of boulders set 0.58 m apart and radially to the kerb. These portal stones are roughly the same height and are lower than the adjacent kerb-stones; they are 0.7 and 0.64 m long by 0.48 and 0.45 m thick, and project 0.5 m. On each side of them are two particularly large kerb-stones, and these six stones are set in an almost straight line. The four kerb-stones do not differ greatly in size; the largest, beside the NW portal stone, is 1.24 m long by 0.68 m thick, and projects 0.94 m. At each end of the setting is another large kerb-stone, but placed at a slight angle to link with the kerb curving round the rest of the cairn; the NW stone has fallen and has been slightly displaced. The kerb is visible round the SE quadrant of the cairn, apart from two small gaps. On the S side cairn material has been removed from the inner sides of the kerbstones; of the four kerb-stones continuing from the southernmost already described, three lean

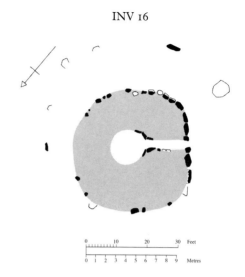

outwards and one lies flat. These are substantial stones about 0.3 m thick. The last eight kerb-stones on this side are almost upright (with one exception), and project 0.2 to 0.3 m, though their true heights are probably about 0.6 to 0.8 m. The kerb-stones diminish irregularly in size from S to E. Six more kerb-stones can be identified round the N side of the cairn, but only their tips are visible in the spread of field-gathered stones. The kerbstones have mostly been set with small gaps between them rather than contiguously.

The cairn was evidently reduced long ago to only a basal layer of cairn material, and subsequently field-gathered stones have gradually been added. It is partly turf-covered and partly bare. The centre of the cairn is hollow, and is filled with loose stones and a stunted tree. On the S side, between the kerb and the chamber area, are several flat boulders with the appearance of displaced corbel stones, and one boulder may have been a lintel.

In 1957 two stones that formed the inner ends of the passage walls were visible, but could not be seen in 1996. However, that year a stretch of the NW wall was partly exposed, consisting of an upright stone 0.3 m square and projecting 0.25 m, with, to the SW, two slabs of which only the upper surfaces and the SE edges could be seen. Midway between these and the NW portal stone there are two flat boulders, one over the other, which almost certainly have been slightly displaced from the wall. The passage is about 4.5 m long including the portal stones.

Three stones belonging to the chamber wall could just be seen in 1957, though not in 1996. They were on either side of the entrance, and the third stone extended the wall-face in a curve to the E.

Six of the stones that once encircled the cairn survive around the SE half, though they are now either reduced in height or prone. On the NE side, on the projected axis of the passage, is the stump of a stone, 0.8 m long by 0.25 m thick, which projects 1.14 m. South of it, the ends of three partly-buried prone slabs project from the edge of the platform. They are evidently substantial blocks, 0.25 to 0.35 m thick and over 0.55 to 0.9 m wide. These slabs have the appearance of fallen standing stones. On the S side of the cairn is the stump of another stone which was broken long ago; it is 1.3 m long by 0.37 m thick, and projects 0.8 m. The most westerly stone lies sloping up towards the cairn. It is 1.7 m long by 1.4 m wide, and is over 0.52 m thick. The spacing of the stones is irregular, between about 2.5 and 6.65 m; of the three prone slabs on the E side, possibly one, or more, has been moved, or was not a standing stone. (The original plan of the circle is discussed in ¶ 8.28.) The two upright stones are about 2.3 and 4.1 m from the cairn kerb.

The cairn was first noted briefly in 1881, as a Druidical Circle similar to that at Corrimony (INV 17) (Grant). In 1943 Childe was told that the passage and chamber had been excavated about fifty years previously, probably by members of the Inverness Scientific Society and Field Club, but no record of this activity is known (RCAHMS, Childe).

INV 17. CORRIMONY

Parish Urquhart and Glenmoriston
Location near the head of Glen Urquhart
Map reference NH 383303

NMRS number NH 33 SE 6
References ONB 1871, No. 56, 15; Mitchell 1874, 643–4; Jolly 1882, 314–15; Grant 1883, 145; RCAHMS 1943, 156–7; Childe 1944, 38; Piggott 1956, 174–84, 197–8, 200–07; Henshall 1963, 368–70
Plan after Piggott 1956 (see also figure 37)
Excavation Piggott 1952
Visited 4.7.55, 22.10.96

Description. Much of Glen Urquhart is steep-sided and afforested, but there is an area of flat cultivated land at the W end of the glen. The cairn is at the S edge of this area, in a field on the flood-plain of the River Enrick, at 150 m OD (plate 16). A by-road passes along the SE side of the monument.

Until the excavation in 1952 the cairn was thought, erroneously, to be intact. It consisted mainly of water-worn stones with some kerb-stones visible within the edge, and a large capstone lying on the summit. The cairn was about 18 m in diameter and 2.43 m high. It was surrounded by a circle of standing stones. Cupmarks had been noted on the capstone and on one of the standing stones. The following account is based on the excavation report (Piggott 1956), supplemented by personal observation. The monument was taken into Guardianship in 1954.

The upper parts of the kerb-stones were exposed by the excavator, and on the SW and NE sides a few were examined in small cuttings taken down to ground level (plate 15). All the kerb-stones (with one exception on the W side, not now visible) were found leaning outwards, varying from nearly upright to completely prone. The kerb-stones were a metre or a little more in height, and up to 1.7 m long, with the longer stones in the SW arc which contains the entrance. The diameter of the kerb is about 14 to 15 m. Behind the kerb-stones there seemed to be a ring of large boulders forming grounders. Against the outer faces of the kerb-stones is a bank of stony material, about 2 m wide and about 0.6 m high, with a gap in front of the entrance. Hundreds of pieces of broken quartz were found behind, between, and in front of the kerb-stones; the quartz had been deliberately scattered during the construction of the monument.

The entrance is 0.73 m wide between a pair of large stones which are aligned with the passage walls and project in front of the kerb. The intact NW stone is 1.1 m long and 1.05 m high, and is much the same height that the adjacent kerb-stone would be if it were upright. The SE stone is broken, and a large block standing on the cairn beside it is probably the detached upper part. The passage is narrowed to 0.42 m by the next pair of stones, after which it gradually widens to 1.22 m at midway, and continues at this width. The passage is about 7 m long, excluding the stones projecting beyond the kerb. The outer half of the passage is built of boulders set on end, the tallest 0.9 m high, with small gaps between them which are filled with cobbles; the upper part of the walls consists of split slabs running back into the cairn.

In contrast, the inner half of the passage is built with three courses of boulders laid flat, supplemented by smaller stones. In 1952 six lintels covered the inner half of the passage at a height of about 0.8 m, though one was displaced; the innermost lintel was cracked and about to collapse. To allow public access to the chamber the upper parts of the passage walls had to be consolidated, and the lintels have been reset; the inner three are now supported by steel bars. About 3.3 m from the outer end of the passage, and near the SE side, a small rounded block had been firmly set in the floor, projecting 0.22 m.

The chamber is 3.6 m in diameter. At the time of the excavation the wall remained up to 2 m high, and some corbel stones which had collapsed onto the chamber filling showed that the wall had been at least 0.45 m higher. The basal course is formed by contiguous boulders,

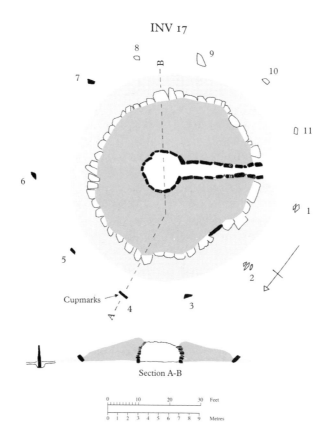

INV 17

Cupmarks

Section A-B

0   10   20   30 Feet

0 1 2 3 4 5 6 7 8 9 Metres

not graded in size, and at most 0.5 m high above the present floor level. They have sunk deeply into the subsoil, which has led to settlement and some displacement in the wall. Above the basal course the wall is rough in appearance, built of boulders and cobbles in the lower part, and mainly with slabs in the upper part. Above about 1 m the wall begins to oversail to reduce the roof span. In 1952 the overhang of the highest part on the NE side was 0.76 m, but it is probable that there had been some distortion of the vertical profile. On the SW side the broken lintel over the entrance and a broken block above it had led to near collapse (see Piggott 1956, plate XXXVIIa). The upper part of the chamber has been rebuilt to produce a stable wall of even height.

A massive block, 2.55 by 1.36 m, and 0.4 m thick, and estimated to weigh about two tonnes, lies on top of the cairn on the E side of the chamber. In 1952 it was moved to this position from above the chamber, where it was resting on rubble. It is irregular in plan with flat surfaces, and it bears over twenty worn cupmarks, some connected by grooves (plate 19). It is almost certainly the capstone of the chamber.

The excavator found that the passage had been deliberately blocked. In front of the entrance the original gap in the bank had been filled in. Between the second pair of stones in the passage walls there was the lower part of a rough wall-face. In front of this, on the S side, were the remains of a bone pin. Behind the wall-face the passage floor was covered by a layer of water-worn stones 0.45 m deep (which had evidently been deliberately introduced because it continued below the lintels). This layer extended over the chamber floor, which was yellow sand. On the centre of the floor was an area of flat slabs, covering about 1 by 0.76 m, and in places the layer was double; both layers were associated with charcoal fragments. Beneath the slabs, the sand retained stains of a crouched burial, lying on the right side with the head to the NW. Stains around the edge of the chamber were unexplained, but are unlikely to have derived from bone. (Details of the soil analyses by A. H. Johnson are in

Piggott 1956, 200–7.) Above the prehistoric deposits was a relatively modern filling of stones and earth, with some fragments of china and glass.

The chamber had probably been broken into in the first quarter of the nineteenth century. In 1830 the capstone, which was then lying on the W side of the cairn, was moved onto the summit by the landowner (Mitchell). Presumably it had been moved from its original position in order to gain access to the chamber, and in 1830 it was presumably returned to roughly its former position, though resting loosely on the recently introduced filling; it was found thus in 1952 (Grant was evidently mistaken in his statement that the capstone had been one of the standing stones outside the cairn).

The cairn is now surrounded by a circle of eleven standing stones, which almost certainly roughly reproduce the original design, though only the five round the N half of the circuit are original and *in situ* (discussed further in ¶ 8.26). Four stones (numbered *3* to *6* on the plan) form a fairly consistent series of split pointed blocks. Excavation showed that they stand in stone-holes with packing of water-worn boulders and pebbles. The first of these stones is triangular in plan with the wider face to the outside of the circle, 0.9 m long and 1.8 m high above the old ground surface (the present surface is about 0.2 m higher). The next standing stone (*4*) is rectangular in plan, 1.1 m long and 1.76 m high. On the flat outer face there are three cupmarks, 60 to 70 mm in diameter and 10 mm deep, and a fourth cupmark which is less clear (illustrated in Jolly, figure 15). The third stone (*5*) is roughly rectangular in plan with the more regular face to the outside, 0.7 m long and 1.57 m high. The standing stone that is on the projected axis of the passage (*6*) is a rather irregular block, 0.9 m long and 1.52 m high. There is a wider gap of about 10 m between this and the next stone to the S, and the possibility that a stone had once stood in this gap was investigated in 1952. No stone-hole was found, but instead, midway between the existing stones, there was an irregular area of cobbles laid on the subsoil. The cobbling was not fully investigated, but it appeared to be an original feature (since the excavation a boulder has been placed in the centre of this gap). The stone on the E side of the circle (7) appeared to be *in situ*, though it was found loose in a socket without packing stones. It is nearly rectangular in plan, 0.76 m long, with the wider face now notably skew to the circumference of the cairn kerb. The stone is 1.08 m high, with a jagged broken top edge.

A sketch plan of about 1860 shows nine standing stones around the cairn, fairly evenly spaced except for one large gap (Mitchell). A note made about ten years later mentions seven standing stones and two lying prone (ONB). A more helpful plan by Grant, published by Jolly in 1882 (figure 39), also records nine stones, six of them standing (*3* to *8* on our plan), two prone, and one evidently moved to between stone *8* and the kerb. In addition there are two composite standing stones on the W side. The composite stones remain (*1* and *2*), and are made up respectively of two and three unrelated slim slabs, patently a spurious arrangement. It is likely, as Piggott suggested, that these slabs were originally lintels over the outer part of the passage.

Excavation showed that stones *8* and *9* on the SE side of the circle have been set in the moved soil of a modern bank edging the drain running NE to SW along the side of the road. Stone *9* is the largest in the circle. It stands 1.4 m high above the surface of the bank and is over 2 m in total height. It is irregular in shape and has probably been damaged. Between 1882 and 1943 two stones (*10* and *11*) were set up on the S side of the cairn. Stones *9, 10* and *11* are presumably the three slabs which are shown prostrate on Grant's plan. Thus it is clear that the exact positions of the four stones now standing in the SE quadrant of the circle are uncertain, but the stones themselves are very probably original.

The five stones that are *in situ* show that the setting was not truly circular, nor were they evenly spaced, nor were they the same distance from the cairn kerb. The stone on the axis is 5.3 m, and the others are about 4 m, from the base of the kerb.

The monument was prepared for public viewing with a minimum of interference beyond the necessary consolidation work on the passage and chamber, already noted. The cairn is of bare stones; the upper edges of the kerb-stones beside the entrance, and of a few elsewhere, are visible. Outside them is a turfed bank of stony material. The standing stones, including the bogus composite stones, remain as they were in 1952. The unroofed chamber is accessible from the passage.

FINDS
Artefact. In the Royal Museum of Scotland.
1. Small piece of bone, calcined and eroded, possibly a pin (EO 956). Not illustrated, but see Piggott fig. 5.

INV 18. CROFTCROY

Parish Daviot and Dunlichit
Location in the upper part of Strathnairn, 10 km S of Inverness
Map reference NH 683331
NMRS number NH 63 SE 2
References Fraser 1884, 333–4; Henshall 1963, 370, 371; Thom, Thom and Burl 1980, 268–9
Plan ASH and JNGR
Visited 8.4.57, 29.4.97

Description. The cairn is on the floor of the strath, near a tributary of the River Nairn. The valley is partly afforested and partly enclosed pasture. The site is level, at 200 m OD. Before houses were built around the cairn the outlook would have been quite restricted up and down the valley. When visited in 1957 the cairn was neglected and overgrown, but in the 1970s it was incorporated into the garden of a house, and it is now exposed in an area of mown grass.

The cairn material has been almost entirely removed, and a depth of probably little more than 0.3 m remains; the surface is fairly level and turf-covered. The cairn was edged by a kerb of heavy boulders and blocks of stone. The kerb is still almost complete, and nearly all of the kerb-stones are intact. Only nine of them remain upright, with the rest either leaning steeply outwards with their bases still in position, or lying where they have collapsed; in some cases the full size of the prone slabs is hidden by the encroaching turf. The outer face of the kerb was not set on an exact circle, and the diameters vary between about 10.3 to 11 m.

The entrance faces S, and it is on the S side that the tallest kerb-stones were placed. A kerb-stone immediately W of the entrance is almost round in plan and projects 1.03 m to a tapered and possibly damaged top. The prone slab beside it is considerably larger, 1.1 m long at the top (which, as with several others, is somewhat longer than the base) and it would have been about 1.7 m high when upright. The other upright kerb-stones on the W side project between 0.85 and 0.56 m. The eight stones in the SW arc of the kerb were set with their outer faces in a fairly regular curve, and the last five of these kerb-stones were set almost touching. Eleven kerb-stones remain round the E side of the cairn. That to the E of the entrance is the largest of all; when upright it would have been 1.3 m long near the top and at least 1.85 m high. A large upright slab on the E side is 1.5 m long by 0.76 m thick, but, like the three upright stones on the NE side, it projects only 0.6 m. The rest of the kerb has been somewhat damaged. Five kerb-stones are slightly displaced, and there are gaps for three or four missing stones.

A number of large stones lie within the kerb, some of which probably derive from the structure. Two very large irregular blocks are particularly striking features, and these appear to be erratics that were incorporated into the base of the cairn (not shown on plan).

The lowest course of the walls of the passage and chamber consists of relatively small boulders and slabs. The entrance is 0.7 m wide between a pair of stones which project forward of the line of the kerb, and which are 0.8 m lower than the adjacent kerb-stone on the W side. The passage walls continue through the kerb, and converge slightly to reduce the width

INV 18

Fallen stones seen in 1884

to 0.5 m. The three stones on each side of the passage project at most for 0.3 m. After a short gap the walls continue, and define the chamber. This is a narrow space, which at its maximum is only 0.72 m wide near its rounded inner end. The stones of the chamber wall are slightly higher than those of the passage. Both the passage and the chamber are about 2.8 m long.

The cairn was already in its present condition when it was recorded by Fraser in 1884. It had been surrounded by a circle of standing stones, of which only three remained, all prostrate. The two on the S side had been removed before 1957. They were 3.8 and 3.65 m long, and it appears from Fraser's plan that the W stone had fallen outwards from a position about 3.9 m from the kerb. The E stone lay obliquely to the assumed line of the circle. The third stone, on the NW side of the cairn, survives. It is 2.3 m long, and roughly rectangular in cross section, 0.75 by 0.55 m. Since Fraser's visit it has been moved nearer to the kerb.

INV 19. CULBURNIE

Ring-cairn, see Appendix 2.

INV 20.

See p. 241.

INV 21. CULDOICH

Ring-cairn, see Appendix 2.

INV 22.

See p. 241.

INV 23   CULLEARNIE
(Upper Cullernie, Culloden Tileworks) (Ring-cairn)

Parish Inverness and Bona
Location 5.5 km ENE of Inverness
Map reference NH 725476
NMRS number NH 74 NW 4
References Anderson 1831, 216; ONB 1870, No. 31, 73; Fraser 1884, 361; RCAHMS 1943, 101-2; Henshall 1963, 372–3; RCAHMS 1979b, 8, no. 16
Plan ASH and JNGR
Visited 10.4.57, 23.10.97

Description. This ring-cairn is on the culti-vated plain which stretches along the S side of the Moray Firth. It is at 25 m OD, in a flat field beside the main road A 96.

The cairn has been partly removed, and the appearance of the surviving part has been distorted by the addition of stones cleared from the field. The remaining cairn material, augmented by the dumped stones, is about 0.7 m high, and more dumped stones extend outside the cairn to the NE. The whole area has an uneven surface covered by coarse grass.

The NW quadrant of the cairn kerb survives, and it is impressive. It consists of intact close-set upright boulders which are fully exposed on the outside, in most cases to a level below their bases. This is due to erosion caused by cattle trampling, and the stones are consequently in a precarious condition. The kerb-stones have an almost uniform height of about 1 m. They have flat or gently convex outer faces, and they mostly have vertical sides. The easternmost stone leans outwards, and on the NW side two stones lie undisturbed where they have fallen. The diameter of the kerb was evidently about 14 m.

Three stones of the inner kerb, which faced the central area of the ring-cairn, remain on its SW arc. They have flat faces to the NE, the side which would have been visible. On the other side the stones are fully exposed, and above ground level two of them project deeply and irregularly to the SW. The stones are 1 m high or a little more. The diameter of the inner kerb can be calculated as about 6.5 m.

There is a standing stone on the NE side of the cairn, about 3.6 m from the assumed line of the kerb. The stone is 0.9 m long by about 0.45 m thick, and is considerably larger above ground level; it is exposed for virtually its full height, 1.55 m. It is a boulder of puddingstone with an almost flat face towards the cairn. Some 4.3 m to the SE is a fallen standing stone. The flat base at the SW end is 0.95 m wide by 0.6 m thick, and the stone is 1.6 m long (its height when upright).

The S end of the cairn kerb is linked to the W stone of the inner kerb by a row of large broken blocks which revet the remains of the cairn. These stones, together with broken blocks lying around the cairn and on the field clear-ance which now links the cairn to the two standing stones, are almost certainly pieces of the standing stones which once encircled the cairn. Some of the blocks are puddingstone, and two have split jumper-holes.

INV 23

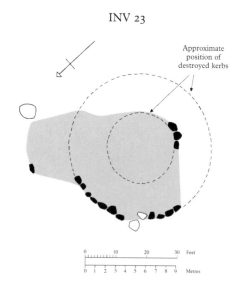

Approximate
position of
destroyed kerbs

0   10   20   30 Feet

0 1 2 3 4 5 6 7 8 9   Metres

The monument was less damaged when Anderson made a sketch plan and notes in 1824 (figure 2, 3). His record fits well with what can still be seen; in particular the diameters of the inner kerb, the cairn kerb, and the circle of standing stones were recorded as seven or eight, fifteen and twenty-four paces. The inner kerb was 'most perfect at the W end, where there are still four upright stones close to each other'. The cairn kerb consisted of '34 or 36 stones, many fallen and greatly displaced, especially on the south-west side.' The smallest stones were on the NE side. Anderson thought there were fifteen standing stones in the circle around the cairn. There were 'two very prominent pillars, each about 5 feet (1.5 m) high' on the NE side, and the remainder were about 0.9 m high, except that 'there are two prostrate stones on the south-west, now greatly broken, which are much larger than any of the others, and which I suspect were once upright.' By 1870, apart from the two remaining standing stones, all of them had been removed and thrown onto the cairn (ONB).

Anderson recorded that close to the NE side of the monument there was a second cairn with a heavy kerb. Nothing remains of this structure.

INV 24–5.

See p. 241.

INV 26. DALCROSS MAINS

Parish Croy and Dalcross
Location 11 km ENE of Inverness
Map reference NH 779484
NMRS number NH 74 NE 15
References ONB 1869, No. 18, 14; Fraser 1884, 361; Piggott 1956, 192, 194; Henshall 1963, 373, 374; RCAHMS 1979b, 9, no. 18; Thom, Thom and Burl 1980, 254, 255
Plan ASH and JNGR
Visited 10.4.57, 23.10.97

Description. The cairn is on the low ridge that separates the Moray Firth from the lower valley of the River Nairn. The area is partly

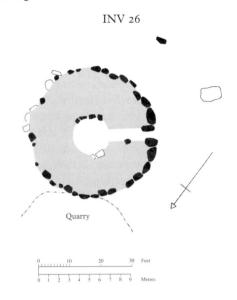

INV 26

Quarry

0 ... 10 ... 20 ... 30 Feet

0 1 2 3 4 5 6 7 8 9 Metres

cultivated and partly afforested. The cairn is located on a small rise between two fields, at 120 m OD, and commands wide views, especially across the firth to the Black Isle and beyond.

The ground slopes down steeply from the cairn on all sides, but the steepness is partly due to ploughing close to its NE and S sides, and more drastically to quarrying for gravel close to the E side, and up to the kerb-stones on the NW side. The latter quarry has exposed a vertical section in which the old ground surface can be identified, and this enables estimation of the true heights of parts of the cairn structure.

There are birch trees around and on the cairn, and the surface of the monument is covered by coarse grass and nettles. Although there appears to be little cairn material remaining, it is in general 0.4 m or so deep, and rather more in the centre of the cairn.

The kerb of the cairn is nearly complete, and has a diameter of 12.5 m. The kerb-stones are substantial intact boulders, and though round most of the circuit their lower parts are hidden, their real heights can be estimated. The cairn material banked against their outer faces, which is not identifiable on surface examination, can be seen in the section exposed at the edge of the NW quarry; in places the bank must be as much as 0.4 m deep. On the SW side the kerb is interrupted by a pair of boulders set radially to form the passage entrance. On each side of these boulders there are two impressive kerb-stones with flat outer faces, and the next two kerb-stones to the N, though less massive, are slightly taller. Above the NW quarry three stones are poised to fall; two of them lean outwards, and another is fully exposed and a little over 1 m high. There is no great variation in the heights of these eleven kerb-stones and the next one to the E. Round the E half of the cairn the kerb-stones are lower; they project only 0.2 to 0.35 m, and their real height is roughly 0.6 m. The quarrying on the E side of the monument has caused three of the kerb-stones to lean steeply outwards, and two are displaced.

The passage entrance is 0.58 m wide between the pair of boulders mentioned above, which were part of the basal course of the passage walls. The boulders are 1.28 and 1.3 m long by 0.8 and 0.65 m thick; they have flat upper surfaces sloping down to the SW, and they project about 0.5 m. Nearer to the chamber the NW wall of the passage is indicated by a boulder which just projects.

The chamber seems to have had a diameter of about 3.4 m. The basal course on the SE side consists of four blocks (formerly five were visible), their flat tops level with the turf and their inner faces hidden. A hole dug recently on the NW side of the chamber has exposed two stones where the wall is to be expected. The stones are of a size and shape suitable for walling, and they are at the same level as the four blocks, but, puzzlingly, they rest on rubble. The S stone is a boulder, 0.95 m long by 0.5 m thick, and 0.4 m deep. A rectangular block that butts its NW end is of the same dimensions except that its length is unknown.

An outer circle of standing stones is represented by two stones on the S side of the monument. The E stone is a boulder, 1.12 m long by 0.75 m thick, and 1.35 m high with a broken top; it is 4.5 m from the cairn kerb. The W stone lies, evidently undisturbed, where it has

fallen outwards due to erosion along its outer side. It is a huge rather irregular block veined with quartzite, 2 m long (the former height), by about 1.26 m wide and about 0.9 m thick. A chunk has recently fallen from the outer end (the horizontal top when upright).

The monument was in its present condition before 1869 (ONB).

INV 27.

See p. 241.

INV 28. DAVIOT

Ring-cairn, see Appendix 2.

INV 29. DELFOUR

Ring-cairn, see Appendix 2.

INV 30. DRUIDTEMPLE (Leys)

Parish Inverness and Bona
Location 1.4 km S of the outskirts of Inverness
Map reference NH 685420
NMRS number NH 64 SE 23
References Anderson 1831, 214–15; ONB 1868–70, No. 19, 2; Cameron 1882, 293; ISSFC 1880b, 155–6; Fraser 1883, 369–70; Fraser 1884, 353, 354–6; Piggott 1956, 185–6; Lisowski 1956; Henshall 1963, 375–6, 377; RCAHMS 1979b, 9, no. 20; Thom 1967, 68–9; Thom, Thom and Burl 1980, 270–1
Plan ASH and JNGR
Excavation Piggott 1952
Visited 9.4.57, 22.5.97

Description. The cairn is on the SE side of the valley of the River Ness, in quite steeply sloping agricultural land, at 130 m OD. The site is a small level area in a patch of woodland, and several oak trees are growing on the actual monument (figure 7). If free of trees, there would be extensive views to the W and N, over the Ness valley and the Moray Firth, to the mountains beyond.

All the cairn material has been removed, and the monument is covered with rank grass (for clarity, the area once covered by cairn material is shown stippled on the plan). Various large displaced blocks of stone lie about the site. The kerb of the cairn survives almost complete and virtually fully exposed. It is not exactly circular because the curve is flattened on the W and NE sides, and the diameters vary between 13.7 and 12.8 m. The kerb is built of very substantial boulders of sandstone or coarse conglomerate, all but one of them undamaged apart for some weathering. Several of the stones have fallen, and others have tilted inwards to varying degrees. Even so, it can be seen that the kerb-stones were carefully selected and placed to achieve a smoothly curved outer face. This is best appreciated on the W side, where the stones abut closely, and a small upright stone even remains between two of them, filling an external crevice. The outer faces of a number of stones slope gently inwards, possibly a deliberate feature, and only five of the kerb-stones in the whole circuit have vertical outer faces. The tops of the stones are rounded or pointed, or occasionally horizontal.

The entrance to the passage is on the S side, between two kerb-stones with vertical outer faces, set 0.7 m apart. The stone on the W side is 1.4 m long by 0.8 m thick, and 1.2 m high; the stone on the E side is only a little smaller. Clockwise round the kerb, the next stone to the W has fallen inwards, and its length (probably its height when in place) is 1.67 m. After a gap there are two more fallen stones, followed by two that lean steeply inwards. Round the NW quarter of the kerb eight stones are in place, or have tilted only slightly. The kerb-stones on the N and NE sides tend to be smaller, but are still substantial, projecting 0.7 m or so. There has been some damage here, and one kerb-stone lies displaced inside the kerb. After a gap on the E side, the SE arc of the kerb contains large stones, one of which leans inwards.

The passage walls had a basal course of quite large and rather shapeless boulders, most of which remain, either leaning steeply or displaced. The passage is 5.7 m long, including a pair of stones at the inner end which were part of the chamber wall; midway along, the passage is 0.87 m wide. On the W side of the passage, immediately inside the entrance and

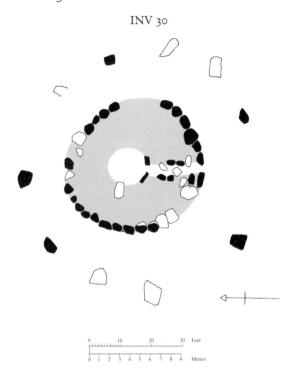

INV 30

0   10   20   30 Feet

0 1 2 3 4 5 6 7 8 9   Metres

set transversely to the wall, is a large block. The upper surface, which slopes down irregularly from 0.75 m high at the W end to ground level at the E end, may have been broken long ago. The next stone has fallen, and would have been 1 m high when upright. The gap beside it was probably filled by a stone which now lies in the passage, and the inner two stones lean to the W. On the E side of the passage, the first stone has fallen, the next leans to the E, followed by an upright stone 0.63 m high; the last stone leans steeply to the W.

The entrance to the chamber is 0.64 m wide between two rectangular blocks. The W stone is 1.2 m long by 0.4 m thick, and projects 0.34 m with a broken top edge (it was intact in 1870, see figure 5). The E stone is 0.8 m long by 0.46 m thick, and 0.75 m high, with its flat upper surface sloping down gently to the E. In 1952 Piggott stripped an area to the N of these stones, representing about three quarters of the presumed extent of the chamber. The position of the destroyed wall was not traced. Piggott found 'that the old surface had been dug over, and was now covered with about 2 ft [0.6 m] of stony debris, among which flat slabs of a type suitable for corbels were relatively abundant, and rounded white quartz pebbles were common. A few small scraps of cremated bone scattered through this disturbed soil were the only finds made.'

A circle of ten stones, five of them upright, surrounds the cairn. The stone to the SW of the entrance is a particularly impressive block. In plan it is almost square, about 1.4 by 1.4 m; the sides are vertical, and it is 2.73 m high. Clockwise, the next stone has fallen outwards. When upright, it would have had an irregular profile, over 1.7 m long above ground level by over 0.6 m thick, and would have been 2.6 m in total height. The next stone is an irregular pointed block of conglomerate which leans so steeply to the E that the base is partly exposed (a sketch in about 1870 seems to indicate that it was then upright, figure 5). It is about 1.6 m long, and before collapsing it would have been 1.5 m high. The fourth and fifth stones are similar irregular blocks, leaning slightly inwards, 1.45 and 1.5 m high. A more shapely block on the NE side leans steeply to the N. It is about 1 m long by 0.3 m thick, and would be 1.35 m high when upright. On the E side of the circle is a rectangular block, about 1 m long by 0.73 m thick, with vertical sides and a flat top, 1.5 m high. Two prone blocks on the SE side have evidently fallen outwards. The first is triangular in cross-section, 1.2 by 0.6 m, and 2.25 long; the other is roughly rectangular in cross-section, 1.2 by over 0.6 m, and 2 m long. The tenth stone is a shapely pointed block, about 1.5 m long by 0.9 m thick, and 1.45 m high.

The standing stones, where measurements can be taken, are between 3.55 and 5.3 m from the kerb. The spacing of the stones seems to have been rather irregular; they are between 3.6 and 5.2 m apart, with wider gaps on the S, SW and NNE sides. A sketch plan made before 1824 (figure 2, 2) shows the monument in its present condition, apart from fourteen stand-

ing stones in the circle. This record is almost certainly inaccurate, but it is likely that there was once an additional stone on both the SW and NNE sides, and that originally there were twelve stones in the circle (see ¶ 8.27, and figure 38, 4). The sketch of about 1870 shows that there were then ten stones, three of them prostrate (figure 5).

A cist containing two vessels and burnt bones was found near the monument before 1824 (Anderson, 215). Another cist is said to have been found in the cairn, and a third cist containing a small vessel was found in 1881 about 13 m NNW of the circle of standing stones (Cameron; Fraser 1884, 356).

FINDS
Human remains.
A small amount of cremated bone, probably from one individual, the sex and age uncertain, was found in the chamber area; there was also a single tooth probably from a young adult (Lisowski).

INV 31. ESSICH MOOR
(Carn Glas)

Parish Inverness and Bona
Location 5.5 km SSW of Inverness
Map reference NH 649383
NMRS number NH 63 NW 14
References ISSFC 1899a, 178; ISSFC 1918, 394; RCAHMS 1943, 93–6; Childe 1944, 36–7; Henshall 1963, 376–8
Plan ASH and JNGR (note differing scales)
Visited 11.4.57, 2.10.96, 21.10.96

Description. The cairn is on an undulating plateau of rough grazing (formerly heather moor), with pools and marshy areas in the hollows. The cairn is in a prominent position at 210 m OD, but is not on the highest point available. The site commands magnificent views, to the N across the Beauly Firth to the Black Isle and the mountains of Easter Ross, to the W to the hills on the NW side of the Great Glen, and to the SE to distant mountains. The cairn occupies a small ridge running N to S, which rises at each end and sinks in the centre. The ground falls away quite steeply along the

E side, and less steeply round the rest of the cairn.

This exceptionally long cairn is a complex structure, of which four elements can be detected on surface examination. At the S end, on the highest part of the ridge, is the large S cairn; a little to the N and at a lower level is the small mid cairn; at the N end is the large N cairn; all three cairns contain a chamber; the low parallel-sided linking cairn combines the separate components into one monument. The size of the long cairn, and the height at each end (exaggerated by the rising ground) remain impressive. The length is about 126 m, and the axis lies E of N to W of S by about 13°. The cairn is partly bare cairn material of small angular shattered stone with some cobbles, and partly covered with coarse grass. The contrasting areas of stone and grass tend to confuse interpretation, and patches of gorse, especially along the E side, cause further difficulties. Although parts of the cairn have suffered considerable disturbance, the damage is evidently much less than was implied in the two earliest notes (ISSFC 1899a, 1918). The outline plan of the long cairn is clear, though the position of the edge can seldom be traced precisely because the turf-covered lower slopes merge into the ground. The four components of the cairn are described below in turn.

The S cairn, because of its position on the highest part of the ridge, appears to be the largest component of the long cairn. The sides of the cairn slope up virtually undisturbed, and the only serious interference is into the S slope where the passage would be expected, and on the top where the chamber has been investigated and hollows have been made to the N and NW of it. The cairn appears to be heel-shaped. The S edge is straight, and the square form of the S end is clearer above ground level where the end slope joins that of the almost straight W and E sides. The sides curve northwards to a round N end. Here the cairn merges with the linking cairn material, but the edge of the cairn can be approximately traced where the two meet. The cairn is about 42.5 m N to S by about 36 m transversely. The height of the

cairn is nearly 2.6 m (calculated from the recorded height of the back-slab of the chamber). The axis of the cairn, judging by the S edge and the probable alignment of the chamber, is nearly SSW to NNE, skew by some 20° from that of the long cairn.

About 7 m S of the centre of the cairn, the back-slab of the S chamber is exposed in the centre of a deep hollow which is partly infilled with loose stones. The back-slab is a large block, 1.56 m long by 0.45 m thick, and was recorded in 1918 as about 2.2 m high; it now projects only 0.9 m above the chamber filling. The E wall of the chamber was formerly partly visible (RCAHMS, Childe). A narrow pointed orthostat butted against the SE corner of the back-slab; it was 0.86 m long, and was about 1.2 m shorter than the back-slab, so its true height was about 1 m. A second orthostat immediately to the S (its top edge still just visible) is 1 m long by over 0.13 m thick; it was a little taller than its neighbour. Above the pointed orthostat there was walling of thin slabs which reached nearly to the top of the back-slab, and also continued behind the second orthostat (illustrated in Childe, pl. II, 2). The awkward alignment of the orthostats in relation to the back-slab strongly suggests that they had been displaced slightly inwards whilst the walling had retained its original position. The chamber was investigated about 1918, when 'distinct indications of a burial, and a few small bones' were found (ISSFC 1918).

About 5 m to the N of the S cairn, and E of the axis of the long cairn, are the reduced and disturbed remains of the mid cairn. It is largely concealed within the linking cairn material of the long cairn, but it is up to 1.6 m high to the N and W of the chamber which it contains, and so is somewhat higher than the surrounding cairn material. Amongst the spread of loose stone the edge of the mid cairn is indicated by boulder kerb-stones the tops of which are just visible, and by the portal stones mentioned below. Some 7.7 m W of the chamber are two kerb-stones, 0.75 and 0.45 m long by 0.5 and 0.4 m thick, and a probable kerb-stone can be seen on the grass-covered S

INV 31

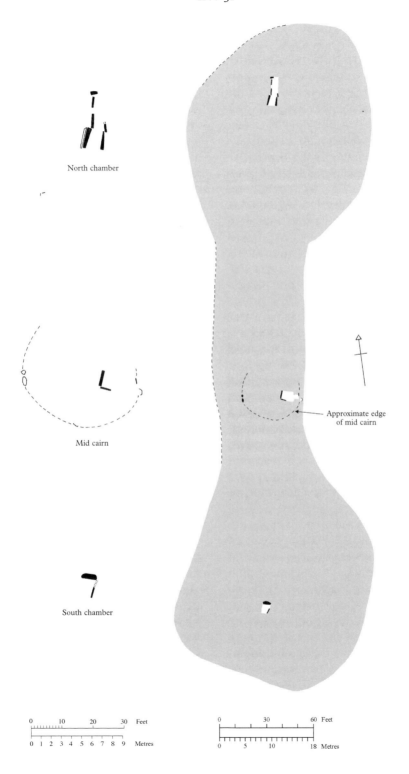

North chamber

Mid cairn

South chamber

Approximate edge
of mid cairn

0   10   20   30 Feet

0 1 2 3 4 5 6 7 8 9 Metres

0   30   60 Feet

0   5   10   18 Metres

side of the cairn. The mid cairn has a diameter of about 12 m.

On the E edge of the mid cairn, and near the edge of the long cairn, is a pair of portal stones 0.54 m apart. They evidently formed the entry to the small chamber, perhaps via a short passage. The taller S stone, which leans to the E, has a worn rounded upper edge; it is over 0.7 m long by 0.2 m thick, and projects 0.3 m. Its partner is 0.6 m long and only the top edge can be seen. The structure to the W of them has evidently been dug out and refilled. Only the back-slab of the chamber, 3.3 m from the N portal stone, and the adjacent S side stone can be seen. The back-slab is rectangular in plan and elevation, 1.53 m long by 0.34 m thick, and projects 1 m. It butts against the side-slab which is 0.45 m shorter; the side-slab is over 1.07 m long (the W end is not visible), and of unknown thickness. The axis of the chamber is SSE to NNW, and is thus unrelated to that of the long cairn, but the former is roughly at right angles to the axes of the other two chambers.

The N cairn is roughly 37 m from the S cairn, and is of similar size, but it differs in being oval in plan. Apart from the investigation of the chamber area and some probably superficial hollows made in the S side, there does not seem to have been any serious interference with the cairn. The edge can be traced with confidence from the centre of the N end for about 20 m to the SW, but beyond this the edge is obscured. On the S side the cairn slopes down gradually and the edge cannot be traced due to disturbance where it merges with the linking cairn. Round the E side and up to the centre of the N end the outer part of the cairn is almost entirely overgrown by gorse. The N cairn is about 44 m NNE to SSW by roughly 36 m transversely. Measured from the N it is 2.3 m high around the inner end of the chamber, and 0.3 m higher than the tallest orthostats, though (due to the rising ground level) the real height of the cairn is almost certainly less.

The axis of the N chamber is not quite straight, but it is roughly parallel with the axis of the S chamber, and differs from the axis of the long cairn by between 10° and 20°. About 9 m from the N end of the cairn is a pillar-like W portal stone, set transversely to the chamber axis, and leaning slightly to the N. It measures 0.6 by 0.3 m, and projects 0.85 m. It is a little taller than the highest part of the chamber at the W end, and its true height is over 1.2 m. The unusual height of the portal stone suggests that it may be part of a façade.

It is not clear whether the structure extending S from the portal stone should be regarded as a passage and chamber, or whether the whole structure should be regarded as a chamber. There is little difference in the widths of the outer part, which is 3.2 m long, and of the inner part, which is 1.8 m long; nor is there any indication that there were any transverse divisional slabs. Nevertheless, it seems preferable to interpret the structure as a long and substantial passage leading to a chamber built with a pair of massive side-slabs. There is no indication that the chamber was ever longer, but no back-slab is visible, and it is possible that the chamber extended further to the S (see ¶ 4. 15, 44).

The passage is completely infilled and turfed over. Two slab orthostats on the W side have been partly exposed by the removal of cairn material from their outer faces. They are over 1 and over 1.37 m long by over 0.18 m thick, and they are exposed for up to 0.6 m. They are about 0.6 m lower than the portal stone, and a little lower than the N ends of the chamber orthostats. The S end of the S passage orthostat has shifted slightly to the E. On the opposite side of the passage, the E portal stone and the orthostat(s) forming the outer part of the wall are missing or hidden, and all that can be seen is part of the top edge of the innermost orthostat. It is over 0.75 m long (neither end is visible) by over 0.2 m thick. It overlaps the E side of the E chamber orthostat, and is somewhat skew to the axis of the passage.

The chamber has been emptied and partially infilled. The side-slabs are intact rectangular blocks with flat upper edges gently sloping up to the S. They are 1.75 and 1.86 m long by up

to 0.33 and 0.35 m thick; they are the same
height, and project 0.9 m. They are not quite
parallel, and give the chamber a maximum
width of 1.3 m at the S end. The W block is at a
slight angle to the orthostats on the W side of
the passage, though the non-alignment is exaggerated by the slight displacement of the S
passage orthostat.

A large flat slab in an almost vertical position
leans against the W side of the W chamber
orthostat. The slab is almost certainly a displaced capstone. It is 2.05 m long by 0.23 m
thick, and over 0.63 m wide (the vertical measurement). Two or three nearly vertical slabs,
of which only the upper edges can be seen, lean
against the E side of the opposite orthostat,
and are probably displaced corbel stones. A
few large flat slabs lie outside the chamber.

The cairn which links the S and N cairns
and encloses the mid cairn is 17 to 18 m wide.
The edge is fairly clear along the W side, but
is less clear along the E side. The cairn is
generally about 1 m high, and has been much
disturbed except where it is grassed over, but
there is no reason to think that any quantity
of cairn material has been removed. In several
places slabs can be seen amongst the small
cairn material and suggest the presence of cists
or other structures, but the slabs are probably
no more than relatively recently disturbed cairn
material which has not yet been shattered by
weathering.

The profile of the long cairn, built along the
saddle-shaped ridge, can be well seen from the
E side. The top of the S cairn is 2.85 m higher
than the top of the N cairn, and 3.85 m higher
than the highest part of the mid cairn, which in
turn is 0.6 m higher than the linking cairn.

INV 32. GASK

Ring-cairn, see Appendix 2.

INV 33.

See p. 238.

INV 34. GRENISH

Ring-cairn, see Appendix 2.

INV 35–6.

See p. 241.

INV 37. KINCHYLE OF DORES
(Scaniport)

Parish Dores
Location in the valley of the River Ness, 6 km SW
of Inverness
Map reference NH 621389
NMRS number NH 63 NW 5
References Boswell 1785, 143; Anderson 1831,
212–13; ONB 1870–1, No. 22, 11–12; Beaton 1882,
491, 492; Fraser 1884, 356, 357; Pitt Rivers 1885b,
1; Pococke 1887, 102; Piggott 1956, 185, 187;
Lisowski 1956; Henshall 1963, 380–1; Thom,
Thom and Burl 1980, 272–3
Plan ASH and JNGR
Excavated Piggott 1952
Visited 11.4.57, 30.4.97

Description. The cairn overlooks a small
valley which is separated from the valley of the
River Ness by a low ridge. Both valleys are
partly cultivated and partly afforested. The
site, at 65 m OD, slopes down gently from W to
E. It is at the edge of a small area which was
formerly woodland, and is now covered by grass,
bracken and gorse. The eighteenth-century
military road, now the A862, runs close to the
NW side of the monument, and a field fence
aligned NW to SE passes immediately SW of the
second standing stone described below. In
appearance the monument has not changed
since it was drawn in 1885 (figure 8).

The greater part of the cairn kerb survives,
built of large intact boulders. It has a diameter
of about 9.5 m. Within the kerb all the cairn
material has been removed, and consequently
all the structural stones are exposed for nearly
their full heights (for clarity, the area formerly
covered by cairn material is shown stippled
on the plan). The entrance to the passage faces
S. On the E side of the entrance is a kerb-stone,
0.9 m long by 0.5 m thick, and 1 m high. A

stone is missing between it and the next two kerb-stones to the NE, which are similar in character but lower, 0.65 and 0.5 m high. A low stone forms the W side of the entrance. To the W of it is a gap, probably for two kerb-stones; one of them, which lies where it has fallen outwards, would have been 1.2 m high when upright. The SW arc of the kerb is particularly impressive with three shapely kerb-stones chosen to allow their sides to fit closely, and set with their outer faces on a slight curve. Another kerb-stone continues the series after a gap for a missing stone. These four kerb-stones are similar in size, 1 m or so long by up to 0.6 m thick, and the tallest is 1.1 m high. The next kerb-stone to the N lies displaced outside the kerb. A series of five stones forms a regular curve round the NW arc. They are somewhat smaller, though still substantial, and are more varied in appearance than those already described; the last of them is the smallest, 0.58 m high. There are eight kerb-stones round the E side of the kerb, of which two have fallen outwards, and another has been displaced to lie outside the kerb. Apart from the northernmost, which is a large block 0.8 m high, these kerb-stones are rather irregular in shape and at most 0.65 m high.

The passage is about 3.3 m long, and 0.83 m wide at the inner end. The basal courses of its walls are of relatively small boulders, the tallest 0.53 m high. The edges of the outermost stone on the W side (mentioned above) are aligned with the passage wall and with the outer face of the kerb, and the intact horizontal upper surface projects only 0.2 m. Four more stones, rather irregularly aligned, complete the basal course of the W wall. The second stone may be displaced slightly to the E, and a flat stone overlapping its W side and sloping down to the W is likely to be the last remnant of an upper course, also slightly displaced. Two stones of the E wall remain; the outer leans to the SE and its N end is probably slightly displaced.

Excavation of the chamber area showed that only three stones of the chamber walls survive. The S stone is a red sandstone slab, 0.9 m long, which leans into the chamber, and the other

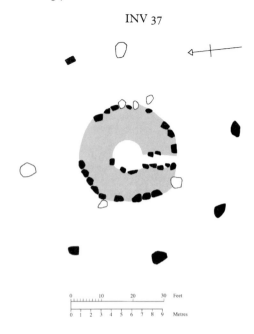

INV 37

two are boulders 0.4 m high. The chamber was evidently about 3 m in diameter. The stone debris covering the floor was found to be less than 0.3 m deep. Towards the NE side there was a small bowl-shaped pit cut into the boulder clay, 0.46 m in diameter and 0.25 m deep, filled with dark soil. Near it, about the centre of the chamber, on the old surface and under a few flattish stones, was a scatter of cremated bone with dark earth.

Of the surrounding circle of standing stones, seven remain, two of them prone. A series of four stones round the SW half of the circuit are spaced fairly evenly at about 6 to 7 m apart, and at between 5.6 and 5.0 m from the kerb. The S stone is an irregular block, the top of which may have been damaged long ago; it is 1.6 m long by 0.9 m thick, and 1.24 m high. The next stone to the W is the most impressive. It is a round-topped block of conglomerate of much the same bulk, and 1.6 m high, set with the wider face to the outside of the circle. The third stone is of similar character, 1.5 by 1.12 m, and 1.35 m high. The fourth stone is a rather irregular block, measuring 1.1 by 0.85 m, and 1.3 m high. The stone lying on the N side of the circle is a boulder, rather irregular in shape though with a flat face, 1.55 m long (its former height) by up to 1.2 m wide and about 0.5 m thick at the base. The NE standing stone is 1 m long by 0.6 m thick, and 1.08 m high; it is rather irregular in elevation, and may have been broken. A block lying on the E side of the circle is tilted up slightly to the W with the W end just free of the ground; it is 1.6 m long by 1.1 m wide, and about 0.4 m thick. (A smaller prone slab on the SE side, shown on Fraser's and Piggott's plans, is loose, and does not appear to have been a standing stone.) A number of large stones lie about the site.

The monument was evidently in virtually its present condition when seen by Pococke in 1760. He noted, perhaps erroneously, seven stones in the circle, 'some of which are fallen', but about fifty years later Anderson recorded nine stones. From his sketch plan (figure 2, 1) it seems that the prostrate stone on the N was then upright, and there were two standing stones in the wide gap on the SE side. These last had been removed by the time of Fraser's visit. The spacing of the stones suggests that there may once have been an additional tenth stone on the NE side of the circle, which was already missing when Anderson made his plan (figure 38, 5).

FINDS
Human remains.
A small amount of cremated bone found in the chamber was probably from one individual, of uncertain age (Lisowski).

INV 38. LEACHKIN

Parish Inverness and Bona
Location on the W outskirts of Inverness
Map reference NH 629441
NMRS number NH 64 SW 8
References Anderson 1831, 213; ONB 1868–72, No. 31, 27; RCAHMS 1943, 103–4; Childe 1944, 36; Henshall 1963, 381–2; RCAHMS 1979b, 9, no. 24
Plan ASH and JNGR
Visited 19.7.56, 23.10.96

Description. The cairn is on the spine of the ridge between the valley of the River Ness and the Beauly Firth. The steep SE slope below the cairn is cultivated, but much of the ridge is afforested. The cairn is just above the cultivated land, at 200 m OD, in an area which is overgrown with gorse and bracken, rowan and birch. The site commands very extensive views across the Beauly and Moray Firths to the N (at present obscured by the vegetation), and across the Great Glen to the E and S.

The cairn material has been almost entirely removed, and the site is heavily overgrown. In 1956, when the cairn was almost free of vegetation, the cairn edge was detected round the N side. A few quite substantial stones which seem to indicate the edge can still be seen in places. The most significant, though it hardly projects, is an almost square block which measures 0.56 by 0.58 m, 4.5 m NE of the entrance. The diameter of the cairn was about 23 or 24 m.

The passage and chamber were built of large blocks of coarse conglomerate, and most of the upright orthostats have irregular upper edges due either to weathering or to deliberate damage. All the orthostats project from a level surface for almost their full heights. The passage faces E. On the N side of the entrance there is a portal stone, 1.05 m long by 0.35 m thick, and 0.5 m high. It leans slightly to the W, and the top edge slopes down to the N. The passage is about 1.45 m long and 1.52 m wide, with an orthostat on each side. These are 1.24 and over 0.8 m long by 0.5 and 0.2 m thick, and 0.85 and 0.4 m high. The S orthostat extends farther to the E than might be expected, which implies that the missing S portal stone (which it is assumed once balanced the N stone) was set at an oblique angle to its partner. The N orthostat is the stump of a larger stone. The entry to the chamber is between a pair of portal stones set 0.7 m apart. The S stone appears to be intact with a horizontal top edge, and leans to the W; the N stone has an irregular and probably broken top. They are 0.86 and 0.7 m long by 0.46 and 0.3 m thick, and 0.6 and 0.2 m high.

INV 38

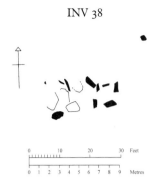

| 0 | 10 | 20 | 30 | Feet |

0 1 2 3 4 5 6 7 8 9   Metres

The N wall of the outer compartment of the chamber was built with two orthostats. The E orthostat, which butts against the adjacent portal stone, is 1.34 m long by 0.45 m thick, and 0.8 m high. The W orthostat has fallen across the chamber to a nearly horizontal position, and only the top part is visible. It is over 0.95 m wide (the original length) by over 0.25 m thick. The outer compartment is 2.7 m long, and was divided from the inner compartment by another pair of portal stones, of which the N stone survives. It has a shattered top and leans slightly to the W; it is 1.42 m long by 0.25 m thick, and 0.35 m high.

Two orthostats of the inner compartment remain *in situ*. On the S side is the most conspicuous feature of the monument, a massive block which leans somewhat to the N. It is about 1.2 m long by 0.7 m thick, and would be 1.9 m high when vertical. Opposite is the stump of a shattered orthostat, over 0.68 m long by 0.17 m thick, and 0.22 m high. The shattered tip of another stone just projects 1.3 m to the W. A prone slab, which probably stood on the N or W side of the compartment, lies across the compartment. Only the SE part is visible, for 0.9 m; the slab is 1 m wide across the SE end and 0.23 m thick. To the E is another fallen orthostat. It slopes down from NE to SW, with the NE part exposed for 0.45 m; it is 1.55 m wide, and 0.2 m thick. South of it is a prone slab, 1.46 by 0.87 m, and 0.26 m thick. (See figure 13 for a tentative reconstruction of the chamber plan.)

The cairn material had evidently been removed well before 1824, when the orthostats

of the chamber were described as 'the fragments of a large circle, the stones of which are visible from the streets of Inverness, at least two miles distant' (Anderson). The chamber was in much its present condition by 1872 (ONB).

INV 39–44.

See pp. 241–2.

INV 45. NEWTON OF PETTY

Ring-cairn, see Appendix 2.

INV 46. REELIG (The Giant's Grave)

Parish Kirkhill
Location on the S side of the Beauly Firth, 4.2 km ESE of Beauly
Map reference NH 558436
NMRS number NH 54 SE 1
References J. M. Joass 1865; ISSFC 1880c, 168; 1925, 199; Henshall 1963, 384; RCAHMS 1979b, 9, no. 22
Plan ASH and JNGR
Visited 2.5.57, 1.10.96

Description. The last remains of what was almost certainly a chambered cairn are situated at 30 m OD in an area of nearly flat agricultural land, which, before drainage operations, was quite restricted in extent. A short distance to the S the hillside rises steeply, and is now extensively afforested. The site, which is in the grounds of Reelig House, was much overgrown in 1996, but when seen in 1957 it was free of vegetation.

Three large contiguous blocks of schist appear to be *in situ*, and may have formed the almost square W end of a chamber which was presumably entered from the ENE. The side-slabs are 1.8 and 1.7 m long, up to 0.33 m thick, and project 0.6 and 0.85 m, almost their full heights. The S side-slab has an irregular upper edge which has probably been damaged long ago, and the N side-slab is intact. The back-slab, set somewhat skew between them, butts against the N face of the S side-slab and against the W end of the N side-slab. The

INV 46

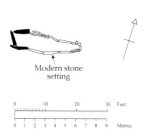

Modern stone
setting

```
0        10        20        30   Feet
|ıılıılıılı|_____|_____|
0  1  2  3  4  5  6  7  8  9   Metres
```

back-slab is 1.54 m long by 0.26 m thick, and projects 0.8 m. The chamber is about 1.1 m wide.

Running eastwards from the orthostats is a setting, 6.2 m long, of slabs on edge. Although the slabs probably derive from the chamber, the present arrangement is modern. There are three low but substantial slabs on the S side, and two on the N side, supplemented by smaller stones, and a small block closes the E end.

There is no sign of the cairn which once covered the chamber. When Joass visited Reelig in 1865 the owner showed him the remains of the chamber (evidently in much the same condition as at present) 'which had formed the nucleus of a Cairn removed 20 years ago – when a vase or Cinerary Urn was found but reinterred'. Thirteen years later visiting members of the Inverness Scientific Society and Field Club were told that demolition of the cairn, which was being used to build walls, had been stopped by the owner's father or grandfather, 'and the large stones that remained were ranged together in a grave-like form' (ISSFC 1880c). On another visit in 1920 the date of the destruction of the cairn was given as about 1780, 'when a flint arrowhead was found, and some other things' which were reburied, but this account is unreliable in other respects (ISSFC 1925).

A large barbed-and-tanged flint arrowhead, believed to have come from the chamber and kept in Reelig House, was described and illustrated in Henshall 1963, 384, 255. Its provenance is now considered to be insecure, and it is not otherwise mentioned in this volume.

INV 47.

See p. 241.

INV 48. TORDARROCH

Ring-cairn, see Appendix 2.

INV 49. TULLOCHGORM
(Boat of Garten)

Parish Duthil and Rothiemurchus
Location in Strathspey, 3.3 km NE of Boat of Garten
Map reference NH 964213
NMRS number NH 92 SE 3
References Grant 1880, 56; Henshall 1963, 385, 386; Thom, 1967, 78–9; Thom, Thom, and Burl 1980, 250–01
Plan ASH and JNGR
Visited 7.4.57, 26.5.97

Description. The cairn is on a slight rise in a field, at 210 m OD, in the undulating agricultural land of the valley floor. There are wide views from the site up and down the valley.

The monument is protected by a square fence which prevents grazing, and consequently the enclosure is covered by rank grass. The cairn remains up to 1 m high with a fairly level surface, and is edged by a kerb of upright stones. Against the outside of the kerb is a bank, of variable height up to 1 m, but ploughed away on the SSE side. The bank is roughly 1.5 to 2.4 m wide, but its outer edge is difficult to define.

The kerb of the cairn is almost complete, and has a diameter of about 14.5 m. It is composed of boulders and occasional split slabs. Round the N half of the circuit these are partly, or sometimes wholly, concealed by the remains of the cairn and the bank. It is not certain that the cairn contained a chamber, but if so, the entrance was probably through one of the gaps between the taller kerb-stones on the SW side. On the WSW side two boulders lean steeply inwards. One of them is intact and is the largest extant kerb-stone, about 1.3 m long by about 0.6 m thick, and if upright it would project 1.26 m. Anticlockwise, they are followed by the stump of a broken slab, a gap, and the tallest kerb-stone which projects 0.9 m, but its true height is about 1.5 m. The rest of the S half of the kerb has been damaged; several stones are missing, and of the ten remaining, two have fallen outwards (one since 1957), and another has broken. The rest of these stones are exposed for almost their full heights, about 1 m, and in one case erosion at the base has exposed chock-stones. Except for a slab that has split vertically, the boulders are set with their outer faces inclining slightly inwards. The stones round the N half of the kerb are all roughly the same height, probably 1 m or a little less, but the height of the bank gives the kerb a misleadingly irregular and insubstantial appearance. Round the E side, as the level of the bank rises, the kerb-stones are increasingly submerged, and in the gap on the NE they are entirely hidden but are present below the turf. On the N side the tops of the kerb-stones barely protrude, but more can be seen round the NW side where their outer faces project up to 0.4 m.

Near the centre of the cairn the tops of several quite large upright stones can be seen, but it is uncertain whether any of them are *in situ*, or are part of the internal structure. In particular, the two largest stones, aligned roughly NE to SW and 4.25 m apart, are about 1 m long and about 0.3 m thick. There is a boulder at the NE end of the SE stone, and there is a larger boulder farther to the N. All four stones are about the same height, and at most they project 0.4 m.

The stump of a standing stone is partly exposed 4.8 m ENE of the kerb. The stone is 0.75 m long by over 0.2 m thick; only the outer face is visible, 0.4 m high. A slab which lies to the NW may be part of another standing stone.

The monument may have been less ruined when seen by Grant about 1876. 'The outer circle is completely gone with the exception of three roundish blocks, which have been rolled upon the inner circles, in order to be out of the way of the plough. The inner circles are 42 ft and 12 ft [12.8 and 3.6 m] in diameter, but

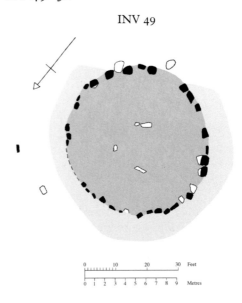

INV 49

without many small stones in the space between them.' The diameter of the internal structure (if correctly observed), and the diameter of the kerb, indicate that the cairn was probably a passage-grave, but lacking any observable diagnostic features, its classification cannot be regarded as certain.

INV 50.

See p. 241.

INV 51. BALVRAID

Parish Glenelg
Location in Glen Beag, W Inverness-shire, between Loch Hourn and Loch Alsh
Map reference NG 845166
NMRS number NG 81 NW 9
References Murchison 1963, 305; Cormack 1964; Corcoran 1965a; 1965b; 1966, 39; 1972, 33–5; Henshall 1967; 1972, 558–9
Plan after Corcoran 1965b (see also figure 30)
Excavation Corcoran 1965
Visited 5.4.65, 24.10.96

Description. The cairn is near the upper end of Glen Beag, a narrow valley running from the kyle that separates the mainland from the island of Skye. There is a limited amount of enclosed pasture in the glen, and the steep sides are rough grazing or afforested. The cairn is on a narrow terrace, a little above the valley floor, at 44 m OD.

The cairn was first identified in 1964 (Cormack) and was excavated in the following year by Corcoran. No report of the excavation was written, though he drew a plan that was intended for publication (figure 30). The following account has been compiled from two published notes (Corcoran 1965a, 1972), the plan (Corcoran 1965b), brief Ms. notes (Henshall 1967), and personal observation (which in 1996 was somewhat limited because the passage and chamber had been partly filled in).

The cairn had been greatly robbed and disturbed before the excavation, particularly so on the W side, and it is known that stones were taken from it in 1917 to repair erosion of the river bank. The shape of the cairn was evident in 1964, and the chamber, with its tilted capstone, was partly exposed (Cormack, Henshall 1972).

The excavator examined more than half of the cairn, though it is unlikely that any great amount of cairn material was removed. It was shown that the cairn was square in plan, and measured about 15 by 15 m. It was revetted by a wall-face built of rounded boulders, which survived to a height of 0.6 m in places. Along the E half of the S side the edge of the cairn had collapsed where it ran along the edge of the terrace. The E side of the cairn was slightly concave, and some irregularly-spaced small orthostats had been incorporated into the façade. The only orthostat to survive was the S portal stone at the entrance to the passage (the stone is no longer visible). About 0.8 m to the S there was the socket of an orthostat with a fragment of the broken stone partly lying over it, and another socket was found 2 m further S. The socket of the N portal stone was identified, and 1.75 m to the N there was another socket. North of the entrance the cairn had been badly ruined, and the NE corner had been destroyed. The revetment of an inner round cairn, 8 to 9 m in diameter, was identified. This inner cairn,

together with the chamber that it enclosed, was interpreted as an earlier structure that had subsequently been surrounded by the square cairn. The cairn is now turf-covered with a very uneven surface. The greatest height, 1.5 m, is on the SW side of the chamber.

The passage is walled by an intact slab-like

INV 51

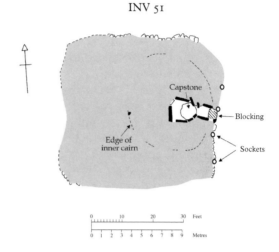

boulder on each side. These were set 0.4 m W of the portal stones in the façade, and their E ends were in line with the wall-face of the inner cairn. The S orthostat, which was already leaning steeply to the N before the excavation, is 1.2 m long. The N orthostat is slightly shorter, and both are about 0.23 m thick; when the S stone was upright both would have been the same height, about 1 m. To the W of the orthostats were two portal stones set 0.6 m apart (they are no longer visible). They were relatively small slabs, both about 0.5 m long, and the height of the S stone was at least 0.6 m. The S stone had evidently fallen inwards as part of the general collapse that occurred along the S side of the passage and chamber. The passage was almost 1 m wide, and about 1.2 m long to the E end of the passage orthostats, and about 2 m long to the entrance.

The polygonal chamber is about 2 m long, and about the same from N to S. It was built of five closely-set slab orthostats, 0.2 to 0.25 m thick, and taller than the portal stones. The SE orthostat (not seen in 1996) was found either prone, or nearly so, on the chamber floor. It was about 0.6 m long and would have been at least 1.4 m high when upright. The S and W orthostats are intact: the former leans acutely, and the latter leans rather less, into the chamber. They are 1.25 and 1.4 m long, and would be 1.27 and 1.25 m high if erect. The N orthostat has a shattered top; it is 1.4 m long and 1.17 m high. The fifth orthostat is almost parallel with the N portal stone, which is only 0.3 m to the E. The orthostat is 0.82 m long and 1 m high, about the same height as the passage walls. A gap of 0.7 m between the orthostats at the NW corner of the chamber evidently retained some walling, as did smaller gaps on either side of the N portal stone. The capstone, which measures 1.7 by 1.67 m, rests on the highest point of the inward-leaning S orthostat and is tilted down steeply to the E. The axis of the passage and chamber differs by some 15° from that of the square cairn (Corcoran 1972).

The entrance to the passage had been closed with walling, behind which the passage had been deliberately blocked (drawn faintly on the plan Corcoran 1965b). Some sherds of neolithic pottery were found in the blocking. The inner end of the passage was divided from the chamber by a thin vertical slab, probably a sill-stone rather than a deliberate blocking (Corcoran 1966). The chamber had been disturbed to ground level, and sherds of a beaker were found above a fallen orthostat (Henshall 1967). There were no skeletal remains.

FINDS
Artefacts. Lost (figure 32).
1. Sherds of undecorated neolithic pottery.
2. Sherds, many very small, from an undecorated beaker, mostly from the rim and neck, which has broken along a building-ring; friable mid-brown fabric with a grey core, 2 to 3 mm thick; rim diameter about 100 mm (Henshall 1967).
3. Lignite beads.
4. Flints, including a small leaf-shaped arrowhead.
5. Stone spindle-whorl (presumably unconnected with the neolithic use of the cairn).
1, 3–5 not illustrated.

INV 52. TOMFAT PLANTATION

Parish Daviot and Dunlichity
Location 6 km S of Inverness
Map reference NH 678374
NMRS number NH 63 NE 5
References Woodham 1963, 37; Woodham and Woodham 1964, 36–8; Henshall 1972, 559–60
Plan ASH and JNGR
Excavation Woodham and Woodham 1963
Visited 4.10.63, 20.10.96

Description. The cairn is in the upland region which separates Strathnairn from the Great Glen. The cairn is almost on the watershed, situated on a small knoll, at 250 m OD. Formerly the region was rough pasture with extensive remains of prehistoric and later settlement, but during the twentieth century much of it has been afforested. In 1963, when the cairn was discovered, the area in which it is sited had been recently replanted, and by 1996 the forest was thick and mature.

The ground falls away from the site on all sides except to the N, where it is level until it rises to a nearby higher knoll. The cairn has been almost completely removed, and only a depth of 0.5 m remains, covered with grass and moss. The edge of the cairn can be traced approximately, giving a diameter of about 17 m. Two stones on the S side, exposed on their outer faces, may be kerb-stones. In an earlier phase of afforestation trees were planted on the cairn and even in the chamber, and in the present phase there are a few trees on the cairn.

Excavation showed that the chamber had been greatly ruined. Afterwards it was left open, and the features described by the excavators can still be seen down to ground level. The chamber now appears as a shallow rectangular hollow, with cairn material flush with the tops of the low side-slabs, the only conspicuous feature being the very tall back-slab. The chamber orthostats are slabs from which rectangular pieces readily shear off.

The axis of the chamber is ENE to WSW (but is described as being E to W). The back-slab is impressive, 2.05 m high, with flat faces and a pointed top. It is 1.52 m long by 0.2 m thick,

INV 52

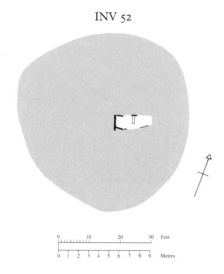

and evidence that originally it was thicker is provided by the base of a sheared-off piece which remains along its foot on the E side. The back-slab leans to the E with an overhang of 0.47 m. Two small side-slabs butt against the back-slab, and lean slightly outwards; they appear totally inadequate for their position. They are 0.82 and 0.78 m long at the top edge and considerably less at ground level, and are very thin. They are about 0.5 m high, and so their horizontal upper edges are 1.5 m below the top of the back-slab. The S wall of the chamber is continued eastwards by two short stretches of disintegrating walling separated by a gap of 1.13 m. The walling is of small slabs, with a small block of intact stone at the E end. It is likely that the gap was once filled by an orthostat. In the N wall of the chamber, opposite the gap, is an orthostat that has obviously suffered considerable flaking; it is 0.5 m long by 0.1 m thick, and 0.76 m high. At the time of the excavation it was upright, but by 1996 it was leaning steeply into the chamber supported by a stone lying across the chamber floor. This stone, 0.7 m long by 0.15 m thick, and only 0.27 m high, was formerly interpreted as a N portal stone dividing the chamber, but it is unlikely to be a structural stone *in situ* because it stretches more than half way across the chamber, and because of its relationship to the adjacent orthostat. The E end of the chamber

seems to have been completely ruined. Amongst a jumble of stones a rather larger slab was interpreted as part of a deliberate blocking of the entrance. The chamber is 1.1 m wide at the W end, and the remaining structure is 3.3 m long.

Various slabs were found lying on the floor of the chamber, and in three cases patches of dark soil had survived where they had been protected. The floor was sand, in which there were a few tiny pieces of charcoal. There were some small sherds on the floor, or just below its surface, in two deposits near the centre of the chamber.

FINDS
Artefact. In the Royal Museum of Scotland.
1. Six small undecorated wall sherds from a small vessel, probably from a beaker; hard fine dark fabric with buff surface, 5 mm thick (EO 1001). Not illustrated.

INV 53. ALLT EOGHAINN
(Lowerbog)

Parish Kiltarlity and Convinth
Location in Glen Convinth, 5 km S of Beauly
Map reference NH 523403
NMRS number NH 54 SW 12
References RCAHMS 1979b, 9, no. 26
Plan ASH and JNGR
Visited 1.10.96

Description. The cairn was built on the steep hillside which forms the E side of Glen Convinth. Beech woods cover most of the lower slopes of the hillside, and above them, where the gradient is less, the land is cultivated. The last remains of the cairn are just within the wood, at 145 m OD, on the spine of a narrow ridge between two burns that run nearly E to W into the valley (plate 8). The ridge slopes down to the W, and on the N side of the site the ground drops steeply to the Allt Eoghainn, while on the S side the drop is gentler.

The cairn material has been almost entirely removed, and what little remains is covered by moss and forest litter. An indefinite edge to the thin spread of stones is detectable in places round the N half of the site, and suggests that the cairn was roughly 18 m in diameter.

The ruined chamber is represented by four upright orthostats surrounded by a group of large prone slabs. The design of the chamber is not altogether clear, but it is likely to have consisted of two relatively small compartments, and to have been entered from the E (the uphill) side. In the centre of the group of prone slabs is an *in situ* pair of portal stones which clearly formed the entry to an inner compartment. They are boulders, set 0.47 m apart, both 0.73 m long by 0.27 m thick, and they project 0.45 and 0.6 m. The westernmost prone slab and that to the SE of it were evidently the back-slab and S side-slab of the compartment; they have fallen outwards, and subsequently have not been moved. They lie almost horizontally with their bases partly exposed and their outer ends clear of the ground. The W slab is intact except that the NE corner seems to have been damaged long ago. It is 1.2 m wide (the original length) by 0.36 m thick, and 1.8 m long (the original height). The base may have been straight before the damage, and the top would have been narrow and horizontal. The S slab appears to be intact; it is 0.9 wide (the original length) by 0.3 m thick, and 1.17 m long (the original height). It would have stood on an almost flat base and would have had a wide slightly rounded top. A third orthostat probably stood on the N side of the compartment. Immediately W of the portal stones is a slab lying flat, 1 m wide by 0.3 m thick, and 1.44 m long. It may have been the third orthostat, and have fallen across the chamber, in which case its straight N end would have been the base; alternatively, it may have been a lintel which rested on the portal stones. To the N of the compartment is a slab that has been damaged round most of its edges, leaving it irregular in shape, and measuring 1.26 by 0.9 m, and up to 0.25 m thick.

To the E of the portal stones, the stones which presumably belonged to the outer compartment are difficult to interpret, mainly because the two upright orthostats indicate an asymmetric plan. These are irregular boulders,

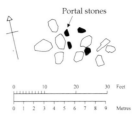

INV 53

Portal stones

roughly 0.64 by 0.65 m and 0.68 by 0.48 m, and they project 0.66 and 0.62 m. They are 1.57 m apart. Between the S orthostat and the S portal stone is an almost horizontal slab which appears to have fallen outwards from the S side of the compartment; the N edge of the slab is almost embedded, and the S end is clear of the ground. The slab is 0.85 m wide by 0.27 m thick, and 1.1 m long. It is likely that this slab and the S orthostat formed most of the S wall of the outer compartment. If so, the N orthostat was part of the N wall (though it has the appearance of a portal stone), and a slab is probably missing from between it and the N portal stone. This tentative interpretation implies that the portal stones, which would be expected between the passage and the chamber, have been removed from immediately E of the two boulder orthostats. (See figure 14 for a reconstruction of the plan.)

An intact but rather irregular slab, 1.5 by about 0.95 m, and up to 0.45 m thick, lies tilted down from S to N between the two boulder orthostats. Three obviously displaced blocks lie to the SE, and that nearest the chamber has been reduced in size.

INV 54. BALBLAIR WOOD

Parish Kilmorack
Location 2.2 km SW of Beauly
Map reference NH 502445
NMRS number NH 54 SW 64
References Coghill and Hanley 1993, 44
Plan ASH and JNGR
Visited 23.10.97

Description. The cairn is on a gravel terrace in the flat lower valley of the River Beauly, at

INV 54

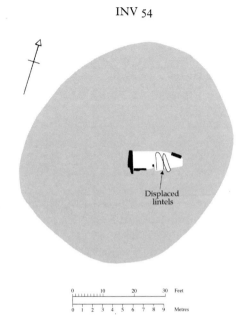

Displaced
lintels

0   10   20   30 Feet

0 1 2 3 4 5 6 7 8 9 Metres

23 m OD. The actual site is on a slight rise on ground that slopes down gently from S to N. It is near the northern edge of a large plantation of pines.

The cairn has been greatly reduced, particularly to the N of the chamber, and at most the cairn material remains about 1 m high near the S side. The approximate limits of the cairn can be traced except where it fades away round the E side, and the diameter appears to have been between 20 and 21 m. The surface of the cairn is uneven, and is covered with moss and forest litter.

The chamber has evidently been cleared out and partly refilled with rubble. The axis is ENE to WSW. The most prominent feature is the impressive back-slab at the WSW end. It is 2.3 m long by 0.5 m thick; it projects 1.25 m above the chamber filling, and its real height is probably about 1.85 m. The E face is flat, and the top is horizontal with rounded corners. On the S side of the chamber, and butting against the back-slab, is a slab with its horizontal upper surface 0.85 m lower than the back-slab and level with the cairn material. The side-slab is over 1.4 m long and over 0.25 m thick. To the E, 1.93 m from the back-slab, the top of a small

upright stone is just visible level with the top of the side-slab. This stone, which measures only 0.2 by 0.16 m, may be part of an inner portal stone. Further to the E, on the N side of the chamber, is a regular rectangular slab set skew to the chamber axis. Its flat upper surface slopes down to the W, and the W end is hidden. It is over 1 m long by 0.3 m thick, and over 0.43 m high. The E end of the slab is presumably at the entrance to the chamber from the passage, of which there is no sign.

Between the last stone and the putative portal stone two lintels lie across the chamber. They rest at the general level of the cairn material, and 0.3 m below the top of the skew slab; their low position indicates that they are not *in situ*. The E lintel is 1.77 m long, and its triangular cross-section measures 0.5 wide by 0.4 m deep. The W lintel is tilted down slightly to the S with the S end hidden; it is over 1.7 m long, and 0.7 m wide by 0.4 m deep.

INV 55. CULDOICH SOUTH

Parish Croy and Dalcross
Location in Strathnairn, 8.5 km E of Inverness
Map reference NH 755428
NMRS number NH 74 SE 37
References Watson and Clarkson 1998; Bradley 2000, 176
Plan after Watson and Clarkson
Visited 28.10.97, 5.4.99

Description. The cairn is on a terrace on the NE side of Strathnairn, at 200 m OD, with wide views to the N and W. The ground drops quite steeply from the terrace to the floor of the valley, and the River Nairn, together with the Balnuaran cairns (INV 8–10) only 1.5 km to the NNE, are not in sight. The cairn occupies the top of a small knoll in an undulating field. The steep sides of the knoll have been accentuated by ploughing up to its base.

The cairn is edged by a fine boulder kerb, 10 m in diameter. Eighteen kerb-stones are *in situ*, projecting up to 0.5 m, and there is little graduation in their size. Nine kerb-stones have fallen outwards and remain undisturbed, and several more lie displaced outside the line of

INV 55

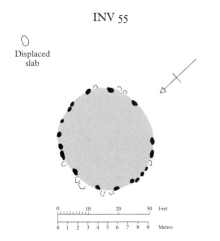

Displaced
slab

```
0        10       20       30  Feet
0  1  2  3  4  5  6  7  8  9   Metres
```

the kerb. Within the kerb, cairn material is at least 0.6 m high. The surface is rather uneven and is covered by coarse grass.

A slab of red sandstone lies on the steep E slope of the knoll, 7.4 m from the kerb. The slab measures 0.9 m by 0.6 m, and its two broken edges indicate that it was once part of a larger block. The slab may be significant because it was brought to the site (the nearest source of sandstone is in the floor of the valley), and because sandstone was used for the major upright stones in the Balnuaran cairns. Thus the slab may have been part of a standing stone which was one of a circle round the cairn, and which was set closer to the kerb than the present position of the shattered slab. If this interpretation is correct, the cairn was a monument of Clava type, and the small diameter implies that it was a passage-grave.

BAN 1. LAGMORE

Parish Inveravon
Location in central Strathspey, near the confluence of the rivers Spey and Avon
Map reference NJ 176358
NMRS number NJ 13 NE 9
References Stuart 1867, II, xxiii; Coles 1907, 141–9; Henshall 1963, 389–90, 391
Plan ASH and JNGR
Visited 15.4.57, 24.5.97

Description. The lower hillside and floor of the valley of the Avon are cultivated or mixed woodland, and the higher ground is afforested. The cairn is on the quite steep S side of the valley, at the edge of a field and a little below the forest, at nearly 200 m OD. There are wide views over the valleys of the Spey and Avon. The site slopes down gently from SW to NE.

The cairn has been severely robbed and disturbed, and is covered by grass (figure 36). Much of the cairn kerb is visible; within it the surface of the cairn material is very uneven, and at most it is about 0.5 m high. Against the outside of the kerb a bank survives round nearly half the circuit. Field-gathered stones have been dumped on and around the cairn, and large stones which presumably derive from the structure lie about the site; together they inhibit and confuse interpretation of the remains.

The kerb-stones are mainly waterworn blocks, generally rectangular in plan, and often with horizontal upper surfaces. They tend to split vertically, and at least some have been reduced in thickness. Many of the stones lean outwards to a greater or lesser extent. The few upright stones indicate that the diameter of the kerb was about 13 m. The entrance to the passage is on the S side of the kerb, between two stones set radially to the kerb and projecting in front of it. The kerb is nearly complete round the S half of the circuit. At the entrance and to the W of it, where the external bank has been largely removed, the structural stones are nearly fully exposed. On each side of the entrance is a large kerb-stone with a horizontal top edge. That on the W side is 1.45 m long by 0.34 m thick, and it has a true height of at least 1.22 m; it is 0.3 m higher than the adjacent stone which forms the entrance. In the SW arc of the kerb the stones are regular in shape; they project up to 0.5 m, and a hollow in the cairn material shows that the true height of some is over 0.9 m. The intact kerb-stone on the E side of the entrance is longer than that on the W side, but is 0.7 m lower, producing a notable lack of symmetry. The kerb-stones in the SE arc are smaller and less regular than those on the SW side. They project 0.3 to 0.57 m, and when upright most of them were about 0.6 m

BAN I

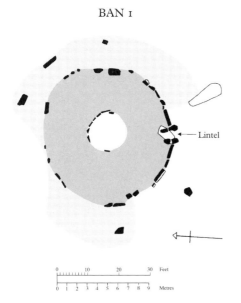

Lintel

0   10   20   30 Feet

0 1 2 3 4 5 6 7 8 9 Metres

or a little more high. Fewer kerb-stones are visible round the N half of the circuit, they vary somewhat in size, and (apart from one large block) they hardly project.

The bank is clearly visible round the E side of the cairn. At its maximum it is about 0.5 m high against the kerb-stones and it merges into the cairn material. It appears to be about 3 m wide extending to just outside the standing stones described below. Its edge here is defined by the limit of ploughing, and by the resultant erosion on the downhill NE side. On the N side the bank has been interrupted by robbing; it is present on the W side, though its edge is ill-defined; on the SW side it has been obscured by field-gathered stones, and it cannot be detected on the S side.

The entrance to the passage is 0.6 m wide between the pair of stones mentioned above (figure 36). They are 0.9 m high with nearly horizontal upper surfaces. The passage walls are continued by a second stone on each side. A lintel, skew to the passage and evidently displaced, rests on three of these stones. The lintel is a waterworn slab with flat faces, 1.9 m long by 0.95 m wide, and about 0.3 m thick. Nothing is visible of the inner part of the passage, and the alignment of the outer part is to the W side of the chamber. The space below

the lintel was cleared of rubble by Coles in 1906, and on the floor was a layer or two of loose slabs, which remain.

The chamber is filled with rubble. On the NE side seven slabs of the basal course of the wall can be seen where cairn material has been pulled away from their outer sides, but their inner faces are hidden. The slabs are all the same height, 0.5 m or a little more. The southernmost slab overlaps its neighbour, and both stones are covered by a horizontal slab; this is probably the last remnant of an upper course. On the W side of the chamber one stone of the wall can be seen, projecting 0.17 m. The diameter of the chamber was about 3.6 m.

Five stones of the surrounding circle remain upright, and all have damaged tops, probably due to natural fracturing. A sixth stone lies where it has fallen outwards. The stone to the W of the entrance is only a stump, measuring 0.86 m by 0.66 m, and projecting 0.44 m. The W stone is the most impressive. It is a vertical-sided block, about 1.1 m long by about 0.65 m thick (and was once thicker because a piece has broken away from one face), and 2.34 m high. The N stone is 1.2 m long by 0.47 m thick, and 1.66 m high; the faces are flat and there is a vertical lengthwise fissure down the centre. At its base the packing stones of its stone-hole are just exposed. The next stone is 1.5 m long by 0.37 m thick. It projects 1.78 m above the ground on its SW side, but erosion up to its NE side has exposed in section its stone-hole and the packing, and the total height of the stone is 2.4 m. Pieces have sheared off both faces of the stone, and another piece is about to break away. The E stone measures 0.45 by 0.3 m, and is 1.35 m high, and it leans slightly to the NE. The fallen slab SE of the entrance is 3.5 m long (the full original height) by 1.25 m wide near the SE (originally the upper) end, and over 0.4 m thick. The stones are between 2.8 and 1.8 m from the kerb, and the three on the NE side of the circle show that the stones were irregularly spaced.

The condition of the monument is unchanged since 1906, and probably since 1864 (Coles, 147; Stuart).

Appendix 1

Structures previously published as chambered cairns (presumed to belong to the Orkney-Cromarty group) or long cairns, but not included in the Inventory

ROS 21. EASTER ALNESSFERRY,
near the N shore of the Black Isle, opposite Alness.
Map reference NH 670662. *NMRS number* NH 66 NE 2. *References* Woodham 1956a, 78–9, 87; Henshall 1963, 346; RCAHMS 1979c, 8, no. 8.

In all three records some doubt has been expressed about the identification of this steep-sided elongated mound as a long cairn. It is composed of stones with quantities of earth, and is turf-covered. It is 17 m long by 10 m wide, and about 1.5 m high. The axis is NE to SW. In recent years the mound has been overgrown with gorse and riddled with rabbit burrows. Most recently the interior has been partly removed during a school project, and the centre is now irregularly hollowed. The structure cannot be interpreted as a prehistoric long cairn, but it does not appear to be merely field gathered stones, and its character is uncertain. Visited 1.5.96.

ROS 26. KINRIVE EAST, *on the N side of the Cromarty Firth*
Map reference NH 699754. *NMRS number* NH 67 NE 5. *References* ISSFC 1899, 363; Childe 1944, 31; Henshall 1963, 350; 1972, 563, 565; RCAHMS 1979a, 8, no. 12.

Although described as a small long cairn in previous publications, when seen in 1994 this interpretation seemed unlikely. The structure is rectilinear, measuring roughly 20 by 11 m, and comprises a large amount of loose stone to which field stones have been added in the past

and again quite recently. In the SW part there is a rectangular hollow, about 5 by 3.5 m, which suggests that the structure is the remains of a building. The rubble forming the NE part seems to derive from further building, probably of more than one period. Visited 24.5.94.

INV 33. GLENBANCHOR, *in Upper Strathspey, 2 km W of Newtonmore*
Map reference NN 689996. *NMRS number* NN 69 NE 1. *Reference* Henshall 1963, 378.

A turf-covered mound, 29 m long, which was recorded as a possible long cairn, is now considered to be a glacial deposit (note corrected map reference). Visited 22.4.58, 24.10.96.

The following structures were not included in Henshall 1963 or 1972, and therefore do not have code numbers, but they have been published either on recent editions of the 1:10,000 OS maps or elsewhere, as chambered cairns, possible chambered cairns, or possible long cairns.

ACHANDUNIE, *2.5 km N of Alness*
Map reference NH 642727. *NMRS number* NH 67 SW 3. *References* Maclean 1886, 338; RCAHMS 1979a, 24, no. 203; *Discovery and Excavation in Scotland 1995*, 44–5.

The site, until recently heavily overgrown with rhododendrons, has been recorded as remains of a chapel, and also as possibly the remains of a chambered cairn. The most obvious feature is a pair of upright parallel slabs, which appear to be relatively modern. Close by is a line of large low boulders, and to one side is an intermittent curved setting of boulders, possibly the base of a tree enclosure. The site is enigmatic, but it does not appear to be remains of a cairn. Visited 29.9.96.

BRAEANTRA, *in Strath Rusdale*
Map reference NH 567779. *NMRS number* NH 57 NE 1. *References* Maclean 1886, 339.

The site is on a turf-covered hillslope strewn with large boulders. Amongst these is a small setting of boulders, too irregular to be part of a chamber, and probably the remains of a bothy or pen. There is no evidence of a cairn, and the surrounding boulders, suggestive of a disturbed stone circle, appear to have been deposited naturally. This is probably the structure that Maclean referred to as a 'Druidical circle'. Visited 26.5.94.

GLENURQUHART NORTH-EAST, *on the Black Isle, near Rosemarkie*

Map reference NH 737628. *NMRS number* NH 76 SW 14. *Reference* RCAHMS 1979c, 8, no. 11. In a large field of pasture, a slight rise covered with grass (with a few stones visible) has been interpreted as possibly a long cairn. The rise measures about 19 m ENE to WSW, by about 10.5 m across the rounded ENE end and about 7 m across the rounded WSW end, and at maximum 0.5 m high. The surface is smooth without any signs of disturbance. The size, proportions, and general appearance of the rise make it very unlikely that this is a long cairn. Visited 29.9.96.

GLENURQUHART SOUTH-WEST, *on the Black Isle, near Rosemarkie*

Map reference NH 733624. *NMRS number* NH 76 SW 13. *Reference* RCAHMS 1979c, 8, no. 10. A parallel-sided mound near the edge of a field of pasture has been recorded as a long cairn. The mound measures 20.5 m ENE to WSW, by 12 m across, and is up to 1 m high. The E end is rounded in plan, and the W end is square. The mound is covered by turf which is broken in places, and it can be seen that it is basically of earth, with an upper layer of stones (probably field-gathered boulders) at the higher E end. The N side is sharply defined, possibly by the base of an old wall, and the W end is defined by an earthy bank, possibly the remains of the W side of a turf structure. The mound has suffered considerable interference, some quite recent. Visited 29.9.96.

LECHANICH, *on the S side of the Dornoch Firth*

Map reference NH 682858. *NMRS number* NH 68 NE 30. *Reference* RCAHMS 1979a, 8, no. 14. The site was thought to be possibly the last remains of a chambered cairn, but there is no cairn material to be seen, and the two upright slabs, at right angles to each other 1.2 m apart, may belong to the corner of a small structure. Visited 22.4.94.

Appendix 2

*Clava-type ring-cairns in the
Central Highlands*

The following monuments were described,
with plans, in Henshall 1963, and only minor
changes were noted when visited by us in 1997:
INV 6 AVIEMORE (now in a landscaped area
within a housing estate), INV 14 BRUIACH,
INV 19 CULBURNIE (now heavily overgrown),
INV 28 DAVIOT, INV 29 DELFOUR, INV 32
GASK, INV 34 GRENISH, INV 48 TORDARROCH.

Additional information is available on other
monuments:

INV 8. BALNUARAN OF CLAVA CENTRE.

A full description and a new plan will be found
in the Inventory.

INV 21. CULDOICH, *in Strathnairn, 8 km ESE of Inverness*

Map reference NH 751437. *NMRS number* NH
74 SE 2. *References* Innes 1860, 48; Jolly 1882,
321–2; Fraser 1884, 338, 340–1; Piggott 1956,
190–2; Henshall 1963, 371–2, 373; Barber
1982.

The monument is heavily overgrown. Its most
striking feature, a single very large standing
stone, fell in 1982. Barber excavated the stone-
hole and adjacent ground, and a resistivity
survey was done, but no evidence of further
standing stones was found. Visited 19.10.97.

INV 23. CULLEARNIE.

A full description and a new plan will be found
in the Inventory.

INV 45. NEWTON OF PETTY, *6 km ENE of Inverness*

Map reference NH 734485. *NMRS number* NH
74 NW 14. *References* Sandby 1750; Anderson
1831, 217–18; Fraser 1884, 359; Henshall
1963, 383–4; Bradley 2000, 131–59.

This greatly damaged cairn was excavated by
John Thawley in 1975–7, and has been published by Bradley. The outer kerb of the cairn,
diameter 16 m, is fairly complete, though some
stones are leaning and some have fallen. The
position of the inner kerb, diameter 6.5 m, was
identified during the excavation, and two
stones survive *in situ*. Between the kerbs cairn
material was up to 0.5 m deep, and subsequently the central area was filled with stones
to a similar depth. A circle of twelve or thirteen
standing stones once surrounded the cairn, of
which six remain, two of them prostrate. Only
one cremation, in the central area, certainly
belonged to the earliest phase. Much later the
cairn was re-used when pits containing cremations were dug into it. Flints and undiagnostic
sherds were not in secure contexts, and most
of them may predate the cairn. Radiocarbon
dates indicate that the cairn was probably built
between 2340 and 2030 BC, and re-use took
place some time between 1100 and 800 BC.
Visited 30.4.97.

Appendix 3

Structures previously published as Clava-type monuments, or possibly Clava-type monuments, but not included in the Inventory nor in the list of ring-cairns in Appendix 2

1. Remains of cairns which are probably of Clava type, but which at present cannot be classified as either passage-graves or ring-cairns

INV 11, 15, 20, 22, 25, 39 (totally destroyed since 1979), have, or had, characteristic heavy kerbs, and some have, or had, an adjacent standing stone. INV 40 and 41, MAINS OF CLAVA NORTH-WEST and SOUTH-EAST, were investigated in 1995 (Bradley 2000, 39–42). At the former it was shown, by means of a resistivity survey, that beside the existing standing stone there was probably a ploughed-out cairn about 20 m in diameter. The latter site, cleared of scrub, was revealed as a greatly denuded ring-cairn lacking its kerb, and without any evidence of standing stones.

2. Cognate monuments which are not Clava-type cairns as strictly defined

INV 43 MILTOWN OF CLAVA NORTH is an enigmatic ruined cairn with an adjacent standing stone in an unsatisfactory relationship to it (excavated in 1990, see Sharples 1993). INV 47 STONEYFIELD is a multi-period kerbed cairn without an open central area or standing stones (excavated in 1972–3, see Simpson 1996) (re-erected at NH 687450). INV 3 and 50 appear to be simple ring-cairns.

3. Destroyed monuments of which there is no adequate record, but which may have been cairns of Clava type

The character of INV 1, 2, 7, 13, 24, 27, 36, 42 is uncertain. Of these monuments INV 7 and 27 are particularly doubtful because they were/are single standing stones, recorded as 'stone circles, remains of' on the 1st edition 6-inch OS maps, and listed by Fraser in 1884; there is no evidence that they were remains of larger monuments. It has been suggested that three more monuments, not listed by Henshall, at Ardersier, Connage and Flemington, all near Fort George on the Moray Firth, and destroyed in the first half of the nineteenth century, may have been Clava-type cairns (RCAHMS 1979b, 7, no. 3; 8, no. 11; 9, no 21).

4. Mis-interpreted sites, which are not Clava-type cairns

ROS 1. ALCAIG MANSE, *on the Black Isle, 3 km ENE of Conon Bridge*

Map reference NH 576567. *NMRS number* NH 55 NE 2. *References* Childe 1944, 34; Woodham 1956, 72–3, 87; Henshall 1963, 333; RCAHMS 1979c, 8, no. 16.

The cairn has an almost complete kerb of heavy boulders, which are more impressive on the S and SW sides, and one on the S side is cupmarked. The cairn is about 1.3 m high with a diameter of about 17.5 m. The centre of the cairn is not hollowed, and thus it does not appear to be of Clava type. Inside the kerb on the SW side two large upright and nearly parallel stones project, set some 2.25 m apart. They are too far apart to be orthostats in a passage leading to a chamber, and are too near to the kerb to be part of an Orkney-Cromarty-type chamber. Inside the kerb on the SE side is a large horizontal slab which has the appearance of a capstone, but which, from its position, cannot be *in situ* over a chamber. Thus there is no evidence that the cairn was chambered, and the upright stones are unexplained. The cairn is surrounded by a platform, the outer edge of which is faced by a boulder kerb. Visited 3.5.96.

ROS 20. CROFTCRUNIE, *on the Black Isle, 6.7 km NW of Inverness*

Map reference NH 611519. *NMRS number* NH 65 SW 6. *References* Beaton 1882, 484–5;

Woodham 1956, 81; Henshall 1963, 346;
RCAHMS 1979c, 7, no 7.
An enigmatic structure in a field at
Croftcrunie was recorded in 1882 (Beaton),
and was destroyed before 1904 (according to
the 2nd edition 6-inch OS map). A wall, 3 m
thick and 0.6 to 0.9 m high, enclosed an oval
area of about 22 by 19 m. There was a gap or
entrance on the NW side. Off-centre within the
enclosure and butting the wall on the NE side
was a circular mound, about 17 m in diameter
and about 1.5 m high. In the centre of the
mound was a circular hollow about 6 m in
diameter and more than 1.5 m deep, faced by
walling. The upper part of the walling oversailed, which suggested to Beaton that the hollow had once had a vaulted roof. It is unclear
whether the enclosure wall and the mound are
contemporary, and if not, which was built first
(see Beaton's plan and section, p. 484).

Woodham suggested that the mound may
have been a Clava-type cairn, and this possibility was accepted in subsequent publications.
However, the diameter of the hole is too great
for it to have been roofed by a stone vault,
and therefore the mound cannot have been a
passage-grave. Further, the location in a gentle
fold in the landscape is not consistent with the
locations of other passage-graves. The purpose
and date of the structure are unknown. Visited
30.9.96.

INV 4. ALTNACARDICH, *7 km W of*
Inverness
Map reference NH 5943. *NMRS number*
NH 54 SE 12, 13. References Wallace 1886,
350; Henshall 1963, 359; RCAHMS 1979b, 7,
nos. 1, 2.
Six structures, rather vaguely described in
1886 in terms suggestive of Clava-type cairns,
were formerly in dense forest. No cairns were

found in 1979 after the area had been cleared
of trees (RCAHMS).

INV 44. MILTOWN OF CLAVA
SOUTH, *0.5 km SW of Balnuaran of Clava*
South-west (INV 10)
Map reference NH 752439. *NMRS number*
NH 74 SE 7. *References* ONB No. 18, 27; Fraser
1884, 341; Henshall 1963, 383; RCAHMS
1979b, 19, no. 31.
The monument consists of the foundations of
a chapel, as has long been recognised, and
which are still clearly visible. There is no evidence that there was also a Clava-type cairn on
the site. This mistake seems to have arisen
from a misreading of Anderson 1834, 449–51,
and was reinforced during the survey work for
the 1st edition 6-inch OS maps. In the ONB the
monument and the adjacent cairn INV 43 were
described together and were almost certainly
confused, resulting in misleading titling on the
map. Fraser continued the error in his descriptions of Clava-type cairns by his conflated
entry for INV 43 and 44. Visited 19.10.97.

BALNUARAN OF CLAVA SOUTH,
100 m E of Balnuaran of Clava North-east
(INV 9)
Map reference NH 758444. *NMRS number*
NH 74 SE 11. *References* Jolly 1882, 302;
RCAHMS 1979c, 18, no. 115; Bradley 2000,
43–4, 85.
A heavily overgrown monument, recorded by
Jolly, OS, and RCAHMS as a round house, was
excavated by Bradley in 1995. He interpreted
the remains as a ring-cairn, with a date in the
late bronze age. When, on invitation, we visited
the excavation, we still favoured the original
interpretation. The monument overlies a
buried soil with radiocarbon dates in the first
millennium BC.

from the long cairn, it may be concluded that the cairn was within a roughly rectangular area measuring 0.7 km NW to SE by 0.3 km NE to SW centred on NH 52256142.

In the S part of the area thus defined there was formerly a standing stone (ONB 1876, No. 9, 64; shown on the first edition of the 6-inch map; NMRS number NH 56 SW 4), which it is tempting to identify as the standing stone which in 1838 stood at the E end of the cairn. A visit to the site showed that this is unlikely because the site of the stone is in a slight hollow, and the cairn was 'on a little rising ground'.

The following information about the Mackenzies of Hilton is provided by D. Warrand (1965) and explains the occurrence of the placename *Hilton* in several locations. In the sixteenth century the family acquired the property of Hilton (just east of Muir of Ord) in Urray parish. In 1660 Alexander Mackenzie of Hilton sold it and moved into Contin parish, but he kept the name *Hilton*; the house of Hilton was on the site of the modern Strathbraan Lodge. In 1731 Roderick Mackenzie, a younger grandson of the Hilton family, acquired the lands of Brae in Cullicudden parish in the Black Isle, and his son John married the daughter and heiress of Mackenzie of Davochmaluag, in Fodderty parish. In 1784 their son Alexander succeeded as heir to his cousin Alexander Mackenzie of Hilton; before this he had inherited Davochmaluag (which included Davochcairn and Davochpollo), which he renamed Brae after the Black Isle property. When he died in 1840 the whole of his estates, including Brae/Hilton in Fodderty parish were sold to meet his debts.

The use, for a short time, of 'Hilton' for the estate of Brae has caused confusion continuing through the nineteenth century. In gazetteers and directories, Hilton in Fodderty parish was recorded as an estate with a large cairn (though the cairn had been totally removed long before 1875). In some gazetteers Hilton in Urray parish, from which Alexander Mackenzie took his title, was not distinguished from Hilton in Fodderty parish, and in a

Appendix 4

Note on the location of the destroyed cairn, Heights of Dochcarty (ROS 58), in Fodderty parish.

The difficulty in identifying the site of this long cairn arises from the placename 'Hilton', which does not appear on the Ordnance Survey maps of Fodderty parish. The only record of the cairn, in 1838, placed it in this parish, on land owned by Alexander Mackenzie of Hilton, and evidently in the neighbourhood of ROS 22 (NSA 14, 1845, 252–3). These facts indicate that it was on the small estate of Brae, bounded on the E by Tulloch Castle estate, on the S by the public road running W from Dingwall, on the W by the lands of the Heights of Fodderty, and on the N by the River Sgitheach. The Brae estate consisted of four farms, Davochcarty (later Dochcarty), Davochcairn, Davochpollo and Davochmaluag (later Dochmaluag) (Watson 1904, 100). The field pattern of the estate is recorded on the first edition of the OS 6-inch map, surveyed in 1875–6, and clearly reflects its former division into four long parallel strips. The strips ran from N to S, from the top of the ridge which separates Strath Sgitheach from Strath Peffer down to the floor of the valley of the River Peffer, and they evidently represent the four davachs of earlier times, each 0.3 km wide. The placenames Davochcairn and Davochpollo were not recorded on the 6-inch map, but on a plan of grazings in 1813 (Signet Library, Edinburgh, 273/8), the sequence of the four davachs from E to W is as given above. The cairn was evidently on the upper part of the estate ('the heights of the property'). On the assumption that Davochcairn took its name gazetteer of 1904 the former was erroneously accredited with a large cairn.

We are grateful to Dr J. Munro for the information on the Mackenzies of Hilton, and to Mr R. W. Munro for providing the reference to the plan of 1813.

References

Anderson, G. (1831) On some of the stone circles and cairns in the neighbourhood of Inverness. *Archaeologia Scotica* 3, 211–22.

Anderson, G. and P. (1834) *Guide to the Highlands and Islands of Scotland*. London.

Anderson, J. (1886) *Scotland in Pagan Times, the Bronze and Stone Ages*. Edinburgh.

Armit, I. (1996) *The Archaeology of Skye and the Western Isles*. Edinburgh.

Armit, I. and Finlayson, B. (1996) The transition to agriculture, in Pollard and Morrison eds (1996) 269–90.

Ashmore, P. J. (1986) Neolithic carvings in Maes Howe. *Proc. Soc. Antiq. Scot.* 116, 57–62.

Ashmore, P. J. (1990) *Maes Howe*. Edinburgh.

Ashmore, P. J. (1996) *Neolithic and Bronze Age Scotland*. London.

Bain, G. (1887) The stone circles at Clava. *Trans. Gaelic Soc. of Inverness* 13, 122–35.

Baldwin, J. R. ed. (1986) *Firthlands of Ross and Sutherland* (The Scottish Society for Northern Studies). Edinburgh.

Barber, J. (1982) A fallen stone at the ring of Culdoich, Clava, Inverness. *Glasgow Archaeol. J.* 9, 31–7.

Barber, J. (1988) Isbister, Quanterness and Point of Cott: the formation and testing of some middle range theory, in Barrett and Kinnes eds (1988) 57–62.

Barber, J. (1992) Megalithic architecture, in Sharples and Sheridan eds (1992) 13–32.

Barber, J. (1997) *The Excavation of a Stalled Cairn at the Point of Cott, Westray, Orkney* (=Scottish Trust for Archaeological Research, Monograph 1). Edinburgh.

Barclay, G. J. (1990) The clearing and partial excavation of the cairns at Balnuaran of Clava, Inverness-shire, by Miss Kathleen Kennedy, 1930–31. *Proc. Soc. Antiq. Scot.* 120, 17–32.

Barclay, G. J. (1992) Are the Clava 'passage graves' really passage graves?: a reconsideration of the nature and associations of the Clava passage graves and ring-cairns, in Sharples and Sheridan eds (1992) 77–82.

Barrett, J. C. and Kinnes, I. A. eds (1988) *The Archaeology of Context in the Neolithic and Bronze Age: Recent Trends*. Sheffield.

Beaton, A. J. (1882) Notes on the antiquities of the Black Isle, Ross-shire, with plans and sections. *Proc. Soc. Antiq. Scot.* 16, 477–92.

Boswell, J. (1785) *The Journal of a Tour to the Hebrides with Samuel Johnson*. London.

Bradley, R. (1993) *Altering the Earth* (=Society of Antiquaries of Scotland Monograph Series, no. 8). Edinburgh.

Bradley, R. (1996) Excavations at Clava. *Current Archaeology* 148, 136–42.

Bradley, R. (1998) Incised motifs in the passage-graves at Quoyness and Cuween, Orkney. *Antiquity* 72, 387–90.

Bradley, R. et. al. (1999) Discovering decorated tombs in neolithic Orkney. *Current Archaeology* 161, 184–7.

Bradley, R. (2000) *The Good Stones* (=Society of Antiquaries of Scotland Monograph Series, no. 17). Edinburgh.

Brown, P. (1816) Reduced plan of the survey of the Commons of Milbuy, Cromarty etc, RHP 4045 housed in the Scottish Record Office.

Brown, W. L. W. (1906) Alness in the eighteenth century. *Trans. Inverness Sci. Soc. and Field Club* 6, 18–25.

Burl, A. (1970) The recumbent stone circles of north-east Scotland. *Proc. Soc. Antiq. Scot.* 102, 56–81.

Burl, A. (1972) Stone circles and ring-cairns. *Scot. Archaeol. Forum* 4, 31–47.

Burl, A. (1976) *The Stone Circles of the British Isles*. New Haven and London.

Burl, A. (1981) 'By the light of the cinerary moon': chambered tombs and the astronomy of death, in Ruggles and Whittle eds (1981) 243–74.

Cameron, D. (1882) Notice of the ancient circular dwellings, hill forts, and burial cairns of Strathnairn. *Proc. Soc. Antiq. Scot.* 16, 288–94.

Cash, C. G. (1906) Stone circles at Grenish, Aviemore, and Delfour, Strathspey. *Proc. Soc. Antiq. Scot.* 40, 245–54.

Cash, C. G. (1910) Archaeological notes from Aviemore. *Proc. Soc. Antiq. Scot.* 44, 189–203.

Childe, V. G. (1935) *The Prehistory of Scotland*. London.

Childe, V. G. (1940) *The Prehistoric Communities of the British Isles*. London.

Childe, V. G. (1944) An unrecognised group of chambered cairns. *Proc. Soc. Antiq. Scot. 78*, 26–38.

Clarke, D. L. (1970) *Beaker Pottery of Great Britain and Ireland*. Cambridge.

Clarke, D. V., Cowie, T. G. and Foxon, A. (1985) *Symbols of Power in the Time of Stonehenge*. Edinburgh.

Close-Brooks, J. (1983) Some early querns. *Proc. Soc. Antiq. Scot. 113*, 282–9.

Coghill, D. and Hanley, R. (1993) Aird Survey. *Discovery and Excavation in Scotland 1993*, 44–5.

Coles, F. R. (1907) Report on stone circles in the north-east of Scotland (Banffshire and Moray). *Proc. Soc. Antiq. Scot. 41*, 130–72.

Coles, J. M. and Taylor, J. J. (1970) The excavation of a midden in the Culbin Sands, Morayshire. *Proc. Soc. Antiq. Scot. 102*, 87–100.

Corcoran, J. X. W. P. (1965a) Balvraid Farm, Glen Beag, Glenelg. *Discovery and Excavation in Scotland 1965*, 20.

Corcoran, J. X. W. P. (1965b) Two plans of the excavated cairn at Balvraid, Inverness-shire, IND 209/1, IND 209/2, housed in the National Monuments Record of Scotland.

Corcoran, J. X. W. P. (1966) Excavation of three chambered cairns at Loch Calder, Caithness. *Proc. Soc. Antiq. Scot. 98*, 1–75.

Corcoran, J. X. W. P. (1972) Multi-period construction and the origins of the chambered long cairn in western Britain and Ireland, in Lynch and Burgess eds (1972) 31–63.

Cormack, E. A. (1964) Balvraid, Glen Beag. *Discovery and Excavation in Scotland 1964*, 30.

Crone, A. (1993) Excavation and survey of sub-peat features of neolithic, bronze and iron age date at Bharpa Carinish, North Uist, Scotland. *Proc. Prehist. Soc. 59*, 361–82.

Cruickshank, J. ed. (1941) *Logan's Collections* (printed for The Third Spalding Club). Aberdeen.

Dalland, M. (1998a) Kinbeachie Farm, Culbokie. *Discovery and Excavation in Scotland 1998*, 60.

Dalland, M. (1998b) Excavations at Kinbeachie Farm, Culbokie. Ross-shire: data structure report, copy housed in the National Monuments Record of Scotland.

Daniel, G. E. (1962) The megalith builders, in Piggott ed. (1962) 39–72.

Daniel, G. and Kjærum P. eds (1973) *Megalithic Graves and Ritual* (=Papers presented at the III Atlantic Colloquium, Moesgård 1969). Copenhagen.

Daniel, G. E. and Powell, T. G. E. (1949) The distribution and date of the passage-graves of the British Isles. *Proc. Prehist. Soc. 15*, 169–87.

Davidson, J. L. and Henshall, A. S. (1989) *The Chambered Cairns of Orkney*. Edinburgh.

Davidson, J. L. and Henshall, A. S. (1991) *The Chambered Cairns of Caithness*. Edinburgh.

DNB (1967–8) *Dictionary of National Biography 12*. Oxford.

Donations (1925) Donations to the Museum and Library. *Proc. Soc. Antiq. Scot. 59*, 71–5.

Edmonds, M. (1999) *Ancestral Geographies of the Neolithic*. London and New York.

Edmonds, M. and Richards, C. eds (1998) *Understanding the Neolithic of North-western Europe*. Glasgow.

Finlayson, B., Hardy, K. and Wickham-Jones, C. R. (1999) *Scotland's First Settlers, 1999 Data Structure Report*, copy housed in the National Monuments Record of Scotland.

Fraser, J. (n.d.) Original surveys of the cairns published in 1884, housed in Highland Council Archive, Inverness.

Fraser, J. (1883) Descriptive notes on the stone circles of Strathnairn and neighbourhood of Inverness. *Trans. Inverness Sci. Soc. and Field Club 2*, 360–79.

Fraser, J. (1884) Descriptive notes on the stone circles of Strathnairn and neighbourhood of Inverness, with plans, etc. *Proc. Soc. Antiq. Scot. 18*, 328–62.

Gill, G. (1975) Look to the rocks, in *The Hub of the Highlands*, Inverness Field Club (1975), 2–16.

Gillen, C. (1984) The physical background, in Omand ed. (1984) 17–47.

Gillen, C. (1986) Geology and landscape of Easter Ross and Sutherland, in Baldwin ed. (1986) 1–22.

Gourlay, R. (1984) The ancient past, in Omand ed. (1984) 99–125.

Grant, A. (1880) Stone circles and other ancient

remains in Strathspey. *Trans. Inverness Sci. Soc. and Field Club 1*, 53–60.

Grant, A. (1883) [address at an excursion to Glen Urquhart in 1881]. *Trans. Inverness Sci. Soc. and Field Club 2*, 145–6.

Hanley, R. and Sheridan, A. (1994) A beaker cist from Balblair, near Beauly, Inverness District. *Proc. Soc. Antiq. Scot. 124*, 129–39.

Harding, A. F. with Lee, G. E. (1987) *Henge Monuments and Related Sites of Great Britain* (=British Archaeol. Reports, British Series, no.175). Oxford.

Hedges, J. W. (1983) *Isbister, a Chambered Cairn in Orkney* (=British Archaeol. Reports, British Series, no.115). Oxford.

Henshall, A. S. (1963, 1972) *The Chambered Tombs of Scotland*, 2 vols. Edinburgh.

Henshall, A. S. (1967) Ms. note and drawing of sherds from Balvraid, and brief notes made at a lecture given by J. X. W. P. Corcoran to the Society of Antiquaries of Scotland in October 1967, titled 'Balvraid and Mid Gleniron: excavation of chambered cairns in Inverness–shire and Wigtownshire'.

Henshall, A. S. and Ritchie, J. N. G. (1995) *The Chambered Cairns of Sutherland*. Edinburgh.

Henshall, A. S. and Wallace, J. C. (1956) Bishop Kinkell. *Discovery and Excavation in Scotland 1956*, 22–3.

Hodder, I. (1992) *Theory and Practice in Archaeology*. London and New York.

Hunter, J. and Ralston, I. eds (1999) *The Archaeology of Britain*. London and New York.

Innes, C. (1860) Notice of a tomb on the Hill of Roseisle, Morayshire, recently opened; also of the chambered cairns and stone circles at Clava, on Nairnside. *Proc. Soc. Antiq. Scot. 3*, 46–50.

ISSFC (1880a) Excursions to Strathnairn, 1876. *Trans. Inverness Sci. Soc. and Field Club 1*, 27–36.

ISSFC (1880b) Excursion to the Mill Burn and Leys Springs, 1878. *Trans. Inverness Sci. Soc. and Field Club 1*, 150–7.

ISSFC (1880c) Excursion to Moniack House and Reelick Burn, 1878. *Trans. Inverness Sci. Soc. and Field Club 1*, 165–71.

ISSFC (1899a) Excursion to Essich and Bunachton, 1897. *Trans. Inverness Sci. Soc. and Field Club 5*, 177–9.

ISSFC (1899b) Excursion to Balnagowan and Strathrory, 1899. *Trans. Inverness Sci. Soc. and Field Club 5*, 359–64.

ISSFC (1918) Excursion to Essich, 1918. *Trans. Inverness Sci. Soc. and Field Club 8*, 393–4.

ISSFC (1925) Excursion to Reelick, 1920. *Trans. Inverness Sci. Soc. and Field Club 9*, 194–199.

Joass, J. M. (1858) Ink and wash drawing of Balnuaran of Clava North-east, housed in the National Museums of Scotland, Ms 499 (iv); an etching in J. Anderson 1886, 301.

Joass, J. M. (1865) Letter to an unknown correspondent, copy housed in the National Monuments Record of Scotland (Inverness Museum and Art Gallery, INV M G 954.031.3).

Joass, W. C. (1865) Notes on cup-and-ring-marked stones in Glenelg, Inverness-shire, and Bakerhill, Tulloch and Mountgerald near Dingwall, Ross-shire, Society of Antiquaries of Scotland Ms 378, no. 9, housed in the library of the National Museums of Scotland.

Jolly, W. (1882) On cup-marked stones in the neighbourhood of Inverness. *Proc. Soc. Antiq. Scot. 16*, 300–401.

Kennedy, K. (1931) Notes, plans and sections of work undertaken at Balnuaran of Clava, 1930–31, housed in the Scottish Record Office, SC 22913/2A (copies in the National Monuments Record of Scotland Ms 590/1, DC 11980).

Kenworthy, J. B. (1972) Ring-cairns in north-east Scotland. *Scot. Archaeol. Forum 4*, 18–30.

Lanting, J. N. and van der Waals, J. D. (1972) British beakers as seen from the continent. *Helinium 12*, 20–46.

Lauder, T. D. (1830) *An Account of the Great Floods of August, 1829, in the Province of Moray*. Edinburgh.

Lisowski, F. P. (1956) The cremations from the Culdoich, Leys and Kinchyle sites. *Proc. Soc. Antiq. Scot. 89*, 83–90.

Logan, J. (1831) Watercolour of 'Clachan more na Taradin' in the portfolio entitled *Primeval Antiquities* (lower part of folio 117) housed in the Library of the Society of Antiquaries of London.

Logan, J. (1834) [Letter from James Logan to the Earl of Aberdeen]. *Archaeologia 25*, 614–16.

Lynch, F. and Burgess, C. eds (1972) *Prehistoric Man in Wales and the West*. Bath.

Macbain, A. (1885) The 'druid' circles. *Trans. Gaelic Soc. of Inverness 11*, 23–50.

MacCarthy, C. (1996) The disclosure of sacred ground: structural developments within megalithic monuments of the Clava group. *Proc. Soc. Antiq. Scot. 126*, 87–102.

McCullagh, R. (1992) *Lairg: the Archaeology of a Changing Landscape*. Edinburgh.

MacGregor, G. and Loney, H. (1997) Excavation at Kilcoy South, chambered cairn. (=Glasgow University Archaeological Research Division Report no. 434.) Glasgow. (Copy housed in the National Monuments Record of Scotland.)

Maclagan, C. (1875) *The Hill Forts, Stone Circles and other Structural Remains of Ancient Scotland*. Edinburgh.

Maclean, R. (1886) The parish of Rosskeen. *Trans. Gaelic Soc. of Inverness 12*, 324–39.

Maclean, R. (1888) Notes on the parish of Alness. *Trans. Gaelic Soc. of Inverness 14*, 217–32.

Maclean, R. (1889) Notes on the parish of Kiltearn. *Trans. Gaelic Soc. of Inverness 15*, 302–10.

MacSween, A. (1992) Orcadian grooved ware, in Sharples, N. M. and Sheridan, A. eds (1992), 259–71.

Masters, L. J. (1997) The excavation and restoration of the Camster Long chambered cairn, Caithness, Highland, 1967–80. *Proc. Soc. Antiq. Scot. 127*, 123–83.

Mercer, R. J. and Midgley M. S. (1997) The early bronze age cairn at Sketewan, Balnaguard, Perth & Kinross. *Proc. Soc. Antiq. Scot. 127*, 281–338.

Mitchell, A. (1874) Vacation notes in Cromar, Burghead, and Strathspey. *Proc. Soc. Antiq. Scot. 10*, 603–89.

Murchison, T. M. (1963) Glenelg, Inverness-shire: notes for a parish history. *Trans. Gaelic Soc. of Inverness 39/40*, 294–333.

NMRS Records housed in the National Monuments Record of Scotland, Edinburgh.

NSA (1845) *The New Statistical Account of Scotland*, 14. Edinburgh.

Omand, D. ed. (1984) *The Ross and Cromarty Book*. Golspie.

Omand, D. ed. (1987) *The Grampian Book*. Golspie.

ONB (1868–76) Object Name Books of the Ordnance Survey, Inverness-shire Mainland, and Ross and Cromarty Mainland, housed in the Scottish Record Office, Edinburgh (microfilm copy in the National Monuments Record of Scotland).

Ordnance Survey Record Card. Records now part of the National Monuments Record of Scotland database.

OSA (1791–9) *The Statistical Account of Scotland*. Edinburgh.

Parker Pearson, M. and Richards, C. (1994) *Architecture and Order: Approaches to Social Space*. London and New York.

Pennant, T. (1771) *A Tour of Scotland in 1769*. Chester.

Perrott, R. (1858) On some groups of stones called dancers, in northern Gaul and Brittany. *Archaeologia Cambrensis*, 3rd series, 4, 388–96.

Phillips, T., Jack, A., and Searight, S. (1999) The Black Isle Fieldwalking Project, typescript report. (Copy in the National Monuments Record of Scotland.)

Piggott, S. (1954) *The Neolithic Cultures of the British Isles*. Cambridge.

Piggott, S. (1956) Excavations in passage-graves and ring-cairns of the Clava group, 1952–3. *Proc. Soc. Antiq. Scot. 88*, 173–207.

Piggott, S. ed. (1962) *The Prehistoric Peoples of Scotland*. London.

Piggott, S. (1973) Problems in the interpretation of chambered tombs, in Daniel and Kjærum eds (1973) 9–15.

Piggott, S. and Simpson, D. D. A. (1971) Excavation of a stone circle at Croft Moraig, Perthshire, Scotland. *Proc. Prehist. Soc. 37*, 1–15.

Pitt Rivers, A. H. (1885a) Field notebook, Work 39/15 housed in the Public Record Office, Kew, London.

Pitt Rivers, A. H. (1885b) Sketch Book 4 illustrating a journey to Scotland, Work 39/6 housed in the Public Record Office, Kew, London.

Pococke, R. (1887) *Tours in Scotland 1747, 1750, 1760*, ed. D. W. Kemp (=Scot. Hist. Soc. 1). Edinburgh.

Pollard, T. and Morrison, A. eds (1996) *The Early Prehistory of Scotland*. Edinburgh.

Prehistoric Society (1957) Notes on excavations in Eire, England, Northern Ireland, Scotland and Wales, during 1956. *Proc. Prehist. Soc. 23*, 220–30.

Price, R. J. (1976) *Highland Landforms*. Inverness.

RCAHMS Royal Commission on the Ancient and Historical Monuments of Scotland.

RCAHMS (1911) Royal Commission on the Ancient and Historical Monuments of Scotland, *Second Report and Inventory of Monuments and Constructions in the County of Sutherland*. Edinburgh.

RCAHMS (1943) Emergency Surveys 1943 (by V. G. Childe and A. Graham), vol. 2, Ms/36, housed in the National Monuments Record of Scotland.

RCAHMS (1979a) *The Archaeological Sites and Monuments of Easter Ross, Ross and Cromarty District, Highland Region* (= The archaeological sites and monuments of Scotland series no. 6). Edinburgh.

RCAHMS (1979b) *The Archaeological Sites and Monuments of North-east Inverness, Inverness District, Highland Region* (= The archaeological sites and monuments of Scotland series no. 8). Edinburgh.

RCAHMS (1979c) *The Archaeological Sites and Monuments of the Black Isle, Ross and Cromarty District, Highland Region* (= The archaeological sites and monuments of Scotland series no. 9). Edinburgh.

Rees, T. (1997) The excavation of Cairnwell ring-cairn, Portlethen, Aberdeenshire. *Proc. Soc. Antiq. Scot. 127*, 255–79.

Renfrew, C. (1979) *Investigations in Orkney* (= Rep. Research Comm. Soc. Antiq. London 38). London.

Richards, C. (1992) Barnhouse and Maes Howe. *Current Archaeology 131*, 444–8.

Richards, C. (1998) 'Centralising tendencies? A re-examination of social evolution in late neolithic Orkney', in Edmonds, M. and Richards, C. eds (1998) 516–32.

Ritchie, A. (1983) Excavation of a neolithic farmstead at Knap of Howar, Papa Westray, Orkney. *Proc. Soc. Antiq. Scot. 113*, 40–121.

Ritchie, A. (1995) *Prehistoric Orkney*. London.

Ritchie, J. N. G. (1970) Excavation of the chambered cairn at Achnacreebeag. *Proc. Soc. Antiq. Scot. 102*, 31–55.

Ritchie, J. N. G. (1974) Excavation of the stone circle and cairn at Balbirnie, Fife. *Archaeol. J. 131*, 1–32.

Ritchie, J. N. G. (1976) The Stones of Stenness, Orkney. *Proc. Soc. Antiq. Scot. 107*, 1–60.

Ritchie, J. N. G. and Crawford, J. (1978) Recent work on Coll and Skye. *Proc. Soc. Antiq. Scot. 109*, 75–103.

Ritchie, J. N. G. and MacLaren, A. (1972) Ring-cairns and related monuments in Scotland. *Scot. Archaeol. Forum 4*, 1–17.

Ritchie, J. N. G., Thornber, I., Lynch, F., and Marshall, D. N. (1975) Small cairns in Argyll: some recent work. *Proc. Soc. Antiq. Scot. 106*, 15–38.

Ross, J. (1880) Druidical circles. *Trans. Inverness Sci. Soc. and Field Club 1*, 146–7.

Ruggles, C. (1999) *Astronomy in Prehistoric Britain and Ireland*. New Haven and London.

Ruggles, C. and Barclay, G. (2000) Cosmology, calendars and society in neolithic Orkney. *Antiquity 74*, 62–74.

Ruggles, C. L. N. and Whittle, A. W. R. eds (1981) *Astronomy and Society in Britain during the Period 400–1500 B.C.* (=British Archaeol. Reports, British Series, no. 88). Oxford.

Sandby, P. (1750) Plan of Newton of Petty, housed in the National Library of Ireland, Ms. LI22 TX(4) p. 30.

Saville, A. (1996) Lacaille, microliths and the mesolithic of Orkney, in Pollard and Morrison eds (1996) 213–24.

Scott, W. L. (1951) The colonisation of Scotland in the second millennium B.C. *Proc. Prehist. Soc. 17*, 16–82.

Sharples, N. M. (1984) Excavations at Pierowall Quarry, Westray, Orkney. *Proc. Soc. Antiq. Scot. 114*, 75–125.

Sharples, N. M. (1993) Excavations at Miltown of Clava, Inverness-shire. *Glasgow Archaeol. J. 18*, 1–9.

Sharples, N. M. and Sheridan, A. eds (1992) *Vessels for the Ancestors*. Edinburgh.

Shepherd, I. A. G. (1986) *Powerful Pots: Beakers in North East Prehistory*. Aberdeen.

Shepherd, I. A. G. (1987) The early peoples, in Omand ed. (1987) 119–30.

Simpson, D. D. A. (1967) Excavations at Kintraw, Argyll. *Proc. Soc. Antiq. Scot. 99*, 54–9.

Simpson, D. D. A. (1996) Excavation of a kerbed funerary monument at Stoneyfield, Raigmore, Inverness, Highland, 1972–3. *Proc. Soc. Antiq. Scot. 126*, 53–86.

Simpson, D. D. A. and Thawley, J. E. (1972) Single grave art in Britain. *Scot. Archaeol. Forum 4*, 81–104.

Simpson, J. Y. (1866) On ancient sculpturings

of cups and concentric rings etc. *Proc. Soc. Antiq. Scot.* 6, Appendix 1–148.

Sissons, J. B. (1967) *The Evolution of Scotland's Scenery*. Edinburgh and London.

Smith, B. (1989) Isbister, an Orkney Islands Council guardianship monument. *Proc. Soc. Antiq. Scot. 119*, 55–9.

Smith, B. B. ed. (1994) *Howe, Four Millennia of Orkney Prehistory* (=Society of Antiquaries of Scotland Monograph Series, no. 9). Edinburgh.

Smith, J. (1975) Geomorphic evolution, in *The Hub of the Highlands*, Inverness Field Club (1975) 17–23.

Somerville, H. B. (1923) Instances of orientation in prehistoric monuments of the British Isles. *Archaeologia 73*, 193–224.

Stewart, B. (1857) Watercolour drawings of Balnuaran of Clava North-east and South-west, housed in the National Museum of Scotland, Ms 499; etchings in Innes 1860.

Stuart, J. (1867) *Sculptured Stones of Scotland*, vol. 2. Edinburgh.

Stuart, J. (1868) Report to the committee of the Society of Antiquaries of Scotland, appointed to arrange for the application of a fund left by the late Mr. A Henry Rhind, for excavating early remains. *Proc. Soc. Antiq. Scot.* 7, 289–307.

Thom, A. (1967) *Megalithic Sites in Britain*. Oxford.

Thom, A., Thom, A. S. and Burl, A. (1980) *Megalithic Rings* (= British Archaeol. Reports, British Series, no. 81). Oxford.

Thompson, M. W. (1960) The first inspector of ancient monuments in the field. *J. Brit. Archaeol. Ass.* 3rd series 23, 103–24.

Tilley, C. (1994) *A Phenomenology of Landscape*. Oxford and Providence.

Tipping, R. (1994) The form and fate of Scotland's woodlands. *Proc. Soc. Antiq. Scot. 124*, 1–54.

Walker, I. C. (1963) The Clava Cairns. *Proc. Soc. Antiq. Scot. 96*, 87–106.

Wallace, T. D. (1886) Notes on ancient remains in the Beauly valley, Inverness-shire. *Proc. Soc. Antiq. Scot. 20*, 340–55.

Warrand, D. (1965) *Information from some Mackenzie pedigrees*. Inverness.

Watson, A. and Clarkson, N. (1998) Culdoich South, Strathnairn. *Discovery and Excavation in Scotland 1998*, 49–50.

Watson, W. J. (1904) *Placenames of Ross and Cromarty*. Inverness.

Whittle, A. (1999) The neolithic period, c. 40000–2500/2200 BC, in Hunter and Ralston eds (1999), 58–76.

Wickham-Jones, C. R. (1990) *Rhum: mesolithic and later sites at Kinloch, excavations 1984–86* (=Society of Antiquaries of Scotland Monograph Series, no. 7). Edinburgh.

Wickham-Jones, C. R. (1994) *Scotland's First Settlers*. London.

Wilson, D. (1851) *The Archaeology and Prehistoric Annals of Scotland*. Edinburgh.

Woodham, A. A. (1953) Four henge monuments in Easter Ross. *Proc. Soc. Antiq. Scot. 87*, 72–9.

Woodham, A. A. (1955) Carn Glas, Kilcoy. *Discovery and Excavation in Scotland 1955*, 26–7.

Woodham, A. A. (1956a) A survey of prehistoric monuments in the Black Isle. *Proc. Soc. Antiq. Scot. 88*, 65–93.

Woodham, A. A. (1956b) (Report on archaeological sites in Ross and Cromarty). *Discovery and Excavation in Scotland 1956*, 23–5.

Woodham, A. A. (1958) Plans, notes and photographs of the excavation of the chambered cairn, Kilcoy South, Ross-shire, Ms to be housed in the National Monuments Record of Scotland.

Woodham, A. A. (1963) Tomfat Plantation chambered cairn. *Discovery and Excavation in Scotland 1963*, 37.

Woodham, A. A. and Woodham, M. F. (1957a) The excavation of a chambered cairn at Kilcoy, Ross-shire. *Proc. Soc. Antiq. Scot. 90*, 102–15.

Woodham, A. A. and Woodham, M. F. (1957b) Kilcoy West. *Discovery and Excavation in Scotland 1957*, 32.

Woodham, A. A. and Woodham, M. F. (1958) (Report on excavation at Kilcoy West). *Discovery and Excavation in Scotland 1958*, 32–3.

Woodham, A. A. and Woodham, M. F. (1964) An Orkney-Cromarty chambered cairn in upper Strathnairn, Inverness-shire. *Proc. Soc. Antiq. Scot. 97*, 35–9.

Wordsworth, J. (1985) The excavation of a mesolithic horizon at 13–24 Castle Street, Inverness. *Proc. Soc. Antiq. Scot. 115*, 89–103.

Index

References to Inventory entries are printed in **bold** type, and to illustrations in *italics*.